TAFSEER OF SURAH AL IMRAN

VERSES 1 TO 100

BY

SERENA HUSAIN YATES

Copyright © *Serena Husain Yates*, 2025

All Rights Reserved

This book is subject to the condition that no part of this book is to be reproduced, transmitted in any form or means; electronic or mechanical, stored in a retrieval system, photocopied, recorded, scanned, or otherwise. Any of these actions require the proper written permission of the author.

DEDICATION TO MY PARENTS MOHAMMED HUBDAR HUSAIN & ZAITOON HUSAIN

MY CHILDREN TARIQ, SALMA, SARAH, SAMEENA

MY GRANDCHILDREN

LAYLA, MUSA, AARON, SETH, YACUB

KEYAAN, LEYAH, EVA, SIYANNA, NOAH

JASMINE, TARIQ ISMAIL, AMELIA,

OMARI, ZAYN, KEIRA, ADAM, AYDEN

Table of Contents

MY LEGACY 1
General Information 3
Historical Context 4
Main Themes 5
Key Messages/Lessons 7
Notable Ayahs from Surah Ali-Imran 8
Topical Analysis of The Verses 11
Verse 1 15
Verse 2 16
Verse 3 & 4 19
Verse 5 30
Verse 6 32
Verse 7 34
Verses 8 46
Verse 9 47
Verse 10 48
Verses 11 52
Verses 12 57
Verse 13 61
Verses 14 73
Verse 15 83
Verse 16 89
Verses 17 91
Verse 18 100
Verse 19 107
Verse 20 114
Verse 21 119
Verse 22 125
Verse 23 131

VERSE 24 & 25	141
Verse 26	145
Verse 27	154
Verse 27	161
Verse 28	168
Verse 29	184
Verse 30	187
Verse 31	189
Verse 32	194
Verse 33	198
Verse 34	204
Verse 35	206
Verse 36	209
Verse 37	213
Verses 38 & 39	217
Verses 40	222
Verse 41	222
Verses 42	226
VERSE 43	229
Verse 44	230
Verse 45	234
Verse 46	238
Verses 47	242
Verse 48	244
Verse 49	245
Verses 50	252
Verse 51	254
Verse 52	259
Verse 53	264
Verse 55	271
Verses 56	273

Verse 57	273
Verse 58	277
Verses 59, 60 & 61	283
Verses 62	288
Verse 63	290
Verse 64	291
Verses 65	294
Verses 66	294
Verses 67	295
Verse 68	299
Verse 69	304
Verses 70	308
Verse 71	310
Verse 72	312
Verses 73	314
Verse 74	317
Verse 75	319
Verses 76	326
Verse 77	328
Verse 78	333
Verse 79	337
Verses 79	342
Verses 80	342
Verse 81	344
Verses 81	353
Verse 82	355
Verse 83	357
Verse 84	366
Verse 85	370
Verse 86	374
Verses 87	380

Verse 88...381

Verse 89...383

Verses 90..385

Verse 91...386

Verse 92...389

Verse 93...396

Verse 94...402

Verse 95...403

Verse 96...408

Verse 97...416

Verses 98..424

Verse 99...426

Verses 100..428

MY LEGACY

My children and grandchildren, I leave this book as a legacy to you.

In this journey of life Allah has chosen me to be your guardian, your protector. Allah has entrusted me, gifted me with the best of treasures, my beautiful family. Live your life in the submission and affirmation to the one God. All that exists belongs to Him as He is the Originator of all. He, subhanahu, alone is worthy of worship and all other deities are to be shunned. Everything happens by the Qader (will) of subhanahu. What was never meant for you will never reach you and what is meant for you, you will nev er have missed. Live your life with kindness, gratitude. Live everyday as the last day of your life. Seek refuge in Allah from the accursed Shaitan who lies waiting to trap you. Fulfil your duties to one another. You might be four different families but live your life as one. There is nothing greater than kinship. Remember that happiness comes with a pure heart free from jealousy, hatred, arrogance. Establish your prayers regularly and with humility. Nothing in your life is more important than your Salaat. Prayer is your connection to Allah. Feel the hunger and thirst of others. Thank Allah in all conditions. He may know a thing that's good for and that what is bad.

Learn the lessons from the Prophets. Put your trust in Allah and avoid those who aim to cause mischief. Speak well of others and avoid slander and backbiting. Live your life with contentment and avoid excess. Have pleasure in giving than receiving. Be charitable to your neighbours and love for yourself what you love for your brother. Live your life with tolerance and be accepting of others, even if their beliefs differ from you. Ask forgiveness from those you harm and repent to Allah. I pray that Allah protect and guide each and everyone one of you and we meet again and live as one family in Jannatul Firdous. AMEEN

Mummy, Nani Serena

Chapter 3: Surah Aal-Imran

The Third Chapter of the Qur'an

In Surah Baqarah we are introduced to a creation who was not created by the laws of reproduction. We learnt about our forefathers Adam and his wife Hawa who were created differently from everyone else. Adam was created from nothing, Hawa was created from Adam.

Surah Imran tells us about Prophet Isa (Pbuh) who was also created differently. This prophet was created without a father.

General Information

Origin of name:

This Surah takes its name from Ayah 33, where Imran is mentioned. According to sources, two different individuals named Imran are mentioned: one is the father of Moses and Aaron, and the other is the father of Mary. While there is some debate over which Imran is intended here, the following verses, especially those concerning Mary's chastity and Jesus' prophethood, suggest that the Imran referred to is Mary's father.

Number of Ayahs (Verses): 200

Surah Imran is a Madani Surah.

Time of Revelation: The Surah was revealed in stages, with parts revealed soon after the Battle of Badr (in A.H. 2-3), during the visit of the Christians from Najran in 9 A.H., and following the Battle of Uhud in 3-4 A.H., making the complete revelation likely between A.H. 3 and A.H. 9.

Historical Context

Surah Al-Imran was revealed in Madinah over several years and addresses key events during the early Muslim community's formative period.

During this time, the Muslims were experiencing external threats from hostile forces such as the Quraysh of Makkah and internal challenges from the Jewish tribes and hypocrites in Madinah. The repercussions of the two significant battles—the Battle of Badr, a victory, and the Battle of Uhud, where the Muslims faced a setback—are directly addressed in the Surah. Both battles influenced the state of the Islamic community, presenting new moral and strategic lessons that required reflection.

Additionally, the Christian delegation from Najran visiting Madinah provides crucial context for parts of the Surah addressing common theological topics between Islam and Christianity, particularly around the figure of Jesus (Isa). The message to Christians here is aligned with the teachings preserved in the Quran, clarifying wrong beliefs they held and inviting them back to the true Abrahamic faith.

The Jewish tribes in Madinah, especially post-Badr, began breaking their alliances with the Muslims, encouraging external enemies like the Quraysh to attack. Thus, the Prophet Muhammad (pbuh) had to confront many challenges from both outside and within his community, as some Jewish tribes conspired with the hypocrites and hostile polytheists.

The Surah seeks to reassure the Muslims by reminding them that patience, unity, and faithfulness are key to overcoming internal weaknesses, which had been exposed during their setback at Uhud. Emphasizing the need for justice and discipline within their community, the Surah warns against greed and moral lapses while providing broader guidance for interacting with the People of the Book—Jews and Christians.

Main Themes

- **Invitation to the People of the Book (Jews and Christians):** The surah continues the invitation started in Al-Baqarah, urging the Jews and Christians to embrace Islam. It clarifies the truth about Prophet Jesus and refutes the Christian belief of his divinity, emphasizing that Muhammad (peace be upon him) brings the same guidance as previous prophets.

- **Truth of Revelation and Monotheism:** The surah reaffirms the teachings of monotheism, stressing that Allah is One, and that all prophets brought the same fundamental message from Allah. The Quran confirms the truth that was revealed in earlier scriptures like the Torah and the Gospel.

- **Lessons from Battle of Badr and Uhud:** The surah reflects upon the victories and challenges faced by the Muslims, particularly in the Battles of Badr and Uhud. It highlights the importance of discipline, unity, and obedience to Allah. The setbacks at Uhud are attributed to greed and disobedience, serving as lessons for the community.

- **Warnings and Guidance for Muslims:** Muslims are cautioned against following the same path of religious and moral decline that previous communities had fallen into. They are reminded of their responsibility to uphold truth, unity, and justice, and their duty to preserve the guidance of the Quran.

- **Strengthening Muslim Community:** The surah provides guidance for building a resilient and cohesive Muslim community. It addresses how to interact with the People of the Book and warns against the influence of hypocrites and enemies of Islam.

- **Prophethood and Divine Guidance:** The surah strengthens the concept of prophethood by explaining the unity and continuity of the prophetic mission, from Adam to Muhammad (peace be upon him). Jesus' birth and role as a prophet are explained, with a focus on clearing misconceptions.

- **Justice and Moral Fortitude:** The surah emphasizes justice in all aspects of life, whether in dealings within the Muslim community or with others.

- **Call for Patience and Perseverance:** Throughout the surah, Muslims are encouraged to remain patient during difficult times, trust in Allah, and maintain their belief in the ultimate success of those who submit to His will.

Key Messages/Lessons

- Emphasizes belief in Allah's oneness and consistent guidance through all prophets.

- Condemns altering divine teachings and warns against misbeliefs about prophets.

- Teaches patience, sincerity, and unity as paths to Allah's help, while warning against greed and disobedience.

- Urges Muslims to reflect on and correct moral weaknesses revealed in trials.

- Advises caution with hypocrites and enemies; unity and fear of Allah protect from harm.

- Encourages following prophets' teachings without elevating them beyond human roles.

- Calls for patience and steadfastness in the face of slander or opposition.

Notable Ayahs from Surah Ali-Imran

- **Verse 19:** *"Certainly, Allah's only Way is Islam. Those who were given the Scripture did not dispute ˹among themselves˺ out of mutual envy until knowledge came to them."* Emphasizes that Islam is the true religion in the eyes of Allah, and highlights the division among the People of the Scripture due to envy.

- **Verse 26:** *"Say, ˹O Prophet,˺ 'O Allah! Lord over all authorities! You give authority to whoever You please and remove it from who You please; You honour whoever You please and disgrace who You please—all good is in Your Hands. Surely You ˹alone˺ are Most Capable of everything.'"* A prayer recognizing Allah's ultimate control over power and positions of honor.

- **Verse 27:** *"You cause the night to pass into the day and the day into the night. You bring forth the living from the dead and the dead from the living. And You provide for whoever You will without limit."* Highlights Allah's power over creation, life, and sustenance.

- **Verse 31:** *"Say, [O Muhammad], 'If you should love Allah, then follow me, [so] Allah will love you and forgive you your sins. And Allah is Forgiving and Merciful.'"* A direct invitation to people to follow the Prophet Muhammad to attain Allah's love and forgiveness.

- **Verse 39:** *"So the angels called out to him while he stood praying in the sanctuary, "Allah gives you good news of ˹the birth of˺ John who will confirm the Word of Allah and will be a great leader, chaste, and a prophet among the righteous."* Refers to the miraculous birth of John (Yahya) to Zechariah, a key part of the conversation with Christians.

- **Verse 42:** *"And [mention] when the angels said, 'O Mary, indeed Allah has chosen you and purified you and chosen you above the women of the worlds.'"* Recognizes the special status of Mary in Islam, refuting any slander against her.

- **Verse 59:** *"Indeed, the example of Jesus to Allah is like that of Adam. He created him from dust; then He said to him, 'Be,' and he was."* Explaining that just like Adam was created without parents, the miraculous birth of Jesus does not make him divine.

- **Verse 64:** *"Say, 'O People of the Scripture, come to a word that is equitable between us and you – that we will not worship except Allah and not associate anything with Him and not take one another as lords instead of Allah.'"* An invitation to unity in the worship of one God, addressed to the People of the Book.

- **Verse 92:** *"Never will you attain the good [reward] until you spend [in the way of Allah] from that which you love..."* Encouragement to give charity from that which is most beloved.

- **Verse 103:** *"And hold firmly to the rope of Allah all together and do not become divided..."* A strong instruction for maintaining unity and avoiding divisions within the Muslim community.

- **Verse 110:** *"You are the best nation produced [as an example] for mankind. You enjoin what is right and forbid what is wrong and believe in Allah..."* Declares the Muslims to be the best community, responsible for promoting good and opposing wrong.

- **Verse 144:** *"Muhammad is not but a messenger. [Other] messengers have passed on before him. So if he was to die or be killed, would you turn back on your heels [to unbelief]?..."* Reminds the community that their faith should not be dependent on the presence of the Prophet Muhammad, but on Allah.

- **Verse 159:** *"So by mercy from Allah, [O Muhammad], you were lenient with them. And if you had been rude [in speech] and harsh in heart, they would have disbanded from about you..."* Highlights the importance of mercy and kindness, especially in leadership.

- **Verse 185:** *"Every soul will taste death, and you will only be given your [full] compensation on the Day of Resurrection..."* A powerful reminder that all humans will face death and accountability in the Hereafter.

- **Verse 200:** *"O you who have believed, persevere and endure and remain stationed and fear Allah that you may be successful."* The conclusion of the Surah, urging patience, endurance, and fear of Allah for ultimate success.

Topical Analysis of The Verses

Verses 1-9

Allah introduces Himself and says that He sent down the three holy books.

Verses 10-20

Allah reveals the end that awaits the unbelievers.

He talks about the things that are beautiful to the eyes of people in this world and the more beautiful things that await those who believe.

The characteristics of those who have taqwa (God consciousness), Allah being the only deity, and Islam being the only acceptable religion.

Verses 21-30

Allah tells about the deeds and lies of the Israelites who have deviated from the truth.

Allah gives examples of His own power and talks about the Day of Judgment.

Verses 31-41

The importance of obedience to Allah and His Prophets.

Zacharias's and Mary's relationship with Allah.

Verses 42-54

Allah talks about the revelations He sent down to Mary (pbuh) and gives her the good news of Jesus (pbuh).

He talks about certain events from the life of Jesus (pbuh).

Verses 55-62

Allah talks about the incident where He has ascended Jesus (pbuh) to the heavens in order to protect him from the Israelites.

Verses 63-71

Allah talks to the people of the book.

There is no god but Allah. Abraham's (pbuh) religion.

Allah asks the people of the book why they deny His verses.

Verses 72-80

Allah exposes the tricks and lies of the hypocrites from the People of the Book.

And Allah explains that neither His prophets nor His angels should be worshipped except Himself.

Verses 81-91

The promise that was given from the Israelites to help the prophets that will come.

That no religion other than Islam will not be accepted in the hereafter.

The torment awaiting those who deliberately fell into disbelief after clear proofs had come to them from Allah.

Verses 92-101

Allah warns the People of the Book who invent lies in the name of Allah and conceal His verses.

He invites people to Abraham's (pbuh) religion and gives information about the Kaaba.

He orders those who can afford to visit the Kaaba.

Verses 102-109

Allah calls out to believers, gives them advice and reminds them of His blessings.

He describes the state of those who believe and those who turn away from their faith on the day of judgement.

Verses 110-120

Allah separates hypocrites and believers from the people of the book and lists their characteristics.

He warns the believers against the hypocrites of the People of the Book and tells them not to take them as friends.

Verses 121-129

Allah mentions that He will help Muslims who trust in their Lord and are patient.

He tells how He sent His angels to help the believers in the battles of Uhud and Badr.

Verses 130-143

Allah explains what the pious people have done and what they have avoided. He also talks about Paradise, which is their reward.

He explains the wisdom behind defeats and victories in wars.

Verses 144-148

Allah gives people what they want in return for the good they do.

Allah says that He rewards those who are grateful, that He loves those who are patient and those who are benevolent, and gives examples of these issues.

Verses 149-155

Allah orders us not to follow the unbelievers and says that the place awaiting those who associate partners with Allah is hell.

Allah tells what happened in the Battle of Uhud from his own point of view.

Verses 156-171

After the Battle of Uhud, Allah warns Muslims about the topics of death and witnessing.

Prophet's forgiving Muslims who fled in the Battle of Uhud; his distribution of the booty with justice; and the Prophet's being a mercy from Allah to all muslims.

Allah is talking about the hypocrites and martyrs whithin the muslims in the Battle of Uhud.

Verses 172-180

Allah speaks of believers who showed heroism in and before the war.

He mentions that the unbelievers only harm themselves, not Allah.

Allah is talking about the unseen and stinginess.

Verses 181-189

Allah speaks about the promises that the Israelites did not keep, the prophets they killed, their denial and the torment that awaits them.

Allah is talking about testing (of life) and death.

Verses 190-200

Allah talks about the prayers of sound believers who see the proofs and lessons of Allah. The promises He has made to them.

He talks about pious people who are from the People of the Book.

The advice that Allah gives to people of faith.

Verse 1

Alif, Lam, Meem.

The chapter begins with three individual letters from the Arabic alphabet: Alif, Lam, and Meem.

The meaning of these letters are only known to Allah swt.

Verse 2

Allaahu laaa ilaaha illaa Huwal Haiyul Qaiyoom

Allah - there is no deity except Him, the Ever-Living, the Ever-Watchful (Chapter 3: Verse 2)

Allah testified that there is no deity except Him before any other creation witnessed the Oneness of His Divinity. He testified to His oneness before He created the angels, and before He created those who have true Knowledge. Thus, the testimony in the verse: 'Allah bears witness that there is no Allah but Him' is the strongest of testimonies and the pure essence of monotheism. Allah is in no need for the testimony of humans, angels, or any other beings.

He says:

Allah bears witness that there is no Allah but Him, as do the angels and those who have knowledge. He upholds justice. There is no Allah but Him, the Almighty, the All-Wise. (3:18)

So when you take a deeper look into the verse "Allah - there is no deity except Him," you will find it extremely easy and simple. Allah did not want to make the case for faith in the supreme power, a complicated philosophical one. Nor did He restrict it to the people of high culture. Faith and the mandates of worship should be equally accessible and understood by all, from the shepherd to the philosopher, and from the street sweeper to the astronaut.

Here is another way to look at the issue of "Allah - there is no deity except Him." Allah has repeatedly declared loud and clear: 'I bear witness that there is no Allah but me.' Either this is true, and thus the matter ends, or it is not. If this is not the truth, then we ask: where are the true Allahs? Didn't they hear the challenge? Why did they remain silent as Allah took away the universe from them and said: I alone am the creator? If these Allahs did not hear the challenge from Allah, then they are not fit to be Allahs. And if they heard but did not act, then again, they are not fit to be Allahs. Thus, the case of lordship and deity belongs to Allah alone until a plaintiff comes forward to contradict Him. Till then, the statement "Allah - there is no deity except Him" remains the ultimate truth supported by ample evidence, prophets, messengers, and heavenly books.

This brings us back to the verse: 'Allah - there is no deity except Him, the Ever-Living.' As long as there is no Allah but Allah, then He is the true Sustainer of the universe and its affairs. This magnificent creation needs an Everlasting power to manage it. Allah must be living life that befits Him as a Creator and Manager. It is an ever-existing life, and it is the source of all life. Allah is the first and the last. Allah is Ever-present and Ever-watchful over His creation. No one gave Him life, and no one takes it away. It is a principal of the Divine self.

The next attribute in the verse is 'the Ever-Watchful' translated from the Arabic origin 'Al Qayyum' 'القيوم' which is in the superlative exaggerated form of the word 'Qa'em'. 'قائم' Why the superlative form? We answer that if Allah the Almighty is the one who manages all matters of the universe, then He must be 'Ever Watchful.'

MONOTHESISM IN ISLAM

The religion of Islam is based on one core belief, that there is no Allah worthy of worship but Allah. When a person embraces Islam or a Muslim wants to renew or confirm his or her faith, they profess their belief that there is no Allah worthy of worship but Allah and that Muhammad is His final messenger. **Ashadu an la ill laha il Allah wa Ashadu anna Muhammadan Rasulullah**, Saying these words, the Testimony of Faith, is the first of five pillars or foundations of the religion of Islam. Belief in Allah is the first of six pillars of faith.

Muslims believe that there is only One Allah. He alone is the Sustainer and Creator of the universe. He is without partners, children, or associates. He is the Most Merciful, the Most Wise, and the Most

Just. He is the all hearer, all seer, and the all knowing. He is the First, He is the Last.

In the religion of Islam belief in One Allah, without partners or associates is essential. It is the focal point of the religion and it is the essence of the Quran. The Quran calls on humankind to worship Allah alone and to give up worshipping false Allahs or associates. The Quran urges us to look at the wonders of creation and understand Allah's greatness and power, and it speaks directly of His names, attributes, and actions. The Quran commands us to reject anything that is worshipped instead of, or along with Allah.

Islam is referred to as **pure** monotheism. It is not adulterated with strange concepts or superstitions. Belief in One Allah entails certainty. Muslims worship Allah alone, He has no partners, associates, or helpers. Worship is directed solely to Allah, for He is the only One worthy of worship. There is nothing greater than Allah Alone.

Verse 3 & 4

Nazzala 'alaikal Kitaaba bilhaqqi musaddiqal limaa baina yadaihi wa anzalat Tawraata wal Injeel

Min qablu hudal linnaasi wa anzalal Furqaan; innallazeena kafaroo bi Aayaatil laahi lahum 'azaabun shadeed; wallaahu 'azeezun zun tiqaam

He has revealed the Book to you with the truth, confirming what was there before it. And He sent down the Torah and the Gospel earlier as a guide for people. And He has sent down the criterion. Those who deny Allah's revelations will suffer severe torment: Allah is almighty and capable of retribution. (Chapter 3, Verses 3 & 4)

In the previous verse, Allah laid the foundation of His lordship: 'Allah - there is no deity except Him, the Ever-Living, the Ever-Watchful.' And as long as Allah is the only Creator, it is logical that He is the One who looks after the affairs of all creation. He says:

He placed firmly embedded mountains on it, towering over it, and blessed it and measured out its nourishment in it, laid out for those who seek it – all in four days. (41:10)

Allah did not only give us the sustenance for material life, He also gave us the values, needed to make life fair and enjoyable. Materialism without values makes life intractable, violent and miserable for most. Thus, the heavenly revelations are most necessary and valuable. Allah says:

He has revealed the Book to you with truth, confirming what was there before it. And He sent down the Torah and the Gospel (Chapter 3, Verse 3)

When something is sent down to you for the Most High, you should not look at it as a burden or an obstacle because they are from the creator of the universe. Thus, following Allah's teachings in submission should make you proud. It does not demean you; rather it elevates you to a higher level.

Let's take a few moments to look at the Arabic origin of the words 'revealed' and 'sent down.' They are translated from one of three Arabic origins: Nazal, Nazzal, Anzal -أنزل, نزّل, and نزل-. Each carries a distinct meaning from the others. We'll take them one by one.

Whenever the word Anzal أنزل is used in the Quran, you will find it referring to Allah. Allah says:

Truly We sent it down on the Night of Power. (97:01)

In the following verse, the word Nazal نزل is used referring to the Archangel Gabriel. Allah says:

The Trustworthy Spirit brought it down (26:193)

Lastly, the word Nazzal نزّل is used for the rest of the angles. Allah says:

on that night the angels and the Spirit descend again and again with their Lord's permission on every task (97:04)

So the use of the verb Anzal أنزل in the Quran is exclusive to Allah, while Nazal نزل is used for Gabriel, and Nazzal نزّل is used for the angels. The Arabic language is a vast language with intricate details and precise meanings hidden within its words, and often within specific letters in these words. The difference between the uses of the words Anzal, Nazal, and Nazzal gives us clues about the revelation of the Noble Quran and the heavenly books that preceded it, namely the Torah and the Gospel.

This brings us back to the verse. When it comes to the Torah and Bible, Allah exclusively uses the verb Anzal, 'And He sent down the Torah and the Gospel.' The use of the verb 'Anzal أنزل' means that both, the Torah and the Bible, were revealed to our beloved prophets Moses and Jesus respectively as two whole books.

When it comes to the Nobel Quran, Allah uses two verbs: Anzal – the same verb used for the Torah and Bible- and then the verb Nazal-. Allah says:

It is with the truth that We have sent it down, and it is with the truth that it was revealed. We have not sent you but as a bearer of glad tidings and to warn. (17:105)

We understand that Allah Almighty revealed the Quran from the preserved slate to the lowest heaven all at once as a single complete book. He says using the verb Anzal: 'And He has sent down the criterion.' Later on, the Quran was revealed to Prophet Muhammad a few verses –and occasionally entire chapters- at a time according to what was appropriate for the circumstances.

So, to those who question: how do you say that Quran was revealed in the month of Ramadan, while you also say that it was revealed little by little over the twenty-three years of Muhammad's Prophethood? We answer that our knowledge of the nuances of the Arabic language clarifies things for us. Allah revealed the entire Quran from His knowledge and sent it down to the lowest heaven in the month of Ramadan. From that moment on, the Quran started its mission in this world in gradual revelations spanning the life of our beloved Prophet Muhammad (PBUH). These gradual revelations were based on the circumstances facing the new faith. A few verses specifying a religious ruling would come down at the time when it was needed. Had the Quran been sent all at once, the rulings and religious teachings might have existed while there was neither need nor hunger for them. But when a teaching is revealed at the time of need, it becomes established and appreciated.

As for those who still question why the Quran was not revealed altogether at once? Allah answers:

The faithless say, 'Why has not the Quran been sent down to him all at once?' So it is, that We may strengthen your heart with it, and We have recited it little by little. (25:32)

Allah revealed the Quran a little at a time to strengthen the heart of the Prophet and the believers. Prophet Muhammad (peace be upon him) faced tremendous challenges from day one of his call to faith. Whenever a tough challenge presented itself, a portion of the Quran -appropriate for that challenge- was revealed to support the Prophet and those standing by him. Each revelation illuminated the path ahead of the Prophet and made him feel tranquil. This also gave the believers time to understand, implement and appreciate each and every new ruling and heavenly teaching.

Prophet Muhammad was often challenged by the non-believers, the Jews, and the Christians. And each time, Allah answered them with clear revelation. Had the Quran been sent down all at once, these rebuttals would have lost some of their impacts. Allah says:

The faithless say, 'Why has not the Quran been sent down to him all at once?' So it is, that We may strengthen your heart with it, and We have recited it little by little. Every time they come to you with a difficult point, We bring you the truth and the best of explanations. (25:32, 33)

He has revealed the Book to you with truth, confirming what was there before it. And He sent down the Torah and the Gospel earlier as a guide for people. And He has sent down the criterion. Those who deny Allah's revelations will suffer severe torment: Allah is Almighty and capable of retribution. (Chapter 3, Verses 3 & 4)

When Allah speaks about the Quran, He says: "confirming what was there before it." Here you may ask: Is Islam confirming Christianity and Judaism? We answer that every heavenly religion confirms the core issue of creed: 'There is no Allah but Allah.' Heavenly religions may differ in matters of social and economic teachings, but never in creed. Each message was sent to address certain societal ills to certain peoples at certain periods of time. As for creed, it never changes. Allah says:

In matters of faith, He has laid down for you the same commandment that He gave Noah, which We have revealed to you and which We enjoined on Abraham and Moses and Jesus (from 42:13)

And in another verse, Allah relays the words of Prophet Jesus to his people, the children of Israel:

I have come to confirm the truth of the Torah which preceded me, and to make some things lawful to you, which used to be forbidden. I have come to you with a sign from your Lord. Be mindful of Allah, obey me (03:50)

Islam, the final message, holds within it the exact creed of all the previous heavenly messages, but its social and economic teachings are for all people till the end of time.

The word 'confirming' is translated from the Arabic origin 'Mussadeqan مُصَدِّقًا' from the root 'Sa Da Qa.' It means 'to match the reality,' or what we call: the truth. If the news does not match reality, we call it a lie.

We had given earlier the example of a car accident that occurred right in front of you. No matter how many times you are asked about the accident, your answer would be the same because you are telling the truth as it occurred in front of you. But if the accident were a lie, then your story would change with time. You would forget some details that you told a month ago, and when you tell the story a third time, it would be different again. Isn't that the same technique investigators use to catch crooks and criminals? They ask a suspect on several occasions about the details of a crime or event. A person with an ever-changing story is a liar. The truth never changes. Thus, we always hear the adage: "No man has a good enough memory to be a successful liar." Allah says: 'He has revealed the Book to you with truth, confirming what was there before it. And He sent down the Torah and the Gospel earlier as a guide for people.'

Here, we should pause and answer some critics of the Quran. A few pointed to verses such as 'We have sent it down as an Arabic Quran so that you may understand' (12:2) then complained that the Quran contains many words that are not of Arabic origin. For example, 'Torah' is a Hebrew word, and 'Bible' is word of Syriac and Greek origins. We answer that such words are actual names of these books in their original language. They are the names the Arabs used to refer to these books. Thus, they became part of the language of the Arabs at the time. For example, in the modern era, the word 'computer' has been introduced into Arabic. It is used by Arabs in everyday life, and because it has become so popular, it has become a part of the language.

Likewise, just because the Quran was revealed in the Arabic language does not mean that every word it contains has to be of pure Arabic origin. It means that the Quran was revealed in the language Arabs used at the time. Allah says: We have sent it down as an Arabic Quran so that you may understand (12:2)

The verse continues: 'He sent down the Torah and the Gospel earlier as a guide for people.' Who are the people referred to in the verse? No doubt they are the people who lived at the time when these books were revealed. If the Qur'an had come to confirm the authenticity of the Torah and the Gospel, then can't we also use these books as guides? Yes, but only what the Quran has authenticated; Only the parts of the scriptures that have been reaffirmed by the Quran hold true to us. Thus, the phrase 'as a guide for people' means as a guide to those who lived at the time of the revelation of these books; and as a guide to us only through the parts explicitly confirmed in the Quran. Allah says: 'And He has sent down the criterion,' referring to the Quran as the standard by which to judge and separate the truth from falsehood.

The use of the word 'criterion' also indicates the presence of a struggle between two parties. Allah assigned you a difficult mission, but He provided you with the best tool to undertake this mission: the Nobel Quran. It is the best tool to differentiate between guidance and misguidance, right and wrong, misery and happiness, integrity and corruption. The 'criterion' –translated from the Arabic Al Furqan- is the standard by which you can measure and distinguishes between good and evil. Evil will always have its supporters, and Allah wants you to be among those who defend the truth.

It was natural for the verse to end with: 'Those who deny Allah's revelations will suffer severe torment: Allah is Almighty and capable of retribution.' Since the Quran is the criterion clarifying truth and falsehood, those who follow it are the forces of good. Likewise, those who ignore its teachings are the forces of evil. Allah gives us the foregone conclusion of this struggle: 'Those who deny Allah's revelations will suffer severe torment.'

POINT OF REFLECTION

We learnt here that the Quran has come to confirm the other heavenly scriptures-the Torah, revealed to Prophet Moses (AS), the Gospel revealed to Prophet Jesus(AS), the Zabur revealed to Prophet David and the Suhuf revealed to Prophet Abrahim) The Quran doesn't reject them but affirm them.

Let us delve into this more deeply.

Quran Confirms Original Revelations of Torah and Gospel, Not Bible

First of all, even though it is common to say that the Quran confirms the Bible, strictly speaking this is not correct. The term Bible does not appear anywhere in the Quran. The term Old Testament and New Testament does not appear anywhere in the Quran. The Quran actually confirms the original revelation that was given to Prophet Moses called the Tawrah (Torah) and the Enjeel (the Gospel) that was revealed to Prophet Jesus. Other scriptures that are mentioned in the Quran include the Zabur revealed to Prophet David and the Suhuf revealed to Prophet Abraham. The idea that the Quran confirms the Bible, the Old Testament or the New Testament is incorrect. Even then when we take a term like Torah, it isn't the exact equivalent in understanding the scriptures between Muslims and Jews and Christians, for example. Among the Jews and Christians the Torah is believed to be the first five books, beginning with Genesis, in the Bible.

Torah in Quran vs. Torah in Bible: What's the Difference?

However, if you look carefully into these books, you'll find many of them don't really represent revelation given to Moses but are biographies of Moses. Also, towards the end of chapter 34 in the book of Deuteronomy, which is part of the Torah it talks of Moses' death and being buried, which obviously is not of the work of Moses nor is it the revelation given to him on Mount Sinai as Muslims believe. As such even the definition of Torah in the Judea-Christian literature is not like the Quranic reference to the Torah, or law, specifically the revelation given to prophet Moses not biographies about him.

Quran's Enjeel: Not the Same as the Four Gospels

Secondly, the term Enjeel, in the Quran, the equivalent of the Gospel (in the singular form) should not be equated with the four Gospels. The Quran speaks of the word of God, not the word of Mark, Luke, Matthew, and John. That is not the word of God, that's their own biographies. What the Quran speaks of is the revelation given to Prophet Jesus, peace be upon him, something that he was guided by divine revelation. Whether he asked people to write it or not we don't know for sure, but it is the same type of divine revelation that was given to Moses, Mohammad, Abraham, or David for that matter, may peace be upon them all.

Quran: The Final Judge of Previous Scriptures

There is another issue here as well. When the Quran speaks of confirming any previous scriptures, it is conditional and indicates in no uncertain terms that the Quran and the Quran alone as the last well preserved revelation is the final judge and the criterion to sift through any previous scripture to discern what is the word of God and what is the word of humans; which parts remained intact and which parts might have gone through some changes throughout history. The term *muhaymen*, which appears in the Quran, in surah number 5 and verses 48 through 51, deals specifically with this issue of the Quran being *muhaymen*. This word, *muhaymen* in Arabic, as Mawlana Mawdudi explains in his Commentary on the Quran, means to uphold, to safe guard or preserve, to watch over and to stand witness. All of these definitions apply to the Quran in its relationship to previous scriptures. First of all, the Quran safeguards and preserves the teachings of previous prophets. It watches over the revelations that God sent before by explaining their true meanings to negate any confusion, misunderstanding or misinterpretation that has arisen throughout history. It stands witness because it bears witness, as Mawdudi says, to the word of God contained in those previous scriptures and helps sort it out from interpretations and commentaries that were later added to them.

The Quran is the Last Revelation, Totally Protected

The revelation of the Qur'an was not an isolated event in time. It was a constant stream of verses descending to Muhammad (peace be upon him) throughout the 23 years of his prophethood in Makkah and Madinah. The Prophet (peace be upon him) appointed numerous companions of his to serve as scribes, writing down the latest verses as soon as they were revealed. Mu'awiya ibn Abu Sufyan and Zaid bin Thabit were among the scribes who had this duty. For the most part, new verses would be written on scraps of bone, hide, or parchment. It is important to note that the Prophet (peace be upon him) would have the scribes read back the verses to him after writing them down so he can proofread and make sure there were no errors.

To further ensure that there were no errors, the Prophet (peace be upon him) ordered that no one records anything else, not even his words, Hadith, on the same sheet as Qur'an. Regarding the sheets that the Qur'an was being written down on, he stated "and whoever has written anything from me other than the Qur'an should erase it." This was done to ensure that no other words were accidentally thought to be part of the text of the Qur'an.

It is important to understand, however, that physical writing down of the Qur'an was not the main way that the Qur'an was recorded. Arabia in the 600s was an oral society. Very few people could read and write, thus huge emphasis was placed on ability to memorize long poems, letters, and other messages. Before Islam, Makkah was a center of Arabic poetry. Annual festivals were held every year that brought together the best poets from all over the Arabian Peninsula. Exuberant attendees would memorize the exact words that their favourite poets recited and quote them years and decades later.

Thus, in this type of oral society, the vast majority of the companions learned and recorded the Qur'an by memorization. In addition to their natural ability to memorize, the rhythmic nature of the Qur'an made its memorization much easier.

The Qur'an was not narrated to just a few select companions. It was heard and memorized by hundreds and thousands of people, many of them travellers to Madinah. Thus, chapters and verses of the Qur'an quickly spread during the life of the Prophet (peace be upon him) to all corners of the Arabian Peninsula. Those who had heard verses from the Prophet (peace be upon him) would go and spread them to tribes far away, who would also memorize them. In this way, the Qur'an achieved a literary status known among the Arabs as mutawatir. Mutawatir means that it was so vastly disseminated to so many different groups of people, who all had the same exact wording, that it is inconceivable that that any one person or group could have falsified it. Some sayings of the Prophet (peace be upon him) are known to be authentic through it being mutawatir, but the entire Qur'an itself is accepted as being mutawatir, because of its wide spread during the life of the Prophet (peace be upon him) through oral means.

We have thus far seen that the way the Qur'an was taught to the numerous Companions of the Prophet (peace be upon him) prevented it from being subject to the protection of a few people. As verses became widespread across the Islamic world, it was impossible for those verses to be changed without Muslims in other parts of the world noticing and correcting them. Furthermore, during the life of Prophet Muhammad (peace be upon him), the angel Jibreel would recite the entire Qur'an with him once a year, during Ramadan. When the Qur'an was finished being revealed near the end of the Prophet's (peace be upon him) life, he made sure that numerous companions knew the entire Qur'an by heart.

During the reigns of the first caliphs, however, a need to compile all the verses into a central book arose. Taking pre-emptive action, the caliphs who ruled the Muslim world after the death of the Prophet (peace be upon him) feared that if the number of people who had the Qur'an memorized dipped too low, the community would be in danger of losing the Qur'an forever. As a result, the first caliph, Abu Bakr, who ruled from 632 to 634, ordered a committee be organized, under the leadership of Zaid bin Thabit, to collect all the written pieces of Qur'an that were spread throughout the Muslim community. The plan was to collect them all into one central book that could be preserved in case the people who had the Qur'an memorized died out.

Zaid was very meticulous about who he accepted verses from. Because of the enormous responsibility of not accidentally altering the words of the Qur'an, he only accepted pieces of parchment with Qur'an on them had to have been written down in the presence of the Prophet (peace be upon him) and there had to be two witnesses who can attest to that fact.

Present day we see how the Quran will be preserved when the Quran is memorized by millions of people living today, even if they burn every last Quran we can bring it back by memory the next day.

Verse 5

Innal laaha laa yakhfaa 'alaihi shai'un fil ardi wa laa fis samaaa'

Indeed, there is nothing in the earth and the heavens that is hidden from Allah

This verse underscores Allah's perfect knowledge and power, including the creation of all living beings within their mothers' wombs. It also emphasizes the importance of believing in the entirety of the Quran, including both clear and ambiguous verses, as all originate from Allah.

Allah tells us he is the Ever Watchful, 'Al-Qayyum.' He manages the affairs of his creation, sustains the entire universe, and sets the most suitable laws for all beings till the end of time. Could Allah do that if He did not have absolute knowledge of everything? Could Allah manage the universe if He is not fully aware of all creations? Of course not.

Allah is all-knowing and free from inclinations. He set laws that transcend time, place, and situation. And because Islam was sent as the final religion -after which no heavenly scripture will be revealed- its laws cover all possibilities. In other words, Islamic heavenly laws were set so changes will not be needed at a later stage. Changing religious rulings may have been logical when messengers and prophets were sent one after another to a specific people in limited geographic areas, but when Allah concluded the heavenly revelations with Prophet Muhammad, it was necessary for Islamic legislations to incorporate all possibilities. Allah says:

Some claim that Islamic rules are not compatible with the modern world. We ask them: Do you believe that Allah had missed something? Do you think that you have more knowledge and expertise? We follow the teachings of our Lord because Allah is the Truth, He is self-sufficient, and He possesses absolute and perfect knowledge. No one can supersede Him or interject His rule. Allah is our Creator, and He is best aware of His creation. He is the only logical source of guidance. He says:

Verse 6

Huwal lazee yusawwirukum fil arhaami kaifa yashaaa';
laa ilaaha illaa Huwal 'Azeezul Hakeem

It is He who fashions you in the wombs however He wishes. There is no Allah except Him, the All-mighty, the All-wise.

Allah created and formed you in the womb. Each human comes into being in a specific form: male or female, different skin and hair colour, height, and much more. Allah says:

Another of His signs is the creation of the heavens and earth, and the diversity of your languages and colours. There truly are signs in this for those who know. (30:22)

Just take one look around your town square; you will quickly realize that people are not the product of a factory that casts all products of a mould. Every person is created differently with his or her distinct identity, unique face, body, voice, fingerprints, and personality. It is proof of Allah's absolute ability. And to dispel any doubt that Allah may only be able to create unique people, He, the All-Capable, creates identical twins. He says:

He is the Originator of the heavens and the earth, and when He decrees something, He says only, 'Be,' and it is. (02:117)

Allah is not bound by physical laws, rules, or norms. A child may be born blind or disabled. This should draw your attention to the immense blessings you have. When you see a person born with extra fingers struggling to do simple daily tasks, you appreciate the wisdom of the creation of five fingers. Beauty is mostly appreciated by its absence. A person who has seven fingers would travel the world seeking the best medical treatment so he or she would have normal hands.

Unfortunately, most of us do not realize the wisdom and beauty of Allah's creation until we see individuals with disabilities. Disabilities are your reminder to help others, and your wake-up call to be grateful for what you have. Do not say: Why did Allah create a disabled person? He, the All-Wise, compensates by granting talents, exceptional abilities, and the support and love of others. Each being is created with Allah's ultimate wisdom; and thus, each is beautiful.

Our beloved Prophet Jesus was walking with his disciples when one of them pointed out an ugly dog and said: 'What a repulsive-looking dog.' Prophet Jesus answered: 'Are you faulting the dog for its looks, or are you faulting the Creator for His work?'

This brings us back to the verses. Allah says: "Indeed, there is nothing in the earth and the heavens that is hidden from Allah. It is He who fashions you in the wombs however He wishes. There is no God except Him, the All-mighty, the All-wise. (3:5, 6)Allah –our Creator- has perfect knowledge and absolute wisdom. He has absolute power, so no one can object or interject on His choice of creation.

Verse 7

Huwal lazeee anzala 'alaikal Kitaaba minhu Aayaatum Muh kamaatun hunna Ummul Kitaabi wa ukharu Mutashaabihaatun fa'ammal lazeena fee quloobihim zaiyghun fa yattabi'oona ma tashaabaha minhubtighaaa 'alfitnati wabtighaaa'a taaweelih; wa maa ya'lamu taaweelahooo illal laah; warraasikhoona fil 'ilmi yaqooloona aamannaa bihee kullum min 'indi Rabbinaa; wa maa yazzakkaru illaaa ulul albaab

It is He who has sent this Scripture down to you. Some of its verses are definite in meaning- these are the cornerstone of the Scripture- and others are ambiguous. Those with deviation in their hearts eagerly pursue the ambiguities in their attempt to foster discord and to pin down a specific meaning of their own: only Allah knows the true meaning; and those firmly grounded in knowledge, they say, 'We believe in it: it is all from our Lord'- only those with real perception will take heed-
(Chapter 3: Verse 7)

In the previous Ayat, we explained that Allah has absolute power and wisdom in creation. 'It is He who fashions you in the wombs however He wishes. There is no God except Him, the All-mighty, the All-wise. (3:6) But Allah does not only create matter and substance; He also creates values to guard the movement of life and guarantee its purity.

Allah created you in the womb as He willed and provided you with all the nourishment needed for your body to grow. More importantly, He did not leave your soul without nourishment. By revealing the Quran,

Allah granted you a system of values for spiritual growth. That is why, right after speaking about creating you in the womb, Allah says: 'It is He who has sent this Scripture down to you.' When you look at religion as nourishment and growth for your soul, you appreciate its wisdom and find everything within it good and beautiful.

What does the phrase 'Some of its verses are definite in meaning' mean? We answer that something definite –translated from the Arabic Muhkamat-is clear, precise, and free of confusion. They are the verses in which people do not differ.

Let us take the following examples. Allah says in the 12th verse of chapter 4:

You inherit half of what your wives leave if they have no children; if they have children, you inherit a quarter. In all cases, the distribution comes after payment of any bequests or debts. If you have no children, your wives' share is a quarter; if you have children, your wives get an eighth. In all cases, the distribution comes after payment of any bequests or debts.

And in another chapter:

Flog the adulteress and the adulterer one hundred times. Do not let compassion for them keep you from carrying out Allah's law—if you believe in Allah and the Last Day—and ensure that a group of believers witnesses the punishment. (24:02)

These clear verses were sent down to make Allah's instructions explicit to humanity. They are easily understood by anyone who reads them. Why? Because they include orders of what to do and prohibitions of what not to do. They consist of actions that, if implemented, will result in reward, and if neglected will result in punishment. Thus, they must be very clear and easy to understand even by the casual reader. It is of Allah's fairness that He made His rulings, and the consequences of these rulings, crystal clear. No one can claim that he or she did not understand.

What is the purpose of Allah's commands? We answer that Allah wants you to curb your whims and desires, so life is orderly and beautiful. When Allah commands you to do something, He is well aware that you are capable of doing the opposite if you wish. Likewise, when He prohibits something, He knows that you can follow or ignore His command even if you so desire.

Take the example of the magnificent gift of eyesight. Allah granted you eyes to see, yet He, the All-Wise, assigned some duties and put some boundaries to safeguard the movement of life. Allah says:

Say, 'Look at what is in the heavens and on the earth.' But what use are signs and warnings to people who will not believe? (10:101)

And in another chapter:

Tell the faithful men to lower their gaze and to guard their private parts. That is more decent for them. Allah is indeed well aware of what they do. Tell the faithful women that they should lower their gaze and guard their private parts and not display their adornments – except for what normally shows – (from 24:30-31)

The command to 'lower your gaze' is Allah's teaching that restricts the movement of the eye.

Similarly, Allah commands you not to use your hand to hit others, or ignite a harmful fire and so on. There is often a struggle between what you desire and what Allah commands you to do. For example, you may want to stay in your warm cozy bed at 5 in the morning, but Allah asks you to get up and pray. Allah's teachings are the nourishment for your soul and the guarantee of a functional and thriving society.

Here we should take a moment to study the phrase: 'these are the cornerstone of the Scripture,' translated from the Arabic origin 'Ummu Al Kitab.' The literal translation is "these are the mother of the Scripture.' Both translations 'mother' or 'cornerstone' share the meaning of a foundation or basis. A basis for what? These verses are out foundation for understating faith and our basis in interpreting other verses.

Take note that Allah used the words 'cornerstone' and 'mother' in the singular form. He says: "these are the cornerstone of the Book" and did not say 'these are the cornerstones of the book.' Why? We answer that not every verse is a foundation or a cornerstone; rather, these verses as a cohesive group are the foundation of the Quran.

Let's clarify with an example. Allah says:

We made the son of Mary and his mother a sign; We gave them shelter on a peaceful hillside with flowing water. (23:50)

Allah referred to Prophet Jesus and his mother, the Virgin Mary, as a sign, not as signs. Because Jesus, peace be upon him, was not a sign except by his birth from his mother without a father. And likewise, Mary did not become a sign until she bore a child while a virgin. Hence, they together are one single sign. Similarly, "these are the cornerstone of the Book" refers to all the clear Quranic verses together.

It is He who has sent this Scripture down to you. Some of its verses are definite in meaning- these are the cornerstone of the Scripture- and others are ambiguous. Those with deviation in their hearts eagerly pursue the ambiguities in their attempt to foster discord and to pin down a specific meaning of their own: only Allah knows the true meaning; And those firmly grounded in knowledge, they say, 'We believe in it: it is all from our Lord'- only those with real perception will take heed- (Chapter 3: Verse 7)

So, in the above, we gave examples of the clear and easy to understand verses of the Quran. These verses are especially important because they contain religious rulings that should be crystal clear to everyone regardless of their education or intelligence. Such matters are associated with reward and punishment, so there should be no ambiguity. Allah says: 'It is He who has sent this Scripture down to you. Some of its verses are definite in meaning- these are the cornerstone of the Scripture- and others are ambiguous.'

Now, let's look into the issue of verses that are not so clear. Such verses require in-depth study understand their meaning fully. The question that comes to mind is: Why? If such verses require so much effort to be understood, then why were they revealed in the first place? The answer is twofold. First, as we explained earlier, you should take everything along with the wisdom of the Lord. Allah is the all-Wise, and He revealed every verse, word, and letter through His knowledge and wisdom.

Second, Allah gave you a thoughtful mind and intellect so you can think and judge matters for your own. When it comes to verses that 'are ambiguous,' you can exercise your mind and grow intellectually and spiritually.

Let's look the following verses as an example. Allah says:

Eyesight cannot perceive Him but He perceives eyesight. He is the All-Subtle, the All-Aware. (06:103)

In another chapter:

On that Day there will be radiant faces, gazing upon their Lord (75:22-23)

And lastly,

No indeed! On that day they will be screened off from their Lord (83:15)

Now, let's think logically through these verses as some verses state that you cannot see Allah, while others state that you can. The first verse states that 'Eyesight cannot perceive' Allah. We understand that this statement is related to our life in this world. While, from the other two verses, we understand that things will be different in the Hereafter.

In our current creation, you and I cannot see Allah. In the hereafter, however, we will be resurrected in a form that is able to see Allah. Just like an eye surgeon maybe able to restore sight to a blind person with surgery, or an audiologist maybe able to help a deaf man hear with a hearing aid. Think about what our Lord Almighty can do. He will recreate you in the Hereafter in a manner that allows you to see Him. He says: 'On that Day there will be radiant faces, gazing upon their Lord' (75:22-23)

Here, I would like you to stop and consider the following: what if you did not understand these verses? What if you thought that Allah can never be seen now or in the hereafter? Or what if you thought that some people could see Him in this world? Would that make any difference to your actions in Islam? The simple answer is: No. These verses can be ambiguous to some because they are not related to Islamic rulings or matters of 'do' and 'do not do.' Thus, your understanding or lack of understanding of such verses will not affect your reward or punishment in the Hereafter.

So what are you supposed to do when you come across a verse that you do not understand? Prophet Muhammad gives you the answer. He, peace be upon him, said: "The Qur'an was revealed free of contradiction. **Thus, implement whatever of it you understand; and believe in whatever of it you do not understand."**

Another simple rule to follow is to use the clarity of the verses you understand to shine a light on the verses you do not. Let me give you an example: Allah says:

Those who pledge loyalty to you are actually pledging loyalty to Allah Himself- Allah's hand is placed over theirs—and anyone who breaks his pledge does so to his own detriment: Allah will give a great reward to the one who fulfills his pledge to Him. (48:10)

Does Allah have a hand? Is it like my hand? How about this verse:

The All-Merciful, Who has settled Himself on the Throne (20:05)

Does Allah have a body that settles on a throne? Does He sit down or stand up? These are examples of ambiguous verses, the meaning of which is not entirely clear. Here, we can refer such verses to something that is very clear in the Quran. Allah says in the 10th verse of chapter 48:

'There is nothing whatever like Him.'

So, when you read a verse talking about 'Allah's hand,' remember: 'There is nothing whatever like Him.' Just as Allah's life is not like yours, just as Allah's knowledge is nothing like yours, so is His hand; it is nothing like yours. Similarly, when you read: 'The All-Merciful, Who has settled Himself on the Throne,' think of it in the clear frame of 'There is nothing whatever like Him.' Do not say that Allah has a chair and He sits in it as you, and I do. We believe in these verses and take them in full faith just as Allah intended. Allah says:

It is He who has sent this Scripture down to you. Some of its verses are definite in meaning- these are the cornerstone of the Scripture- and others are ambiguous. Those with deviation in their hearts eagerly pursue the ambiguities in their attempt to foster discord and to pin down a specific meaning of their own: only Allah knows the true meaning; And those firmly grounded in knowledge, they say, 'We believe in it: it is all from our Lord'- only those with real perception will take heed- (Chapter 3: Verse 7)

Let's study the phrase 'Those with deviation in their hearts eagerly pursue the ambiguities in their attempt to foster discord and to pin down a specific meaning of their own.' 'Deviation' is translated from the Arabic origin 'Zaigh.' It is the same word used to describe maligned crooked teeth. Nowadays, people with crooked teeth seek cosmetic and orthodontic treatments to align their teeth back in their natural straight position.

Similarly, the natural state of the human heart is pure and straight. Allah created all of us with healthy dispositions. What corrupts the heart, you may ask? We answer that deviation develops from blindly following every whim and desire. By letting your desires prevail over what Allah asks of you, you are, in fact, corrupting your heart. A corrupt heart often clouds thought and logic. Prophet Muhammad said: "But there is in the body an organ, if it is upright, the whole body is upright, and if it is corrupt, the whole body is corrupted. That organ is the heart." And in another narration, he, peace be upon him, said: "None of you truly believes until his or her desires are subservient to Allah's teachings."

Here, I would like to bring your attention to a simple truth: those who are perverse at heart and follow their desires over Allah's teachings are well aware of their deviation. They know right from wrong even if they act otherwise. You see many people, who immersed themselves in sin, come to regret their actions and declare repentance later. This is because deviation goes against human nature. Even those who do not repent still know right from wrong. Take the example of a group of young men who spend their nights drinking, gambling, and chasing women. They mock and make fun of those who behave well, attend the mosque, or spend their time working and studying. But what happens when one of the corrupt young men tells his friend that he likes his sister and he is thinking about getting engaged to her? The young man would feel angry and run to his sister to prevent her from seeing his friend!

Interestingly, this man would not object, and may indeed feel happy if one of the upright young men asks to be with his sister. He would normally join his friends in making fun of this upright man, but deep down he knows what is right and what is wrong. He knows that none of his friends are decent enough to be a good husband for his sister. Put simply: people know that Allah's teachings are aligned with healthy and pure instincts, while whims and desires are often objectionable.

This brings us back to the verse. Allah says: 'Those with deviation in their hearts eagerly pursue the ambiguities in their attempt to foster discord and to pin down a specific meaning of their own.' The phrase 'to pin down a specific meaning of their own' is an affirmation that the goal of such people is to interpret the Quran in a way that serves the deviation in their hearts. They want to bend the scripture to match their whims.

Here, we should pause and address a critical issue as some people claim that they cannot stop themselves from in as Allah has created them this way. Listen to the following verse. Allah says:

Remember when Moses said to his people, 'My people, why do you mistreat me when you know that I am the Messenger of Allah to you?' So when they deviated, then Allah made their hearts deviate. Allah does not guide the corrupt. (61:05)

Allah does not create anyone who is evil or corrupt by nature. To the contrary, Allah created you with a pure heart and then gave you free choice. He also sent prophets and scriptures to show you right from wrong. But be careful! If you choose corruption, Allah will not stand between you and what you chose. He says:

Whenever a chapter is revealed, they look at each other and say, 'Is anyone watching you?' and then they turn away- Allah has turned their hearts away because they are people who do not use their reason. (09:127)

Allah treats you as you want to be treated. If you turn away from him, He turns away from you. If you close your heart to faith, Allah places a seal on your heart to ensure that faith does not enter.

Similarly, those who pick and choose verses from the Quran to match their whims and lead people to corruption will not be guided by Allah. Whatever action you choose for yourself, whether good or evil, Allah will facilitate it for you. Allah says in a sacred narration: "I am free from all kinds of partners and associates. Whoever does an act associating partners to me, I abandon him to whatever he associated me with."

The verse continues: 'only Allah knows the true meaning.' The first question that comes to mind is: If some verses are ambiguous in meaning, why did Allah reveal them to begin with? We answer that had Allah wanted these verses to be clear, He would have sent them as such. But it is of Allah's wisdom to reveal these verses and encourage us to ponder over them. Mystery fosters research and investigation. Monotony and clarity, on the other hand, are often taken for granted and stifle human creativity. A person who exercises his or her mind is a person who innovates and prospers.

Allah wants you to sharpen your thinking skills, and not take things for granted or at face value. He says:

Will they not contemplate the Quran? Or do they have locks on their hearts? (47:24)

It is He who has sent this Scripture down to you. Some of its verses are definite in meaning- these are the cornerstone of the Scripture- and others are ambiguous. Those with deviation in their hearts eagerly pursue the ambiguities in their attempt to foster discord and to pin down a specific meaning of their own: only Allah knows the true meaning; And those firmly grounded in knowledge, they say, 'We believe in it: it is all from our Lord'- only those with real perception will take heed- (Chapter 3: Verse 7)

Let us look at the phrase:

"only Allah knows the true meaning; And those firmly grounded in knowledge, they say, 'We believe in it: it is all from our Lord.' Interestingly, the difference comes down to the punctuation.

There are two opinions on this.

Some scholars gave the following interpretation:

'only Allah knows the true meaning' then stop; Then they start a new sentence with: 'And those firmly grounded in knowledge, they say, 'We believe in it: it is all from our Lord.' Hence, they explain that Allah alone knows the interpretation of the ambiguous verses. As for those who are firm in knowledge and who are not tempted by personal desires, they say, 'We believe in it: it is all from our Lord.' Prophet Muhammad, peace be upon him, said:

"The Qur'an was revealed free of contradiction. Thus, implement whatever of it you understand and believe in whatever of it you do not understand."

Other scholars read the verse as follows:

'only Allah knows the true meaning, and those firmly grounded in knowledge' is read as one single sentence. Hence, they explain that those who have been blessed with true knowledge from Allah understand the ambiguous verses. And as a result of their knowledge and understanding, they say: 'we believe in it: it is all from our Lord.'

Regardless of where you choose to stop as you recite, the meaning of the verse holds true. Those who have knowledge and faith affirm their love to Allah and say, "we believe in it: it is all from our Lord."

We believe and implement all verses, the ones we fully understand, and the ones we don't because they are from our Lord and He knows the wisdom behind them.

Allah wants you to believe in Him. He is your Creator, the All-Knowledgeable All-Wise. If you demand to understand the reasoning behind every command before you do it, then you have no faith in Allah. The true essence of faith is to trust your Lord even when implementing matters that you do not fully understand.

Allah forbade the consumption of pork over fourteen centuries ago. Nowadays, modern science tells us that pig meat is harmful, and some people have stopped consuming it. Will they be rewarded for not eating pork? No. Allah's reward is reserved for those who abstain from eating pork products because Allah has forbidden them. The believer says: Allah created me, and He is best aware of which fuel is suitable for my body; thus, I follow His teachings even when I do not fully understand them. A person who abstains from drinking alcohol in obedience to Allah attains Allah's rewards. But a person who abstains from Alcohol out of fear of liver damage will not be rewarded. That is the difference between implementing an order out of reason and implementing it out of faith.

The verse ends with: "only those with real perception will take heed.' Perception requires mindfulness and contemplation -the exact opposite of whimsical desires-. The phrase 'those with real perception' is translated from the Arabic origin "Albab الالباب." The root 'lub لب' means 'the mind' or 'the core': Allah is informing you that your mind should examine the core of all matters, and should not be fooled by superficialities.

Let's look at the example of theft: Allah orders cutting the hand of the thief who steals for luxury, not out of dire necessity. The representatives of human rights and compassion say: 'this is brutal and cruel!' We answer that this is a superficial understanding of the law; the core of understanding says that the mere possibility of losing one's hand is a very effective deterrent preventing anyone from stealing. More importantly, this rule is only applied when the thief is not stealing out of hunger or out of dire necessity. It only applies to those who make theft their profession. Thus, the true purpose of the penalty prescribed by Allah is to prevent the act of theft from occurring in the first place. The actual punishment is rarely prescribed. A bus accident may result in more disfigurements of the face, limbs and hands than the number of people who lost their hands due to theft since the beginning of Islam. Do not assume that you are more merciful than Allah. Allah wants to protect the movement of life among people and deter them from doing anything that harms society. Look at the entire picture, not at how the punishment afflicts the sinner. A thief can instil fear in an entire neighbourhood. When you deter people from stealing, you protect everyone's safety. This is the core of understanding. Allah says:

And there is life for you in Fair retribution, people of understanding, so that you may guard yourselves against what is wrong. (2:179)

The ultimate goal is for both: the crime and the punishment to disappear. Thus, you should know that laws and punishments are legislated not with enforcement in mind; rather, they are set with prevention in mind.

Verses 8

Rabbanaa laa tuzigh quloobanaa ba'da iz hadaitanaa wa hab lanaa mil ladunka rahmah; innaka antal Wahhaab

'Our Lord, do not let our hearts deviate after You have guided us. Grant us Your mercy: You are the Ever Giving.'

In the previous verse, Allah taught us that when it comes to the Quran, 'those firmly grounded in knowledge, they say, 'We believe in it: it is all from our Lord.' When it comes to Quranic verses that are not entirely clear, true believers follow the advice of our beloved Prophet Muhammad (SWS).

He taught us: "The Qur'an was revealed free of contradiction. Thus, implement whatever of it you understand and believe in whatever of it you do not understand." Isn't this the true essence of guidance? Isn't it something worth hanging-on to? We supplicate: 'Our Lord, do not let our hearts deviate after You have guided us. Grant us Your mercy: You are the Ever Giving.'

We ask Allah for the gift of mercy because we know that we are not entitled to mercy. It is a great privilege not a right. Why, you may ask? We answer that no creature has a right to anything from Allah, except for what Allah grants him or her. We ask Allah to grant us the mercy to be free from enslavement to our whims and desires. We ask for sound judgment, and for the strength and wisdom to know right from wrong.

But you should not assume that your responsibilities stop at studying and understanding Allah's teachings. You also have the responsibility of sharing your knowledge, because this knowledge is the key to the ultimate success in the hereafter.

Verse 9

Thus, in the very next verse, Allah reminds us to supplicate:

Our Lord, You will gather all people on the Day of which there is no doubt: Allah never breaks His promise.'

The phrase "Our Lord" is beautiful in its meaning. It is translated from the Arabic origin 'Rubbana.' The root 'Rub' or 'Lord' means the caretaker who nourishes, educates, and protects. In the Arabic language, the father is called the Rub of the family. The same word 'Rub' is the root of the word 'tarbia' which means to raise and educate a child. Allah created you from nothing and put the entire universe at your service. Shouldn't you be the least bit appreciative and follow His advice? The Lord's teachings are the sure path to reach your full potential.

Allah reminds you that this world will come to an end, and as He promised, He will gather all people for Judgment Day. Allah never breaks His promises, because anyone who breaks or cannot fulfill a promise is not fit to be Allah. Thus, as believers, we pray for the ultimate goal: to be protected against the torment of the Hereafter.

Let's take a moment to compare our promise to Allah's promise. Allah has perfect ability and complete knowledge. As for us humans, when we plan to do something in the future, we say: 'Insha Allah' or 'Allah willing' Why? Because we do not possess the power or the knowledge to fulfill our promise. Allah says:

Do not say of anything, 'I will do that tomorrow' without adding: 'Allah willing.' And, whenever you forget, remember your Lord and say, 'May my Lord guide me closer to what is right.' (18:23-24)

Our Lord, You will gather all people on the Day of which there is no doubt: Allah never breaks His promise.' (Chapter 3: Verse 9)

Verse 10

Innal lazeena kafaroo lan tughniya 'anhum amwaaluhum wa laaa awlaaduhum minal laahi shai'anw wa ulaaa'ika hum waqoodun Naar

Indeed, those who disbelieve - neither their possessions nor their children will be of any use against Allah. The disbelievers will be fuel for the Fire

In the previous verse, the believers affirmed their faith in Allah's promise:

Our Lord, You will gather all people on the Day of which there is no doubt: Allah never breaks His promise.' (3:9)

But why? Why the resurrection and the gathering? We answer that as believers, we follow Allah's book, and have full faith even in the parts of the Quran that are not entirely clear to us. We do our best to curb our whims in honour of Allah's teachings, and we supplicate the Lord to keep our feet firm on His path. We do all of this is out of love for Our Lord and hope for success on the last day.

As for the disbelievers, they hope that life ends at death; and they claim that all talk about resurrection and the Hereafter is a fantasy. But deep down, all humans know that this universe has a creator. It is part of the human instinct. Allah says:

Did you think We had created you in vain and that you would not be brought back to Us? (23:115)

So why do many people dismiss the Hereafter? We answer that people who want to follow their desires and not abide by any rules know that their deeds would not save them. Thus, the most comfortable thought is the thought that there will be no accountability. However, even such people fancy themselves with the idea that even if they are wrong about resurrection, they have insurance. There is something that could save them that day; maybe their lineage or vast wealth. Just as money and connections are the ticket to power in this world, maybe they can be used to buy favours in the hereafter. Allah answers:

Indeed, those who disbelieve - neither their possessions nor their children will be of any use against Allah. The disbelievers will be fuel for the Fire (Chapter 3: Verse 10)

The phrase 'will be of any use' is translated from the Arabic origin 'toughni.' The root 'ghena' is often used for wealth and riches. But the true meaning is much deeper. To be rich or 'Ghani' means to be free of need and fully independent from others. Today, every day, and on the Day of Judgment, the One true 'Ghani' is Allah. He has no needs. As for wealth and children, they will neither benefit anyone nor fulfill any of the dire needs on the Day of Judgment. There is no one in power but Allah, and paradise is not for sale.

The disbelievers at the time of the Prophet used to claim that since Allah has given them wealth and children in this world, He must be pleased with them, and will grant more in the Hereafter. They looked at Allah's bounty as a sign of approval. Allah answers:

Let not the prosperous dealing of the unbelievers in the land deceive you. This is only a brief enjoyment, after which, Hell will be their home- a miserable resting place! (3:196, 197)

And in another chapter:

We tempt you with evil and with good as a trial, and to Us you will return. (from 21:35)

Allah created means in this world for people to work and excel. The believer and the disbeliever alike are governed by the same means. If you work the land, plant seeds and take care of your crops, you will have a good yield. If you study hard and work hard, you will earn a good living regardless of your faith. But the matter is different in the Hereafter. No one will possess any means and all matters are in Allah's hands. He says:

The Day when they will come out and nothing about them will be concealed from Allah. 'To whom belongs all control today?' To Allah, the One, the All-Powerful. (40:16)

In this world, people live in varying levels of luxury according to their means, efforts, and circumstances. In the Hereafter, you are no longer dependant on means, effort or circumstance; rather, as a believer, you are under the care of the Creator of means and circumstances. As soon as you think of something in paradise, it will come to you. As for the disbelievers, all the wealth and children that preoccupied them away from Allah in this life will not avail them in the hereafter. Allah says:

The desert Arabs who stayed behind will say to you, 'We were busy with our property and our families: ask forgiveness for us,' but they say with their tongues what is not in their hearts. Say, 'Whether it is Allah's will to do you harm or good, who can intervene for you?' No! Allah is fully aware of everything you do. (48:11)

The verse ends with: 'The disbelievers will be fuel for the Fire.' Isn't that the greatest loss and the most severe torment? Those who are punished in fire fuel the fire with their flesh. It is the revenge of the flesh against its owner. How, you may ask? We answer that each cell that forms the body of the disbeliever is a believing cell. The cells of the disbeliever believe in Allah, and the atoms of the sinner are obedient to Allah. The tongue that utters the words of disbelief curses its owner while doing it. Likewise, the hand that steals does so while cursing its owner. But on the day of judgment, all control belongs to Allah. Even your body parts will no longer be subject to your will. They will be witnesses against their owner of the evils he or she used to commit.

Allah put our body parts under our control in whatever we choose to do. But if you choose to do wrong, keep in mind that your body parts will tell on you when you are returned to Allah, the Creator. He says:

And the day when the enemies of Allah will be raised up and gathered for the Fire. They will be driven in arrays. Until when they reach it, their ears, and their eyes, and their skins will bear witness against them as to all that they did. They will say to their skins, 'Why did you testify against us?' and their skins will reply, 'Allah, who gave speech to everything, has given us speech- it was He who created you the first time and to Him you have been returned-You did not think to shield yourselves from your hearing, sight and skin testifying against you and you thought that Allah would never know much of what you did. So were the thoughts you entertained about your Lord that led to your ruin, and you became losers.' (41: 19-23)

Verses 11

Kadaabi Aali Fir'awna wallazeena min qablihim; kazzaboo bi Aayaatinaa fa akhazahumul laahu bizunoo bihim; wallaahu shadeedul 'iqaab

Just like the custom of Pharaoh's clan and those who were before them, who denied Our signs. So Allah seized them for their sins, and Allah is severe in retribution.

In the previous verse, Allah told us about the disbelievers who disregard faith while chasing after worldly possessions. All they chase after: family, connections, and wealth will be useless in the hereafter. Who was the best example of chasing after greed and power? Perhaps Pharaoh.

Allah used the word 'custom' to describe the actions of such people. To be accustomed to doing something means that you worked hard without interruption to establish a habit. We say: so and so is accustomed to gossip and backbiting. Does this mean that all of this person's actions are limited to gossip and backbiting? No, but gossip is his or her most notable trait. Allah says: "Just like the custom of Pharaoh's clan and those who were before them, who denied Our signs.'

Allah wants you to consider what happened to such people as their punishment was not postponed to the Hereafter. He says:

Just like the custom of Pharaoh's clan and those who were before them, who denied Our signs. So Allah seized them for their sins, and Allah is severe in retribution.

(Chapter 3: Verse 11)

On the other hand, just because they were seized in this world, Allah does not want you to think that they escaped the punishment of the Hereafter. He says:

There is a punishment for them in this world, but the punishment of the Hereafter will be harder- no one will shield them against Allah. (13:34)

Here you may ask, if Allah has reserved the severe punishment for the hereafter, then why are people also punished in this world? We answer that if all punishment was postponed to the Hereafter, people's lives would become wretched from the sinners who see no consequences to their actions. Thus, Allah gives us many real-life examples from Pharaoh to modern oppressors. Anyone who makes a habit out of greed and transgression is subject to Allah's retribution, and such punishments are limited to ancient history. Listen to Allah's words:

By the dawn, by the ten nights, by the even and the odd, and by the passing night. Is this oath strong enough for a rational person? Have you considered how your Lord dealt with the people of 'Ad of Iram, the city of lofty pillars, the likes of which has never been made in any land? and the people of Thamood, who hollowed out the rocks in the valley? and Pharaoh of the Stakes in the ground? All of them committed excesses in their lands and spread corruption. So your Lord poured a scourge of punishment over them. Behold! Your Lord is always on the watch. (Chapter 89: 1-14)

Our Lord is always on the watch for people who make denial, greed, and transgression their custom. Allah will reward their behaviour with severe punishment.

When you hear the words 'guilt' and 'punishment,' you immediately think that a crime or sin was committed. But there is something else I would like you to think about: before sin and crime, there must be laws and teachings that specify which acts are criminal and sinful. There is no sin without a text. A person cannot be punished except by a pre-existing law clarifying what is considered a crime. You cannot start arresting people and say: we decided that what you were doing is a punishable crime. Rather, it is necessary to pass laws, give warnings, and present a clear text explaining criminal behaviour. Only then, punishment can be exercised. Put simply: there is no punishment without a crime; there is no crime without a law; and there is no law without a text. Allah says:

Whoever accepts guidance does so for his own good; whoever strays does so at his own peril. No soul will bear another's burden, nor do We punish until We have sent a messenger. (17:15)

The Quranic text about any sin or punishment confirms the legal process that we all recognize around the world: Allah informs, sends ample signs and messengers, and only after repeated warning does the punishment fall. He says:

Just like the custom of Pharaoh's clan and those who were before them, who denied Our signs. So Allah seized them for their sins, and Allah is severe in retribution.

(Chapter 3: Verse 11)

Let's look at another example from the Quran. Allah says:

Indeed Allah does not forgive that any partner should be ascribed to Him, but He forgives anything besides that to whomever He wishes. And whoever associates any partner with Allah has indeed fabricated a most heinous sin. (4:48)

Again, the law is clear: Allah may forgive all sin except for ascribing partners unto Him, because partnership with Allah is declared as the greatest crime. Now listen to the following verse:

Say, 'My servants who have committed excesses against their own souls, do not despair of Allah's mercy. Allah forgives all sins: He is truly the Most Forgiving, the Most Merciful. (39:53)

Some people claim that there is inconsistency. In one verse, Allah proclaims that He does not forgive ascribing partners to Him. Yet in the second verse, He says: "do not despair of Allah's mercy. Allah forgives all sins." Isn't that a contradiction? We answer that, to the contrary, if you take time to study the verses properly, you will find beautiful consistency. Allah starts verse 53 of chapter 39 with the phrase 'Say, 'My servants.' In other words, Allah is addressing His followers and worshippers who believe in His Oneness; yet they have sinned. Their sins have not reached the highest level where they ascribe partners to Allah. Thus, they have hope in Allah's mercy. As for those who ascribe partners to Allah, they are not among Allah's servants, and their sins will not be forgiven.

LET US PONDER AND REFLECT

THE ILLUSION OF THIS WORLD

This world is nothing just an illusion. This world is like a dream. The purpose of our creation is to be tested. Each and everything is our exam whether Allah is blessing us or depriving us of things. In every hurdle and smooth road we are being examined by Allah.

The judgment day is the real day in which our eyes will open, where all our deeds of this dream would get their rewards or punishments. At that day no person of this dream will recognize us. Leaders, friends and even enemies are not closer than your parents. At this day even the closest relation of father and son won't matter. When the son is punished, father would not come to rescue him. Even the son, whose father sacrificed whole life to bring him up, would not go and ask to transfer his father's sin to his. In this type of situation when father and son would refuse to recognize each other, what can you expect from someone else to help?

"O mankind! Fear your Lord, and fear the Day in which no father will benefit his child; nor will any good child be of any benefit to the father; indeed Allah's promise is true; so never may the worldly life deceive you; and never may the great cheat deceive you in respect of Allah's commands. Al- Quran (31:33)"

On that day, everyone will try to escape, where no one will ever be able to escape. So, that person who ruins his life after death for the people living in this temporary world or who chooses the wrong path following the world is innocent or idiot.

"And if they contend with you that you should associate with Me what you have no knowledge of, do not obey them, and keep company with them in this world kindly, and follow the way of him who turns to Me, then to Me is your return, then will I inform you of what you did—Al- Quran- (31:15) "

We are unaware of our deaths. We are not afraid of the day when our nama-e-amal will be presented before Allah. This life has indulged us in many misunderstandings; some think that every breath is to be taken in this world so whatever one want to do, do it here. Others are so much busy in collecting money and spending it that they forget that one day they all will be buried deep in the ground without even one penny in their Coffin.

A person is not born in this world to enjoy and to do whatever he wishes to do but this world exists to do hard work and to tolerate the hurdles and obstacles which come between the ways to achieve the desired goal i.e. to follow teachings of Islam. Every night while you dream, you see many achievements and many downfalls, you also see some scenes which you refuse to see again after you wake up and there are also many situations which you wish to change in your dream. Like movie "Inception", You are living dream in a dream. And one day you will wake up regretting the ending of this dream.

Quran has explained the dream world and the world's existence in some words which are more than enough to conclude this article.

" Verily the likeness of (this) worldly life is as the water (rain) which We send down from the sky, so by it arises the intermingled produce of the earth of which men and cattle eat until when the earth is clad with its adornments and is beautified, and its people think that they have all the powers of disposal over it, Our Command reaches it by night or by day and We make it like a clean-mown harvest, as if it had not flourished yesterday! Thus do We explain the *Ayat* (proofs, evidences, verses, lessons, signs, revelations, laws, etc.) in detail for the people who reflect. " Al-Quran (10:24)

Verses 12

Qul lillazeena kafaroosatughlaboona wa tuhsharoona ilaa jahannam; wa bi'sal mihaad

Say to the disbelievers, 'You will be defeated and driven together into Hell, a foul resting place.

Allah instructs Prophet Muhammad, the conveyer of His message, to issue a warning to the disbelievers. Who are these people? Are they the disbelievers of Quraysh? Maybe. Are they the Jews of Medina who fought the Prophet? This is also possible. In fact, the true warning is to all disbelievers.

Let's take a moment to study the word 'Say.' It is a word that many verses of the Quran start with. But why? We answer that the Quranic literary style is different from the speech you and I use daily. Let me give you an example. You say to your child: "Son, go to your uncle and say: my father will come to visit you tomorrow." So, your son goes to his uncle and says, "My father will visit you tomorrow." Isn't that what 99% of us would say? But if you want to be absolutely accurate and faithful to the message that you were entrusted with: you would go to your uncle and deliver the message as follows: "My father said: Say to your uncle that I will visit him tomorrow."

Our beloved Muhammad is the trustworthy and the truthful. These were the names Meccans gave him before the message of Islam. So, when Muhammad become the Messenger of Allah, he, peace be upon him, delivered Allah's message in the most authentic and accurate form exactly as he received it:

Say to the disbelievers, 'You will be defeated and driven together into Hell, a foul resting place.

It would have been sufficient for the Prophet to go to the disbelievers and say to them: 'You will be defeated and driven together into hell.' But, he peace be upon him, did not want to leave any room for doubt as to the source of the message. Maybe someone would question whether this threat is from Prophet Muhammad(pbuh) or Allah. Thus, by delivering the message accurately, the Prophet informed everyone that he was conveying a command from Allah. He did not convey the gist of the message; rather He passed the entire text verbatim exactly as it was delivered to him by the Angel Gabriel.

Say to the disbelievers, 'You will be defeated and driven together into Hell, a foul resting place.

Here is another point to consider. When Allah instructs the Prophet to convey a message to the disbelievers, he, peace be upon him, is sometimes addressed first, and then he is tasked with sharing the message.

Let us read the following verse:

Say to the faithless, if they relinquish faithlessness, what is already past shall be forgiven them. But if they revert, then the precedent of the ancients has already passed. (08:38)

99% of us would deliver this message as follows: 'if you relinquish faithlessness, what is already past shall be forgiven you.' But the verse states: 'Say to the faithless, if they relinquish faithlessness, what is already past shall be forgiven them.' This indicates that when the verse was revealed to Prophet Muhammad, the disbelievers were not present, so they were mentioned in the third person pronouns 'they' and 'them.' It is interesting to note that heavenly messages are sometimes addressed to the disbelievers in the third person, while in other occasions, such as the verse under study, the message is delivered in the second person.

It is also interesting to consider the timing of the message: "you will be defeated and driven together into Hell.' When was this message delivered to the disbelievers? We answer that Allah revealed this verse when the Muslims were few in numbers and heavily persecuted in Mecca. Every believer lived either under the protection of another or was forced to migrate to a safe place away from Mecca. The logical question to ask is: How can a message promising defeat in this world and dire consequences in the Hereafter be delivered to a great political and military power by a group incapable of protecting itself? For such a message to hold any weight, it can only come from the One who possesses absolute power, all knowledge, and has control over time, space and creation.

Our beloved prophet conveyed Allah's message, while the Muslims were in a state of severe weakness. Moreover, once delivered, this message put a huge burden of proof against Islam. In other words, if the weak Muslims did not prevail over the much stronger Quraysh, the Quran would have been proven inauthentic. But, with Allah's help, this matter came to fruition during the battle of Badr.

The verse under study was not the only one that threatened the disbelievers. Allah says in another chapter:

Their forces will be routed, and they will turn tail and flee. (54:45)

When Omar ibn Al Khattab heard this verse in Mecca, he wondered loudly: "What army?" He knew that the Muslims were persecuted and could not safely assemble in a small group to worship, let alone put together a force to face Quraysh, the largest Army in Arabia. But Prophet Muhammad was not talking about the means available to the believers; rather, he was talking about the Lord of the means who was supporting the message of Islam. In a few short years, events came to prove the authenticity of Allah's words: 'Their forces will be routed and they will turn tail and flee.'

Thus, the battle of Badr should have been a wakeup call for the disbelievers. Why? We answer that there are two warnings in the verse under study: the first was warning was of the disbeliever's defeat in this world, and the second warning was of the gathering and punishment in hellfire in the Hereafter. When, against all the odds, the Prophet's first warning became evidently true in the battle Badr, the authenticity of the Prophet's second warning about the Hereafter should have been taken more seriously. The disbelievers' defeat in Badr confirmed that they would also be 'driven together into Hell.'

Some scholars noted that the Jews of Medina who conspired against the Prophet were meant in the verse under study. They did not think that Islam would prevail against Quraysh. Some saw the Muslim's victory as a sign of Allah's support and believed in Prophet Muhammad, while others decided to wait for another battle. We answer that the verse is general to all disbelievers, polytheists, and anyone who opposes Allah's message.

The phrase 'resting place' is translated from the Arabic origin 'Mihad.' It refers to a lined flattened surface that is comfortable for sitting, walking, and living. In fact, a child's cradle is called 'Mahd.' Here, the question that comes to mind: Is the word 'Mihad' appropriate for a place like Hellfire? We answer: yes it is because he who sits in a crib has no strength to leave or even move. If an infant is uncomfortable in a crib, all he or she can do is cry for help. If no one helps, the infant will remain in the crib forever. Thus, the person whose resting place is hellfire has truly ended up in the most dreadful of resting places.

Verse 13

Qad kaana lakum Aayatun fee fi'atainil taqataa fi'atun tuqaatilu fee sabeelil laahi wa ukhraa kaafiratuny yarawnahum mislaihim ra' yal 'ayn; wallaahu yu'ayyidu bi nasrihee mai yashaaa'; innaa fee zaalika la 'ibratal li ulil absaar

There was certainly a sign for you in the two groups that encountered each other: one group fighting in the way of Allah and the other faithless, who saw them visibly twice as many. Allah strengthens with His help whomever He wishes. There is indeed a lesson in that for those who have vision.

The verse starts with 'There was certainly a sign for you.' Who is being addressed here? The verse is primarily addressing anyone who lived after the battle of Badr, whether a believer or a disbeliever. Allah assures the believer that His aid can overcome any odds, and warns the disbeliever that without ALLAH, numbers and equipment count for little. Allah has made this battle a sign because its events fell out of the normal human convention.

The lesson is also general to anyone who belongs to a party of combatants, whether believers or disbelievers. The people of faith should understand that the physical means of war are not everything in the battle between the truth and falsehood. Moreover, this verse is a warning to the disbelievers who might be under the illusion that superiority in numbers and munitions all but guarantee victory. Battles between a disadvantaged truth and a superior falsehood have taken place before, and, with ALLAH's help, the truth became victorious.

The phrase "two groups that encountered each other" suggests that there was a conflict. When you take a closer look at the Quranic text, you find that Allah gave you a unique description of each group, and left it up to you to draw the full picture. ALLAH explains: "one group fighting in the way of Allah and the other faithless." He described the first group as 'fighting in the way of Allah,' and did not mention that they were believers. At the same time, Allah made clear that the other force was 'faithless,' yet did not mention whose cause they were supporting. By eliminating a description of the first group while reflecting it in the description of the second, and vice-a-versa, Allah gave you a more complete picture. We understand that there was a force of believers fighting in ALLAH's cause against a group of disbelievers who were fighting in satan's cause. Moreover, this Quranic style cemented the link between fighting for ALLAH's cause and faith on the one hand, and fighting for the devil's cause and infidelity on the other.

The verse continues: 'who saw them visibly twice as many.' We have two armies here, but which one is the verse referring to? Who is looking, and who is seen? If the observing army were the Muslims, then the disbelievers were the observed. The opposite is also true. Let's look at the matter from both angles.

In the battle of Badr, the disbelievers numbered close to one thousand, while the Muslim force was three hundred and fourteen fighters. If the disbelievers were the ones who were seeing the Muslims 'visibly twice as many,' then this opens two possibilities. The first is that the disbelievers saw the believers double their own number. Since the disbelievers numbered a thousand fighters, then they saw the believers as two thousand fighters. The second possibility is that the disbelievers saw the believers twice their actual number -double 314 is 628 fighters-.

Let's consider the other angle where the believers were the ones who were seeing the disbelievers 'visibly twice as many.' Again, they may have seen the disbelievers twice their actual number (double 1000 is 2000 fighters.) Or they may have seen them double their own number, that is, 628 disbelievers. In the latter scenario, the number of disbelievers in the eyes of the believers was less than the disbelievers' actual number, which is more in-line with ALLAH's promise to the believers in the Quran. He says:

But ALLAH has lightened your burden, for now, knowing that there is a weakness in you—a steadfast hundred of you will defeat two hundred and a steadfast thousand of you will defeat two thousand, by ALLAH's permission: ALLAH is with the steadfast. (08:66)

ALLAH promised the believers victory even when they were weak. Allah reminds us all: 'Allah strengthens with His help whomever He wishes. There is indeed a lesson in that for those who have vision.'

Some critics have used the verse under study in their attempts to find faults in the Quran. The argument goes: How come the Quran says: "who saw them visibly twice as many" -regardless if the increase was in the believers or disbelievers eyes- while another verse in the Quran says:

Remember when Allah showed them to you in your dream as only a few. If He had shown you them as many, you would have lost heart and quarreled about the matter; but Allah saved you. He knows what your hearts contain. When you met He showed them to you as few, and He made you few in their eyes, so that He might bring about what has been ordained; for all things rest with ALLAH. (08:43-44)

Isn't that a contradiction in the Quran? We answer that there is a difference between courage and enthusiasm before engaging in battle, and morale and bravery during battle. Allah spoke of both situations: He made each party appear small in the eyes of the other before engaging in battle. This allowed the Muslims —who were at a great disadvantage in numbers- to see the disbelievers less. It made the Muslims feel better about their odds in battle. It also gave them hope that victory, while hard, is achievable if they go in with full force. When the disbelievers saw the believers even less than their already low number, they felt so assured of victory. They relaxed and did not take the battle too seriously. ALLAH says:

When you met He showed them to you as few, and He made you few in their eyes so that He might bring about what has been ordained; for all things rest with ALLAH. (08:44)

But what happened to morale when the two groups engaged in actual battle? The believer entered the battle with intense readiness while the disbeliever entered almost careless. Once the battle started, everything was turned on its head. The believers saw the disbelievers as many, yet they were defeating them. This gave the Muslim even more courage and confidence. The disbelievers found themselves in a battle they were not prepared for, and as they were pushed back by the smaller army, their morale deteriorated. ALLAH says:

One group fighting in the way of Allah and the other faithless, who saw them visibly twice as many. Allah strengthens with His help whomever He wishes.

So before the battle, ALLAH reduced the numbers of both parties to encourage both to fight. And during the battle, ALLAH made both appear greater in number in the eyes of each other. Thus, boosting the morale of the advancing Muslims and decimating the morale of the retreating army. Allah, the All-Capable, can manipulate emotions from one end of the spectrum to the other and grant victory to whomever he wills. He says:

There was certainly a sign for you in the two groups that encountered each other: one group fighting in the way of Allah and the other faithless, who saw them visibly twice as many. Allah strengthens with His help whomever He wishes. There is indeed a lesson in that for those who have vision.

(Chapter 3: Verse 13)

This verse carries glad tidings to every believer in conflict, and a warning to every disbeliever fighting the truth: Do not measure matters solely by means and numbers. Prepare all you can, and then leave the rest to your Creator. Do not be deceived by numbers and munitions, for there is plenty of precedents where a small number of believers overcame a large number of disbelievers.

The Great Battle of Badr took place on the seventeenth of Ramadan, two years after the Hijra. This was the first battle that the believers ever engaged in with the disbelievers, and it is, by far, the most famous and most renown, because of the several extraordinary events that occurred during it. Prophet Muhammad (saws) had encouraged the Muslims to oppose the Quraysh caravan which was returning to Mecca from Sham. The Muslims went out with 300 and some soldiers not intending to meet a caravan of about 40 men, not intending to fight but only to overpower them. The caravan escaped, but Abu Sufyan had already sent word to Quraysh to come and protect it. The Quraysh marched with enormous army of 1000 men, six hundred wearing shields, 100 horses, and 700 camels, and luxurious provisions to last for several days. The disbelievers wanted to make this a victory that would put fear into the hearts of all the Arabs. They wanted to crush the Muslims once and for all and the odds were overwhelmingly in their favour. Imagine that the believers with their small army (including only 2 horses), going out with the intent of meeting a mere 40 unarmed man and instead meeting a well- prepared army of *3 times* their size.... Prophet Muhammad (saws) could have easily ordered the believers to fight and they wouldn't have hesitated to comply, but, he (saws) wanted to emphasize to his followers that they should fight out of conviction and iman and to teach us a lesson in the process. He gathered his followers to conduct shura (consultation). Many of the muhajireen (the Muslims who emigrated from Mecca to Medinah) spoke up, using the most eloquent of words to describe their dedication. But there was one of the sahabah whom all the others envied for his statement to Prophet Muhammad (saws). He, Miqdad ibn al Aswad, rose up in front of the crowd and said, 'Ya Prophet Muhammad! We will not say to you like Bani Israel said to Musa, 'Go you and your Lord and fight, we are here sitting (waiting).' (surat al maa'idah). Go by Allah's blessing and we are with you!" And so Prophet Muhammad (saws) was very pleased, but in his great wisdom, he waited silently, and some among the Muslims knew what he intended. So far only the muhajiroon had given their consent, but it was the Ansar (the Muslims who lived in Medinah and welcomed the Muslims into their city) who had the most to loose in this stake and it was not a part of the pledge (that Prophet Muhammad had taken from the Ansar at 'Aqabah) for the Ansar to fight with the Muslims in foreign territory. So, the great leader of the Ansar, Sa'd ibn Mu'adh spoke up, "Ya Prophet Muhammad! Maybe you mean us." Prophet Muhammad (saws) responded in the affirmative. Sa'd proceeded to give a beautiful speech in which he said, among many things: "O Messenger of Allah, we have believed in you and we believe that you are saying the truth. We give you, based on that, our covenant to listen to and obey you.....By Allah, the One Who sent you with the truth, if you were to enter the sea, we would rush into it with you and not one of us would stay behind...May Allah show you in our actions what will satisfy your eyes. So march with us, putting our trust in Allah's blessings." Prophet Muhammad (saws) was very pleased by this and said, "Forward and be of cheer, for Allah has promised me one of the two (the caravan or the battle), and by Allah, it is as if I now saw the enemy lying prostrate." The Muslims marched forward and encamped at the nearest spring of Badr (closest to Medinah, which is north of Mecca). One of the companions, Al-Hubab ibn Mundhir, asked Prophet Muhammad (saws), " Has Allah inspired you to choose this very spot or is it stratagem of war and the product of consultation?" Prophet Muhammad (saws) said, "It is the product of stratagem of war and consultation." So Al-Hubab suggested that the Muslims encamp further south on the nearest water well, make a basin of water for themselves, and destroy the other wells to thereby restrict to Quraysh's access to the water. Prophet Muhammad (saws) approved of his plan and carried it out. Then, Sa'd ibn Mu'adh suggested that a trellis or hut be built for Prophet Muhammad (saws) as a protection for him and to serve as a headquarters for the army. Prophet Muhammad (saws) and Abu Bakr stayed in the hut while Sa'd ibn Mu'adh and a group of his men guarded it. Prophet Muhammad (saws) spent the whole night preceding the battle in prayer and supplication although he (saws) knew that Allah (swt) had promised him victory. It was out of his (saws) love for and worship and submission to Allah (swt) that he did this.

That same night, the night when tensions were mounting for one of the biggest events in history, the night before the battle that would signify the progress or defeat of Islam, instead of being nervous, worried and unable to sleep, the Muslim army enjoyed a sound and refreshing sleep. That night was the night of the 17th of Ramadan, the year 2 A.H. This was a Divine favour which Allah (swt) mentioned in the Quran: "(Remember) when He covered you with a slumber as a security from Him, and He caused rain to descend on you from the sky, to clean you thereby and to remove from you the Rijz (whispering, evil suggestions, etc.) of Satan, and to strengthen your hearts, and make your feet firm thereby." [8:11] The second favour Allah (swt) mentioned in this verse is the rain that Allah (swt) sent upon the believers that very night. The place where the Muslims were to encamp was made of sandy ground which was hard to walk on because one's feet could easily sink in it. Allah (swt) sent the rain to make the ground firm under their feet and sent the sleep to make their hearts firm. The next morning, Prophet Muhammad (saw) was still asleep when Quraysh was very closely approaching. Abu Bakr (ra) was very hesitant to wake the noble Messenger (saws), but was forced to do so because the Quraysh were approaching quickly. The Muslims were arranged in ranks. When the two parties were closer and were visible to each other, Prophet Muhammad (saws) began supplicating to Allah swt. The Quraysh were haughty and arrogant and confident in their superior numbers, weapons, and provisions but it is Allah (swt) who would decide the matter: "(O disbelievers) if you ask for a judgement, now has the judgement come unto you and if you cease (to do wrong) , it will be better for you, and If you return (to the attack), so shall we return, and your forces will be of no avail to you, however numerous it be, and verily, Allah is with the believers." [8:19]

The battle began with a confrontation between three men from each side:

In the former two cases, Hamza and Ali killed their opponents, but 'Ubaidah (despite killing his opponent) was severely wounded and died about four or five days later. The fighting intensified, and many more duels broke out. In the midst of all of this, Prophet Muhammad (saws) continued to supplicate his Lord. He (saws) said, "O Allah! Should this group (of Muslims) be defeated today, You will no longer be worshipped."Abu Bakr witnessed this incessant supplication so He said to Prophet Muhammad (saws), "O Prophet Muhammad, you have cried out enough to your Lord. He will surely fulfill what He has promised you."

Immediate was the response of Allah (swt), Who sent down angels from the heavens for the help and assistance of Prophet Muhammad (saw) and his companions. The Quran marks this miraculous occurrence:

"I will help you with a thousand angels each behind the other (following one another) in succession." Quran [8:9] Prophet Muhammad (saws), in his hut, dozed off a little and then raised his head joyfully crying and said, "O Abu Bakr! glad tidings are there for you. Allah's victory has approached. By Allah, I can see Jibreel on his mare in the thick of a sandstorm." Then he came out of the hut and exclaimed: "sayuhzamul jam'u wa yuwwalloonad-dubur" Quran [54:45] (Their multitude will be put to flight, and they will show their backs.) This is in fact one of the miracles of the Quran because this verse was revealed in Mecca before any of these events at Badr had taken place. Omar (ra), upon hearing Prophet Muhammad (saws) proclaim this verse on this occasion said, "When this verse was first revealed, I asked Prophet Muhammad what it means. What multitude? What defeat? And Prophet Muhammad (saws) didn't answer me. But when I saw him recite it on that occasion, I then understood." Then Prophet Muhammad (saws) took a handful of dust and cast it at the enemy and said : Confusion seize their faces!" As he flung the dust, a violent sandstorm blew like furnace blast into the eyes of the enemy. About this, Allah says: "And you (i.e. Muhammad - saws) threw not when you did throw, but Allah threw." [8:17] It was at this point that Prophet Muhammad (saws) gave orders to launch a full counter-attack. He incited the believers reciting the following verse: "And be quick for forgiveness from your Lord, and for Paradise as wide as are the heavens and earth." [3:133] The spirit of the Muslims was at its peak and they fought with the utmost courage and bravery severely wounding the Quraysh army, killing many of their men and instilling fear in their hearts. The Muslims did not know that Allah's help was about to descend upon them. They only knew the odds that were apparent to both sides: 100 against 300, 700 camels against 70 camels, 100 horses against 2, enormous provisions against none, an intent and preparation for war against an unprepared group of believers. Still, despite all odds, they had trust in Allah (swt) and His Messenger and they were willing and even hoping to give their lives of this dunya for the ever-lasting abode of Jannah. Because of their devotion Allah (swt) sent His help and victory.

In addition to sending down angels, Allah (swt) also brought another miraculous occurrence to ensure the Muslim victory. Allah says: "(And remember) When Allah showed them to you (Muhammad) as few in your dream, if He had shown them to you as many, you would have surely have disputed in making a decision. But Allah saved (you). Certainly, He is the All Knower of what is in the breasts.'" [8:43] And indeed, Allah (swt) did fulfill His promise: "And (remember) when you met (the army of the disbelievers on the Day of the battle of Badr), He showed them to you as few in your eyes and He made you appear as few in their eyes, so that Allah might accomplish a matter already ordained (in His Knowledge), and to Allah return all matters (for decision)." [8:44] Many of the disbelievers were killed in this battle, the most noteworthy one was Abu Jahl, the archenemy of Islam. When Prophet Muhammad (saws) set out to look at his corpse, he (saws) said, "'This is the Pharaoh of this nation.'" And so the Muslims defeated the disbelievers in a humiliating defeat by the Help of Allah (swt). Indeed Allah, again, fulfilled His promise, "'Their multitude will be put to flight, and they will show their backs'" [54:45] The disbelievers, with all their might, turned their backs and ran away from the Muslims in disgrace and utter humiliation.

VICTORY BELONGED TO THE MUSLIMS

REFLECTING ON VERSE 13

There was certainly a sign for you in the two groups that encountered each other: one group fighting in the way of Allah and the other faithless, who saw them visibly twice as many. Allah strengthens with His help whomever He wishes. There is indeed a lesson in that for those who have vision.

(Verse 13)

Let's take a few moments to study the word 'lesson,' translated from the Arabic origin 'Ebra' 'عِبْرَة.' The root of the word 'عِبْرَة' is 'ر ب ع' which means to cross from one place to another. For example, the ship that ferries people from one shore to the other is called 'Abbara' 'عبّارة.' In literature, 'Ebara' 'عبارة' is a phrase we use to convey our ideas to other people. 'Abeer' 'عبير' is the beautiful aroma that fills the air, traveling from the source, such as a flower, to your nose. All these words share the core meaning of transfer from one place to another. Similarly, a lesson 'Ebra' 'عِبْرَة' is a remarkable tool that takes you from a place of ignorance to a place of understanding. A really good lesson gives you a whole new outlook on life.

Thus, when Allah says: "There is indeed a lesson in that for those who have vision," we should pay close attention. Allah transfers the believers from a place of fear to a place of victory, from the conventional thoughts of battle -where a poorly armed few stand no chance against the well-equipped many-to victory by ALLAH's support. Likewise, Allah transfers the disbelievers from sure victory to defeat despite their clear advantage on the battlefield; and from a place of confidence to utter humiliation. Allah wants you to understand that His support overrides all convention.

The phrase 'Allah strengthens with His help whomever He wishes' should draw your attention to the fact that ALLAH wants you to work and prepare. Had ALLAH wanted to torment the disbelievers without having the believers fight them, He would have ruined them with an earthquake, a storm, or disease. But ALLAH wanted to punish the disbelievers at the hands of the believers. He says:

How could you not fight a people who have broken their oaths, who tried to drive the Messenger out, who attacked you first? Do you fear them? It is ALLAH you should fear if you are true believers. Fight them: ALLAH will punish them at your hands. He will disgrace them. He will help you to conquer them, He will heal the believers' feelings. (09:13,14)

Allah wants you to learn the lesson of hard work and preparation, and only then, Allah would complete the process of victory. ALLAH says: 'There is indeed a lesson in that for those who have vision.'

Some people have questioned: Is the lesson for people who have vision, or people who have insight? We answer that the lesson here is for those who have vision because what the verse talks about is a tangible matter which can be observed. Anyone who has eyes can see.

If you look at the battle of Badr, you find it full of evidence of the authenticity of this lesson. The believers were few in numbers and equipment, and they were not even prepared for war. They went out looking to seize a caravan carrying goods, food, and clothing for Quraysh who seized all their possessions in Mecca. Had they only captured the caravan, the victory would not have been small because caravans are lightly defended. But ALLAH intended proper victory for them over a formidable force. He says:

Remember how ALLAH promised you that one of the two enemy groups would fall to you: you wanted the unarmed group to be yours, but it was ALLAH's will to establish the truth according to His Word and uproot the disbelievers—(08:07)

Had the Muslims raided the caravan –as they wished-, people would have said that Muhammad and his followers confronted a group of unarmed merchants. ALLAH, however, wanted to give the Muslims a true triumph, so he set them against a fully prepared enemy. Then, He Almighty gave them victory and made it a lesson for all.

Let's take a few moments and consider other lessons from the battle of Badr. One of the more interesting facts is that Badr had members of the same family –often a father and son- fighting on opposite sides. Take the example of Abu Bakr, who was fighting next to the Prophet, and his son, who had not accepted Islam yet, fighting with Quraysh.

Before Abu Bakr migrated to Medina, he had a very close relationship with his son. Later, when the son entered Islam, he said to his father: "I saw you on the day of Badr, but I turned my face away from you." Abu Bakr responded: "Son, if I saw you that day fighting the faithful, I would have killed you." This statement may seem extreme, but both positions are logical. How, you may ask? We answer that if the son of Abu Bakr came face to face with his father in battle, he would have to weigh his love for his father against his ties to Quraysh. The son knew that Quraysh was corrupt and had illegally seized the properties of those who accepted Islam. Abu Bakr, on the other hand, would have compared his love for his son on the one hand, and his ties to ALLAH, Prophet

Muhammad, and justice on the other. He knew the truth and the value of faith.

Mus'ab met his brother Abu 'Aziz –a disbeliever- on the battlefield. After the battle, Mus'ab saw his brother captive to another companion, Abu al-Yusr. He said to him: "O Abu al-Yusr, be tough on your captive, for his mother is rich, and she will pay a handsome ransom to set him free." Abu Aziz was astonished. He turned and said: "My brother, is this how you treat me?" Mus'ab replied, pointing to Abu al-Yusr: "He is a much closer brother to me than you."

Faith permeated the soul of the believers. It made it possible for a small army to triumph over the people of disbelief; it was the love for ALLAH and the truth that eclipsed the bonds of brotherhood, paternalism, and tribalism. ALLAH says:

The indelible marking of Allah. And who marks better than Allah! And for Him we are worshipers. (2:138)

Another lesson to learn from Badr is that many of Quraysh's leaders and fearsome warriors escaped death that day. This made the Muslims angry. ALLAH, however, had wisdom behind preserving the life of the disbelievers. ALLAH had reserved many of these men for great tasks serving the future of Islam. For example, had Khalid ibn al-Walid died on the battlefield when he was supporting the disbelievers, Muslims would have lost a great future leader. ALLAH saved Khalid for the future, where his sword would be aimed at the enemies of Islam. This was another form of victory.

From all the lessons above, we find that the phrase "There is indeed a lesson in that for those who have vision," is a perfect end to a verse that started with 'There was certainly a sign for you in the two groups that encountered each other.'

Verses 14

Zuyyina linnaasi hubbush shahawaati minannisaaa'i wal baneena walqanaateeril muqantarati minaz zahabi walfiddati walkhailil musawwamati wal an'aami walhars; zaalika mataa'ul hayaatid dunyaa wallaahu 'indahoo husnul ma-aab

Beautified for people are the love of desires of women, sons, heaped piles of gold and silver, and pure bred horses, cattle, and tilth; Such are the enjoyments of the worldly life; yet with **ALLAH** is the best resort.
(Verse 14)

This verse comes right after the discussion of the historical battle of Badr. It may seem off-topic: a verse talking about women, children and riches right after discussing war. In reality, Allah is alerting you that proper faith demands that you devote yourself to ALLAH and abandon the pleasures of life. This is especially important when you are called to defend Islam. Faith should override greed and make the faithful sacrifice wealth and self to safeguard ALLAH's teaching. A person who is chasing life's pleasures usually shies away from participating in war. So the placement of this verse makes perfect sense following talk about war.

Let's take a moment to discuss the pleasures of life, whether money, the opposite gender, property, and so on. Life is inherently unfair; you may work hard and do everything right only to see a criminal or a drug-dealer do far better than you in life. Even if you attain all your desires in life, one of two things is guaranteed to happen: either you will depart these pleasures in death, or these pleasures will depart you in a loss. Life's pleasures are fleeting.

This is in sharp contrast to the pleasures of the hereafter. If you work hard and follow ALLAH's teachings, ALLAH guarantees you amazing results. The luxuries of life are according to the abilities and resources of humans; whereas, the luxuries of paradise are according to the infinite ability and resources of the Almighty. Lastly, in the hereafter, you will never die and leave the pleasures behind, nor will paradise disappear and leave you behind. The pleasures of the hereafter are far superior and everlasting.

ALLAH says:

The life of this world is merely an amusement and a diversion; true life is in the Hereafter, if only they knew. (29:64)

Thus, when the call to defend Islam arises, ALLAH made it a sign of proper faith to leave life behind and stand up to secure faith. He says:

Say, 'Do you expect something other than one of the two best things to happen to us? Well, we expect ALLAH to inflict punishment on you, either from Himself or at our hands. So wait; we too are waiting.' (09:52)

The 'two best things' mentioned here are both triumphs for the believer: either victory over the disbelievers in battle, or attaining the status of martyrs in Paradise; both are beautiful.

This brings us back to the verse. The word 'Beautified' should alert you that something is being artificially embellished beyond its true nature. Beautification is often the dividing line between the pleasures that ALLAH permits and the pleasures that He forbids. For example, a woman is naturally beautiful and attractive; but if she further beautifies herself in public with makeup, surgery, or revealing clothes, then this adornment is something above the essence of her natural beauty, and it is prohibited in Islam.

Does that mean that you should live an ascetic life? No, Allah wants you to embrace life, not shun it. The key is to embrace life's necessities and not to lust after its embellishments. ALLAH says:

Seek the life to come by means of what ALLAH has granted you, but do not neglect your rightful share in this world. Do good to others as ALLAH has done good to you. Do not seek to spread corruption in the land, for ALLAH does not love those who do this,' (28:77)

The second word we should study is 'desires.' What is desire? It is a strong craving of one's self towards something. Here we should distinguish between reasonably following the desires that are necessary to sustain life –which ALLAH likes-, and foolishly lusting after these desires –which ALLAH hates-.

This brings us back to the verse. ALLAH says: 'Beautified for people are the love of desires of women, sons, hoarded treasures of gold and silver, and purebred horses, cattle, and tilth' But who exactly is beautifying these desires? We answer that Allah placed beauty in everything, but if beauty is artificially enhanced in excess of the natural and necessary, then it is the work of Satan.

The verse continues: "Beautified for people are the love of desires of women, sons.' You may find it interesting that ALLAH mentions the desire for male children, and did not mention 'daughters.' Why? We answer that throughout the ages, cultures have preferred sons over daughters because they believed that sons are the only ones capable of carrying the family name and honour. Before Islam, some of the Arabs used to bury their newborn daughters alive because they feared a daughter may bring shame to the family. Islam put an end to this horrendous practice. Even in our modern era, when China instituted a one-child policy, the practice of aborting female foetuses became common because the family would rather have a son as the only child. ALLAH says describing the scene on the day of judgment:

When the sun is shrouded in darkness, when the stars are dimmed, when the mountains are set in motion, when pregnant camels about to deliver are abandoned, when wild beasts are herded together, when the seas boil over, when souls are sorted into classes, And when the female infant, buried alive, is asked: For what offense was she killed? (81:1-9)

Beautified for people are the love of desires of women, sons, heaped piles of gold and silver, and distinguished horses, cattle, and tilth; Such are the enjoyments of the worldly life, yet with Allah is the best resort. (Verse 14)

We continue down the list of worldly glamour that draws men away from defending their land and standing up for their faith. The next item on the list is 'heaped piles of gold and silver.' The word 'heaped' is translated from the Arabic origin 'Quanateer' 'القناطير' the plural of 'Quintar.' 'Quintar' is a unit for measuring weight which equals about 144kg or 317lbs.

Here is a little history of the word: before 'Quintar' was used as a unit for measuring weight, it was used as a unit for volume. In ancient times, a sign of a person's wealth was when he or she would own enough gold to fill the skin of a bull. This volume was called Quintar. Later on, rather than using the word Quintar to refer to the volume of gold needed to fill a bull's skin, people started using it to refer to the weight of that gold.

At first glance, the phrase "heaped piles," sounds redundant: A heap, after all, is a pile. We answer that such expressions —common in the Arabic language- are used for emphasis. Usually, a word is followed by a very similar word -often derived from the same root- to give it strength.

Allah says:

As for those who believe and do good deeds, We shall admit them into Gardens graced with flowing streams and there they will remain forever. They will have pure spouses there, and We shall admit them into a cool shaded shade. (4:57)

A 'shaded shade'?! Let's clarify with an example. When the sun is high in the sky and its heat is beating down on your head, you look for shade. You can seek cover under the shade of a solid wall; The wall will protect you from the sun, but it will not provide you with cool breeze. However, if you sit under a tree, where there are many levels of shade, you are protected from the sun and you get a nice breeze. Each leaf provides a shade, and each leaf under it provides additional shade and so on. The space between the leaves allows air and coolness in; that is why we all love sitting under trees. Don't we use the same concept in our homes? We often have two or three layers of curtains to allow just the right amount of air and sunlight in.

This brings us back to the verse, Allah described the 'heaped piles of gold and silver' emphasizing the insatiable desire for hoarding wealth.

The next item on the list of life's adornments is 'distinguished horses.' A fine horse has always been an instrument of pride and a sign of wealth. In today's modern world, a man's cars and pure-bred horses are an indication of status and wealth.

The phrase 'distinguished horses'-translated from the Arabic origin 'Musawamah-'carries many meanings. It means that these horses have pastures where they are free to roam and eat wherever they like. They are not work-horses that are only offered hay. 'Musawamah' also means that these horses have markings distinguishing them from other horses, such as fancy names, known heritage, and physical traits. Another meaning is that these horses are well trained to be proud rides.

The verse continues with 'cattle, and tilth.' Allah says about cattle in chapter 6:

There are eight in pairs: A pair of sheep and a pair of goats – Say: 'Is it the two males He has made unlawful, or the two females, or what the wombs of the two females contain? Tell me with knowledge if you are being truthful.' And a pair of camels and a pair of cows – Say: 'Is it the two males He has made unlawful, or the two females, or what the wombs of the two females contain? Were you then witnesses when Allah gave you this instruction?' Who could do greater wrong than someone who invents lies against Allah thus leading people astray without any knowledge? Allah does not guide the people of the wrongdoers. (06:143-144)

There is a common misconception regarding this verse. Many people mistake the phrase 'There are eight in pairs,' for 'There are eight pairs.' In other words, they assume that the verse is talking about sixteen animals; however, the proper understanding is:'there are eight animals arranged in four pairs.' They are two sheep, two goats, two camels, and two cows. The total is four pairs because a pair consists of two items. For example, a pair of shoes consists of two shoes, a left, and a right.

Cattle have always been a sign of wealth and a source of pride for the owner.

So are prime pieces of land. When you hear the word "tilth," you think of crops and yield. But Allah wants to remind you that tilling the land is the only part you and I have in producing crops. Allah does the rest.

Allah says:

Consider the seeds you sow in the ground- Is it you who make it germinate or are We the Germinators? (56:63-64)

Take note that Allah referred to our part in agriculture as merely plowing and sowing. Plowing is the process of loosening the soil to allow air and water to penetrate the top layer freely. Allah, the Creator, has deposited in the cotyledon of each seed all the elements needed to support the germinating plant until the roots grow enough to leach nutrients from the soil. As the roots strengthen, the cotyledon withers or become the plant's first leaf. In other words, Allah deposited in the cotyledons the perfect amount of nutrients to feed the plant until –given the right circumstances- the plant can feed itself from the ground.

Good farmers know that the ideal soil to plow and sow seeds in is one that is not sandy –as it does not hold water-, nor clay-like or Muddy –as it does not allow air in-.

The value of all of the pleasures mentioned in the verse, from the desire of women, children, heaps of gold and silver, fine branded horses, cattle, to crops are summarized in the phrase: "Such are the enjoyments of the worldly life; yet with Allah is the best resort."

So when it comes to choosing between sub-bar and temporary pleasures on the one hand, and Allah's company in Paradise on the other, the choice should be a clear, easy one. A true believer would never sacrifice eternal pleasure for worldly one.

REFLECTING ON VERSE 14

Beautified for people are the love of desires of women, sons, heaped piles of gold and silver, and distinguished horses, cattle, and tilth; Such are the enjoyments of the worldly life; yet with Allah is the best resort. (Verse 14)

What makes people deviate away from the path of their Lord into ruin? We answer that every human being has a weakness; a key or desire that can easily lead down the wrong path. For some, the key is the opposite gender, while for others, the key maybe money, or children. There are many examples of men who steal from their jobs to give their children a better life. How many people you know who go into usurious debt to buy a luxury car?

Look at the vast majority of advertisements on TV and in magazines. They are specifically designed to lure people into following their desires. They dangle the keys of riches, and countless other traps to seduce you. Here you may ask: If Allah wanted us to stay on His path, then why did He create all these distractions? We answer that the key word you have to understand is 'Beautified.' It is the act of artificially embellishing something beyond its true nature. Allah mentioned it in the passive voice, because this 'beatification' can come from many sources.

Allah created a world full of beauty and assigned each blessing in life a suitable task. He created the opposite gender to provide comfort through compassion and kindness in marriage. Allah says:

Another of His signs is that He created spouses from among yourselves for you to live with in tranquillity: He ordained love and kindness between you. There truly are signs in this for those who reflect. (30:21)

Allah wants us to enjoy long-term relationships under the umbrella of marriage. A lawful relationship satisfies desires, protects the society from the ills of promiscuity, and provides a healthy environment for raising children. Compare that to illicit relationships that often leave behind single parents unable to properly provide for the child.

What about the desire for family and children? Allah teaches how to properly channel it for our benefit and the benefit of the society.

Prophet Zachariah supplicated:

'Lord, my bones have weakened and my hair is ashen grey, but never, Lord, have I ever prayed to You in vain: I fear what my relatives will do when I am gone, for my wife is barren. So grant me a successor –a gift from You– to be my heir and the heir of the family of Jacob. And make him, my Lord, pleasing to You.' (19:4-6)

Zachariah (peace be upon him) prayed for a son that would inherit the wisdom and teachings of the family of Jacob. He asked for an obedient child who reveres Allah and preserves His message on earth. Prophets and messengers do not leave wealth to their heirs; rather they leave the treasures of Allah's word.

Similar is the case of wealth, tilth and livestock. Each can be used for the sake of Allah, and help the poor.

In fact, each desire can be directed either towards Allah or towards sin. You have the power to make you desires work for you rather than against you. Listen to the supplication of the righteous as they direct their desires in the right direction:

Those who pray, 'Our Lord, give us joy in our spouses and offspring. Make us good examples to those who are aware of You'. (25:74)

Allah ends the verse with: 'Such are the enjoyments of the worldly life; yet with Allah is the best resort.' An enjoyment is typically something temporary and superficial. For something to be a true pleasure, it should satisfy four requirements: First, it has to be of a good nature; second, it has to increase with time. Third, it has to be continuous; and lastly, it has to follow you wherever you go. In other words, true pleasure –that is good and everlasting- can only be given to you from an everlasting power that does not change.

Let's measure the supposed pleasures of this life against these four requirements: If you look at the opposite gender, money, children, cars, horses, cattle, and property, you will quickly find that none of them satisfy any of the requirements of true pleasure. Your spouse can be evil in nature. Your car can give you trouble. Your children –even if they are the best- may die any time. Your farm may cost you all your savings and so on.

Let's say that you are lucky enough to have the best spouse, tons of money, the best cars, and livestock, all living on the best piece of land on earth; let us also concede that none of these things will be taken away from you. How long do you think this will last? At the very most a few decades until you die.

The worldly life is measured by your age, not by the age of the universe itself. Your life lasts 75 on average –in reality you may die today-. If the universe lasts for one day or a million years after you die, it does not make any difference. No one lives forever, thus, the enjoyments of this life are of little value. As for those who wish to live for a hundred years or more, Allah reminds them:

And whomever We give a long life, We cause him to decline in wellbeing. Then will they not apply reason? (36:68)

It is of Allah's wisdom that He does not inform you of the time you will remain on earth. When a child is born, he or she does not bring down a card specifying how many years he or she will live. It is said that the concealment of your lifespan is the loudest form of declaration. Let me explain this further: Allah had concealed the time of death and its cause from every man and woman. Thus, each person can anticipate death at every moment. This uncertainty about death makes it omnipresent at every moment of every day. It is the loudest form of declaration. This, in turn, makes any life desire –whether for the opposite sex, money, or property- of very little value.

Perhaps, the best indicator of the small value of this world is its name in the Noble Quran. Allah calls our life in this world: 'The Dunya,' which translates literally into: 'The lowest.' It's opposite, then, must be the highest. Allah calls the afterlife: 'The Akhera' which means 'the destination,' or the 'true goal.'

Now let's examine the pleasures of paradise. Remember the four criteria for true pleasure? A truly good nature that is continuous, increases with time, and follows you wherever you go. Isn't that the definition of paradise? It is good because Allah created it pure and perfect in every way. It is everlasting and, more importantly, you are guaranteed immortality in it. Allah says:

On the Day when you see the believers, both men and women, with their light radiating out ahead of them and to their right, 'Glad tidings to you this day, there are Gardens graced with ?owing rivers where you will stay forever: that is truly the supreme triumph!' (57:12)

So when the Allah asks you not run after the desires of this world, is He burdening you or setting you free? We answer that Allah teachings may look like a burden to the superficial. But in reality, Allah teachings give you the ultimate benefit and freedom. Let me explain. Take a moment to think about all the luxuries and pleasures in our world…..the fancy hotels you want to stay in, the fine restaurants you would like to eat at, the beach resorts and spas you would love to visit, the designer clothes, luxury and sport cars and so on. All these items and experiences are the work of humans, and they are limited by our capabilities and imagination. Now compare that to the pleasures and luxuries that Allah Almighty, who is limitless in his knowledge and capability, has prepared for you in Paradise. Everything pales in comparison.

So when Allah asks you to lower your gaze from the opposite sex, it is not a limitation of your freedom, because Allah wants to give you your eye's fill in the eternity of the Hereafter. Similarly, when Allah asks you to give a small share of your wealth to feed the poor, it is not an assault on your wealth, because Allah wants to give you far superior things limitlessly in the Hereafter. Indeed, 'with Allah is the best resort.'

Verse 15

Qul a'unabbi 'ukum bikhairim min zaalikum; lillazeenat taqaw 'inda Rabbihim jannaatun tajree min tahtihal anhaaru khaalideena feehaa wa azwaajum mutahharatunw wa ridwaanum minal laah; wallaahu baseerum bil'ibaad

**Say: "Shall I announce to you far better alternatives? For the Allah-conscious, with their Lord, theirs shall be Gardens underneath which rivers flow, where they shall live forever, and purified spouses and pleasure from Allah. Allah is ever-watchful over His servants.
(Verse 15)**

The phrase "Shall I announce" is translated from the Arabic origin "Unabeukum." It prepares the listener for the big news. When, for example, you say to someone, "I want to tell you something," he or she would expect ordinary conversation; but when you say: "I want to make an announcement," people anticipate something major. You do not announce that you will be having lunch at 2 pm today, you announce that you are moving to another city. How about if the Almighty is the one making the announcement? It must be something monumental. Allah says:

What are they asking each other about? Of the mighty Announcement (78:1-2)

The verses in chapter 78 are referring to the Day of Judgment, a matter that will alter the fabric of the entire universe. So when Allah says "Say: "Shall I announce to you far better alternatives?" we should expect enormous good, far superior to the worldly pleasures of wealth, family, children, and property.

The phrase 'with their Lord' holds another clue to the scale of the pleasures Allah will inform you about. This phrase should give every believer a great deal of comfort. Why? We answer that 'the Lord' is the caretaker, the provider, and the protector. The Lord is the one who nourishes and provides.

What has the Lord prepared for the God-conscious? "For the God-conscious, with their Lord, theirs shall be Gardens underneath which rivers flow, where they shall live forever, and purified spouses and pleasure from Allah."

Let's compare the pleasures of the Hereafter to those of this world to find out if they are truly 'far better.' In the 14th verse of Al-Imran, when Allah referred to the pleasures of owning land, He used the word 'tilth.' We explained how tilth involves ploughing and planting. In the Hereafter, Allah uses the word 'gardens' to inform us that paradise is fully prepared and does not require any work. Things do not stop here, if you own land in this world, you always worry about rain and water supply. Paradise, on the other hand, is self-sufficient 'underneath which rivers flow.' Most importantly, life in paradise is eternal; it never leaves you, and you can never be kicked out.

Let's compare the second item. Allah says: 'and purified spouses.' Ask any happily married man or woman if their spouse is perfect, and you will often get a long list of complaints. Even people who fall madly in love find faults after a while, either in looks or in character. On some occasions, faults can ruin the entire marriage. The most beautiful woman starts getting wrinkles in a decade or two, and the strongest man grows weaker with age.

Things are different in the Hereafter. Spouses will be cleansed from every defect that afflicts them in this world. Why? Because Allah will purify them in creation and character. More importantly, everyone in paradise enjoys eternal youth.

When you compare verse 14 of Al-Imran to verse 15, you notice that many items are missing in verse 15. When talking about the pleasures of the hereafter, Allah mentioned gardens and spouses, but omitted piles of gold and silver, horses, livestock, or children –all mentioned in verse 14-. Why? We can answer this question in two ways. First, in verse 15, Allah talked about spouses and gardens because these were the first and the last items mentioned in verse 14. It is as if the spouses who were mentioned first in verse 14 represented the opening parenthesis, and the gardens that were mentioned last were the closing parenthesis. By only mentioning the first and last items in verse 15, the verse became inclusive, covering everything in between. Allah wants you to know that paradise is far superior in every way, and it is inclusive of all pleasures.

The second way to answer the question is as follows: Allah's bounties are in everything that benefits us. Good character is a bounty, so are knowledge, food, and clothes. Sometimes Allah's provision is direct, and at other times it is indirect. For example, money –like gold and silver- are just a medium of exchange and do not directly benefit you. Say, for example, that you were very hungry, and you had a pile of Gold. Does the pile do your hunger any good? It does not. But if you had a loaf of bread, you would benefit directly. Likewise, if you had millions in cash and you were dying of thirst in the desert, would your cash offer you any direct benefit? No, but a bottle of water would save your life.

Money is a means to an end; and means will not be needed in the Hereafter because you now live with the Creator of means. Things will come to by the Almighty's command 'be.' In heaven, you will not need money or piles of gold and silver to get what you desire. Neither will you require horses or cars to get around. Anything that comes to your mind will be presented to you immediately without any work or effort. Thus, such things were not mentioned in the verse.

Say: "Shall I announce to you far better alternatives? For the Allah-conscious, with their Lord, theirs shall be Gardens underneath which rivers flow, where they shall live forever, and purified spouses and pleasure from Allah. Allah is ever-watchful over His servants.

(Verse 15)

Many people ask why the verse starts with a question: 'Shall I announce to you far better alternatives?' Why didn't Allah tell us directly instead of asking us a question? We answer that this type of introductory question adds beauty and anticipation. It shows Allah's compassion for us. Allah did not wait for us to wonder about the pleasures of the Hereafter. He rushed to tell us. And just in case some people were not paying attention, Allah started with a question. It is a very effective method to grab attention, because as soon as someone offers to tell you about something better than what you have, your mind starts anticipating a superb deal. Do you want me to tell you how you can earn a lot more money than your current job? This type of question gets your attention every single time.

But in order to qualify for far better rewards in paradise, you have to be 'God-conscious.' Why, you may ask? You can find the answer in verse 14 of Al Imran. All the worldly pleasures mentioned in the verse –from women to sons, wealth, and land- are very easy to abuse if you are not Allah-conscience. Piety in needed in all these areas. Some believers think that the solution is to shun life's pleasures and live an ascetic life. In other words, they want to limit their activities to worship and leave everything else behind. We say to such people: No, your work in life helps you become more pious. Allah put all these blessings at your disposal not for you to shun, but to enjoy properly within Allah's limits and to use them for the benefit of others. This is how we show true appreciation to Allah, and Allah, in turn, will gift you the enormous pleasures of Paradise.

Keep in mind that all the pleasures of paradise from food to drink and amazing gardens are not required for the sustenance of life. In paradise, you enjoy eternal youth that does not require any nourishment. The only longing is to be in Allah's pleasure and company.

Let us look at the following verses. Allah says:

On that Day there will be radiant faces, gazing at their Lord. (75:22-23)

Those who were preoccupied with the Lord in life attain a superior level of paradise called 'illiyoun.' It is a place where there is only the one overconsuming pleasure: being in Allah's company.

So there are multiple levels in heaven for you to attain. Thus, Allah ends the verse with 'Allah is ever-watchful over His servants' because He will give each person according to his or her deeds. Those who followed Allah's teachings to earn the luxuries of Paradise will attain them, and those who obeyed Allah because He is worthy of worship will be granted the pleasure of seeing Him. Rabia al-'Adawiyyah said:

"Allah, if you know that I am worshiping you out of greed for paradise then deprive me of it, and if you know that I am worshiping you out of fear of hellfire then admit me into it, for I am only worshiping you because you deserve to be worshipped."

So the phrase 'Allah is ever-watchful over His servants,' means that Allah will give every believer according to his effort and intention. One of the highest degrees of devotion to Allah is to put the love of Allah and His Messenger over all things in life. Prophet Muhammad, peace be upon him, said:

"Whoever has the following three qualities will experience the true sweetness of faith in his or her heart:

The one to whom Allah and His Messenger become dearer than anything else; the one who loves a person only for Allah's sake; and the one who hates to fall back into disbelief after Allah had saved him as much as he hates to be thrown into fire."

Allah praises His servants in front of the angels and says: 'They worship me for my sake,' The angels reply: 'Our Lord, they worship you for the sake of your blessings.' Allah says: 'Then, I will withhold my blessings from them, they will still love me. Amongst My servants are those whose supplication is very dear to me. I afflict them with adversities so that they invoke me and supplicate: 'O our Lord, O our Lord'.

Now you understand why some of the most afflicted people with trials are the prophets, then the most righteous of the believers. Their patience and acceptance is evidence of the purity of their love for Allah. We like the people who are good to us; but we do not accept any hardship except from the ones we truly love.

The following verse says:

Say, 'I am only a human being, like you, to whom it has been revealed that your God is One. So let him who hopes to meet his Lord act rightly and not associate anyone in the worship of his Lord.' (18:110)

Take note that Allah says: "So let him who hopes to meet his Lord act rightly,' and did not say 'let him who hopes to enter paradise.' Because Allah does not want anything to distract you form your Creator, even the great blessing of paradise.

Verse 16

Allazeena yaqooloona Rabbanaaa innanaaa aamannaa faghfir lanaa zunoobanaa wa qinaa 'azaaban Naar

Those who say, "Our Lord, indeed we have believed, so forgive us our sins and protect us from the punishment of the Fire" (Verse 16)

The statement of the believers: 'Our Lord, indeed we have believed, so forgive us our sins,' is the first step towards getting closer to Allah. When you declare your faith in Allah, you entrust Him with your affairs, and you take on the responsibilities of following His teachings. Faith has a right that must be fulfilled. Thus, the believer says: 'Dear Lord, I am human, and I cannot perfectly fulfil the right of faith. My Lord, forgive me that which I have done out of negligence or arrogance.' Prophet Muhammad, peace be upon him, taught us: "Worship Allah as if you see Him, for if you cannot see Him, then rest assured that Allah sees you."

Allah says to us in a sacred narration: "O my servants, if you think that I do not see you, then the fault is in your faith. And if you think that I see you, yet you still disobey Me, then why do you treat Me as the least important observer?" As if the Almighty is asking you: Am I less than my servants? You do not dare to disobey your boss in his or her presence; how dare you offend your Creator?!

The believers acknowledge that the requirements of faith are difficult. Thus, they turn to Allah and ask for forgiveness over and over. But what do the believers rely on when they ask for forgiveness? We answer that they count on faith and say 'Our Lord, indeed we have believed' because Allah has legislated repentance as part of faith. Allah knows that you may weaken and deviate away from His teachings; thus, He legislated repentance, so you do not despair. Allah is the Most-forgiving, Most-Merciful. A saying goes: "Perhaps a sin that causes humility and regret is better than obedience that provokes pride and arrogance."

Allah legislated repentance to protect the entire community from great evil because if a single sin meant that the sinner would never be forgiven, he or she would lose hope and go wild in evil doings. Without repentance and forgiveness, the whole community would suffer. Prophet Muhammad says: "All of the children of Adam are sinners, and the best of sinners are those who repent."

So, if you sin, then rush to seek forgiveness from your Lord. Allah says:

I said: 'Ask your Lord for forgiveness, for surely He has always been All-Forgiving. (71:10)

Allah does not want you to live in fear or despair. Once you repent, you can reproach His commands with love. This is the true beauty of Islam. Islam is not mere words; it is a practical religion that recognizes the nature of humanity. Allah knows that we will sin, so He opens the door to forgiveness. In fact, when you ask Allah for forgiveness, He will not only forgive you, but He will also reward you each time you remember your sin in regret. Allah says:

Except those who repent, believe, and do good deeds: Allah will change the evil deeds of such people into good ones. He is most forgiving, most merciful. (25:70)

The verse concludes the supplication of the believers with: 'and protect us from the punishment of the Fire.' Here, we note that forgiveness from sin is one thing, and protection from Hellfire is something different. How, you may ask? Doesn't forgiveness mean being spared from punishment? We answer that Allah made repentance a part of faith. It is an obligation. He knows that we often forget and commit sin. But what happens when a believer forgets to repent? Allah teaches you to ask not only for forgiveness from the sins you remember but also to ask for His protection from hellfire from all the sins you did not repent for.

Verses 17

Assaabireena wassaa diqeena walqaaniteena walmunfiqeena walmus taghfireena bil as-har

Those who are patient, truthful, genuinely devout, who give, and who pray before dawn for forgiveness.'
(Verse 17)

Who are the people described in the verse? They are the believers who will be rewarded in the hereafter as discussed in verses 15 and 16 'with their Lord, theirs shall be Gardens underneath which rivers flow, where they shall live forever, and purified spouses and pleasure from Allah.' They are the believers who supplicate, "Our Lord, indeed we have believed, so forgive us our sins and protect us from the punishment of the Fire."

Would you like to be one of them? Would you like to earn the wonderful rewards of paradise? Let's study what they do to earn this great honour. We start with patience. Implementing Allah's teachings is not easy because obligations require hard work and determination. Religious obligations feel difficult because they limit your freedom. Allah created you and gave you free will. So when it comes to actions, you can choose to do or not do. When, for example, Allah says to you 'pray at dawn,' then He has limited your freedom in staying asleep. This creates two levels of difficulty. First, if you usually wake up late, then you must push yourself to get up and pray. Second, you must resist the temptation of falling into sin by abandoning Allah's command. Both these matters require a great deal of patience.

Likewise, you have to exercise patience when Allah commands you 'not to do' something that you desire. For example, when it comes to the opposite gender, Allah asks you to lower your gaze. Abstaining from sin requires a great deal of patience.

We covered two scenarios that require patience. The first was following Allah's teachings in doing something, and the second involves following Allah's teachings in not doing something. This leaves out one possibility: events that do not fall within the scope of do and do not do, but are destined to happen to you. You may face a situation where you have no choice, such as being involved in a car accident or falling ill. How are you supposed to handle the ugly events of life? A believer is patient over the pains of life because he or she has trust in the Lord. Allah is your creator, and no one ruins his or her creation. To the contrary, Allah takes ultimate care of us. So when He afflicts you with a sickness or an emergency, then rest assured that there is divine wisdom behind it.

Patience is the ultimate expression of believing in the wisdom of the Creator. If a problem befalls you that is not the result of your actions, then certainly Allah has wisdom behind it. In such cases, you should remain patient, and this is not an easy matter. In fact, one of the doors of heaven is reserved for those who were patient.

To summarize, patience falls under one of three categories: patience over obedience and its hardships, patience over sins and its temptations, and patience over the fateful events of life. If you happen to know someone who showed patience in all three areas, then realize that he or she is truly devoted to Allah.

The second characteristic of the believers who will be handsomely rewarded by Allah is the 'truthful.' If you ask your friends, what does it mean to be truthful? Most would answer that being truthful is saying something that matches reality. It is the opposite of lying. We answer that being truthful goes a bit deeper than that. Every time I speak, my speech passes through three different levels. The first level is mental where, before I speak, I run the issue in my mind. The second level is lingual which happens after my brain gives the signal to my tongue to speak. The third level is a question whether what I say matches reality or not. Only when there is agreement on all three levels, I am being truthful.

To better understand this concept, let us read the following verse:

When the hypocrites come to you, they say, 'We bear witness that you are the Messenger of Allah.' Allah knows that you truly are His Messenger and He bears witness that the hypocrites are liars (63:1)

This verse is often pointed out by the critics of the Quran. It relates the incident of the hypocrites coming to the Prophet Muhammad to declare their faith. Allah affirms that their statement is correct, yet at the same time, He calls them liars. How could this be? The answer is found within the hypocrites' hearts.

Let's measure the statement of the hypocrites against the three levels of speech. Does the statement 'you are the Messenger of Allah' match reality? It does. Allah affirmed it in the verse: 'Allah knows that you truly are His Messenger.' Did the hypocrites voluntarily say this statement to Prophet Muhammad? Yes they did. So where is the lie? It is in the statement 'We bear witness.' The hypocrites only testified with their tongues that Muhammad is the Messenger of Allah, while their hearts denied it. For a person to be truthful, what he or she says must match what is in the heart. Thus, although the statement 'you are the Messenger of Allah' is true, the hypocrites were liars.

This brings us back to the verse. Allah praised the truthful because their words and actions are not only aligned with the teachings of Allah, but they are also affirmations of what is in their hearts. They believed and testified that "there is no one worthy of worship but Allah," then they fulfilled the obligations of faith to the best of their ability.

As for the one who says with his tongue, 'there is none worthy of worship but Allah' and then opposes the Lord's teachings day in and day out, we say to him or her: you are a liar and a hypocrite. Allah says:

You who believe, why do you say things and then do not do them? It is deeply abhorrent to Allah that you should say what you do not do. (61:2, 3)

It is interesting to learn that both the believer and the disbeliever are honest with themselves. How, you may ask? We answer that the believer has faith in his or her heart, and then declares that faith with the tongue: "I testify that there is none worthy of worship except Allah, and I testify that Muhammad is His messenger." The belief in the heart and the words of the tongue are then reflected in everyday actions. The disbeliever is also honest with him or herself. He or she denies Allah in the heart, and then, words and actions reflect faithlessness honestly.

Now we come to the hypocrite, whom we discussed in detail at the beginning of Chapter 2 -Surah Al Baqarah-. A hypocrite is not truthful to the people around, not even to him or herself.

Allah says:

Wavering all the time between this and that, belonging neither to one side nor the other. And whomever Allah leads astray, you will never find any way for him. (04:143)

The hypocrite says, "there is no God but Allah," yet this statement does not match what is in the heart. A hypocrite acts one way in public and the opposite in private. He or she is not sincere to himself, his Lord, or the people.

To fully appreciate the value of truthfulness in Islam, listen to what Prophet Muhammad, peace be upon him, taught us. He said, "The adulterer is not a believer at the moment when he is committing adultery; the wine-drinker is not a believer at the moment when he is drinking wine, and the thief is not a believer at the moment when he is stealing." In other words, the moment a believer violates the requirements of his or her faith, it does not matter what he or she says, because actions speak louder than words.

Those who are patient, truthful, genuinely devout, who give, and who pray before dawn for forgiveness.' (Verse 17)

In the previous verse, we started with the qualities of the believers who will enjoy Allah's company in paradise. The next trait on the list is the 'genuinely devout,' translated from the Arabic origin 'Qaniteen.' A devout person is the one who worships with reverence, tranquillity, and steadfastness. We explained that in order to be true to yourself, your actions must reflect what your heart feels and what your tongue says. When it comes to worship, the devout rush to be with their Lord, and implement His teachings even when they do not know the wisdom behind them. A devout believer implements Allah's command simply because it came from Allah.

Reflect on the following verse:

Believers, if you remain mindful of Allah, He will give you a criterion to tell right from wrong, and wipe out your evil deeds, and forgive you: Allah's favour is great indeed. (08:29)

Did you notice the order of events? You should be mindful of Allah first, and only then would He clarify things for you, and forgive your mistakes. Some people expect the exact opposite. They want a full explanation from Allah before they follow His teachings. A devout believer said: 'If you truly want to understand a command the Almighty has ordered, then fully implement it as He intended. Allah will soon enlighten your mind with the wisdom you are looking for.' Allah says in the 282nd verse of 'Surah Baqarah':

Be mindful of Allah, and He will teach you: He has full knowledge of everything

Allah asks you to follow His teachings first so He can enlighten your heart with knowledge. This is the difference between receiving a command from your equal on the one hand, and from the one who is higher than you on the other. If another human -who has the same knowledge as you- gives you an order, you can argue because you are his or her equal. But if the order comes from someone that you trust and who is more knowledgeable, then you should follow the order without argument. Take the example of a doctor advising his patient. Your doctor's advice should be followed even if you don't understand the reason behind it. You trust your doctor and know that he spent years acquiring the knowledge to treat your illness. You can only discuss the doctor's recommendations if you have the same degree he does. More importantly, if a friend asks you: Why are you taking this medicine? You are quick to give the perfect answer: because my doctor told me to.

How about if the command comes from the Most-high, the All-Wise, and the All-Knowledgeable? Do you need an explanation for every act of worship? If you answered yes, then you do not truly believe in Allah, you only believe in the explanation. In such case, there would be no difference between a believer and a non-believer as neither of them is doing anything for Allah's pleasure. If a friend asks you: why do you pray five times a day? The simple answer should be: because Allah told me to.

Allah is the Creator and the Manager of everything in the universe, and to Him belongs absolute wisdom. In the example, where you went to the doctor, the doctor is human and he or she may make a mistake. But Allah is free of all flaws, and His judgment is never wrong. We have full trust in Allah, who is the Most-High above all creations.

Some people ask: what does Allah want from me? To pray, pay almsgiving, and fast? Fine, I will do it. We answer: No, Allah wants you to seek Him out of love and reverence, not fear or duty. Faith was instituted for your benefit and the benefit of the society, not for Allah's benefit. If you find yourself delaying your prayer, and the rushing to pray at the last minute with an absent mind, then you do not value Allah's company. It is as if you tried Allah and did not find Him worthy of your time. 'Qanit' refers to the person who worships the Lord with humility and tranquillity. He or she looks forward to prayer because it brings the sweetness of faith to the heart. The heart of the believer longs for Allah's company in worship. It is a virtuous cycle that brings the believer back to worship again and again.

Those who are patient, truthful, genuinely devout, who give, and who pray before dawn for forgiveness.' (Verse 17)

We continue down the list of qualities that will earn the believers immense rewards in Allah's company in paradise. Let's talk about those 'who give' translated from the Arabic origin 'Munfiqeen.' The root 'nafaqa' refers to an animal that has just died. When talking about a market, the word 'nafaqa' refers to bare shelves because people have just purchased everything. If you apply the same root to spending, you realize that Allah is asking you to spend generously, and to completely forget about the money you donated. In other words, don't say to yourself: 'I did so and so a favour', such thoughts should not circle in your mind.

The only person you did a favour for with your charity is yourself, because charity is your salvation.

In order to give, you must work beyond your basic needs. If Allah granted you time and ability, you should work extra to provide for your family and to help others. Allah guarantees the poor families sustenance from the excess of the rich.

Always keep in mind that Allah made ability a symptom of life. It is temporary and subject to change at any moment. While Allah may be asking you to help the poor today, He will ask everyone to help you if you fall on hard times. In an ever-changing world, if you become weak, Allah's commands become an asset on your side, not the burden that you may see them today. So as you help others, remind yourself 'If I, or my children, become helpless, there will be someone to help us.' Isn't this the best insurance policy? The believer gives when he or she is capable, trusting that all the believers will be there if he or she is in need.

More importantly, when the day comes where you need the help of others, wouldn't you love for that help to come fast with no strings attached? Wouldn't you like the relief to be honourable and not accompanied by arrogance or hurtful words? If you answered yes, then this is how you should act now while helping others. Be the best insurance policy for your brothers and sisters: give generously, forget about your gift, and do not mention to anyone that you helped so and so.

Prophet Muhammad –peace be upon him- said: "There are seven types of people to whom Allah will provide shade on the day when there will be no shade except the shade of the Almighty. They are: a just ruler; a young person who grew up in the worship of Allah; a person whose heart is attached to mosques; two people who befriend each other in Allah's cause and separate in Allah's cause; a man who was seduced by a woman with status and beauty, yet he said 'No, I fear Allah'; a person who conceals his charitable giving so his left-hand does not know what his right hand gave, and a person who remembers Allah in solitude and his eyes fill with tears."

Here is another way to look at your charitable giving: It is your personal savings account. You are guaranteed to collect your investment in one of two ways. First, if your circumstances change and you become in need, your brothers and sisters in faith will step forward with their charitable giving to pay you back. Second, you will collect your charity in the hereafter many folds over directly from Allah's hand. Either way, by giving now, you are securing your future in this world and the next. Allah says:

The example of those who expend their wealth in the way of Allah is that of a grain of corn from which grow seven ears, each ear containing a hundred grains. Truly Allah multiplies for whomsoever He will, for Allah is infinite and all-wise. (2:261)

Allah created all of us. Some are capable and others are incapable; and our abilities are always changing. The power you have today may be taken away at any moment. Everything, including your own body, is not yours; It is a gift from Allah. Thus, the only true refuge for the believer is with the One who is the possessor of all power, the Ever-Living, Ever-Capable. Allah says:

Humankind! you are the poor in need of Allah whereas Allah is the Rich Beyond Need, the Praiseworthy. (35:15)

Allah made charitable giving a sign of piety, and He promised the donor heavenly gardens. Now, every believer makes it a goal of his or her to work hard, earn extra, and then seek the poor to help. This is how Allah insured the livelihood of the weak and the poor.

Hard work requires intellect to think and plan; it requires land, natural materials, and energy. Whether you a are harvesting crops, or running a machine, everything you work with comes from Allah. Thus, you should always work with the mindset that you are the custodian of Allah's gifts, and you should give Allah His due right from whatever you earn. Allah does not take this right for Himself, He only wants it for your helpless brothers and sisters.Allah, in turn, will collect His right from the believers for you and your family if you become helpless. Allah says:

Who will lend Allah a good loan, which He will increase for him many times over? It is Allah who withholds and Allah who gives abundantly, and it is to Him that you will return (2:245)

Then Allah turns our attention to those "who pray before dawn for forgiveness." Let's recall the detailed description of the believers Allah gave us so far. They affirm their faith, supplicating the Lord for forgiveness, and ask for protection against hellfire. They are patient, devout, and charitable. All these deeds are meant to fulfill the right of worship; Yet, a true believer still longs to spend part of the night in prayer to connect with Allah. Why? We answer that a servant either seeks Allah for forgiveness because he or she made a mistake or because he or she feels that more could have been done to seek Allah's pleasure.

The word "before dawn" draws our attention towards the hour of the day when most of us rest in comfort. A person who wakes up before dawn must have had his or her share of rest. Isn't this one of the major problems of our lifestyle? Work occupies the day, and then the night is wasted watching pointless shows or socializing. People often go to sleep late and exhausted. How can anyone with this lifestyle expect to wake up before dawn? If you genuinely value time with your Lord, you would organize your life around it. You would rest after work, spend time with your family, then go to bed early skipping the nightly entertainment.

What's the big deal in waking up early, you may ask? We answer that Allah distributes His mercy in the calm hours of the night. When you wake up before dawn, supplicate Allah, and seek forgiveness, you will earn the lion share of this amazing blessing. A mercy with no limits. Allah says:

What you have runs out but what Allah has endures, and We shall certainly reward those who remain steadfast according to the best of their actions. (16:96)

Verse 18

Shahidal laahu annahoo laa ilaaha illaa Huwa walmalaaa'ikatu wa ulul 'ilmi qaaa'imam bilqist; laaa ilaaha illaa Huwal 'Azeezul Hakeem

Allah bears witness that there is no Allah but Him, as do the angels and those who have knowledge, upholding justice. There is no Allah but Him, the Almighty, the All-Wise. (Verse 18)

In the previous verses, Allah taught us the characteristics of those who are mindful of Him. They affirm their faith, ask for forgiveness, and seek Allah's protection from hellfire. They are patient, truthful, devout, and charitable. They arrange the affairs of their day to spend the night in Allah's company.

All these qualities are fruit of 'There is no God but Allah.' Allah wants everyone to reap these marvellous rewards, thus, He did not leave it to you and me to reach the conclusion 'There is no God but Allah.' Allah filled our universe with evidence of His existence and His ultimate power. Doesn't this serve to prove that there is no God but Him? Moreover, Allah testified that there is no God but Him, and He is sufficient as a witness. He says:

Allah bears witness that there is no God but Him, as do the angels and those who have knowledge, upholding justice. There is no God but Him, the Almighty, the All-Wise.

(Verse 18)

The phrase 'bears witness 'means to testify and share knowledge. Allah testified that there is no deity except Him before any other creation witnessed the Oneness of His Divinity. He testified to His oneness before He created the angels and before He created those who have true

Knowledge. Thus, the testimony 'Allah bears witness that there is no Allah but Him' is the strongest of testimonies and the pure essence of monotheism. And there is strong evidence to support it.

Look at the following verse:

He is the Originator of the heavens and the earth, and when He decrees something, He says only, 'Be,' and it is. (02:117)

If Allah had not witnessed to Himself that there is no God but He, the He could not have proclaimed that 'when He decrees something, He says only, 'Be,' and it is.' Let's clarify. The moment Allah says 'be,' it means that He has full knowledge that there is no other God who can say 'do not be.' Allah wants to reassure you that there is no God but He, so you have peace in your heart that He is in full control, and there is no one to contradict Him. He says:

Allah has never had a child. Nor is there any God beside Him- if there were, each Allah would have taken his creation aside and tried to overcome the others. May Allah be exalted above what they describe! (23:91)

One of Allah's names is 'the Believer.' What does the Almighty believe? He believes that there is no God but Him, and He is the One who owns and controls everything with no one to oppose Him.

Similarly, it was not enough for our beloved Muhammad to be the first believer in Allah, he, peace be upon him, also had to believe that he is the messenger of Allah. There were many occasions where Muhammad would joyfully say: 'I bear testimony that I am the messenger of Allah.' If he did not bear witness to his Prophethood, how could he risk delivering Allah's message to others?

There was a wise woman at the time of the Prophet who correctly understood the value of bearing witness to one's self. It was her glimpse into the Prophet's belief that caused her to accept Islam. Listen to her story. This woman, who was a disbeliever, lived close to the Prophet. She used to see a group of believing men as guards surrounding the Prophet and protecting him from the disbelievers at all times. Then, one day, she saw Muhammad dismissing all his guards for good. She was surprised and wondered what happened. A neighbour told her that the following verse was revealed to Prophet Muhammad. Allah says:

Messenger, proclaim everything that has been sent down to you from your Lord- if you do not, then you will not have communicated His message- and Allah will protect you from people. Allah does not guide those who disbelieve. (5:67)

This wise woman thought to herself. These armed men were guarding the Prophet's life, yet he sent them home for good after receiving the verse that stated, 'Allah will protect you from people.' Even if Prophet Muhammad had managed to deceive everyone around him with Islam, he would not risk his own life based on a lie. The woman realised that the prophet truly believed in Allah, truly believed in his own Prophethood, and put down his personal safety as proof. No one goes as far as putting his or her life on the line for a lie. She rushed to the Prophet and said: 'I testify that there is no God but Allah and that you are the Messenger of Allah.'

Allah testified to His oneness before He created the angels, and before He created those who have true Knowledge. Allah is in no need for the testimony of humans, angels, or any other beings. His testimony is that of the self for the self. The angels are true first hand witnesses. They have never received any orders from anyone but Allah.

The verse continues with 'and those who have knowledge.' The people of knowledge are those who take time to look and contemplate the overwhelming evidence that such a magnificent and exquisitely managed universe must have a creator. Their intellect confirmed the authenticity of the testimony of the angels and the Almighty. Take note that those who take time to contemplate Allah's signs in the universe gain a high status as Allah has associated them with the angels in this verse.

Here is another simple way to look at Allah's oneness. Allah has repeatedly declared loud and clear: 'Allah bears witness that there is no Allah but Him.' Either this is true, and thus the matter ends, or it is not.

If this is not the truth, then we ask: where are the true Allahs? Didn't they hear the challenge? Why did they remain silent as Allah took away the universe from them and said: I alone am the Creator? If these Gods did not hear the challenge from Allah, then they are not fit to be Gods. And if they heard but did not act, then again, they are not suited to be Gods. Thus, the case of lordship and deity belongs to Allah alone until a plaintiff comes forward to contradict Him. Till then, the statement "there is no God but Him" remains the ultimate truth supported by ample evidence, Prophets, messengers, and heavenly books.

Allah bears witness that there is no Allah but Him, as do the angels and those who have knowledge, upholding justice. There is no Allah but Him, the Almighty, the All-Wise.

(Verse 18)

In the previous session, we reviewed the case for "there is no God but Him." Now, let's examine the most beautiful phrase in this verse; Allah says: 'upholding justice.' Allah, with all His majesty and power, can rule anyway He sees fit. He can be a tyrant, and no one would be able to interject. He can be an oppressor, and no one would be able to stop Him. Yet, Allah gives you the ultimate piece of mind and assures you that he runs the affairs of the universe based on justice and mercy.

Another beautiful side of the phrase 'upholding justice,' is that in the Arabic origin, it is mentioned in the singular form. What does that mean? It means that Allah bears witness that there is no Allah but Him; He rules justly. The angles and those who have knowledge only came afterward, confirming Allah's oneness and justice. Allah was the Creator before He created anything. He was the all-merciful before the existence of those who seek His forgiveness. Likewise, Allah was just even before He created anyone to rule over.

Allah created people and distributed different talents and abilities amongst them. No single person has all the talents needed to thrive. We all need one another. If you have a special skill that I do not possess, then I am forced to seek your help. Likewise, you would seek my advice in matters I excel at. There are people in your community who perfected the craft of agriculture to produce enough food for themselves and meet the needs of others. Some people plant cotton, others who harvest it, others who spin it, and manufacture it into clothes. This sort of cooperation builds societies and progress, and this is part of Allah's justice.

There is deep integration between all people on earth, even when they do not like each other. Take a moment to think about the people who live far away from you across the globe, most likely, they are working and doing something that makes your life better and more comfortable. This should fill your heart with love and appreciation to your fellow man. Allah says:

O Humankind! We created you from a male and female and made you into peoples and tribes so that you might come to know each other. The noblest among you in Allah's sight is the one most mindful of Allah. Allah is All-Knowing, All-Aware. (49:13)

Quite often, the talents of others benefit you more than it benefits them. A saying goes: 'The door of the carpenter is always broken.' When a person asked, "why do you think that is?" a wise person replied,"because it is the only door the carpenter will not get paid for fixing" Again, this should fill your heart with love and appreciation for others instead of envy and hatred. It is part of Allah's justice.

It is interesting to note that the verse that started with 'Allah bears witness that there is no Allah but Him, as do the angels and those who have knowledge, upholding justice,' ends with "There is no Allah but Him, the Almighty, the All-Wise." As if Allah is telling us: if the testimony of the self for the self, the testimony of the angels, and the testimony of the scholars are upheld, then the logical conclusion is - without any doubt- 'There is no Allah but Him.'

Rest assured that since Allah is One, you will not need the help of anyone else; you can rely on Him alone. He is 'the Almighty' that cannot be overcome. Our beloved Prophet, peace be upon him, said: "If you ask, then ask Allah alone; and if you seek help, then seek it from Allah alone. Rest assured that if the entire world were to come together to benefit you with something, they would not benefit you except with what Allah had already prescribed for you. And if they were to conspire together to harm you, they would not harm you except with what Allah had already prescribed against you. The pens have been lifted, and the ink has dried."

This sometimes goes against our human logic. If I am in trouble and I seek refuge with someone influential, that is good. But isn't it better to seek refuge with twenty additional people? Doesn't that offer me more protection? We answer that when it comes to Allah, the word 'alone' holds an entirely different meaning. We seek Allah, and Allah alone, because He is the Creator, the Possessor of All Power, the Provider, the All-Capable, and the Almighty that cannot be overcome. We seek Allah alone because none other than can genuinely help.

Our Lord is 'the All-Wise.' What is wisdom? It is to place each matter in its rightful place and give it its rightful measure. It is translated from the Arabic origin: 'Hikma.' The word 'Hikma حكمة' originated from the 'bridle' which is the piece of leather and iron placed in a horse's mouth so the rider can control and aim the animal towards the desired destination. Without it, the animal may stray from the rider's goal. Allah, the all-Wise, is the one who identifies for each creation its bounds and mission. Who is better than your Creator, the One who knows you best, in determining your goal in life? Allah takes the utmost care of His creation. If you are patient over hardships, Allah will enlighten you with knowledge and amaze you with His wisdom in running the affairs of the universe.

Let's pause and think about the beauty of our Lord. Long before you were born, Allah prepared a universe to welcome you and support all your basic needs. Allah, the One, the All-Powerful, created you from nothing. He kept all the essentials of life under His control. The sun, the moon, the rain and the wind serve all of us justly. Your organs work for you tirelessly form the time you are born, well before you learned about their function. He gave you means to work and earn. Through His ultimate wisdom, He assigned your goals in life. Allah gave you a thinking mind, sent you Prophets and messengers, revealed the Quran for you, and laid before you the consequences, so you can freely choose what you want for yourself. Allah guaranteed for you all the necessities of life, yet, He did not force you to guarantee Him His due right. You have full control of your beliefs and actions. The scale of justice is in His Hands, so no one can tip it against you, even an atom's weight. Isn't that the epitome of justice?

Verse 19

Innad deena 'indal laahil Islaam; wa makhtalafal lazeena ootul Kitaaba illaa mim ba'di maa jaaa'ahumul 'ilmu baghyam bainahum; wa mai yakfur bi Aayaatil laahi fa innal laaha saree'ul hisaab

Indeed, the true religion in the sight of Allah is Islam. Those who were given the Book did not differ except after true knowledge had come to them, out of envious rivalry among themselves. Whoever disbelieves in the revelations of Allah should know that Allah is swift to take account. (Verse 19)

In the previous verse, Allah laid out the case for 'there is no God but Him' 'upholding justice.' It was further confirmed by the angels and by anyone who took time to contemplate the wonders of the universe. Wouldn't it be logical for you to follow the One Allah who is fair? Why would you go anywhere else?

Since Allah is one and Allah is just, we should ask ourselves: What are His teachings? Allah answers 'Indeed, the true religion in the sight of Allah is Islam.' The word 'religion' is translated from the Arabic origin الدين" Deen.' The verb 'dana' means 'to return to' or 'surrender to.'Al deen' is also used for accountability; in fact, the Day of Judgment is called 'Yaoum Al-Deen' 'the day of recompense.' It is a day of reward and punishment.

The word 'Deen' is sometimes used for religion and sometimes for religious law. The system of rules which Islam recognizes for regulating the actions of Muslims is what we call Shariah Law, while belief in Allah, obedience, and creed, are what we call faith. Both fall under the umbrella of 'religion.'

When you hear the phrase 'Indeed, the true religion in the sight of Allah is Islam, you understand that there are other religions out there that people follow that are not considered valid in the sight of Allah. Allah instructed our beloved Prophet Muhammad(saws) to say to the disbelievers:

Nor will you worship who I worship; you have your religion, and I have mine. (109:5,6)

The word 'Islam' comes from the Arabic root 'Sa La Ma,' the meaning of which revolves around peace and protection from corruption. It also holds the meanings of harmony between a person and his soul, his Lord, and the universe. It refers to integrity and righteousness, which are the opposite of corruption. Since the word 'Islam' holds all these meanings within, isn't it worth following?

Furthermore, Islam means submission and surrender; Islam means to be a servant of Allah, a slave of Allah. I understand that these words hold very negative connotations in human terms, but when it comes to Allah, they mean the exact opposite. How, you may ask? Let's compare the most negative of these term 'slavery' as it related to humans and to Allah. A human slave is held against his or her will. He or she is exploited for the benefit the master who reaps all the rewards, while the slave gets the absolute minimum for sustenance. The children of slaves are born into slavery, and they are often denied education to keep them ignorant about their condition. A slave is severely punished for every mistake, often unreasonably. In short, the human master-slave relationship is most unjust.

On the other hand, submission to Allah is a source of pride and elevation. I am a proud slave of Allah because my Lord is just. Allah sent me prophets and messengers to educate me so I can choose Him freely. He prepared for me an entire universe and put it at my service. Allah did not ask anything of me until I chose to come to Him. Allah does not need my labour; rather, my labour earns me immense rewards. Allah does not pay me the bare minimum; He rewards me ten times or more for every deed I do. I have made countless mistakes, and I found my Lord to be the most forgiving. My children are free to choose their way in life. Allah does not ask anything of them until they reach the age of maturity so they can make a thoughtful decision. They have the Quran to show them the exact consequences of their choices. Yes, I am a very proud servant of Allah, and I willingly submit to Him and only to Him. It brings me peace and harmony. This is the essence of the word 'Islam.'

As for those who choose to associate partners to Him. Allah says:

Allah puts forward an example: can a man who has for his masters several partners at odds with each other be considered equal to a man devoted wholly to one master? All praise belongs to Allah, though most of them do not know. (39:29)

Indeed, the true religion in the sight of Allah is Islam. Those who were given the Book did not differ except after true knowledge had come to them, out of envious rivalry among themselves. Whoever disbelieves in the revelations of Allah should know that Allah is swift to take account. (Verse 19)

We should start with the question, If "the true religion in the sight of Allah is Islam," then how about all the previous prophets and messengers? How about Jesus, Moses, David, Abraham, peace be upon them all? In the previous session, we explained how the word "Islam" means submission to the One Allah who created and provided us with all things. In that sense, Islam is the essence of all the religions of all prophets and messengers.

Read Allah's words as He relays to us the supplication of Prophets Abraham and Ishmael,

Our Lord, make us both Muslims submitted to You, and our descendants a Muslim community submitted to You. Show us our rites of worship and turn towards us. You are the Ever-Returning, the Most Merciful. (2,128)

And in another verse, the words of Prophet Jacob on his death bed,

Or were you present when death came to Jacob, and he said to his sons, "What will you worship when I have gone?" They said, "We will worship your Allah, the Allah of your forefathers, Abraham, Ishmael, and Isaac – one God. We are Muslims submitted to Him." (2,133)

Lastly, the supplication of our beloved Prophet Muhammad, may peace and blessings of Allah be upon him.

Say, "My Lord has guided me to a straight path, an upright religion, the faith of Abraham, a man of pure faith. He was not a polytheist." Say, "My prayers and rites, my life and death, are all for Allah, Lord of all the Worlds; He has no partner. This is what I am commanded, and I am the first of the Muslims." (6,161-163)

The spirit of Islam -which is submission to Allah and harmony with the universe- is common to all heavenly messages; the word Muslims applies to all those who submit to Allah from the beginning of time till the last Day. In other words, Islam is not limited to the message and teachings of Prophet Muhammad.

Here is the distinction, however, in the use of the words "Islam" and "Muslim" across religions. The words "Islam" and "Muslim" were occasionally used to describe previous heavenly messages and their followers. As for the nation of Prophet Muhammad, peace be upon him, "Islam" and "Muslim" were the defining characteristics because our beloved Muhammad embodied true and permanent submission to Allah. His faith is the perfect expression of harmony between man and the universe. The religion of Prophet Muhammad earned the name "Islam" because his message reached the summit of how a true believer should live. Allah says in the 3rd verse of chapter 5,

Today I have perfected for you your religion, completed My blessing upon you, and have been pleased to assign for you Islam as religion.

Islam became the global religion for all people until the end of time. It was our beloved Prophet Abraham who called us Muslims. Allah says,

Strive hard for Allah as is His due, He has chosen you and placed no hardship in your religion, the faith of your forefather Abraham. This is the way of your father, Abraham. He named you Muslims previously, and in this Book, that the Messenger may be a witness for you, and that you may be the witnesses for Humankind. So establish the prayer, pay the prescribed alms, and hold fast to Allah. He is your Guardian. How excellent a Guardian and Helper. (22, 78)

Take note that the verse specified "He named you Muslims," and did not say "He described you as Muslims" because a name is something permanent, whereas a description is temporary. Followers of previous heavenly messages were occasionally described as Muslim, but the followers of Muhammad earned that name. An adjective only becomes a name when the description takes on absoluteness and permanency. For example, you may be fair, and you may be generous; but these are only descriptions that may change with time. Only Allah has the names "The Just" and "The Generous."

Another interesting observation is that the followers of previous heavenly religions are often attributed to their prophet. For example, Christians are named so because they are the followers of Jesus Christ, son of Mary. We, the nation of Prophet Muhammad, do not go by "Muhammadi;" we say, "We are Muslims," and that is a great honour for us. Allah says,

Indeed, the true religion in the sight of Allah is Islam.

The verse continues, "Those who were given the Book did not differ except after true knowledge had come to them." Here we should ask, why the disagreements between those who have heavenly revelations? If divine religions mean submitting to the teachings of Allah, and since Allah is One who maintains justice, then there should be no conflict. Where did the disagreements come from? Did another God appear to contradict Allah in His kingdom? No, Allah answers, "Those who were given the Book did not differ except after true knowledge had come to them, out of envious rivalry among themselves." The key phrase -and the tragic calamity- is that differences only came "after true knowledge had come to them." Had people differed before knowledge came to them, we would have said, "they are excused; they did not know."

Divine knowledge came directly from the One God who rules justly; Allah is a constant that never changes. Worldly whims and desires must have entered religion and became the sources of conflict. A group adopts one path, while a second group adopts another.

In any conflict, whether between people or nations, there are only two possibilities. The first is that one party holds to the truth, while the other deviates towards falsehood. The second -and most common- possibility is that both parties have deviated towards falsehood. There are many falsehoods out there, so the options for conflict are limitless. You will never find two parties fighting each other while both are holding to the truth because there is one truth.

Let's take the example of the Jewish people. Allah sent the heavenly message of Judaism to our beloved Moses. Despite the many changes people introduced over the centuries, there was a group of Jews who held firm to their true faith. When the message of Islam was revealed to Muhammad, they rushed to embrace it because they recognized it from their books. Allah says in the 157th verse of chapter 7,

Those who follow the Messenger- the unlettered Prophet they find described in the Torah that is with them, and in the Gospel- who commands them to do right and forbids them to do wrong

Allah's message is not vague; it was clearly laid out in the Torah and the Gospel. He says about Prophet Muhammad,

Those to whom We gave the scripture know him as they know their own sons. But indeed, a party of them conceal the truth while they know (2,146)

It is of Allah's mercy that He gave the glad tidings of Islam in the Gospel and the Torah. Some held on to it while others concealed it and changed the scripture to match their whims. Allah says,

Yet, they are not all alike. There are some among the People of the Book who are upright, who recite Allah's revelations during the night, who bow down in worship, who believe in Allah and the Last Day, who order what is right and forbid what is wrong, who are quick to do good deeds. These people are among the righteous (3,113, 114)

Allah treated all fairly. Those who held to their true faith were guided to the truth when Islam came. Those who followed their whims were lost.

Allah refers to the people of previous religions as "those who were given the Book." When something is given to you, it means that it came from someone else. Similarly, the scripture was given; it is not the work of humans. Had it been the work of humans, they would have differed regarding its content. Allah gave us a clear book, with no contradictions or disagreements. He says,

Will they not ponder over this Quran? Had it been from anyone other than Allah, they would have found much inconsistency in it. (4, 82)

Allah is warning us that any system of governance produced by humans will create conflicts. These conflicts can be avoided if we turn to Allah, the only source that is fair and consistent. So when you see conflict within a religion, rest assured that whims got involved, and people started adding and attributing falsehoods to Allah.

Verse 20

Fa in haaajjooka faqul aslamtu wajhiya lillaahi wa manit taba'an; wa qul lillazeena ootul Kitaaba wal ummiyyeena 'a-aslamtum; fa in aslamoo faqadih tadaw wa in tawallaw fa innamaa 'alaikal balaagh; wallaahu baseerum bil 'ibaad

If they argue with you, say, "I have devoted myself to Allah alone and so have my followers." Ask those who were given the Scripture, as well as those without one, "Do you too devote yourselves to Him alone?" If they do, then they are indeed rightly guided, but if they turn away, your only duty is to convey the message. Allah is All-Seeing of His servants.

Allah revealed the phrase "if they argue with you" to prepare our beloved Muhammad for the reality he is about to face. The Prophet was confronted by three camps, The first was the idol worshippers of Quraish, at the peak of their political and military power. The second camp was the people of the book -namely the Jews and Christians-. Lastly, there were the hypocrites. Surprisingly, the fiercest arguments came from the second camp. The people of the book had a connection to the heavens and should have been the first to recognize Allah's new message. The idol worshipers, on the other hand, did not claim to have a heavenly religion, so their opposition was understandable.

Since this debate was between the truth and falsehoods, Allah was not about to leave the Prophet without support.

Allah says, "If they argue with you, say, "I have devoted myself to Allah alone and so have my followers." Is this a proper response to the argument? We answer, Yes, this is proper because of what the Quran tells us about the people of the book and the idolaters. Allah says,

And if you ask them, "Who created the heavens and earth?" they are sure to say, "The Almighty, the All-Knowing created them." (43:09)

And in another verse,

And if you asked them who created them, they would say, "Allah." How, then, have they been perverted? (43:87)

Hence, the phrase, "I have devoted myself to Allah" is the perfect answer because it asks everyone to submit to the One they uniformly recognize as the Creator.

The phrase "devoted myself," is translated from the Arabic origin "Aslamtu Wajhee." The literal translation is, "I have submitted my face." Why? Because the face is the most distinctive and honourable feature; it expresses emotions of pleasure and sadness. If you prostrate unwillingly, your face will show it. Likewise, the signs of contentment and happiness are apparent on your face when you feel closeness to Allah.

By submitting your face to Allah, you submit your entire being. In fact, "the face" as an expression is sometimes used when the whole being is intended. Allah says,

Do not call out to any other Allah beside Allah, for there is no God but Him. Everything will perish except His Face. His is the Judgement, and to Him you shall all be brought back. (28:88)

Everything will perish except He the Almighty; this is what is meant by "His Face" in the verse. Always remember that all the attributes that are common to humans and Allah come under the principle we find in verse 11 of chapter 42,

There is nothing whatever like Him.

Some scholars explain phrases such as "Allah's Face" to mean Allah's essence, and the "hand of Allah" to mean the power of Allah. We answer that we do not need to go into such explanations. We believe that there is nothing whatsoever like Allah. Hence, we have protected ourselves from making an error in understanding Him. We do not equate Allah with His creation; neither do we strip the Quranic text from its literal meaning.

This brings us back to the verse. "The face" is used to refer to the self because people are identified by their faces, not their body parts. The phrase, "I have devoted myself to Allah alone, and so have my followers," indicates that Prophet Muhammad, peace be upon him, submitted himself to Allah after he received the heavenly revelations. Likewise, anyone who follows the message of the prophet has submitted to Allah. Prophet Muhammad is the messenger of the truth who delivers Allah's teachings to all humanity; so, there is no need for each individual to receive a separate memo from Allah.

Allah commands His Messenger, "Ask those who were given the Scripture, as well as those without one, "Do you too devote yourselves to Him alone?" Here we should recognize that there are two types of questions. First, some questions are asked to investigate and search for the truth.

Let's look at an example from the Quran. Allah says,

With intoxicants and gambling, Satan seeks only to incite enmity and hatred among you, and to stop you remembering Allah and prayer. Will you not give them up? (5:91)

The question "Will you not give them up?" is a command to refrain from drugs and gambling because of their social and personal harms. Similarly, the question, "Do you too devote yourselves to Him alone?" is a call to unity in submission to the One Allah because of the overwhelming evidence of His existence.

Prophet Muhammad, peace be upon him, invited the disbelievers and the people of the book to devote themselves to Allah. Allah says, "If they do, then they are indeed rightly guided." To be guided means to know the path that leads you to your true goal of success in the hereafter.

How about the word "devotion', translated from the Arabic origin "Aslamtu," what does it mean? We answer that devotion signifies submission, and submission can only be through actions. Imam Ali, who inherited a wealth of the Prophet's eloquence in expression said, "I will describe to you the lineage of Islam like no one has done before me, Islam is a conviction, and conviction comes through belief; Belief is confirmation, and confirmation is a calling that comes through actions. The believer's faith can only be recognized through his or her actions.

Allah says, "If they do, then they are indeed rightly guided, but if they turn away, your only duty is to convey the message."

Our beloved Prophet Muhammad worried himself sick over every person who turned away from Allah. Allah wanted to comfort His Messenger. He says,

Perhaps you may worry yourself to death with grief, chasing after them, if they do not believe in this Message. (18:06)

The Prophet's only responsibility is to deliver Allah's message. But that responsibility also falls on you. Let us look at the Prophet's words, "I have devoted myself to Allah alone, and so have my followers." And in another verse, Allah explains,

You were the best nation brought forth for humankind, you bid what is right and forbid what is wrong, and have faith in Allah. And if the People of the Book had believed, it would have been better for them. Among them are faithful, but most of them are transgressors. (3:110)

Prophet Muhammad was the final messenger because his message remains alive within His nation. We are all responsible for delivering the message of Islam and standing up to corruption. He, peace be upon him, said, "The scholars are the heirs of the prophets."

So when Allah says, "your only duty is to convey the message," we clearly understand that the responsibility of conveying Allah's teachings does not stop with the Messenger, rather it includes each one of us. Allah says,

Indeed, you have in Allah's Messenger an excellent example to follow for whoever looks forward to Allah and the Last Day, and remembers and mentions Allah much. (33:21)

Prophet Muhammad patiently endured harm and ignorance as he delivered the message to the people. As our role-model, we must follow his example. He worked tirelessly to deliver Allah's message, and so should we.

The inheritance of prophethood is the great honour of delivering Allah's message. This means that you must convey the message of the Prophet Muhammad to those around you. It is a difficult task that requires plenty of patience and endurance. Allah says,

Strive hard for Allah as is His due, He has chosen you and placed no hardship in your religion, the faith of your forefather Abraham. Allah has called you Muslims—both in the past and in this —so that the Messenger can bear witness about you and so that you can bear witness about other people. So keep up the prayer, give the prescribed alms, and seek refuge in Allah, He is your protector—an excellent protector and an excellent helper. (22:78)

The verse ends with, "Allah is All-Seeing of His servants." This phrase gives us a true insight about Islam. Allah did not say that He is all-knowing of His servants. Why? Because knowledge is for matters of faith and matters of the heart. But Allah is not asking you for belief; He is asking you for action. In other words, Allah wants to see that your movement in life corresponds with your Islamic beliefs; A movement that everyone can see, not a feeling in your heat that no one knows about.

The second benefit of the phrase "Allah is All-Seeing of His servants" is to stop you from doing anything wrong. You should be ashamed to be seen doing something wrong by your Lord. Take the example of a teenager who smokes. He is ashamed of being seen by his elders while smoking. So, he refrains from smoking when they are around. How about a servant who believes that Allah Almighty can see him or her at all times? Allah says in a sacred narration, "O my servants, if you think that I do not see you, then the fault is in your faith. And if you think that I see you, yet you still disobey Me, then why do you treat Me as the least important observer?"

Verse 21

Innal lazeena yakfuroona bi Aayaatil laahi wa yaqtuloonan Nabiyyeena bighairi haqqinw wa yaqtuloonal lazeena ya'muroona bilqisti minannaasi fabashirhum bi'azaabin aleem

Those who disbelieve in Allah's signs and kill the prophets unjustly, and kill those who call for justice from among the people, give them the glad tidings of a painful torment.

The phrase "Those who disbelieve in Allah's signs" is interesting because it makes a distinction between a person who disbelieves in Allah and one who disbelieves in the signs of Allah. Faith in Allah only comes through observing the evidence which proves His existence in the universe. Proofs of the presence of a magnificent creator are all around us. People who ignore such signs naturally disbelieve in Allah. Allah is unseen, whereas the evidence to His existence is everywhere, thus the phrase "Those who disbelieve in Allah's signs" also includes those who disbelieve in Allah.

The verse continues with "and kills the prophets." It is worth noting that the word "kill" is associated with prophets in the Quran, but never with messengers. Why? To answer this question, we must understand the difference between prophets -translated from the Arabic نبي (Nabi)- and messengers -translated from the Arabic رسول (Rasoul).

Allah sent prophets and messengers to convey His teaching to humankind. A messenger carries a new heavenly message, teaches it to his people, and practices it among them. A prophet, on the other hand, does not carry a new message. He only serves as a practical example and as a reminder to his people of previous messages. Thus, every messenger is a prophet, but not every prophet is a messenger.

Let's clarify. Prophet Muhammad, Jesus, Moses, Abraham, David (peace be upon them) brought new heavenly messages and new scriptures; thus they were all messengers. They were also prophets because they practiced the new message and led by example. Prophets Solomon, Lot, John, and many others, peace be upon them, were sent to bring people back to the right path and adhere to the scriptures they already had. They were not messengers because they did not bring new revelations.

Allah protects both His prophets and His messengers from sin and mistakes. They are infallible in delivering and practicing Allah's teachings. Since messengers are the carriers of new revelations, Allah gives them the added protection from being killed. It does not make sense for Allah to choose the best of His creation, send him as a messenger to deliver new heavenly revelations, and then give people the power to kill him. However, people may have power over prophets who are sent as role models.

Here we should ask, why do people kill prophets? Understandably, they may want to kill a messenger. A messenger, after all, carries with him a new religion, and people may be intolerant of change; they may be zealots for the old religion. But prophets do not bring anything new; they only re-establish the faith people already have. So why kill them? We answer that a prophet's actions highlight the hypocrisy of the people of his time. Prophets properly adhere to Allah's teachings, and thus expose those who only do so superficially. Prophets subject their whims to Allah's will, while those around them lust after life's pleasures. And lastly, the model behaviour of prophets often exposes the clergy who abuse religion to grab power and amass wealth.

In a corrupt society, people dislike anyone who exposes their hypocrisy. They often feel anger and hatred towards him or her and see a need to remove this obstacle from their way. There is a big difference between merely declaring faith and actually practicing it. Thus, you often see those who properly practice their faith ridiculed in their community.

Take the example of a lazy student who sees her friend studying and preparing for exams. She starts wondering, "Why is my friend disciplined to study and succeed, and I cannot bring myself to sit down and focus?" No one likes to feel inferior to others. Sadly, for many people, the solution is not to sit down and study, but to distract the good student from studying and make fun of her. This is exactly what happens to upright people in a corrupt society. Allah says:

The wicked used to laugh at the believers, wink at one another as they passed by them, and joke about them when they got back to their folks. When they saw them, they said, "They have indeed gone astray;" though they were not sent to be their keepers. (83:29-33)

Don't we see this scenario play out in our societies today? People who adhere to Allah's teachings are often called crazy and out of touch with modernity. Allah responds with the scene from the Hereafter:

So today, the believers are laughing at the disbelievers as they sit on couches, gazing in wonder. Have the disbelievers been repaid for what they used to do? (83:34-36)

If this is how sinners are punished, then can you imagine the punishment of those who kill the prophets?

Here we should ask, why did Allah describe the killing of the prophets as "unjust"? Is there any just way of killing a prophet? We answer that the killing of prophets can never be justified. The description "unjustly" is used as an introduction to the following phrase: "and kill those who call for justice from among the people." Allah turns your attention to the fact that those who kill prophets are not satisfied until they remove all the prophets' followers out of their way. Anyone who acts upright and calls for justice is a target.

There were many attempts by the enemies of Prophet Muhammad(pbuh) to kill him. The assassination plots -some were very sophisticated- started in Mecca in the early days of Islam. However, all the efforts of the Messenger's enemies were foolish. Why? Because they ignored the fact that he, peace be upon him, was not only a prophet but also a messenger of Allah. As a prophet, Muhammad led by example, and as a messenger, he was the carrier of a new divine message. Had he only been a prophet, they may have succeeded in killing him as they killed many prophets before. But as the carrier of a new religion, he had Allah's full protection. Allah says:

Messenger, proclaim everything that has been sent down to you from your Lord -if you do not, then you will not have communicated His message- and Allah will protect you from people. Allah does not guide those who defy Him. (5:67)

Allah, however, reassured the believers and informed the opponents of the Messenger that there is no way to kill him. He says:

When it is said to them, "Believe in Allah's revelations," they reply, "We believe in what was revealed to us, "but they do not believe in what came afterwards, though it is the truth confirming what they already have. Say: "Why did you kill Allah's prophets in the past if you were true believers?" (2:91)

The phrase "in the past" explained to our beloved Muhammad and to his enemies that the practice of killing the prophets is now over. From this point forward, no one will ever succeed. Regardless of the wishes and the schemes of the disbelievers, Allah has power over everything, and He will protect His Prophet. Allah says:

And they plot and Allah plots. But Allah is the best of plotters. (3:54)

Here we should ask, why is Allah issuing a warning against those who killed the prophets before? These people were not even alive at the time of Muhammad! Who exactly is Allah addressing? We answer that Allah's warning is mainly directed towards some of the people of the Book. More specifically, to the Children of Israel who follow in the footsteps of their ancestors who killed their prophets. The Children of Israel had killed over forty-three of their prophets and hundreds of their followers. This verse is a rebuke of the Jews of Medina who rejected Prophet Muhammad's message and insisted on following the faith which was corrupted by their ancestors. Allah says:

And in Surah Al-Baqarah:

But when it is said to them, "Follow the message that Allah has sent down," they answer, "We follow the ways of our fathers." What! Even though their fathers understood nothing and were not guided? (2:170)

The phrase "give them glad tidings" should give us pause. How could anybody give glad tidings of a painful torment? "Glad tidings" is usually reserved for pleasant surprises. Allah gives the believers glad tidings of paradise as an encouragement to implement His teachings. We answer that using a term like "give glad tidings" for punishment is meant to inflict psychological pain. How? We explain that when you come up to somebody and tell them that you have great news, they anticipate hearing something pleasing. But when you follow that with something horrible, the devastation is doubled. The sudden fall from happiness to despair is psychologically damaging.

Similarly, had Allah warned the killers of prophets -and those who follow them- directly, the news of the painful punishment would have been expected. But by starting with "give glad tidings" then following with the punishment, the sense of calamity is heightened. Here is another example from the Quran. Allah says in the 29th verse of chapter 18:

We have prepared a Fire for the wrongdoers that will envelop them from all sides. If they call for relief, they will be relieved with water like molten metal, scalding their faces. What a terrible drink! What a painful resting place!

When the residents of hellfire cry for help and then hear that help is on the way, they feel better immediately. But what do you think happens when the relief is worse than the punishment? The psychological damage is devastating. Allah says:

We shall send those who reject Our revelations to the Fire. When their skins have been burned away, We shall replace them with new ones so that they may continue to feel the pain: Allah is mighty and wise. (4:56)

Such is the glad tiding for those who killed the prophets and the righteous. Allah gives them glad tidings of a painful punishment, and His warning extends to anyone who believes that what they did was appropriate.

Verse 22

Ulaaa'ikal lazeena habitat a'maaluhum fid dunyaa wal Aaakhirati wa maa lahum min naasireen

The deeds of such people will come to nothing in this world and the next, and for them, there will be no helpers. (Chapter 3: Verse 22)

In the previous verse, Allah promised severe punishment to the people who ignore His signs, kill the prophets, and kill those who advocate for justice. In this verse, Allah adds that the deeds of such people -and whoever follows in their footsteps- will become worthless in this world and the Hereafter. The phrase "will come to nothing" means that their work in life will bear no fruit.

Why do you get out of bed in the morning? It is to achieve a goal. You usually have an objective to accomplish for the day. You may have a plan to learn something or earn money for your family. This is how productive people run their lives. Any action without a goal is a crazy waste of time. So when Allah says, "The deeds of such people will come to nothing in this world and in the next," He is clarifying to us that regardless of how good the actions of such people may appear to be, it is considered useless because there is no faith behind it. Faith is the bedrock underneath any good deed.

Some people criticize Islam and ask, "How come Allah does not reward the disbelievers who do wonderful services for humanity? Is it conceivable that a person who creates a medicine that saves millions of lives would not benefit on the Day of Judgment? Could great inventors and researches who elevate humanity end up in Hellfire if they are disbelievers?" We answer that Allah is fair. You earn your reward from the one you worked for. If, for example, you work as an engineer for BMW and you design a great new safety feature, would you expect to get a salary from Mercedes Benz or Pepsi? Of course not, that is not who you worked for. Let's apply this concept to great inventors who happen to be disbelievers. Did they come up with all these inventions while keeping Allah in mind? Or were humanity, money, and fame their goals? If they worked for humanity, then they have received their fair reward. They have university halls named after them, statues, and books commemorating their work, and some earned great wealth. They should not expect a reward from Allah if they did not work with Him in mind.

This also applies to Muslims. Listen to the words of the Prophet Muhammad. He, peace be upon him, said:

"Verily, amongst the first people to be judged on the Day of Resurrection will be a man who was martyred. He will be brought forth and shown the blessings Allah gave him on Earth, and he will acknowledge them. Allah will ask, 'What did you do with those blessings?' The man will answer, 'I sacrificed all in your cause until I was martyred.' Allah will say, 'You have lied, for you only fought so people would say, 'He is a brave man,' and so it was said.' Then, Allah will order him to be dragged upon his face until he is cast into Hellfire. Another man will be brought forward. He was a scholar who studied, taught others, and recited the Quran. He will be shown the blessings Allah gave him on Earth, and he will acknowledge them. Allah will ask, 'What did you do with those blessings?' The man will answer, 'I learned religious knowledge, taught others, and I recited the Quran for your sake.' Allah will answer, 'You have lied, for you only studied so people would say, 'What a great scholar,' and so it was said.' Then, Allah will order him to be dragged upon his face until he is cast into Hellfire. Another man who was immensely wealthy will be brought forth. He will be shown his wealth, and he will recognize it. Allah will ask, 'And what did you do with your wealth?' The man will answer, 'I sought every path in which You like money to be spent and gave for Your sake.' Allah will say, 'You have lied - you spent so people would say, 'What a generous man,' and so it was said.' Then, Allah will order him to be dragged upon his face until he is cast into Hellfire."

Similarly, do not expect a reward from Allah if you did not seek Him in the first place. Allah says:

If anyone desires the harvest of the life to come, We shall increase it for him; if anyone desires the harvest of this world, We shall give him a share of it, but in the Hereafter, he will have no share. (42:20)

Here is another proof that Allah was not on the minds of the disbelievers even when they were doing beneficial deeds. Allah says:

But the actions of the disbelievers are like a mirage in the desert. A thirsty man mistakes it for water, but when he reaches it, he finds it to be nothing at all, and he finds Allah there. He will pay him his account in full. Allah is swift at reckoning. (24:39)

The phrase "and he finds Allah there" informs us that such people are surprised by the existence of Allah. As if Allah says to the person of such good deeds: I was not in your mind at the time you performed the deed, so go and collect your reward from whomever you worked for.

Thus, those who dedicate their life's work to fight Allah, fight His messengers, and fight people who call for justice, will see their efforts go to complete waste. Allah's religion will triumph even if faced against overwhelming odds. Allah says:

Those who disbelieve spend their possessions on turning people away from Allah; they will go on spending more, but all they will reap is regret. Then they will be overpowered and led to Hell. (8:36)

Deep Hadith - The disbelievers are rewarded in this world...

Narrated Anas ibn Malik: The Messenger of Allah ﷺ said: "Allah does not wrong a believer for any good deed; He gives him reward for it in this world and recompenses him for it in the Hereafter. As for the disbeliever, he is given provision in this world for the good deeds he performed for Allah, until when he reaches the Hereafter, there will not be any good deed for which he is rewarded."

[Commentary]

All praise is due to Allah, I say this is amongst the most beautiful and deepest hadiths as it is filled with so much wisdom, and I've explained this hadith many times before as well.

No doubt Allah is the best of judges, and it's not possible that He will be unjust to anyone, and that includes those who believe in Him and obey Him, as well as those who reject Him or associate partners with Him. There is no judge like Allah, Glory be to Him.

"Allah does not wrong a believer for any good deed" means that Allah will not let the reward of the good deeds of a believer go to waste. Rather, as Allah is the best judge, "He gives him reward for it in this world and recompenses him for it in the Hereafter." Meaning whenever a believer does a good deed, Allah rewards him not only in the Hereafter, but rather in this world as well! Reward in this world can come in the form of provision, ease, blessings, and the like. But when they (the believers) meet Allah on the Day of Judgment, they will also have their reward for the good deeds they performed, so this way they received benefits and rewards in this world as well as the Hereafter! However, it is possible that Allah might also save the entire reward for the Hereafter.

I say this is justice, and this is also love. This is like the hadith in which the Prophet ﷺ said: "When Allah wants good for a servant, He hastens the punishment for his sin. And if He wants evil for him, He withholds punishment for his sin until he meets Him…" [Sharh Majmu' al-Ahadith al-Sahihah 105] So just like when Allah wants bad for a servant, He saves the punishment for his sins, until they pile up into a huge pile, then Allah will punish the person in the next life for all of his sins with a way more significant punishment compared to the punishment of this life.

Similarly, it's possible that when Allah wants good for someone and He loves someone, He saves all of his reward for his good deeds, and out of love, He will give it to him in the Hereafter, which is even better!

This is like if a parent gives their child some money, and while on the street the child sees a shop and wants to buy a toy. But the parent tells him to save your money right now, there is a better shop with better toys that you will love much more than these ones! So the only thing the child has to do is trust his parents and also be patient. This is out of love, not out of hate!

"As for the disbeliever" means those who died in a state of disbelief, whether they rejected Allah, or associated partners with Him, and the like. "He is given provision in this world for the good deeds he performed for Allah" meaning the good acts they did which do not require any intention to be valid, like maintaining family ties, feeding the poor, helping the needy, facilitating good deeds, and the like. Some of these were mentioned by An-Nawawi and some by Mulla Ali al-Qari.

However, the deeds are not accepted from them, meaning they will not get any reward for it in the Hereafter as they don't believe in Allah nor the Day of Judgment or Resurrection. But as Allah is the best judge, Allah Knows who will die in disbelief and who will die on faith, so Allah rewards the disbelievers for their good deeds in this world. This can mean Allah gives them wealth, health, children, and other blessings that might make their life easier.

"Until when he reaches the Hereafter, there will not be any good deed for which he is rewarded." Meaning when they reach the Hereafter, they will have zero good deeds for which they can be recompensed. That's because whatever good deeds they did, Allah already rewarded them in this life, so they will be out of good deeds to be recompensed for in the Hereafter. So no matter how great their good deeds are in this world, the punishment for disbelief is much greater. This is why Allah forgives the sins of a Muslim, but He does not forgive someone who died in the state of disbelief. This is the biggest sin in the sight of Allah as His signs are extremely clear!

Plus, how can the disbeliever expect something from Allah when he rejected Him and rejected that one day he will be resurrected and asked about every single thing he did?

This is like someone who tries to grow a beautiful flower, he puts soil and waters it every day and spends a lot of time on it, yet as he didn't plant the seed, nothing will grow. All the effort without planting the seed is useless. Similarly, no matter how many good deeds one does, if they don't believe in Allah, they won't get the reward in the Hereafter.

This is also like a person offering you a gift, but you don't believe and trust them. But later, you expect to get that same gift, even though you never placed trust in that person in the first place. Similarly, the disbeliever rejects Allah and doesn't believe in the reward of Paradise. They make fun of it, they make jokes about it, mocking it. But when they find out on the Day of Judgment that Paradise exists and so does Hell, all the things we mocked are indeed true. So how can such people expect to receive Paradise when they didn't believe in the One who promised Paradise for those who believed in Him?

May Allah guide us and allow us to die on Islam (faith). Ameen

Verse 23

Alam tara ilal lazeena ootoo naseebam minal Kitaabi yud'awna ilaa Kitaabil laahi liyahkuma bainahum summa yatawallaa fareequm minhum wa hum mu'ridoon

Didn't you see those who were given a share of the Scripture? When they are called to Allah's Book to arbitrate between them in their disputes, a group from them turns away objecting. (Verse 23)

There are many verses of the Quran that address our beloved Prophet Muhammad with the phrase "Didn't you see?" In the verse under study, the matter was very clear to the Prophet Muhammad. He saw those who were invited to Allah's Book to solve their disputes turn away over and over. However, in many other verses, the question "Didn't you see?" does not seem to make any sense because it asks the Prophet about events that happened before his time. There is no way that Prophet Muhammad could have seen them.

Let us read the following verse from Surah Al-Baqarah:

Didn't you see those who abandoned their homes, though they were in the thousands, for fear of death? Allah said to them, "Die." Then He restored them to life. Truly, Allah shows real favour to people, but most of them are ungrateful. (2:243)

Allah chose to ask the Prophet Muhammad and the companions "Didn't you see?" about an event that happened hundreds of years prior. No one reciting the Quran could have seen these events. They might have heard or read about it, but none could have seen it. What is the point of the question then? It would have made more sense to ask, "Haven't you heard?" or "Didn't you read?" We answer that eyesight is the most certain of our senses. You may hear from someone you trust about an event that happened, but there is always room for doubt. You may read about an event from a trusted news source, but there is still room for bias and error. However, when you see something with your own eyes, you become certain. So are the words of our Lord. To the believer, what Allah says is as real and sure as one's own eyesight. The Quran is Allah's word, and the phrase "Didn't you see?" implies that we should believe in what Allah tells us with the same certainty as if we were there witnessing the event first hand. A believer sees through his or her faith what his or her eyes fail to see. This vision and certainty are continuous for every believer who recites the verse until the Day of Judgment.

In another example, Allah addresses the Prophet in the following verse:

Have you not seen how your Lord dealt with the people of the elephants? (105:1)

Some critics of Islam cite this verse to challenge the authenticity of the Quran. Prophet Muhammad was born in the year of the battle of the elephant. Allah addressed him by using the phrase "Didn't you see?" although the Prophet, an infant at the time, could not have seen the incident. We answer that when we hear the words of Allah, we believe in them as if we were physically there. So let your Lord be more trustworthy to you than your own eyes. When Allah informs you about an event, you should believe in it as if it has happened right in front of you.

Allah says:

Allah's command has already come, so do not ask to bring it on sooner. Glory be to Him, and highly exalted be He above what they associate with Him! (16:01)

How is it that "Allah's command has already come," yet we are asked to be patient and not to hasten it? The phrase "has already come" is in the past tense, meaning that it has happened. We answer that Allah is the All-Powerful, All-Knowledgeable, and when He decrees a matter, no one can stop it. Thus, Allah's will, even for future matters, will come to pass with absolute certainty. No power can oppose the Almighty to bring forward a different matter.

This brings us back to the verse. Allah says, "Didn't you see those who were given a share of the scripture?" What is a share? It is a part of something, less than the whole. For example, if you have twenty pounds and you divide them amongst four people, each will receive a share of five pounds. So, the phrase "those who were given a share of the scripture" is a beautiful gesture from Allah. Why? Because Allah is reminding our beloved Muhammad that some of the Jews and Christians of Medina are excused because only a small part of their original scriptures reached them. Allah says:

When they dishonoured their pledge, We condemned them and hardened their hearts. So they distort the words of the Scripture out of context and have forgotten some of what they were reminded with. You will always hear of treachery on their part except that of a few. But forbear and forgive them, for Allah loves those who do good. (5:13)

Of course, that does not apply to everyone. Some of the scholars had full access to true knowledge. Allah says:

Those We gave Scripture know it as well as they know their own sons, but some of them hide the truth that they know. (2:146)

The scholars who had full access to the original scriptures hid it from their followers. Thus, many commoners were deceived, but that was not all. Allah says:

Among them is a group who distort the Book with their tongues so that you think it is from the Book when it is not. They say, "It is from Allah," but it is not from Allah. They tell a lie against Allah, and they know it. (3:78)

So the heavenly scriptures that were revealed before the Quran were subjected to more than one type of assault until only a fraction of the truth remained. The Quran is inviting the Christians and the Jews to uphold the remaining truths in their disputes, and discard the parts that were tainted by corrupt clergy over the centuries.

LET US TO BACK TO THE VERSE UNDER STUDY

Didn't you see those who were given a share of the scripture? When they are called to Allah's Book to arbitrate between them in their disputes, a group from them turns away objecting. (Verse 23)

The verse under study is related to an incident that happened at the time of Prophet Muhammad as the Jews and Christians argued endlessly. One of their arguments was over the religion of Prophet Abraham. Allah sent the following verse to resolve the matter:

You argue about some things of which you have some knowledge, but why do you argue about things of which you know nothing? Allah knows, and you do not. Abraham was neither a Jew nor a Christian. He was upright and devoted to Allah, never an idolater. The people with the strongest claim to Abraham are those who followed him and this Prophet and those who have faith. Allah is the Protector of the believers. (3:66-68)

Judaism and Christianity came well after the time of Abraham. How could they argue over something that defies history? Maybe we should ask, what are these disagreements truly about? Allah answers in verse 19 of chapter Al-Imran, "Those who were given the Book did not differ except after true knowledge had come to them, out of envious rivalry among themselves." Such conflicts were commonplace, not only across religions but also within Judaism and Christianity.

When arguments arise, we should look to Allah and the scriptures for answers. But which scripture is this verse referring to? Is it the Quran? That is a possibility. Our beloved Muhammad invited the people of the book to use the Quran to solve their disputes, because the Quran confirms all the heavenly books sent previously. The Jews and the Christians of the time were called to measure what they knew to be true in their books against the Quran, and then adopt the Quran as the prevailing heavenly revelation. However, most of them were not interested in the truth. They were busy chasing after worldly rivalries out of hatred and envy.

Another possibility is that the disagreements were regarding the Torah and the Gospel. But which share of the scripture is Allah referring to? Were the disagreements about the share of the Torah and the Gospel that were available at hand? Or about the share they lost and neglected? We answer that the disputes were about the portion of the scriptures the Jews and Christians had at hand. They had little confidence in the authenticity of their scriptures, and on many occasions they ignored them altogether.

For example, at the time of Prophet Muhammad, two Jewish residents of Medina, a woman and a man from the tribe of Khyber, committed adultery. They were from prominent respectable families. Feeling the social pressure, the rabbis who adjudicated the matter tried to conceal the ruling in the Torah, which is stoning. They wanted to spare the elites from public humiliation. So, they resorted to trickery and suggested that the families should go to Prophet Muhammad, peace be upon him. The action of the rabbis raises two questions: why Prophet Muhammad, and did they really trust him to solve all their disputes? We answer that seeking Prophet Muhammad for this dispute gives you a clear idea of the kind of clergy the rabbis were. They only went to him to circumvent the Torah and find a solution that was socially acceptable despite Allah's teachings. In short, stoning was too harsh for their elites; maybe Muhammad would judge differently.

When the Jewish group sat with Prophet Muhammad, two men spoke: Numan bin Awfa and Bahry ibn Amru. They said, "O Messenger of Allah, judge between these people." He, peace be upon him, responded, "Don't you have a clear ruling for this matter in the Torah? I will judge according to your scripture." They reluctantly replied, "That would be fair."

Prophet Muhammad first explained that the ruling for adultery in Islam is stoning, and then he asked for one part of the Torah to be brought in. He asked, "Which of you has the most knowledge of the Torah?" They named Abdullah bin Suriya, who was brought forth and given the section of the Torah that Prophet Muhammad had specified. Bin Suriya began to read, but when he reached the verse about stoning he covered it with his hand and skipped ahead. A companion named Abdullah bin Salam said, "O Messenger of Allah, did you see him covering the verse!?" Bin Salam moved the man's hand and revealed the hidden verse about stoning.

This showed everyone that, when it came to adultery, the judgment was identical both in the Quran and the Torah. It also revealed that Prophet Muhammad, peace be upon him, was guided by the Divine Power to the exact part of the Torah that contained Allah's ruling. Moreover, Abdullah bin Salam, a Jewish convert to Islam, knew very well his people's trickery to forge and falsify.

The story of Abdullah bin Salam accepting Islam is wonderful. After faith had settled in his heart, he came to the Messenger of Allah and said,"Allah has opened my heart to Islam, and the words "There is no God but Allah and Muhammad is His Messenger" are always on my tongue. But, before I declare my faith publicly, I would like you to meet with the Jewish leaders so that you can ask their opinion of me. I know my people, and I want to see how they act." Prophet Muhammad met with the Jewish leaders and asked them about Abdullah bin Salam. They said, "Our chief, the son of our chief, and our rabbi. He is among the best of us." They kept on showering him with praise. Then Abdullah bin Salam stood and announced, "I testify that there is no God but Allah and that Muhammad is His Messenger." In an instant, the Jewish leaders turned on Abdullah, cursed him, and accused him of bad traits. They contradicted everything they had said just a few moments ago. Abdullah bin Salam turned to Prophet Muhammad and said, "O Messenger of Allah, didn't I tell you that they are maligned corrupt people? By Allah, I wanted you to know what they truly thought of me before I become a Muslim."

It was Abdullah bin Salam who moved the palm of Abdullah bin Suriya away from the stoning verse in the Torah. Allah says:

Didn't you see those who were given a share of the scripture? When they are called to Allah's Book to arbitrate between them in their disputes, a group from them turns away objecting.

LET US REFLECT ON VERSE 23

Why would anyone refuse Allah as a judge? In the previous verses, we gave the example of the rabbis of Medina who ignored stoning as a punishment when the adulterers were from the social elites. They desperately searched for a lesser sentence and went as far as consulting Prophet Muhammad, hoping for a better outcome for the prominent Jewish families.

It is a classic example of "worldly authority", known also as "temporal authority." What is the "worldly authority?" It is a power grab that comes from abusing religion. People take from the sacredness of religion what benefits them, then cast themselves as righteous, and abuse this authority. In fact, all the transgressions made against the Torah and the Gospel stem from this type of greed for power.

Here is an example. Before the advent of Islam, the Jews of Medina used to say to the pagan Arabs, "A prophet will soon come. We will follow him, fight you with him, and kill you as our ancestors killed the pagans of Iram and Aad." Moreover, when Prophet Muhammad came, they immediately recognized him from their books. Yet, they disbelieved and fought the Muslims. Allah answers:

Those who disbelieved say, "You are not a messenger." Say: "Allah is a sufficient witness between you and me, and anyone else who has knowledge of the Book." (13:43)

Allah singled out "anyone else who has knowledge of the Book" because such people knew, without a shadow of a doubt, who Prophet Muhammad was. Many priests and rabbis had accurate descriptions of the prophet and proofs of the authenticity of his message. They should have been the first to believe. Sadly, they viewed Prophet Muhammad as a threat to their religious authority and status in the community. Their temporal authority was at risk!

Corrupt preachers often try to build up their temporal authority by one of two tactics. The first tactic is to ease religious rulings which people find stressful. They steer religion away from actions into empty rituals. For example Musaylama, the liar, who claimed prophethood after the death of our beloved Muhammad, lightened the obligation of prayers and lessened the amount of Zakat almsgiving. He hoped to attract followers by easing difficult matters. People can now claim to be religious without having to adhere to any obligation. That is how most religions are gutted from their real value.

Allah is the All-Wise and All-Knowing. He is best aware of His creation. Look how He addressed the issue of our weakness when it comes to adhering to our daily prayers. Allah says:

Seek help through patience and through prayers. Indeed prayer is burdensome, but not for those humbled by their reverence of Allah. (2:45)

And in another chapter:

Instruct your family and community to establish the prayer, and be diligent in its observance. We do not ask you to provide for Us; rather, it is We Who provide for you. And the best outcome is gained through righteousness. (20:132)

The second tactic employed by corrupt preachers to boost their temporal authority is to ease the restrictions on unlawful matters. You can easily attract followers if you make sin permissible, or at least, lessen its punishment. Look at the words of some rabbis as narrated in the Quran:

They say, "The Fire will not touch us at all except for a few days." Say, then: "Have you made a covenant with Allah and received a promise from Him? If so, Allah will never break His covenant. Or do you say things against Allah that you do not know?" (2:80)

To understand the trickery of such clergy, let's break down their statement, "The Fire will not touch us at all except for few days." We know that every event has a time, a place, and a scale. The corrupt clergy tried to assault Allah's prohibitions at every level. When it came to time, they claimed that their status after the Day of Resurrection, which is eternal, will only affect them for a few days. Hence, there is no immortality in punishment. When it came to the place and scale of the punishment, they tried to play down Hellfire for their followers. By using the word "touch," people were misled into thinking of Hellfire not in terms of immersion, but in terms of a mere touch of fire. How did they justify this special treatment? The rabbis answered, "We are the children of Allah and His beloved. Have you ever seen anyone torturing his children and loved ones?" This is how their followers were led to indulge in sin with little consideration for the repercussions.

Often, corrupt clergy misrepresent the stories of the prophets to support their false claims. A favourite of theirs is the story of our beloved Prophet أيوب (Job), who suffered terribly from a debilitating physical illness. In the depth of his misery, Job lost his temper and made an oath to strike his wife a hundred times once he is cured of his ailments. Job's wife was the only person who stood by him throughout his terrible ailments. He deeply loved her and regretted his words, but felt bound by the oath. Job prayed for Allah's help. Allah answered:

He has ordained a way for you to release you from such oaths. Allah is your helper: He is the All-Knowing, the Wise. (66:2)

And in another verse:

"Take a small bunch of grass in your hand, and strike with that so as not to break your oath." We found him patient in adversity, an excellent servant! He, too, always turned to Allah. (38:44)

Allah helped Job fulfill his oath with an expression of love, not anger. Job's wife was the only person to stand by him during the years of his illness. Allah ordered Job to take a bundle of grass that contained one hundred leaves, and then gently strike his wife's arm with it. Thus, one stroke with green grass absolved Job from his oath. Some of the Israelites said, "We are the grandchildren of Jacob and Job, and we will only be punished for our sins as Job's wife was struck with the grass. The fire will not touch us at all except for a few days." Allah says:

That is because they said, "The Fire shall not touch us, except for a few days," and so the lies they forged in their religion have deluded them. (3:24)

VERSE 24 & 25

Zaalika bi annahum qaaloo lan tamassanan naaru illaaa ayyaamam ma'doodaatinw wa gharrahum fee deenihim maa kaanoo yaftaroon (Verse 24)

Fakaifa izaa jama'naahum li Yawmil laa raiba fee wa wuffiyat kullu nafsim maa kasabat wa hum laa yuzlamoon (Verse 25)

That is because they said, "The Fire shall not touch us, except for a few days," and so the lies they forged in their religion have deluded them. (Verse 24)

How will they then fare when We gather them together for a Day of which there is no doubt, when every soul will be paid in full for what it has done, and they will not be wronged? (Verse 25)

Let's take a moment to study the verb "deluded." The Arabic origin غَر (Ghar) comes from الْغَرُورُ (Al-Gharour), which refers to the desire to attain something unattainable or inappropriate to have. The word مغرور (Maghrour) is used to describe someone arrogant and egotistical. An inexperienced, naive person is called غَر (Ghar) because he or she can easily be fooled. In fact, Allah uses the word الْغَرُورُ (Al-Gharour) to describe Satan in the Quran. The Devil is the master deceiver. Allah says:

People! Allah's promise is true, so do not let the present life delude you, and do not let the Deceiver delude you about Allah: Satan is your enemy, so treat him as an enemy. He invites his followers so that they may become the inhabitants of blazing fire. (35:5-6)

Satan adorns sin to people and urges them to chase after insatiable desires only to end up in misery. How many celebrities do you know who fulfilled every desire only to fall into depression or worse? All they pursued turned to be the delusion of happiness. Allah says:

Know that the present, worldly life is but a play, vain talk and ostentation, and mutual boasting among you while competing in wealth and children. It is like when the rain comes down, and the vegetation grown by it pleases the farmers, then it dries up, and you see it turning yellow, then it becomes straw. In the Hereafter, there is a severe punishment, but also forgiveness from Allah and His good pleasure, whereas the present, worldly life is but a transient enjoyment of delusion. (57:20)

Allah called Satan "the Deceiver" because he tempts us into chasing after illusions against our interest. Allah paints for us the picture on the Day of Judgment where Satan disowns those who followed him. Allah says:

When everything has been decided, Satan will say, "Allah gave you a true promise. I, too, made promises, but they were false: I had no power over you except to call you, and you responded to my call, so do not blame me; blame yourselves. I cannot help you, nor can you help me. I reject the way you associated me with Allah before." A bitter torment awaits such wrongdoers. (14:22)

The phrase "I had no power over you except to call you" gives you valuable insight about your battle with the devil. Always keep in mind that Satan does not possess the authority to compel you to do what you do not want, nor does he have the power to make you feel comfortable with sin. In fact, Satan does not have any power or authority over any human being.

Authority is of two types. The first type is forcing one to do an act he or she does not want to do; this is known as the "power of compulsion." The second type is convincing a person to voluntarily do an act while he or she is content; this is known as the "power of persuasion." Satan does not have the power of compulsion nor the power of persuasion. Sadly, his whispers often find an inclination and a desire within us, and thus we lend them an attentive ear and pursue them.

However, we should always keep in mind the end result of this struggle. Satan will declare the facts to his followers on the Day of Resurrection, after it is too late. He will say, "I had no authority over you, I had no arguments to convince you to do sins, nor did I have the power to force you to act, but you were flirting with sin and all I had to do was to give you a little nudge." Perhaps even more devastating, Satan will confirm that he will not come to the aid of any of his followers.

This brings us back to the verse. Allah says, "and so the lies they forged in their religion have deluded them." In order to hoard wealth and power, some of the people of the book resorted to deception. They fabricated words, attributed them to Allah, and then believed their own lies. This is a terrible calamity because their lies involved people's faith. Let me clarify. If you deceive people in worldly matters and scam them out of their money, for example, the damage is limited. But if you deceive people in their religion and change Allah's teachings, the damage is eternal. Allah sent the scriptures to run the affairs of His creation. Corrupting the scriptures ruins the lives of millions in this world and the next.

Look at how the actions of a few corrupt clergies destroyed the lives of the Jews of Medina centuries later. Allah says:

Didn't you see those who were given a share of the scripture? When they are called to Allah's Book to arbitrate between them in their disputes, a group from them turns away objecting. That is because they said, "The Fire shall not touch us, except for a few days"; and so the lies they forged in their religion have deluded them. (3:23-24)

The Jews of Medina rejected Prophet Muhammad's call to resort to Allah's Book in their disputes. They reasoned that "The Fire shall not touch us, except for a few days." This was one of the fabrications added to the scriptures by their ancestors. They further claimed that the number of days they would suffer in the Hereafter would be equal to the number of days their ancestors worshipped the golden calf. These were all lies, and many of them knew it. Allah answers:

How will they then fare when We gather them together for a Day of which there is no doubt, when every soul will be paid in full for what it has done, and they will not be wronged? (Chapter 3: Verse 25)

All lies will come to an end. Allah will expose every liar, cheater, and corrupt preacher. He asks, "What will all these people do on the Day of Judgment?" Throughout life, Allah had given them freedom of choice. They did as they wished and were well aware of the consequences of their actions. Allah made the reward for those who implement His teachings very clear and the punishment for those who do not clear as well. How will such people behave when the Almighty will take away their freedom of choice on the Day of Judgment?

Verse 26

Qulil laahumma Maalikal Mulki tu'til mulka man tashaaa'u wa tanzi'ul mulka mimman tashhaaa'u wa tu'izzu man tashaaa'u wa tuzillu man tashaaa'u biyadikal khairu innaka 'alaa kulli shai'in Qadeer

Say: "O Allah, Master of all dominion! You give dominion to whom You will, and extract dominion from whom You will, and You honor whom You will, and abase whom You will; in Your hand is all good; surely You have full power over everything." (Verse 26)

Let's start with the phrase "Master of all dominion," translated from the Arabic origin الْمُلْكِ مَالِكَ (Malek Al Mulk). The word مُلْك (Mulk), which means "ownership" or "control," has a couple of variations. مِلك (Melk) refers to personal belongings such as the clothes, books, and phones you own. Mulk, on the other hand, refers to the property of those who hire or rule people. Everything you see around you falls under the dominion of Mulk, or "the observed world." There is another dominion that is hidden from us, which we call the "Dominion of Malakout."

So, to review, there are three levels of dominion or ownership. The first level is personal Melk, which applies to the simplest things a person may own. Then there is the larger Mulk, which refers to the property of figures of authority and of those who have people working for them. Lastly, there is Malakout, which is a vast world beyond what we see. Listen to Allah's words as He revealed to Abraham, peace be upon him, some of His hidden dominions:

Thus We showed Abraham the visible and invisible dominions of the heavens and the Earth, that he could be among those who believe. (6:75)

Allah wanted Abraham to see the Malakout of the heavens and the Earth, including the parts hidden from our eyes.

Along with these three levels of ownership come three levels of owners. A person who has مُلك (Melk) is called مَالِك (Maalek.) Maalek is the lowest level of ownership because you can be called Maalek even if your only possession in life is the shirt on your back. As for a person who has people working under him or her -in other words, has Mulk- he or she is called مَلِك (Malek). Malek is the same Arabic word used for a king. It is the highest level a human can attain. In the divine realm, Allah is the One who owns every owner and king. He is the "Master of all dominion," مَالِكُ الْمُلْكِ (Maalek Al Mulk).

It is interesting to note that Allah, the Exalted, the Almighty, used the word Maalek to describe Himself on the Day of Judgment. When you recite the fourth verse of Al-Fatiha in your prayers, you say, "Maaleke Youme Al-Deen." "Maalek", if you recall, is the lowest level of ownership! Why would Allah use "Maalek" to describe Himself on that day? We answer that, on the Day of Judgment, no one except Allah Almighty owns anything at all. You will not have any possessions, not even a grain of sand. In fact, you will not even have control over your limbs. Allah is the one and only Owner, so the word "Maalek" is sufficient. It is the strongest expression of Allah's exclusive rule. Listen to the following verse:

The day when they will come forth and when not one thing about them will be hidden from Allah. To whom does the kingdom belong today? To Allah, the One, the Conqueror! (40:16)

And in another chapter:

On that day We shall seal up their mouths, but their hands will speak to Us, and their feet bear witness to everything they have done. (36:65)

The verse continues, Say: "O Allah, Master of all dominion! You give dominion to whom You will, and take away dominion from whom You will." You should never think that anyone has any rule over Allah's creation without His will. No one takes a grain of sand forcefully from the Almighty. But, when a tyrant assumes power, people mistakenly think that matters are outside Allah's will. They wonder, "How can Allah allow such a thing to happen?" We answer that Allah is best aware of His creation, so He appoints rulers based on their condition. When people turn away from Allah's teachings, He appoints an unjust ruler over them. Allah says:

In the like manner do We let some of the unjust have power one over another because of their wrongful deeds. (6:29)

Allah puts the oppressor in charge of the unjust. Prophet Muhammad, peace be upon him, narrated to us: "Allah, the Exalted, the Glorious, will fold the Heavens on the Day of Judgment and then place them on His right hand and say, "I am the King. Where are the tyrants today? And where are the arrogant today?"

Now, we turn our attention to the word "O Allah," translated from the Arabic origin اللَّهُمَّ (Allahumma). The word "Allah" is full of linguistic wonders! The Quran descended from the heavens in Arabic. The Arabs at the time were known for their eloquence and superb mastery of the language. Interestingly, the word of majesty "Allah" had a very distinguished position in the Arabic language well before the advent of Islam.

Let me explain. In Arabic, the preposition used to call on someone is "Ya." For example, if you wanted to call your son into the room, you would say, "Ya Hasan, come here." It is equivalent to the English "Hey", or "O." The preposition "Ya" can be used to call on someone as long as the name is not preceded by the definite article ال (The). You can use "Ya" to call on Omar, but you cannot use it to call on "the policeman," or "the neighbor." Any noun preceded by the definite article cannot be joined with "Ya." The only exception in the Arabic language is the word of majesty "Allah." You can always call on Allah and say يا الله (Ya Allah).

It is also important to note that the preposition "Ya" is used to call someone who is far, or not present with you. Thus, it is not proper to use it to supplicate Allah, because He is with you all the time. Allah teaches us to supplicate him by اللَّهُمَّ (Allahumma). The preposition "Ya" is omitted and replaced by the letter م (m, Meem) at the end of the word.

This letter adds a sense of love and closeness to the call. In the Arabic language, Allah alone is the One summoned without using the vocative preposition "Ya."

Lastly, the only word that accepts the letter ت (Ta) before it as the article of an oath is the word "Allah." Hence, you can say تالله (Ta Allah) to make an oath, but you cannot use "Ta" with any other word. All these linguistic honors to the word "Allah" were bestowed well before the advent of Islam. Even the pagans who denied Allah gave the name of the Almighty a special status!

Say: "O Allah, Master of all dominion! You give dominion to whom You will and extract dominion from whom You will, and You honor whom You will, and abase whom You will; in Your hand is all good; surely You have full power over everything."

(Verse 26)

There is a fascinating story behind this verse. It started when the enemies of Prophet Muhammad formed a coalition to defeat Islam once and for all. They gathered their forces and headed towards Medina. Moreover, the Jews of Medina —who had signed a defense treaty with the Muslims— engaged in spying and sabotage to weaken the Muslims from within. When Prophet Muhammad, peace be upon him, heard of the large army headed his way, he consulted with his companions. Salman al-Farisi, a companion from Persia, recommended digging a trench around Medina as a defense line to halt the invading army's progress. Experienced soldiers knew that cavalrymen on horses could jump a maximum of a few meters, and a wide trench was needed to impede their ability to cross.

Let's look at how the Messenger managed this challenging situation. He, peace upon him, sought advice from the best people around him. When Salman suggested digging a trench, as the Persians did in battle, the Prophet adopted the idea to be implemented by the Muslims. We learn not to automatically reject everything that the disbelievers do. The Messenger of Allah, peace be upon him, would weigh the matter and see its advantages and disadvantages, and then act accordingly. On many occasions, Prophet Muhammad initiated and signed fair defense and trade treaties with the non-believers for the benefit of all.

Now the Muslims were facing the daunting task of manually digging a long trench in the desert heat. Furthermore, the land allocated to the trench was hard and challenging to manage. Prophet Muhammad assigned forty cubits of land to every group of ten companions. A cubit is an ancient measuring unit roughly equal to the length of a forearm. The Prophet explicitly distributed the work and responsibility and did not leave matters vague. He assigned a manageable amount of work to a manageable number of people. The distribution of responsibility means that each group of ten knew exactly what they were expected to do. Clarity fostered friendly competition between the groups for who could finish first.

Here you may wonder, why didn't the Prophet divide the task further to each person? Rather than giving ten companions forty cubits, he could have given each companion four cubits to dig. We answer that there is wisdom behind the Prophet's decision. He, peace be upon him, knew that not all diggers are equal in ability and experience. Thus, he wanted weak companions to be supported by their strong brethren. The Prophet did not make the entire task open to all, nor did he make it an individual burden. Rather, there were clear responsibilities assigned to each small group of individuals: the weak got help, groups competed among each other, and the spirit of affection grew between the companions.

Amr ibn Auf was among the nine companions in Salman al-Farisi's group. As they were digging, they encountered a solid piece of rock, which completely halted their progress. After trying for a while, the group said to Salman, "Go to the Prophet and bring this matter to his attention." Salman explained the problem to Prophet Muhammad, who then accompanied him back to the location of the rock. From this incident, we learn that when those assigned a task encounter a problem, they should bring it up the chain of command to get help.

Our beloved Muhammad took a pickaxe and struck the rock with it causing sparks to fly. He, peace be upon him, loudly said, "Allah is the Greatest, the palaces of Bosra in Syria have been conquered." Then he struck the rock a second time and said, "Allah is the Greatest, the Roman palaces of Al-Hamra have been conquered." He struck it a third time and said, "Allahu Akbar, the palaces of Sana'a in Yemen have been conquered." Each time our beloved Muhammad hit the rock, Allah showed him a place that would be conquered by the Muslims.

When the army of Quraish heard of the incident, their leaders laughed and said, "Muhammad promises his followers the palaces of Caesar and Khosrow, but he has to dig a hole in the desert because he is afraid of our army!" At this juncture, Allah revealed the following verse to our beloved Muhammad:

Say: "O Allah, Master of all dominion! You give dominion to whom You will and extract dominion from whom You will, and You honor whom You will, and abase whom You will; in Your hand is all good; surely You have full power over everything."

(Chapter 3: Verse 26)

You should always keep in mind that Allah asks you to do your best first, and then leave the rest to Him. Do not look at challenges based solely on your ability. If you are Allah-conscious and [you] do your best, Allah will be with you. Is there any matter that is difficult if Allah, the Greatest of all Helpers, is by your side? It is the Almighty who gives rule and sovereignty. He is the One true Allah who takes control away from Persia, Rome, and Sana'a and gives it to Muhammad and his followers. He takes it away from Quraish and the Jews of Medina and grants the spoils to the Muslims.

The word "extract" should grab your attention because it seems out of place. The verse starts with "You give dominion to whom You will," then Allah talks about the opposite. But the opposite of "give" is "to take," not "to extract." Why did Allah use the verb "extract"? We answer that extracting something means removing it with force against the person's will. Presidents and kings are happy to assume power, but they often fight to the death before giving it up. Rule is often a great job that brings in wealth, fame, and countless perks. Rulers quickly embrace the easy life and forget the heavy responsibility of caring for their people.

When you see a king, president, or ruler clinging to power at all costs, then know that he or she has disregarded their responsibilities to the people and are too busy chasing wealth and power.

LET US PONDER AND REFLECT

A man came to Omar ibn al-Khattab, the second caliph of the Muslims, and said, "O Omar, if we lose you, we should appoint your son Abdullah as caliph. He is a humble Allah-fearing man." Omar got upset and replied, "Do not do that! Isn't it sufficient for the family of Al-Khattab to have one man questioned before Allah about the nation of Muhammad?" Omar felt the heavy burden of responsibility and did not want his son to be under that mountain of stress. Omar once said, "I fear that if a goat stumbled on a road in Iraq, my Lord would ask me, 'Omar, why wasn't the road paved properly?'" Compare that to most rulers today who cling to power and appoint their family to high positions to loot the people.

Yet, you should always keep in mind that "Allah, Master of all dominion! You give dominion to whom You will, and extract dominion from whom You will." There are many examples in history of ruthless rulers and powerful civilizations that worked tirelessly to secure power, only to lose it for the most trivial reasons. How? It was the will of the Supreme Creator. Allah either takes governance away from rulers or removes rulers from life altogether.

The verse continues, "You honor whom You will, and abase whom You will." It is a known fact that power is not limited to those who govern. Every president and king is surrounded by people who enjoy their reign and amass vast wealth. Such enablers are not always visible to the public. Quite often, they are the most corrupt people in the society. They hide in the shadow of authority and do as they wish. Thus, to restore justice, it is not enough for Allah to remove the unjust ruler: it is also necessary to expose and demean all those who enabled him or her. Hence, Allah says, "You give dominion to whom You will and extract dominion from whom You will," and then immediately follows with "You honor whom You will, and abase whom You will."

Here, we should pause and think about a critical issue. Most people assume that being installed as a ruler is wonderful, while losing power is terrible. We answer that every matter has two sides. The removal of an oppressive ruler is bad for the ruler and those around him, but good for the people. The removal of a just ruler is terrible for the people, except the corrupt. And, in some instances, the removal of an oppressive ruler is good for the ruler. Why? Because Allah saves him or her from further sin and punishment. Allah sometimes relieves the oppressor from his or her own injustice and opens the door of repentance.

You and I may have limited knowledge about the people's affairs, but Allah is the All-seeing, All-Knowledgeable. Thus, when you consider all things, you will find that whatever is happening in the universe is good; all those who are granted power and honor, and all those who lost power and were publically humiliated fall under the wisdom of our Lord. Allah teaches us to say: "O Allah, Master of all dominion! You give dominion to whom You will and extract dominion from whom You will, and You honor whom You will, and abase whom You will; in Your hand is all good; surely You have full power over everything."

Since Allah Almighty is the Master of all dominion, who gives it and then extracts it from whom He wills, then there must come a day when Allah takes back all that is His. He says:

He is exalted in rank, the Lord of the Throne. He sends revelations with His teachings to whichever of His servants He chooses to warn of the Day of Meeting, the Day when they will come out and nothing about them will be concealed from Allah. "Who has control today?" Allah, the One, the All Powerful. (40:15-16)

When Allah gives a person or a group rule over others, He also gives them enormous responsibility. Thus, there must come a day when Allah takes all rule away and questions those who temporality had it about that responsibility. For example, some of the people of the book who were given religious authority ignored Allah's commands and chased after worldly gains. All the while, they were claiming that the fire would not touch them but for a few days, because they were Allah's children and His beloved.

Every ruler has a free choice to follow Allah's command or his or her own desires. Allah gives us a stern warning of the day, which is sure to come, where no one will have any power or choice. The ability to choose is here and now, so make the best choices every moment in your life and use the light of Allah's scripture as your guide.

Reaching a position of power often involves decades of planning and preparation; sometimes, a person grabs power by a military coup. Likewise, removing someone from power requires a similar effort —this how we measure things in human terms. But do not despair when you see a powerful unjust ruler because Allah has infinite power and ability. When He decrees a matter, He commands it, "Be," and it becomes.

Verse 27

Toolijul laila fin nahaari wa toolijun nahaara fil laili wa tukhrijul haiya minalmaiyiti wa tukhrijul maiyita minal haiyi wa tarzuqu man tashaaa'u bighari hisaab

"You merge night into day and day into night; You bring the living out of the dead and the dead out of the living; You give provision to whom You will without account." (Verse 27)

Allah ended verse 26 of Al-Imran with the phrase, "Surely You have full power over everything," then He gave us ample evidence of His power in verse 27. He says:

"You merge night into day and day into night; You bring the living out of the dead and the dead out of the living; You give provision to whom You will without account." (3:27)

Allah turns our attention towards two wonders of the universe: night and day, and life and death. We are all familiar with the phenomenon of night and day because it is one of the greatest wonders of nature. The phrase "merges night into day and day into night" does not only apply to sunrise and sunset, but it also includes the fact that Allah did not give the day a fixed duration throughout the year. Day and night vary by as much as five to six hours between summer and winter.

Do these shifts in duration happen suddenly? Do you have a six-hour night one day, and then a thirteen-hour night the next? No, it is a gradual, almost unnoticeable process. This type of change is seamless because it happens in infinitely small increments. Contrast that to human-made mechanical movements, such as that of a hand watch. A watch keeps time using an intricate system of springs, gears, and cogs. The second, minute, and hour hands do not continuously move; instead, each hand stops then jumps to the next location, and then stops again. There is stillness in the minute hand from one minute to the next. Allah's creation is different. Time flows between day and night, and the changes between the seasons are seamless.

You can also find the same type of change as humans, plants, and animals grow. A newborn baby does not grow suddenly from one morning to the next. He or she grows ever so slowly with the parents hardly noticing. The baby's height may increase by a fraction of a millimeter each day. This growth is almost imperceptible as each cell grows ever so slightly. Such a process requires infinite precision in the distribution of growth between cells and atoms over time. This is the magnificence of our Creator! Change happens all around us while we enjoy the perception of stability.

Here we should ask, why did Allah give us the examples of "You merge night into day and day into night; You bring the living out of the dead and the dead out of the living" right after He spoke about rule, kingship, and authority? We answer that Allah drew our attention to His infinite ability to merge night into day slowly but surely, so that we do not despair. When you see an oppressive ruler established in power, or a civilization spreading injustice, rest assured that Allah will bring them to an end. Just as He injects precise –almost unnoticeable– changes in the day and night, He injects decay into the rule of the unjust. This is how civilizations decline after reaching the height of their progress, then collapse from within. Allah draws our attention to the majesty of His ability and the precision of His creation. The One who can turn night into day, and death into life and growth, can depose kings and dictators.

The verse continues, "You bring the living out of the dead and the dead out of the living." What is life? There have been endless discussions among philosophers about the meaning of life. Some said that life is awareness: if you are aware of yourself and your surroundings, you are alive. Others said that life is movement, and so on. All these definitions are based on our human experience. We answer that the broadest and most comprehensive meaning of life is the ability and the fitness to perform your intended task. Take a tree, for example. As long as it is growing and producing fruit, it is alive. Once it stops growing or producing, it no longer performs its task, and it is dying. A man is alive as long as he can perform his duties. We refer to a man in a coma as entering a vegetative state because he can no longer do any tasks. We also refer to a lazy man as a deadbeat. You can apply the same to inanimate objects. Go to the beach and look at the smooth pebble stones. You will see that each has a different shape and size. Some are big, others very small. This indicates change. With time, even the most massive rock turns into grains of sand. This is the lifecycle and function of a rock. If you remove a pebble from its natural environment, the change will stop, and the stone is no longer performing its intended task. So each being and object is alive as long as it can perform its intended task in life. Allah says in the 42nd verse of chapter 8:

It happened so that Allah could settle a matter whose result was preordained: so that those who perished would perish with clear proof, and those who lived would live with clear proof. Allah is All-Hearing, All-Knowing.

Take note that Allah used the verb "to perish" opposite to the verb "to live." Then we find the following verse:

Do not call out to any other Allah besides Allah, for there is no Allah but Him. Everything will perish except His Face. His is the Judgement, and to Him you shall all be brought back. (28:88)

"Everything will perish except His Face" refers to all beings such as people, angels, and jinn; it also refers to all plants, animals, planets, stars, objects, and matter. Since all these things will perish, it means that each was alive before. Each had a life, maybe not like yours and mine, yet a life suitable for its purpose.

Modern science showed us that individual atoms are full of movement and change and that a drop of water is full of living bacteria. Even when matter drastically changes, such as when we make sand into glass, it merely moves from one form of life and function to another. Allah is ever-present, ever-watchful over His creation. No one gave Him life, and no one takes it away from Him. He is ever fit and capable of watching over and running the universe. Thus, His life is the one true life. It is a principal of the Divine self.

Scientific discoveries allowed us to peek into the secrets of the universe, from the leaves interacting with the sun to electrons moving about a nucleus. There is a difference in what the layperson sees and perceives as life, and what life means in the eyes of those who study science. A farmer in a remote village may not know that the dry and shriveled seed is alive, but he or she understands that Allah will sprout life out of it once it is sown in healthy soil. Now, let's consider the atoms of the soil. They may not grow as a tree, but within each of them is an awesome amount of energy. If properly harnessed, the energy trapped in the atoms of a grain of sand is enough to power an entire city for weeks.

Thus, when a scientist reads the verse "You bring the living out of the dead and the dead out of the living," he or she will have a different understanding than when an ordinary person reads it. Each appreciates Allah's power based on their level of knowledge. This is part of the beauty of the miraculous words of the Noble Quran. It can be read, understood, and appreciated by a person in a remote village, as well as by a Ph.D. university professor. It satisfies the scientific and spiritual needs of a janitor and an astronaut. This is the power of Allah's words.

You merge night into day and day into night; You bring the living out of the dead and the dead out of the living; You give provision to whom You will without account.

(Verse 27)

In a single verse, Allah gave us two examples of His power, one about changing night into day, and one about life and death. The phenomenon of morphing day into night is clear for all to see. It is one of the wonders of the universe. On the other hand, Allah expressed the matter of life and death in a manner that can be understood differently by the public and the scientists.

Allah gave us examples of His capabilities because He wants you to have peace of mind of His ability to give power and take it away from whom He wills. The One who can move the sun and create life can easily grant rule and remove it. The cosmic signs are a small piece of evidence of Allah's capability.

But why do unjust rulers exist? This is best explained with an example. If your child fell ill, you would rush her to the doctor and you would do everything necessary to cure her illness, even if surgery is required. You would approve the procedure for the benefit of your child, even if you know that she will suffer from pain for a week or two. Isn't how we care for our loved ones? What would you expect of Our Generous Creator who loves His creation? Allah chooses what is good and necessary for us, even if it involves temporary pain.

The verse continues with "You give provision to whom You will without account." This phrase is specifically addressing the people who do not pay attention to Allah's cosmic signs and to matters of life and death. They may be busy, preoccupied with their daily problems, or chasing life's pleasures. Even if a person never takes time to contemplate Allah's creation, he or she is surely paying close attention to earning money and putting food on the table. It is the common preoccupation of all human beings, rich or poor. Thus, Allah mentioned it clearly in the verse. He says, "You give provision to whom You will without account."

The word "account" distinguishes between what is for you and what is against you. Keeping account requires three elements; first is the one who takes account, second is the one is being accounted, and last is the item being counted. Let's apply that to the phrase "You give provision to whom You will without account." Provision is the item being counted. It comes from Allah, the accountant who grants it to whomever He wills. Allah is the true Provider of sustenance, and He is the One who will take all of us to account on the Day of Judgment.

Allah created the means by which we earn our daily provisions, but He did not abandon us to these means. Sometimes He provides for us exactly according to our efforts and the means available, and at times He provides us without any means or effort. And every now and then, all our time and effort seem to go to waste. Anyone who ponders over these matters will conclude that Allah grants without account. He has the absolute ability because there is no higher authority to question, "Why did you do it?" Or "What did you give so and so?"

Here is the most important lesson from verses 26 and 27 of Al-Imran. If our Lord is the One who "merges night into day and day into night," and the One who "brings the living out of the dead and the dead out of the living," and "gives provision" "without account;" If our Lord is the One who gives dominion and extracts it, honours and abases whom He wills, then isn't the ultimate stupidity for you to seek help from anyone else? Isn't it foolish to ally with someone who has zero control and leave Allah who has power over everything? Allah says:

You who believe, do not take for your intimate allies such outsiders as spare no effort to ruin you and want to see you suffer: their hatred is evident from their mouths, but what their hearts conceal is far worse. We have made Our revelations clear for you; will you not use your reason? (3:118)

Allah warns us against putting our trust in anyone but Him. Muslims should never rely on the enemies of Allah in hopes for protection or prosperity because there is no power above the power of the Almighty. Allah says in the very next verse of Al-Imran,

Let not the believers take the disbelievers as allies rather than the believers. And whoever does that would isolate himself entirely from Allah, except when taking ample precaution against them in prudence. Allah warns you of Himself, and to Allah is the final destination. (3:28)

Your freedom to do as you like is a great blessing from Allah. But it is also a heavy responsibility. Allah made your body parts subject to your will. You can use your hand to give charity, or you can use it to steal or strike an innocent person. On the Day of Judgment, however, your body parts will no longer obey your commands. Instead, they will act independently and report your actions to Allah. He says:

On the Day when their own tongues, hands and feet will all bear witness against them in regard to what they used to do. On that Day, Allah will pay them in full their just due, and they will come to know that Allah is the Absolute Truth. (24:24-25)

The disbeliever's tongue was the instrument that proclaimed disbelief, but on the Day of Resurrection it will testify against him or her. Similarly, the hand that was an instrument of disobedience will testify against its previous owner. The skin, eyes, legs will all reveal to Allah the sins they were forced to do. What a terrible scene! Allah treats people justly based on their actions. It is the people who treat themselves unjustly in this world.

Allah says:

How will they then fare when We gather them together for a Day of which there is no doubt, when every soul will be paid in full for what it has done, and they will not be wronged?

(Chapter 3: Verse 25)

Verse 27

Toolijul laila fin nahaari wa toolijun nahaara fil laili wa tukhrijul haiya minalmaiyiti wa tukhrijul maiyita minal haiyi wa tarzuqu man tashaaa'u bighari hisaab

"You merge night into day and day into night; You bring the living out of the dead and the dead out of the living; You give provision to whom You will without account." (Verse 27)

Allah ended verse 26 of Al-Imran with the phrase, "Surely You have full power over everything," then He gave us ample evidence of His power in verse 27. He says:

"You merge night into day and day into night; You bring the living out of the dead and the dead out of the living; You give provision to whom You will without account." (3:27)

Allah turns our attention towards two wonders of the universe: night and day, and life and death. We are all familiar with the phenomenon of night and day because it is one of the greatest wonders of nature. The phrase "merges night into day and day into night" does not only apply to sunrise and sunset, but it also includes the fact that Allah did not give the day a fixed duration throughout the year. Day and night vary by as much as five to six hours between summer and winter.

Do these shifts in duration happen suddenly? Do you have a six-hour night one day, and then a thirteen-hour night the next? No, it is a gradual, almost unnoticeable process. This type of change is seamless because it happens in infinitely small increments. Contrast that to human-made mechanical movements, such as that of a hand watch. A watch keeps time using an intricate system of springs, gears, and cogs. The second, minute, and hour hands do not continuously move; instead, each hand stops then jumps to the next location, and then stops again. There is stillness in the minute hand from one minute to the next. Allah's creation is different. Time flows between day and night, and the changes between the seasons are seamless.

You can also find the same type of change as humans, plants, and animals grow. A newborn baby does not grow suddenly from one morning to the next. He or she grows ever so slowly with the parents hardly noticing. The baby's height may increase by a fraction of a millimeter each day. This growth is almost imperceptible as each cell grows ever so slightly. Such a process requires infinite precision in the distribution of growth between cells and atoms over time. This is the magnificence of our Creator! Change happens all around us while we enjoy the perception of stability.

Here we should ask, why did Allah give us the examples of "You merge night into day and day into night; You bring the living out of the dead and the dead out of the living" right after He spoke about rule, kingship, and authority? We answer that Allah drew our attention to His infinite ability to merge night into day slowly but surely, so that we do not despair. When you see an oppressive ruler established in power, or a civilization spreading injustice, rest assured that Allah will bring them to an end. Just as He injects precise —almost unnoticeable— changes in the day and night, He injects decay into the rule of the unjust. This is how civilizations decline after reaching the height of their progress, then collapse from within. Allah draws our attention to the majesty of His ability and the precision of His creation. The One who can turn night into day, and death into life and growth, can depose kings and dictators.

The verse continues, "You bring the living out of the dead and the dead out of the living." What is life? There have been endless discussions among philosophers about the meaning of life. Some said that life is awareness: if you are aware of yourself and your surroundings, you are alive. Others said that life is movement, and so on. All these definitions are based on our human experience. We answer that the broadest and most comprehensive meaning of life is the ability and the fitness to perform your intended task. Take a tree, for example. As long as it is growing and producing fruit, it is alive. Once it stops growing or producing, it no longer performs its task, and it is dying. A man is alive as long as he can perform his duties. We refer to a man in a coma as entering a vegetative state because he can no longer do any tasks. We also refer to a lazy man as a deadbeat. You can apply the same to inanimate objects. Go to the beach and look at the smooth pebble stones. You will see that each has a different shape and size. Some are big, others very small. This indicates change. With time, even the most massive rock turns into grains of sand. This is the lifecycle and function of a rock. If you remove a pebble from its natural environment, the change will stop, and the stone is no longer performing its intended task. So each being and object is alive as long as it can perform its intended task in life. Allah says in the 42nd verse of chapter 8:

It happened so that Allah could settle a matter whose result was preordained: so that those who perished would perish with clear proof, and those who lived would live with clear proof. Allah is All-Hearing, All-Knowing.

Take note that Allah used the verb "to perish" opposite to the verb "to live." Then we find the following verse:

Do not call out to any other Allah besides Allah, for there is no Allah but Him. Everything will perish except His Face. His is the Judgement, and to Him you shall all be brought back. (28:88)

"Everything will perish except His Face" refers to all beings such as people, angels, and jinn; it also refers to all plants, animals, planets, stars, objects, and matter. Since all these things will perish, it means that each was alive before. Each had a life, maybe not like yours and mine, yet a life suitable for its purpose.

Modern science showed us that individual atoms are full of movement and change and that a drop of water is full of living bacteria. Even when matter drastically changes, such as when we make sand into glass, it merely moves from one form of life and function to another. Allah is ever-present, ever-watchful over His creation. No one gave Him life, and no one takes it away from Him. He is ever fit and capable of watching over and running the universe. Thus, His life is the one true life. It is a principal of the Divine self.

Scientific discoveries allowed us to peek into the secrets of the universe, from the leaves interacting with the sun to electrons moving about a nucleus. There is a difference in what the layperson sees and perceives as life, and what life means in the eyes of those who study science. A farmer in a remote village may not know that the dry and shriveled seed is alive, but he or she understands that Allah will sprout life out of it once it is sown in healthy soil. Now, let's consider the atoms of the soil. They may not grow as a tree, but within each of them is an awesome amount of energy. If properly harnessed, the energy trapped in the atoms of a grain of sand is enough to power an entire city for weeks.

Thus, when a scientist reads the verse "You bring the living out of the dead and the dead out of the living," he or she will have a different understanding than when an ordinary person reads it. Each appreciates Allah's power based on their level of knowledge. This is part of the beauty of the miraculous words of the Noble Quran. It can be read, understood, and appreciated by a person in a remote village, as well as by a Ph.D. university professor. It satisfies the scientific and spiritual needs of a janitor and an astronaut. This is the power of Allah's words.

You merge night into day and day into night; You bring the living out of the dead and the dead out of the living; You give provision to whom You will without account.

(Verse 27)

In a single verse, Allah gave us two examples of His power, one about changing night into day, and one about life and death. The phenomenon of morphing day into night is clear for all to see. It is one of the wonders of the universe. On the other hand, Allah expressed the matter of life and death in a manner that can be understood differently by the public and the scientists.

Allah gave us examples of His capabilities because He wants you to have peace of mind of His ability to give power and take it away from whom He wills. The One who can move the sun and create life can easily grant rule and remove it. The cosmic signs are a small piece of evidence of Allah's capability.

But why do unjust rulers exist? This is best explained with an example. If your child fell ill, you would rush her to the doctor and you would do everything necessary to cure her illness, even if surgery is required. You would approve the procedure for the benefit of your child, even if you know that she will suffer from pain for a week or two. Isn't how we care for our loved ones? What would you expect of Our Generous Creator who loves His creation? Allah chooses what is good and necessary for us, even if it involves temporary pain.

The verse continues with "You give provision to whom You will without account." This phrase is specifically addressing the people who do not pay attention to Allah's cosmic signs and to matters of life and death. They may be busy, preoccupied with their daily problems, or chasing life's pleasures. Even if a person never takes time to contemplate Allah's creation, he or she is surely paying close attention to earning money and putting food on the table. It is the common preoccupation of all human beings, rich or poor. Thus, Allah mentioned it clearly in the verse. He says, "You give provision to whom You will without account."

The word "account" distinguishes between what is for you and what is against you. Keeping account requires three elements; first is the one who takes account, second is the one is being accounted, and last is the item being counted. Let's apply that to the phrase "You give provision to whom You will without account." Provision is the item being counted. It comes from Allah, the accountant who grants it to whomever He wills. Allah is the true Provider of sustenance, and He is the One who will take all of us to account on the Day of Judgment.

Allah created the means by which we earn our daily provisions, but He did not abandon us to these means. Sometimes He provides for us exactly according to our efforts and the means available, and at times He provides us without any means or effort. And every now and then, all our time and effort seem to go to waste. Anyone who ponders over these matters will conclude that Allah grants without account. He has the absolute ability because there is no higher authority to question, "Why did you do it?" Or "What did you give so and so?"

Here is the most important lesson from verses 26 and 27 of Al-Imran. If our Lord is the One who "merges night into day and day into night," and the One who "brings the living out of the dead and the dead out of the living," and "gives provision" "without account;" If our Lord is the One who gives dominion and extracts it, honours and abases whom He wills, then isn't the ultimate stupidity for you to seek help from anyone else? Isn't it foolish to ally with someone who has zero control and leave Allah who has power over everything? Allah says:

You who believe, do not take for your intimate allies such outsiders as spare no effort to ruin you and want to see you suffer: their hatred is evident from their mouths, but what their hearts conceal is far worse. We have made Our revelations clear for you; will you not use your reason? (3:118)

Allah warns us against putting our trust in anyone but Him. Muslims should never rely on the enemies of Allah in hopes for protection or prosperity because there is no power above the power of the Almighty. Allah says in the very next verse of Al-Imran,

Let not the believers take the disbelievers as allies rather than the believers. And whoever does that would isolate himself entirely from Allah, except when taking ample precaution against them in prudence. Allah warns you of Himself, and to Allah is the final destination. (3:28)

LET US PONDER AND REFLECT

Day and Night in the Quran

One of the most important and talked about things by Allah in the Quran is the matters of the universe, the solar system, the sun and the moon so that people understand the world that they see around them and appreciate the science behind everything.

Researchers and scientists are still discovering massive things which Allah has already mentioned in the Quran for us to gather ourselves, using our own intelligences. The process of day and night is one of them.

"And the sun runs [on course] toward its stopping point. That is the determination of the Exalted in Might, the Knowing." [36:38] Muslims are told by Allah in the Quran the science behind day and night.

However, one thing that Allah mentions again and again in the Quran is that He has made day for us to work and go about our normal business and He has made night for us to rest. Allah has said in the Quran: "He it is Who made for you the night that you should rest therein, and the day to see. Surely in those are signs, indications of His Oneness, exalted be He, for folk who are able to hear (those who think deeply)."

Allah tells us that there are signs for us in this. There are benefits of working in the day which include health and well being benefits. For example, when people work during the day they receive the sun, the light of which has a positive effect on the mind and body, giving us energy. Sunlight also gives us vitamin D which is important for our bones and muscles. These are the signs that we should take note of. During the night, the sunshine is taken away from us leaving our bodies to relax and rest.

Allah says in the Quran, "And a sign for them is the night. We remove from it [the light of] day, so they are [left] in darkness." [36:37]The darkness is not a sign of misery. Rather it is a sign from Allah to take a rest and then wait for sunshine once again, where you will get back to your routine chores.

Hence Allah has made day and night, constellations and galaxies, the milky way and the planetarium and left it open for us to explore and study. Allah has made day and night and asked us to discipline our bodies and minds to follow the correctness of our routines in it. May Allah enable all of us to follow his instructions in the Quran, Ameen.

Verse 28

Laa yattakhizil mu'minoonal kaafireena awliyaaa'a min doonil mu'mineena wa mai yaf'al zaalika falaisa minal laahi fee shai'in illaaa an tattaqoo minhum tuqaah; wa yuhazzirukumul laahu nafsah; wa ilal laahil maseer

Let not the believers take the disbelievers as allies rather than the believers. And whoever does that would isolate himself entirely from Allah, except when taking ample precaution against them in prudence. Allah warns you of Himself, and to Allah is the final destination.
(Verse 28)

This is a very mis –understood verse.

To explain this verse we have to look at its historical context.

This verse has a historical context surrounding the issue of taking disbelievers as protectors or allies instead of believers. It was revealed in Medina and cautions against forming bonds of friendship with those who reject the faith, unless for strategic reasons. The verse emphasizes that Allah will not help those who prioritize disbelievers over believers

This was at a time when the Muslims were surrounded by polytheists and Jews who waged wars against Muslims. Their aim was to destroy the Muslims and to bring an end to Islam.

At this critical time, there were relatives and friends of the Muslims who were on the non-Muslims side. This verse is ordering them not to take disbelievers as their allies to prevent them from leaking information.

Here is the explanation of this from the Quran itself:

O you who have believed, take not those who have taken your religion in ridicule and amusement among the ones who were given the Scripture before you nor the disbelievers as allies. And fear Allah, if you should [truly] be believers. 5:57

O you who have believed, do not take My enemies and your enemies as allies, extending to them affection while they have disbelieved in what came to you of the truth, having driven out the Prophet and yourselves [only] because you believe in Allah, your Lord. 60:1

Allah does not forbid you from those who do not fight you because of religion and do not expel you from your homes - from being righteous toward them and acting justly toward them. Indeed, Allah loves those who act justly.

Allah only forbids you from those who fight you because of religion and expel you from your homes and aid in your expulsion - [forbids] that you make allies of them. And whoever makes allies of them, then it is those who are the wrongdoers. 60:8-9

From these verses, it is clear that the Quran is only commanding Muslims not to make allies with the non-Muslims who are enemies of Islam. As quoted in the verse above, Allah says in the Quran "Allah does not forbid you from those who do not fight you because of religion", clearly showing that Islam does not encourage the isolation/segregation of Muslims from non-Muslims. **Further clarification on Muslims being friends with disbelievers.**

Let us begin on what the word "friend" in this context means.

Can I be friends with the disbeliever in the sense that he is not my enemy (as a war combatant, let's say) and that I can hold peace treaties with him? The answer is yes.

Can I be friends with the disbeliever in the sense that I can hang around with them by going by going to haram places? The answer to that is a no. However, this is not discriminatory to disbelievers. It can also be applied to Muslims as well.

I am going to elaborate on the above two in separate sections.

Does Islam Prohibit Friendship With Disbelievers In The Form Of Being Peaceful With One Another?

We will analyze some Qur'anic verses that speak about us Muslims not being able to take the disbelievers as friends, allies, and patrons.

Quranic verse no.1

Surah 4:144

O ye who believe! Take not for friends (*awliyaa*) unbelievers rather than believers: Do ye wish to offer Allah an open proof against yourselves?

Imam Tabari states in his commentary:

This is a prohibition from Allah on the believers **that their character should not be like the hypocrites who take the disbelievers as allies instead of the believers.** So they (the hypocrites) will become like them (the disbelievers) if they do what Allah forbade them, which is allying themselves with the disbelievers. **(Ibn Jarir al-Tabari,** *Jami' al-bayan fi ta'wil al-Qur'an,* **Commentary on Surah 4:144, Source)**

So Allah is warning the believers not to act like the hypocrites because the hypocrites would secretly aid the disbelievers against the Muslims. It is clear in the context of the passage that it is referring to the hypocrites when you read the next verse:

Surah 4:145

The Hypocrites will be in the lowest depths of the Fire: no helper wilt thou find for them;-

The Arabic word *awliyaa* used in the verse could mean "patrons, friends, allies, etc." and it seems most appropriate to say that the word means ally in this verse.

So, the verse really means that we cannot aid the disbelievers against the Muslims.

Quranic verse no.2

Surah 3:28

Those who believe shall not take misbelievers for their patrons, rather than believers, and he who does this has no part with Allah at all, unless, indeed, ye fear some danger from them. But Allah bids you beware of Himself, for unto Him your journey is.

Imam Tabari says in his commentary of this verse that this means that we should not go around supporting the disbelievers in their religion and that we should support ours. Allah will make Himself innocent from those who apostatize from Islam. **(Ibn Jarir al-Tabari,** *Jami' al-bayan fi ta'wil al-Qur'an,* **Commentary on Surah 3:28, Source)**

Ibn Abbass states:

(Let not the believers take) the believers ought not to take [the hypocrites:] 'Abdullah Ibn Ubayy and his companions [and] (disbelievers) the Jews (for their friends) to become mighty and honorable (in preference to believers) who are sincere. (Whoso doeth that) seeking might and honor [by taking the hypocrites and disbelievers as friends] (hath no connection with Allah) has no honor, mercy or protection from Allah (unless (it be) that ye but guard yourselves against them) save yourselves from them, (taking (as it were) security) saving yourselves from them by speaking in a friendly way towards them with, while your hearts dislikes this. (Allah bideth you beware (only) of Himself) regarding the shunning of unlawful killing, unlawful sex, unlawful property, consuming intoxicants, false testimony, and associating partners with Allah. (Unto Allah is the journeying) the return after death. **(Ibn Abbaas,** *Tanwîr al-Miqbâs min Tafsîr Ibn 'Abbâs,* **Commentary on Surah 3:28, Source)**

Here, we see that Ibn Abbass says that this verse actually refers to people like Abdullah Ibn Ubayy and his cohorts who were enemies of the Prophet (peace be upon him) and were conspiring against Islam.

Quranic verse no.3

Surah 3:118

O you who believe! Take not as (your) Bitanah (advisors, consultants, protectors, helpers, friends, etc.) those outside your religion (pagans, Jews, Christians, and hypocrites) since they will not fail to do their best to corrupt you. They desire to harm you severely. Hatred has already appeared from their mouths, but what their breasts conceal is far worse. Indeed We have made plain to you the Ayat (proofs, evidences, verses) if you understand.

This verse tells us to take precautions against letting out secrets to non-Muslims, which could be used against Muslims and Islam if the non-Muslim was capable of deciding to use the information or power that he has obtained to hurt the Muslim nation.

This verse states that we must take this precaution. Also, this does not mean that we can trust any Muslim. We can only trust a pious and trustworthy Muslim.

You won't put your baby in the hands of a babysitter who is known to dislike babies. Now, it is possible that the babysitter who does not like babies might actually end up caring for the baby pretty well and not harming it. However, that doesn't mean that we take the risk.

Similarly, we Muslims are not to risk putting the safety of the Muslims in the hands of non-Muslims who could potentially have a motive to harm the Muslims and Islam.

This verse is not saying that we can't have friendly relations with non-Muslims. It only says that we should not depend on them and be at their mercy and under their control.

Quranic verse no.4

Surah 5:51

O ye who believe! take not the Jews and Christians for your patrons: they are patrons of each other; but whoso amongst you takes them for patrons, verily, he is of them, and, verily, Allah guides not an unjust people.

One explanation is that this is referring to the hypocrites: 'Oh ye who believe outwardly,' and that they used to assist the polytheists and tell them about the secrets of the Muslims. Al Suddi said that this verse came down during the Battle of Uhud when Muslims were afraid that they were going to lose the battle and wanted to ally themselves with the Jews and Christians. **(See Abu 'Abdullah Al-Qurtubi,** *Tasfir al Jami' li-ahkam al-Qur'an,* **Commentary on Surah 5:51 Source)**

The verse could also refer to true, sincere believers who do not ally themselves with the enemy against the believers.

Reading the passage in context clearly indicates that it was in a certain context where the people being warned were afraid of something:

Surah 5:52

Thou wilt see those in whose hearts is a sickness vieing with them; they say, 'We fear lest there befall us a reverse.' It may be Allah will give the victory, or an order from Himself, and they may awake repenting of what they thought in secret to themselves.

So, it makes sense to say that it was referring to those people who were afraid of defeat and then sided with the enemy.

Also, if one continues to read on, he will see who we are not supposed to befriend:

Surah 5:57

O ye who believe! take not for patrons **those who take your religion for a jest or a sport, from amongst those who have been given the Book before and the misbelievers;** but fear Allah if ye be believers.

So here we see a greater emphasis on whom we are not supposed to take CERTAIN people from the People of the Book (Jews and Christians) as patrons and allies.

However, as I mentioned previously, we are not supposed to be dependent upon any non-Muslim, regardless of whether they outwardly are kind to us or not.

Until now, we still haven't seen a verse that prohibits Muslims from having peaceful relations with those who do not harm the Muslim Community or disparage Islam.

Quranic verse no.5

Surah 5:80-81

Thou wilt see many of them taking those who disbelieve for their patrons; evil is that which their souls have sent before them, for Allah's wrath is on them, and in the torment shall they dwell for aye. But had they believed in Allah and the prophet, and what was revealed to him, they had not taken these for their patrons; but many of them are evildoers.

Ibn Abbas said:

(Thou seest many of them) many of the hypocrites (making friends with) by seeking their assistance and help (those who disbelieve) Ka'b and his followers; it is also said that this means you see many Jews, such as Ka'b and his followers, making friends with the disbelievers, the disbelievers of Mecca, Abu Sufyan, and his followers, (surely ill for them is that which they themselves send on before them) in their state of Judaism and hypocrisy: (that Allah will be wroth with them and in the doom they will abide) never to die or be removed. (If they) i.e., the hypocrites (believed in Allah) genuinely believed in Allah (and the Prophet) Muhammad (and that which is revealed unto him), i.e., the Qur'an (they would not choose them), i.e., the Jews (for their friends) seeking their assistance and help. (But many of them) from among the people of the Book (are of evil conduct), they are hypocrites. It is also said that this means that the Jews genuinely believed in Allah and Allah's divine Oneness and believed in the Prophet (pbuh). That which was revealed to him, i.e., the Qur'an, they would not have taken Abu Sufyan and his followers for friends, seeking their assistance and help. Nonetheless, many among the people of the Book are disbelievers. **(Tanwîr al-Miqbâs min Tafsîr Ibn 'Abbâs, Commentary on Surah 5:80-81, Source)**

Again, we see that it is prohibited to take those who are fighting against Islam, such as Kab Al Ashraf, as supporters and allies.

Quranic verse no.6

Surah 11:113

Lean not unto, those who do wrong, lest the Fire touch you, for ye have no patrons but Allah; and, moreover, ye shall not be helped!

Ibn Abbass said in his commentary:

(And incline not towards those who do wrong) themselves by means of disbelief, idolatry and transgression (lest the Fire touch you) as it has touched them, (and ye have no protecting friends) no relatives to help you (against Allah) against Allah's chastisement, (and afterward ye would not be helped) you will not be prevented from what is wanted with you. **(Tanwîr al-Miqbâs min Tafsîr Ibn 'Abbâs, Commentary on Surah 11:113, Source)**

We are not too inclined towards those who do wrong by imitating their habits (common sense).

Quranic verse no.7

Surah 58:22

Thou shalt not find a people who believe in Allah and the last day loving him who opposes Allah and His Apostle, even though it be their fathers, or their sons, or their brethren, or their clansmen. He has written faith in their hearts, and He aids them with a spirit from Him; and will make them enter into gardens beneath which rivers flow, to dwell therein for aye! Allah is well pleased with them, and they well pleased with Him: they are Allah's crew; ay, Allah's crew, they shall prosper!

We cannot have feelings of love towards those who oppose Allah and His messenger. Here, 'opposing' is actually to the degree of fighting against and wanting to hurt us. This verse came down in a certain context.

Ibn Kathir has it in his commentary:

(even though they were their fathers), was revealed in the case of Abu 'Ubaydah, when he killed his father **during the battle of Badr,** while the Ayah,

(or their sons) was revealed in the case of Abu Bakr As-Siddiq when he intended to kill his (disbelieving) son, 'Abdur-Rahman, **(during Badr),** while the Ayah,

(or their brothers) was revealed about the case of Mus'ab bin 'Umayr, who killed his brother, 'Ubayd bin 'Umayr, during Badr, and that the Ayah,

(or their kindred) was revealed about the case of 'Umar, who killed one of his **relatives during Badr,** and also that this Ayah was revealed in the case of Hamzah, 'Ali and Ubaydah bin Al-Harith. They killed their close relatives 'Utbah, Shaybah and Al-Walid bin 'Utbah that day. Allah knows best. A similar matter is when Allah's Messenger consulted with his Companions about what should be done with the captives of Badr. Abu Bakr As-Siddiq thought that they should accept ransom for them so the Muslims could use the money to strengthen themselves. He mentioned the fact that the captured were the cousins and the kindred, and that they might embrace Islam later on, by Allah's help. 'Umar said, "But I have a different opinion, O Allah's Messenger! Let me kill so-and-so, my relative, and let 'Ali kill 'Aqil ('Ali's brother), and so-and-so kill so-and-so. Let us make it known to Allah that we have no mercy in our hearts for the idolators." Allah said,

(For such He has written faith in their hearts, and strengthened them with Ruh from Himself.) means, those who have the quality of not befriending those who oppose Allah and His Messenger , even if they are their fathers or brothers, are those whom Allah has decreed faith, meaning, happiness, in their hearts and made faith dear to their hearts and happiness reside therein. **(Tafsir of Ibn Kathir, Commentary on Surah 58:22, Source)**

Imam Suyuti states:

You will not find a people who believe in Allah and the Last Day loving, befriending, those who oppose Allah and His Messenger, even though they, the opposers, were their fathers, that is to say, the believers' [fathers], or their sons or their brothers or their clan, **rather [you will find that] they intend to do them harm and they fight them over [the question of] faith,** as occurred on one occasion with some Companions, may Allah be pleased with them. [For] those, the ones who are not loving of them, He has inscribed, He has established, faith upon their hearts and reinforced them with a spirit, a light, from Him, exalted be He, and He will admit them into gardens underneath which rivers flow, wherein they will abide, Allah being pleased with them, for their obedience of Him, and they being pleased with Him, because of His reward. Those [they] are Allah's confederates, following His command and refraining from what He has forbidden. Assuredly it is Allah's confederates who are the successful, the winners. **(Tafsir Jalalayn, Commentary on Surah 58:22, Source)**

So, as we can see, this was in the context of those who were opposing Allah and his Messenger by FIGHTING against the Muslims.

Until now, we still don't see a verse that prohibits Muslims from having friendly relations with non-Muslims who do not attack Islam.

Surah 60:1

O ye who believe! take not my enemy and your enemy for patrons, encountering them with love for they misbelieve in the truth that is to come to you; **they drive out the Apostle and you for that ye believe in Allah your Lord!** If ye go forth fighting strenuously in my cause and craving my good pleasure, and secretly show love for them, yet do I know best what ye conceal and what ye display! and he of you who does so has erred from the level path.

Surah 60:13

O ye who believe! take not for patrons a people whom Allah is wroth against; they despair of the hereafter, as the misbelievers despair of the fellows of the tombs!

These verses are just simply telling us not to support those who fight us and to assist the disbelievers against the Muslims:

Ibn Abbass states:

And from his narration on the authority of Ibn 'Abbas that he said concerning the interpretation of Allah's saying (O ye who believe!): (O ye who believe!) referring to Hatib, (**Choose not My enemy) in religion (and your enemy) who fight you,** i.e. the people of Mecca (for friends) seeking their assistance and help. (Do ye give them friendship) you send them a letter to assist and help them (when they disbelieve in that truth which hath come unto you) i.e., to Hatib, (driving out the messenger) Muhammad (pbuh) from Mecca (and you) i.e., Hatib (because ye believe) because of your faith (in Allah, your Lord? If ye have come forth) if you have, O Hatib, come forth from Mecca to Medina (to strive in My way) for the sake of My obedience (and seeking My good pleasure, (show them not friendship). Do ye show friendship unto them in secret) do not send letters to them in secret to assist and help them, (when I am best Aware of what ye hide) i.e. of what you hide, O Hatib, regarding the letter; and it is also said that this means: regarding your faith (and what ye proclaim) O Hatib, of excuse; and it is also said: of profession of Allah's divine Oneness? (And whosoever doeth it among you) whoever of you, O believers, does as Hatib did, (he verily hath strayed from the right way) he has indeed strayed from the path of guidance. **(Tanwîr al-Miqbâs min Tafsîr Ibn 'Abbâs, Commentary on Surah 60:1, Source)**

(O ye who believe!) referring here to 'Abdullah Ibn Ubayy and his fellow believers (Be not friendly) i.e. seeking their help and assistance and divulging to them the secrets of the Prophet (pbuh) (with a folk with whom Allah is wroth) twice; this refers to the Jews when they said: "Allah's Hand is uptight" and again when they disbelieved in Muhammad (pbuh) ((a folk) who have despaired of the Hereafter) who have despaired of the bliss of Paradise (as the disbelievers) the disbelievers of Mecca (despair of those who are in the graves) i.e. of the return of the people of the graves; and it is also said that this means: of the questioning of Munkar and Nakir; and it is also said this means: do not be friendly with a folk with whom Allah is wroth, but rather be of those who glorify Allah and pray to Him.' **(Tanwîr al-Miqbâs min Tafsîr Ibn 'Abbâs, Commentary on Surah 60:13, <u>Source</u>)**

Imam Qurtubi states:

يَعْنِي الْيَهُود . وَذَلِكَ أَنَّ نَاسًا مِنْ فُقَرَاءِ الْمُسْلِمِينَ كَانُوا يُخْبِرُونَ الْيَهُود بِأَخْبَارِ الْمُؤْمِنِينَ

This is referring to the Jews, because some poor people amongst the Muslims used to spell out the secrets of the Muslims to the Jews. **(Abu 'Abdullah Al-Qurtubi,** *Tasfîr al Jami' li-ahkam al-Qur'an,* **Commentary on Surah 60:13 <u>Source</u>)**

We have to read the whole Surah in order to understand exactly what Allah is saying:

<u>Surah 60:8-9</u>

<u>Allah forbids you not respecting those who have not fought against you for religion's sake</u>, and who have not driven you forth from your homes, that ye should act righteously and justly towards them; verily, Allah loves the just! **<u>He only forbids you to make patrons of those who have fought against you for religion's sake, and driven you forth from your homes, or have aided in your expulsion;</u>** and whoever makes patrons of them, they are the unjust!

So when the Quran says that we cannot be *awliyaa* of the disbelievers it means that we cannot ally ourselves and support them against the Muslims. We cannot be friends or supporters of those who mock our religion. We cannot risk the security and fate of the Muslims under the power and control of the non-Muslims and be dependent upon them.

Shakyh Saalih Aal ash-Shaykh said:

And the principle concerning Tawalle is to help the kuffar against a Muslim during the time of war between a Muslim and a Kaafir with the intent and purpose (qasd) of allowing the Kuffar to gain ascendancy over the the Muslims. And the basis (asl) of Tawallee is complete love, or aiding a kaafir against a Muslim, so whoever loved a kaafir for his religion (deen), and then he turned to him with tawallee, and this is kufr. **(Shakyh Saalih Aal ash-Shaykh, *Concerning Tawallee and Muwaalaat*, Source)**

However, there is absolutely nothing wrong with showing kindness and having peaceful relations with those who do not fight and attack us and our faith.

Does Islam Prohibit Friendship with Disbelievers in the Form of Being Companions with Them?

The position that I will argue is yes.

The Prophet (peace be upon him) said:

Sunan Abu Dawud

Book 41, Number 4814:

Narrated AbuSa'id al-Khudri:

The Prophet (peace_be_upon_him) said: Associate only with a believer, and let only a Allah-fearing man eat your meals.

Book 41, Number 4815:

Narrated AbuHurayrah:

The Prophet (peace_be_upon_him) said: A man follows the religion of his friend; so each one should consider whom he makes his friend. **(There is some minor dispute regarding the authenticity of this narration; see *Awn Al Ma'bood*, however the meaning of this hadeeth is correct)**

When the Prophet (peace be upon) said, "Associate only with a believer," the Arabic phrase is لا تصاحب إلا مؤمنا, which means that you should not be the companion or close friend of anyone except a believer.

The reason for this is given in the next hadith, which says "A man follows the religion of his friend", which means that a man follows the habits and customs of his friends.

The Prophet (peace be upon him) is also reported to have said:

Saheeh Muslim

Book 032, Number 6361:

Abu Musa reported Allah's Messenger (may peace be upon him) as saying: The similitude of good company and that of bad company is that of the owner of musk and of the one (iron-smith) blowing bellows, and the owner of musk would either offer you free of charge or you would buy it from him or you would. smell its pleasant odour, and so far as one who blows the. bellows is concerned, he would either burn your clothes or you shall have to smell its repugnant smell.

The Prophet (peace be upon him) is telling us that we should not be friends or companions of people who can have a negative influence on our faith. If a person wants to be friends with a non-Muslim, then this should only be done out of necessity. For instance, if you have a Non-Muslim friend who you meet and constantly have interfaith dialogues with, and you intend to bring him to Islam, then there is nothing wrong with this. If you have a Non-Muslim friend whom you have to meet outside for any important matters (e.g., work-related), then again, there is no problem with this.

However, if you simply want to hang around with a non-Muslim while there is no necessity to do so, then this is prohibited. The reason for this is that it could have a negative impact on your faith. Just think about what things you would be doing with this individual. You are not working on anything important with him, nor are you talking about religion. So what are you doing then? If you are wasting your time going out to the movies, picnics, etc., with this person, then there is a big chance that you would be committing sins since he does not believe that everything that is haram for you is also haram for him.

Also, over time, your heart might soften too much for the person, and you may begin to disbelieve that Allah could possibly place such a person in Hellfire. To have such a belief is kufr. Thus, it is advised to avoid these kinds of friendships to protect one's faith.

I must also stress the fact that this same logic applies to Muslims as well. It is forbidden for you to be friends with a non-practicing Muslim who could negatively influence you regarding practicing your faith. I would associate with a non-Muslim who is willing to speak about matters of faith rather than associate with a Muslim who drinks alcohol and wants to drag me down to his level as well.

We should be friends with people who would encourage us to stay away from inequities and not the other way around.

Allah punished those Israelites who did not positively influence their friends:

Surah 5:78-79

Curses were pronounced on those among the children of Israel who rejected faith, by the tongue of David and of Jesus the son of Mary: because they disobeyed and persisted in excesses. **Nor did they (usually) forbid one another the iniquities which they committed:** evil indeed were the deeds which they did.

Thus, we ought to choose not to befriend and be close to those who will not try to positively influence us. This applies to non-practicing Muslims (they are sinning and will influence you to sin) and to non-Muslims (what interest do they have in ensuring that you practice your faith?).

In conclusion, we are allowed to be friends with non-Muslims in the sense that we don't have to wage war against them, and we can have peaceful relations with them and engage in friendly dialogue with them. However, we are not permitted to be close friends with them in the sense that they are our companions because this might have a negative impact on ourselves. The exception to this is that you can be close friends with them if you have the ability to influence and not be influenced and try to have the person come to Islam, or you can also associate with them for important matters such as work.

Verse 29

Qul in tukhfoo maa fee sudoorikum aw tubdoohu ya'lamhul laah; wa ya'lamu maa fis samaawaati wa maa fil ard; wallaahu 'alaa kulli shai'in Qadee

Say: "Whether you conceal or reveal what is in your hearts it is all known to Allah, as is known to Him all that is in the heavens and the earth; and Allah has the power over all things." (Verse 29)

Allah knows the feelings, emotions and intentions of our hearts. Why is the heart mentioned in this verse and not the brain? The heart is the place of iman (faith) and the part of our body that makes the decisions (such as whether to believe or disbelieve, obey or disobey, etc.). The brain hears the commands of Allah, witnesses His signs, receives and gathers information and transmits them to the heart. The heart then understands and comprehends the information and orders the brain, which in turn instructs the limbs.

So who is the king of the body, the decision-maker? It is the heart. That is why Allah directed our attention towards His Knowledge of what is in our hearts. We must constantly monitor our intentions, faith and feelings towards others. We must ask ourselves questions such as: Am I sincere to Allah? Do I love Allah? Who am I relying upon? Do I intend evil for others? Do I consider myself superior? Do I feel envious of others? Am I selfish? All of this is in our hearts and none knows our true intentions and feelings except Allah alone.

So the most important thing to take care of, to nurture and purify is our heart and without this, we will never be able to get close to Allah. If there is even an ounce of wickedness and evil in a person's heart it will become a barrier between him and Allah. That is why a person must not just prostrate, give zakah, and memorise the Quran while leaving his heart evil and sick. No! Rather, we need to realise that Allah will look at our hearts and not our appearances.

How can we know what Allah would be pleased with to see in our hearts? No doubt, through the Quran and Sunnah. We must learn about what pleases Allah and then put it into practice. For example, Allah would be pleased to see our hearts loving and glorifying Him and His commands, loving and respecting His Prophet, peace be upon him, and the Companions, desiring good for our fellow Muslims, and having humility, etc.

We all regularly face subtle situations that show us the reality of our hearts. For example, a young woman who eagerly desires marriage, hears that her friend is getting married. Now, in this situation, she must pay attention to her heart. Is she envious of her friend, or is she genuinely happy for her while asking Allah for the same? There is a great difference between both!

Similarly, when we encounter a hardship or calamity, we must be vigilant regarding how we react. Do we say "All praise is due to Allah Alone (alhamdu lillah), to Allah we belong, and to Him we return", or do we say; "What did I do to deserve this, Allah?!" Are we patient and content with the Decree of Allah? Thus, due to what Allah sees in us, He will either love us or hate us, and we ask Allah to enable us to purify our hearts for Him, and only for Him, ameen.

The Scholars say:

"Dealing with your heart by rectifying it and nurturing it upon good is something very special because. No one knows what is going on in your heart, and your struggle to get rid of envy, hatred or arrogance. This is a very discrete battle that exists only between you and Allah. As for outward actions, such as praying or teaching, you might question your sincerity, and in addition to this, the Shaytan may throw in doubts about your sincerity. However, when you are dealing with correcting your heart, there is no scope for insincerity because no one can see this except Allah!

He knows what is in the heavens and what is in the earth.

Allah's knowledge, hearing, and sight encompasses everything. There is nothing in the universe except that Allah is knowledgeable about it. Each grain of sand, each leaf that falls from a tree, each feather of a bird, Allah knows about it, Glorified and Exalted is Allah! Even if you tried to gather every piece of knowledge about one, single creature, you would not be able to do so, but Allah is the Creator and The All-Knower of everything.

When you say that Allah is The All-Knower, then this statement must have an effect on you. You must fear Allah wherever you are and in whatever you do. You do not whisper or conceive an evil thought, but Allah knows it. Never try to hide from Allah because there is no place to hide from Him.

Verse 30

Yawma tajidu kullu nafsim maa'amilat min khairim muhdaranw wa maa 'amilat min sooo'in tawaddu law anna bainahaa wa bainahooo amadam ba'eedaa; wa yuhazzirukumul laahu nafsah; wallaahu ra'oofum bil'ibaad

On the Day when every soul finds all the good it has done present before it, it will wish all the bad it has done to be far, far away. Allah warns you to beware of Him. Allah is compassionate towards His servants.
(Verse 30)

Our natural assumption is that time flows in one direction, so when things are in the past, they are gone never to come back again. Thus, for the longest time, scholars interpreted the phrase "On the Day when every soul finds all the good it has done present before it" as: "In the hereafter, every person will find the consequences of his or her deed, either punishment or reward." This is still a valid interpretation. However, as science advances, we can look at things differently. Technology allows us to record every moment of our lives and replay it at any time. If humans can do this with their limited means, then what about the Almighty? Certainly, His ability is above all abilities, and on the Day of Judgment, Allah can bring our deeds physically in front of us to see. He says:

He has the keys to the unseen: no one knows them but Him. He knows all that is in the land and sea. No leaf falls without His knowledge, nor is there a single grain in the depths of the earth, or anything, fresh or withered, that is not written in a clear Record. (6:59)

The verse ends with, "Allah warns you to beware of Him. Allah is compassionate towards His servants." This is a second warning! It is an emphasis of the previous verse. Allah knows what we conceal within our hearts, and He sees and records what we do. So before you do any action, keep in mind the absoluteness of His power. More importantly, remember that as long as you are alive, the door of repentance will remain open before you.

Verse 31

Qul in kuntum tuhibboonal laaha fattabi' oonee yuhbibkumul laahu wa yaghfir lakum zunoobakum; wallaahu Ghafoorur Raheem

Say: "If you love Allah, follow me, and Allah will love you and forgive you your sins; Allah is most forgiving, most merciful." (Verse 31)

After reading this verse, we understand that some people must have claimed to love Allah, but their actions did not support what they said. In other words, they did not follow Allah's teachings or the example of our beloved Muhammad. Allah brought us into existence and provided for us, and that is a great blessing. He also sent us a clear system to manage our lives. He does not benefit when we follow His teachings; the benefit is all ours, which is also a great blessing.

Why Love for Allah is Part of the Muslim Faith?

When we love Allah, that love draws us closer to Him and helps us build a strong relationship that can help us in this life and in hereafter. As Muslims, our faith requires that our love for Allah and his prophet supersedes any other type of love for any other object or creation. Many scholars agree on the basis of sound ahadith that Allah creates a person (and his heart) in such a way that he has the natural inclination to love Allah. However, as a person's heart gets corrupted by doubts, desires and other temptations, that love has to be rekindled through faith and knowledge.

Let us ask the question-

What Does it Mean to Love Allah?

We answer that the love of Allah requires us to follow the Quran and the Sunnah. To follow his commands and to stay away from his prohibitions.

We must actualize that love in real behavioural commitments.

Let's review various aspects about the love of Allah and how we can build and nurture that love in our hearts. The Obligation to Love Allah has made His love obligatory on the believers. Many of us find it easy to express that love verbally but unfortunately our actions don't.

How can we claim to love Allah when we take what He has revealed lightly, don't follow His commands, and fail to make our behaviours reflect what pleases Him? Many times we find that love missing from our hearts because our hearts are filled instead with doubts, vain desires, and temptations of temporal life. One of the reasons for this has to do with the lack of right knowledge. To counter doubts, therefore, we need to firm up our beliefs, and we need a better overall spiritual perspective in order to counter desires and temptations. We also need to clear those doubts that hinder the instilling of that love for Allah by learning more and asking questions.

Consider one of the ahadiths which shows the prophet getting angry with a group of people for taking a decision that resulted in someone unnecessarily losing his life. On that the prophet said,

"Could they not have asked if they didn't know? Indeed the cure for ignorance is to ask" [Sunan Ibn Majah and classified as Hasan]. When we don't make that effort and don't plant that love in our hearts, our actions too come out short and empty and we risk His anger and making our deeds fruitless.

Allah says in the Quran :

"That is because they followed that which angered Allah, and hated that which pleased Him. So He made their deeds fruitless" (Surah Muhammad :28). What do we have to do specifically to love Allah? Take the example of the companions of Prophet who used to say that "We love Allah". In response to that and to provide them a yardstick to know whether they indeed loved Allah, Allah revealed the verse understudy:

"Say (O Muhammad SAW to mankind): "If you (really) love Allah then follow me (i.e. accept Islamic Monotheism, follow the Quran and the Sunnah), Allah will love you and forgive you of your sins. And Allah is Oft-Forgiving, Most Merciful." (Surah Aal-e-Imran:31)

What pulls us away from loving Allah? To properly answer this question, we need to search deep within our souls about the motivations that drive our lives and our understanding (explicit or implicit) of the purpose of our lives. That is because the purpose of our life drives our goals, actions, and behaviours in general. For many of us, earning a living tends to be the focal point of our lives, including a total immersion in building our dwellings, families, and so on while neglecting our duty and love for Allah. The time that we spend on various activities reflects our priority and love for each of those activities.

For those of us who exhibit that behaviour, Allah says the following:

"Say: If it be that your fathers, your sons, your brothers, your mates, or your kindred; the wealth that you have gained; the commerce in which you fear a decline: or the dwellings in which you (seek) delight – are dearer to you than Allah, or His Messenger, or the striving in His cause; then wait until Allah brings about His decision: and Allah guides not the rebellious" (Sura At-Taubah : 24).

We can, therefore, infer that while we do have an obligation to attend to our responsibilities, that should not divert us from building our relationship with Allah.

As He says in the Quran:

"Let not your properties or your children divert you from the remembrance of Allah. And whosoever does that, they are the losers" (Al-Munafiqoon 63:9).

Love of Allah triggers sweetness of faith. The prophet had said as narrated in both Sahih hadith ,

"Whoever possesses the following three qualities will taste the sweetness (delight) of faith: the one to whom Alláh and His Messenger become dearer than anything else, the one who loves a person and he loves him only for Alláh's sake, and whoever hates to revert to disbelief, after Alláh has saved him from it, as he hates to be thrown into the Fire." Love of Allah can keep us away from sins.

Today, when the hearts of most of us are filled with lusts, desires, temptations and fantasies, we need to remind ourselves that it is not possible to have those take room in the same heart where we want to plant our love for Allah. Always ask yourself whether what lives in your heart makes you neglect Allah, and is worth more than the love of Allah? When we start replacing the lusts, desires, and fantasies that live in our heart with Allah's love, then we will see ourselves regaining that love back from Allah. Love of Allah stimulates our emotions the vagaries of this life generate emotions which must be channelled appropriately for us to retain our positive mental states. No matter how we express and channel those emotions to various people in this life, there are emotions trapped in our system that we simply can't express with an open heart to even the most beloved of His creations. But it is different with our creator. When we do succeed in planting that love for Allah in our hearts and build that relationship, it can make our repressed emotions pour out with a pleasing force.

The relationship that we establish with our creator out of that love for Him and His love for us can make us say what is in our hearts, complain about our situations, express profuse apologies, and so on – all without worrying about demeaning ourselves because He is our creator and sustainer who controls everything in this universe. In fact, what we humans go through and what manifests as hidden emotions can come flooding back when we sit in front of our creator with that love for Him. This can help us in reconciling matters within ourselves and, most important of all, lets Allah respond and listen to us. Thus, the more we love Allah, the better we will be able to engage with Him at this level and the better we will be able to feel and expect his mercy in return. When we love Allah, He will put our love in others' hearts.

Many of us spend a lot of our efforts to gain the love and pleasure of others and sometimes we may do that at the expense of disobeying Allah's commands. We should realize that such tactics are short lived (even if achieved) and earn us nothing but Allah's displeasure. On the other hand, if we focus on planting Allah's love, then we will not only get His love but He will instill our love in others' hearts as well.

Allah says in the Quran:

"Verily, those who believe [in the Oneness of Allah and in His Messenger (Muhammad SAW)] and work deeds of righteousness, the Most Gracious (Allah) will bestow love for them (in the hearts of the believers)" (Surah Maryam : 96).

How do we get love of Allah in our hearts and lives?

How can we increase our love for Allah?

- Recitation of the Quran with reflection and Understanding.
- Optional acts of worship, after the obligatory ones
- Constant remembrance in every circumstance by the tongue, the heart, actions.
- Acknowledging the Almighty favours and always be in a state of gratitude.
- Being alone at the Time of the Descent of Allah (during Tahajjud) for having private conversations with Him, reciting His Words, investigating the heart, displaying the manners of servitude whilst sealing all of that with forgiveness and repentence.
- Keeping good company – those who reminds you of Allah swt.
- Keeping distant from everything that goes against the commands of Allah swt.

Verse 32

Qul atee'ul laaha war Rasoola fa in tawallaw fa innal laaha laa yuhibbul kaafireen

Say: "Obey Allah and the Messenger." But if they turn their backs, Allah does not love the disbelievers.
(Verse 32)

The issue of obedience is mentioned in the Quran in one of three forms. The first form is to "Obey Allah and the Messenger," the second is to "Obey Allah and obey the Messenger," and the third is "Obey the Messenger." Each of these forms has a very distinct and essential meaning.

Let's take them one by one. In the 32nd verse of Al-Imran, Allah says, "Obey Allah and the Messenger." Take note that Allah did not repeat the verb "obey" in this verse. So we may ask, who are we supposed to obey here? The answer is that we are asked both to obey Allah and follow the example of the Messenger. Our beloved Muhammad informs us of Allah's commands, and then we follow his example in implementing these commands. The Prophet, peace be upon him, did not command us to obey him; he only asked us to obey Allah. When the verb "obey" is not repeated, then there is no separation between Allah and His Messenger. Prophet Muhammad delivered a command from Allah, and we implement it just as the Prophet did. This is similar to what we discussed in verse 31 of Al-Imran, "If you love Allah, follow me, and Allah will love you." Our obedience to Prophet Muhammad only stems from his obedience to Allah's commands.

The second way obedience is mentioned in the Quran is as follows. Allah says:

Say: "Obey Allah and obey the Messenger but, if you turn away, he is only responsible for the duty placed upon him, and you are responsible for the duty placed upon you." (from 24:54)

Take note that in this verse the command "obey" is repeated twice, once in regards to Allah and once to the Prophet. So we ask again, who are we supposed to obey here? The answer is both Allah and the prophet. There are times when a command from Allah is general and vague. Then, Prophet Muhammad gives us the details and asks us to follow him. For example, Allah says:

Keep up the prayer, pay the prescribed alms, and obey the Messenger, so that you may be given mercy. (24:56)

No one amongst us could have known the number of prayers in a day or the number of rak'ahs in each prayer. In fact, none of us could have known how to pray! But our beloved Muhammad explained the details. Hence, the believer obeys Allah in general and obeys the Prophet in the details. In such cases, there are two forms of obedience: first is the obedience to Allah, and second is the obedience to the Prophet; this is why the word "obey" was repeated twice. Allah issues a brief command, and the explanation is left to the Prophet.

The third way obedience is mentioned in the Quran is as follows. Allah says in the 7th verse of chapter 59:

Whatever the Messenger gives you, you should accept, and whatever he forbids you, you should forgo. (from 59:7)

Allah gave our beloved Prophet Muhammad full and independent authority to legislate as he saw fit. He gave him the authority to command the believers, and we are under the obligation to obey, even in matters where Allah did not rule. This was a great honour exclusive to our beloved Prophet Muhammad that none of the previous messengers had. For example, the Athan call to prayer was fully legislated by Prophet Muhammad.

To review, the issue of obedience occurred in the Quran in three forms. The first was a unified "obey Allah and the Messenger," indicating that we should obey Allah Who delivered His message through Prophet Muhammad; there is no separate obedience to Muhammad outside of Allah's command. The second form is to "obey Allah and obey the Messenger," which means that we should obey Allah in general and look to Prophet Muhammad for guidance in the details. The third form is to "obey the Messenger," where Allah gave our beloved Prophet Muhammad a general authorization to legislate as he, peace be upon him, saw fit.

Allah is asking of you:

You who believe, obey Allah and obey the Messenger and those in authority among you. If you are in dispute over any matter, refer it to Allah and the Messenger, if you truly believe in Allah and the Last Day: that is better and fairer in the end. (4:59)

This verse is a perfect example of the meaning behind the command "obey" in the Quran. Take note that "obey" was repeated before the words "Allah" and "the Messenger," but absent before "those in authority." Allah is an independent legislator that ought to be obeyed, and Muhammad is an independent legislator that ought to be obeyed. However, those in authority, such as presidents and kings, are to be followed only when their actions conform to Allah's teachings and His Messenger. Our obedience to figures of authority is not independent. Instead, it stems from their obedience to Allah and His Messenger. So, when a dispute arises, Allah and His Messenger are the only references.

In the previous verse of Al-Imran, we learned the elements and benefits of Allah's love. He says:

Say: "If you love Allah, follow me, and Allah will love you and forgive you your sins; Allah is most forgiving, most merciful." (3:31)

If you claim your love for Allah, you have to prove it through actions; words are not enough. Remember that your love for Allah does not benefit Him, but His love for you is a gift that keeps on giving. You express your love through following His teachings, and Allah expresses His with mercy and guidance. But matters can also move in the other direction. Listen to the strong warning Allah issues at the end of verse 32:

Say: "Obey Allah, and the Messenger." But if they turn their backs, Allah does not love the disbelievers." (3:32)

Those who receive the message of Muhammad and choose to ignore it are equivalent to the disbelievers. Is there anything more terrible than this? The phrase "turn their backs" suggests that those who heard Allah's teachings did not discard them out of laziness or misunderstanding; rather, they willingly chose to turn away.

Here I would like to take a moment to remind you: beware of rejecting Allah's commands. For example, if you do not pray, do not say, "I do not pray because there is no benefit to prayers." If you take a usurious loan, do not say that the prohibition of usury is unfair or incompatible with modern life. Because if you say any of these things – in essence, you turn your back to Allah's teachings– you will become a disbeliever and lose all access to Allah's mercy.

Instead, if you cannot bring yourself to implement Allah's teachings, then say, "My Lord, the obligation of prayers or the prohibition of usury is the truth, but I cannot bring myself to do these duties because my faith is weak. My Lord, please shower me with mercy and help me come back to Your path in this life and the next." If you sincerely mean these words, you will only be considered disobedient, not a disbeliever, and you will have access to Allah's mercy. So, be very mindful of distinguishing between sinning while accepting Allah's orders on the one hand and rejecting Allah's commands altogether on the other.

Verse 33

Innal laahas tafaaa Aadama wa Noohanw wa Aala Ibraaheema wa Aala Imraana 'alal 'aalameen

Indeed, Allah chose Adam, Noah, the family of Abraham, and the family of Imran over the worlds. (Verse 33)

In the preceding verses, Allah laid down the principles of faith, starting with the creed. He says:

Allah bears witness that there is no God but Him, as do the angels and those who have knowledge. He upholds justice. There is no God but Him, the Almighty, the All-Wise. (3:18)

Then the Almighty gave the believers glad tidings that He is in full control of all matters:

Say: "O Allah, Master of all dominion! You give dominion to whom You will and extract dominion from whom You will, and You honour whom You will, and abase whom You will; in Your hand is all good; surely You have full power over everything. You merge night into day and day into night; You bring the living out of the dead and the dead out of the living; You give provision to whom You will without account." (3:26-27)

Lastly, Allah illustrated to us the path of love and the key to the treasures of His mercy:

Say: "If you love Allah, follow me, and Allah will love you and forgive you your sins; Allah is most forgiving, most merciful." Say: "Obey Allah, and the Messenger." But if they turn their backs, Allah does not love the disbelievers. (3:31-32)

But were all these verses just theories and assumptions? Of course not. In the verse under study, Allah gives us the example of people who upheld the principles of faith and walked His path of mercy. They serve as practical models for all of us. If there were no prior examples, then people may give up and say, "We do not know how to do this," or "this is too difficult." Thus, Allah gave you examples of people who carried the responsibilities of faith. He says:

Indeed, Allah chose Adam, Noah, the family of Abraham, and the family of Imran over the worlds. (Chapter 3: Verse 33)

Prophet Muhammad, peace be upon him, was sent to an illiterate nation that did not study history, so it was necessary for Allah to introduce examples from the past. The Quran uses examples from previous prophets and religions, which clearly shows that there is no bigotry in Islam. Islam is the conclusion of all prior religions that started with Adam and continued through Abraham, the family of Imran, Moses, and Jesus, peace be upon them all. Islam honours previous heavenly religions and builds on their scriptures. Allah says:

We sent you the scripture with the truth, confirming the scriptures that came before it, and with final authority over them: so judge between them according to what Allah has sent down. Do not follow their whims, which deviate from the truth that has come to you. We have assigned a law and a path to each of you. If Allah had so willed, He would have made you one community, but He wanted to test you through that which He has given you, so race to do good: you will all return to Allah, and He will make clear to you the matters you differed about. (5:48)

Allah reminds us of the purity of our forefathers. Wouldn't it be a shame if we abandon such a connection to the heavens?

When you read the phrase "Allah chose Adam, Noah, the family of Abraham, and the family of Imran over the worlds," you may wonder, did Allah choose these messengers because He knew that they were obedient? Or did they become obedient because Allah chose and favored them? We answer that Allah knew, through His perfect and eternal knowledge, that these people were sincere. Likewise, such honest and respectful people became even more observant after they were assigned the task of delivering Allah's message. Thus, they were the perfect choice to become the bearers of the divine scripture. Allah narrates how our beloved Abraham longed for a connection with his Creator well before receiving Allah's revelations. He says:

Then, when he beheld the sun rising in all its splendor, he said, "This is my Lord. This one is the greatest of all!" But when it set, he said, "O my people, I am through with those you associate with Allah. I have truly turned my face towards Him Who created the heavens and the earth, inclining to the truth and I am not an idolater." (6:78-79)

We understand that when Allah chose Noah, He chose him out of millions of people. Similarly, Allah chose Abraham, Jesus, and David from all the people at the time. But how about when Allah chose Adam? Adam was the first human, with no one else around. Does that mean that Allah singled him out for Himself? We answer that Adam was chosen as a trustee of Allah's teachings on earth. He was selected as the forefather of all future prophets and messengers.

When the word "Imran" is mentioned in the Quran, it could be referring to one of two people. First, there is Imran, the father of Prophets Moses and Aaron. Second, there is Imran, the father of Miriam (Virgin Mary, the mother of Prophet Jesus). Which Imran is the title of Chapter 3 referring to? There has been some confusion among scholars.

We answer that this confusion is easy to resolve. Let's look into the family tree of each of the two Imrans. First, we start with Imran, the father of Moses and Aaron. His father was Yashar, and his grandfather was Fahath. His great grandfather was Lawa, who was in turn the son of Prophet Jacob, the grandson of Isaac, and the great-grandson of our beloved Abraham, peace be upon them all.

Now we look into the lineage of Imran, the father of Miriam, the mother of Prophet Jesus. His father was Mathan, who was a descendant of Prophets Solomon and David. Prophet David was the son of Awsha, grandson of Yahootha. Yahootha was the son of Jacob and the grandson of Isaac, peace be upon them all.

What added to the confusion was that the sister of Prophets Moses and Aaron was named Miriam. So we have Miriam, daughter of Imran, who was the sister of Moses and Aaron. Then we have Miriam, daughter of Imran, who was the mother of Prophet Jesus. The children of Israel loved the name Miriam because it means "the devoted worshipper."

Chapter 3 of the Quran discusses the story of Miriam, daughter of Imran, mother of Jesus. From that, we know that the namesake of this chapter, "Al Imran," is referring to the family of our beloved Prophet Jesus, not to the family of Moses and Aaron.

Indeed, Allah chose Adam, Noah, the family of Abraham, and the family of Imran over the worlds. (Verse 33)

Allah chose Adam and his descendants to be the carriers of His teachings on earth. Adam and Eve, peace be upon them, passed Allah's teachings to their children, who in turn passed them to their children, and so on. One of Allah's messengers was Noah. For centuries the elites and the disbelievers rejected him, so Allah sent the flood and drowned them while saving Noah and his followers. The Almighty says:

When Our command came, and water gushed up out of the boiler, We said, "Place onboard this ark a pair of each species, and your own family -except those against whom the sentence has already been passed- and those who have believed," though only a few had believed with him. (11:40)

All those who survived with Noah were believers. Allah gave humanity a fresh start! His teachings should have passed from this generation on unchanged. However, some descendants did not uphold the values of their forefathers. Corruption and disbelief crept in. The big question to ask is: why? Allah created Adam and provided him with all the knowledge he needed to live peacefully on earth. All we had to do was carry on this knowledge from generation to generation.

We have always succeeded in passing on material knowledge. People have used the wheel from the day of its invention without fail. Every generation after Edison enjoyed light and electricity. No one disregarded the invention of the phone and went back to using tin cans and strings.

Then we must ask, why did we fail over and over in passing on Allah's teachings to the next generation?

The answer is simple. Humans are short-sighted and look for instant gratification. We value material progress because we can enjoy its benefits immediately. But we often fail to see the advantages of Allah's teachings, even though ignoring them usually ends in wars and poverty.

It is of our Lord's mercy that He renewed His message by sending new prophets and messengers. Each new message perfectly preserved the creed from previous ones: there is no God but Allah. In addition, each message had new rulings appropriate for the issues of its time. As long as the society upheld Allah's values, the heavens would not interfere.

How can a society preserve itself? We answer that, when a person commits sin, he or she may regret it later and then vow not to do it again. This is the normal action of the righteous self. However, sometimes individuals lose their moral compass and blindly chase after desires with no remorse. If the people around the sinner step in to advise, correct the injustice and punish when necessary, the society remains upright. Sadly, there are instances where the society as a whole is corrupted. People follow their desires and even attack anyone who tries to stop them. At that point, Allah interferes with a new prophet or messenger supported by miracles to bring people back to the path of their Lord.

It was the will of the Almighty that made Prophet Muhammad the final messenger. No new religion will come after Islam. This is a testimony that Muhammad's nation is entrusted to uphold Allah's teachings till the end of time. Allah says:

You were the best nation brought forth for humankind: you bid what is right and forbid what is wrong, and have faith in Allah. And if the People of the Book had believed, it would have been better for them. Among them are faithful, but most of them are transgressors. (3:110)

Allah's directive for us is to stay vigilant and uphold justice. Even when evil is widespread, there will always be a few from the nation of Muhammad who stand up for the truth and invite people back to the path of their Lord. This is the true inheritance of the prophets and messengers.

Allah says:

Verse 34

Zurriyyatam ba'duhaa mim ba'd; wallaahu Samee'un 'Aleem

They are the descendants of one another, and Allah is the All-Hearing, the All-Knowing.

What is the phrase "they are the descendants of one another" referring to? Is it genealogy or faith? Allah taught us from the stories of Abraham and Noah that lineage through bloodline does not apply to prophets. It is only the lineage of faith and values that counts.

Allah says in the 124th verse of Surah Al-Baqarah:

When Abraham's Lord tested him with certain commandments, which he fulfilled, He said, "I will make you a leader of people." Abraham asked, "And will You make leaders from my descendants too?"

Allah replied to Abraham with,

"My pledge does not hold for those who are unjust."

Why? Because a leader is a role model for others. Thus there is no inheritance by blood, only by values. We find a similar case in the story of our beloved Noah. Allah says:

Then it was said, "O Earth, swallow up your water, o sky, hold back," and the water subsided, the command was fulfilled. The ark settled on Mount Judi, and it was said, "Gone are those evildoing people!" Noah called out to his Lord, saying, "My Lord, my son is one of my family, and Your promise is the truth; You are the most just of all judges." He said, "Noah, he is definitely not of your family. He is someone whose action was not righteous. Do not, therefore, ask Me for something about which you have no knowledge. I admonish you lest you should be among the ignorant." (11:44-46)

Hence, in the verse under study, the phrase "they are the descendants of one another" refers to the inheritors of faith, not bloodline. Similar is the case for the disbelievers. Allah says:

The hypocrites, both men and women, are all the same: they order what is wrong and forbid what is right; they are tight-fisted. They have ignored Allah, so He has ignored them. The hypocrites are the disobedient ones. (9:67)

Whether related by lineage or not, the hypocrites are undoubtedly related by their values, and that is what matters. Allah is fully aware of everyone's actions and intentions; He is "the All-Hearing, the All-Knowing."

Verse 35

Iz qaalatim ra atu 'Imraana Rabbi innee nazartu laka maa fee batnee muharraran fataqabbal minnee innaka Antas Samee'ul 'Aleem

When Imran's wife said, "My Lord, I have vowed what is growing in my womb entirely to You, so accept this from me. You are the One Who hears and knows all."
(Verse 35)

The verse starts with the word "when," which implies "to remember." For example, if I say to you, "When I came to visit you at the store, I gave you my phone," it means "Remember that I came to visit you at the store." The word "when" can also be used to join two sentences together, such as in the phrase "Raise your hand when you're finished."

In the verse under study, the word "when" serves both meanings. First, it means "Remember that Imran's wife said," and second, it joins verse 34 with verse 35. Verse 35 ended with Allah being "the All-Hearing, the All-Knowing," and because Imran's wife's deeply believed that the Lord was listening, she supplicated, "My Lord, I have vowed what is growing in my womb entirely to You, so accept this from me. You are the One Who hears and knows all."

The phrase "entirely to You" is translated from the Arabic origin مُحَرَّرًا (muharraran), which means "free and not owned by anyone." It is the same word used to describe a freed slave or an edited book ready for publishing. But what was the reason behind Imran's wife's supplication? We answer that, just like today, Imran's wife lived in an environment where people were proud of their children: they spent their lives raising them and planning their future, worked hard to bring comfort to them, and were proud of their accomplishments. However, Imran's wife did not find all of this pleasing: she wanted to free the child in her womb from chasing after life's pleasures. In other words, she did not want her son or herself as a mother to be preoccupied with other people's expectations and approval.

But Imran's wife had even more in mind. In the olden days, people could decide to vow a son to the service at the Temple. Such a vow would continue as long as the parents had guardianship over the child or until he reached the age of maturity. At that point, the son had the right to choose whether to continue serving at the Holy House -as his parents wanted- or to live his life as he wished. Imran's wife did not wish for her unborn child to be a comfort for her eyes or to have to help her in her old age. She wanted him to be free from all worldly obligations and completely dedicate himself to the Temple's service. This necessitated her unborn child to be a boy because only males were allowed to serve the Holy House.

The verb "to vow," translated from the Arabic word نَذْرْتُ (Nuthr) means to make a promise to yourself or assign yourself the duty of a specific good deed beyond what Allah has obligated you with. For example, you can vow to pray every night a particular number of prayers, which goes above and beyond the five obligatory prayers. By vowing to pray more, you make it incumbent upon yourself to perform these extra prayers nightly. You can vow to fast two days a week, which is above and beyond the obligatory fast during the month of Ramadan. Similarly, you can vow to give 10% of your wealth rather than the required 2.5% Zakat almsgiving. When you make a vow, it shows that you have tasted the sweetness of worship and want to get closer to your Lord. It is an acknowledgment that Allah is worthy of far more than what He obligated you with. Allah has been extraordinarily generous and merciful because, if He had imposed what He deserves from us, no one could have fulfilled His right. He says:

Can He Who creates be compared to one who cannot create? Why do you not take heed? And should you attempt to count Allah's blessings, you could not compute them. Allah is indeed All-Forgiving, All-Compassionate. (16:17-18)

You have the freedom to make a vow or not, but keep in mind that a vow has to be of the same types of worship prescribed by Allah, such as prayer, fasting, Hajj, and so on. Once you make one, it becomes an obligation. Thus, it is wise not to get carried away and make a too difficult vow to abide by.

Righteous people who have true knowledge of Allah say to those who violate a vow, "Didn't you find Allah worthy of your continuous love?" No one among us has any doubts that Allah deserves deep affection. Therefore, it is better to take your time and think deeply before making a vow.

Imran's wife knew the sweetness of faith and wanted to extend that blessing to her unborn child. So she continued her supplication with "accept this from me." Acceptance means to approve something with pleasure, in contrast, to approve something reluctantly and out of obligation. In the next verse, Allah responded to her prayers with, "Her Lord accepted her with gracious favor and blessed her with a good upbringing."

Imran's wife knew how to supplicate properly. She called out "My Lord," translated from the Arabic ربي (Rubbi), not "Dear Allah" or "O Allah." Here you may ask, what is the difference? We answer that the Lord is the Caretaker, the Provider, and the Protector. Thus, calling to the Lord is calling to the One Who nourishes and provides, while the call to Allah is a call of worship and duties. The wife of Imran said, "My Lord, I have vowed what is growing in my womb entirely to You, so accept this from me. You are the One Who hears and knows all." And the response was "Her Lord accepted her with gracious favor and blessed her with a good upbringing, and entrusted her to the care of Zachariah." Allah spoke about a good upbringing in a nourishing environment under the care of a prophet: all these are gifts of Lordship. Moreover, the word "gracious" indicates a higher level of approval because, while the word "accepted" gives us only a sense of approval with pleasure, "gracious" is definitely a step above. In the next few verses, you will see how Allah's favours will manifest in this child's life for all the world to see till the end of time.

Verse 36

Falammaa wada'at haa qaalat Rabbi innee wada'tuhaaa unsaa wallaahu a'lamu bimaa wada'at wa laisaz zakaru kalunsaa wa innee sammaituhaa Maryama wa innee u'eezuhaa bika wa zurriyyatahaa minash Shaitaanir Rajeem

But when she gave birth, she said, "My Lord! I have given birth to a girl." Allah knew best what she had given birth to; the male is not like the female. "I name her Mary, and I commend her and her descendants to Your protection from the rejected Satan." (Verse 36)

The wife of Imran had pledged her unborn child to the service of the House of Allah and, at the time, this task was exclusive to males. So, when she gave birth to a girl, she was surprised. How could she fulfill the vow now? "She said, 'My Lord! I have given birth to a girl.'" This doesn't mean that she was informing Allah; rather, she wanted to express her sorrow that her vow would go unfulfilled.

The verse continues with "the male is not like the female." Whose words were these? Did Allah answer Imran's wife with "the male is not like the female"? Or did Imran's wife say, "My Lord! I have given birth to a girl; the male is not like the female"? Let's explore both possibilities.

Imran's wife may have said, "My Lord! I have given birth to a girl....The male is not like the female" because she was disappointed that a female couldn't serve at the Holy House as she hoped for her newborn. In this case, Allah's words "Allah knew best what she had given birth to" would be an exclamation affirming His knowledge.

The second possibility is that Imran's wife said, "My Lord! I have given birth to a girl," and then Allah answered with "Allah knew best what she had given birth to; the male is not like the female." In this case, Allah wanted her to know that the male, which she had wished for, could never reach this female's rank. Her newborn girl would have a significant task and an exceptional stature till the end of time. We find this meaning preferable. Allah heard Imran's wife's prayers and respected her vow to deliver a servant of the Holy House, but He answered those prayers with something far better than a male. Allah granted her a blessed female with a task superior to service at the Temple. How? We answer that serving at the House of Allah is limited to a few rituals performed over a few decades, but Mary would serve as a sign of the absoluteness of Allah's ability for the entire humanity. No one else could fulfill this role.

Let's look into Allah's limitless power. Our abilities as humans come from utilizing materials and the laws that underpin them to produce results. But where do these materials and laws come from? Allah is the Creator! Thus, if He wanted to create without these materials and laws, then that is His will! Allah gave us a look into His absolute power because this matter should be front and center in our faith.

Let's take the four logical possibilities of creating a human being. The first possibility is that Allah creates a new individual through the normal reproduction between a male and a female, as he created the vast majority of us. He says:

And all things We have created in pairs, so that you may reflect and be mindful. (51:49)

The second possibility is that Allah creates a new individual in the absence of both the male and female elements: this is how He created Adam from nothing. The third possibility is that Allah creates a human from the male element alone, just as Eve was created from Adam. The last logical option is the creation of a human from a female alone, without a male. Prophet Jesus, peace be upon him, was that creation and Mary, may Allah be pleased with her, was that female. Allah says:

Verily, the case of Jesus in the sight of Allah is as the case of Adam. He fashioned him out of dust, then He said to him, "Be," and he came to be. (3:59)

Allah's blessings were far higher than what Imran's wife had asked for, and this is a reminder to all of us. Allah says, "Allah knew best what she had given birth to: the male is not like the female."

The verse continues with the words of Imran's wife: "I name her Mary, and I commend her and her descendants to Your protection from the rejected Satan." The name Mary or Miriam reflects what was in the heart of her mother. When Imran's wife saw that she gave birth to a girl and missed the opportunity that her child could serve at the House of Allah, she prayed for an obedient and devoted worshipper. And this is what the name Miriam means: "the devoted worshipper."

Another insight into the heart of Imran's wife lies in her supplication, "I commend her and her descendants to Your protection from the rejected Satan." Satan is the main obstacle on the way to devotion. If you want to dedicate some of your time to worship, Satan comes to beautify sin for you. Imran's wife wanted to protect her daughter from Satan because she knew from experience that most sins start with one of his whispers.

Here the story of Abu Hanifa, a famous Muslim scholar, comes to mind. A very distraught man came to him and said, "O Abu Hanifa, I really need your help. You are our scholar!" Abu Hanifa welcomed the man and asked about his troubles. The man said, "I had a small treasure that I buried in the desert. I had marked the place with a few shrubs and rocks, but everything scattered after last week's flood. I cannot find my coins anymore. Please help me!" Abu Hanifa replied, "My son, I am a man of knowledge, and there is no knowledge in this. But come back to me later today; maybe I can figure out a trick for you."

The man returned in the afternoon for Abu Hanifa's instruction. The scholar said, "When the night comes, stand and pray to Allah. Remain in your prayers all night. The Messenger, peace be upon him, used to spend his nights in prayer when a matter bothered him." The man was unhappy with Abu Hanifa's solution; nonetheless, he did as he was told. The next morning, the man came rushing to Abu Hanifa with a big smile on his face. He said, "I found it! I found it! As soon as I began my prayer, I remembered to take twenty steps east of the large palm tree and dig there. I collected my coins and went back to sleep." Abu Hanifa smiled and said, "My son, that was the devil that guided you. By Allah, I knew that Satan would not let you complete a night with your Lord in worship. So make sure you go back home tonight to spend a night in worship and thank Allah for the bounties He blessed you with."

This brings us back to the verse. Imran's wife understood Satan's ways, and she also understood how to stop him in his tracks. She prayed, "I commend her and her descendants to Your protection from the rejected Satan."

When the devil whispers to you to adorn sin, it is you against him. This is a fight that Satan can win. But he cannot enter into a battle with the Almighty. That is why, as soon as Satan hears the name of Allah, he backs off. The Quran described him as the "retreating whisperer" because he only secludes himself with you when your heart is away from Allah. As soon as you seek Allah, Satan retreats. Take the example of a child being bullied in a playground. She may feel overwhelmed and overpowered but, as soon as she turns around and calls her father, the bullies run away. Now, this little girl feels strong and can better stand up for herself against all the bigger kids. If a child feels invincible in her father's company, how should a person in the company of his or her Lord feel? When you are in Allah's company, you are safe and tranquil under all circumstances. Allah says:

If Satan should prompt you to do something, seek refuge with Allah -He is all-hearing, all-knowing. (7:200)

The devil trembles when you seek refuge in Allah, but he does not abandon the battle: he comes back again and again. However, if he finds you always turning to your Lord, he realizes that you are a lost cause and a waste of his time.

The wife of Imran extended her supplication to future generations. She said, "I name her Mary, and I commend her and her descendants to Your protection from the rejected Satan." The descendant of Miriam was no other than our beloved Prophet Jesus, peace be upon him.

Verse 37

Fataqabba lahaa Rabbuhaa biqaboolin hasaninw wa ambatahaa nabaatan hasananw wa kaffalahaa Zakariyyaa kullamaa dakhala 'alaihaa Zakariyyal Mihraaba wajada 'indahaa rizqan qaala yaa Maryamu annaa laki haazaa qaalat huwa min 'indil laahi innal laaha yarzuqu mai yashaaa'u bighairi hisaab

Her Lord graciously accepted her and made her grow in goodness, and entrusted her to the care of Zachariah. Whenever Zachariah went in to see her in her sanctuary, he found her supplied with provisions. He said, "Mary, how is it you have these provisions?" And she said, "They are from Allah: Allah provides limitlessly for whomever He will." (Verse 37)

In verse 35, we explained the meaning of good acceptance and upbringing. Let's begin with the phrase "and entrusted her to the care of Zachariah." Take note that Allah accepted Mary, blessed her nurture, and when it came to her care, He chose Zachariah. In other words, the matter of how Prophet Zachariah came to care for Mary was through divine guidance.

The story started when the village elders gathered to discuss who would be in charge of caring for Mary. Each member was eager to take on the honour. The discussions went on without an agreement, tempers flared, and the leaders feared chaos, so they resorted to drawing lots. People often resort to chance when they differ in opinion and fear that making a decision would result in conflict and hurt feelings. By doing so, they completely remove personal desires and undue influence and leave the final decision to Allah. Allah says:

This is an account of things beyond your knowledge that We now reveal to you. You were not present among them when they cast lots to see which of them should care for Mary; you were not present with them when they argued. (3:44)

Prophet Zachariah was married to Eshaa, the sister of Mary's mother, Hannah. Being the husband of her maternal aunt put Zachariah in an excellent position to care for Mary. It is said that the lots were the pens used to write down the Torah. The elders threw them in the sea, then watched whose pen floated to the top and whose pen sunk. Mary would be entrusted to the person whose pen drowned. By abandoning desires and turning to something over which there is no control, such as drawing lots, there is no room for anger and resentment. Had someone taken on Mary's responsibility by force or coercion, he would have left the others with bitter feelings. Drawing lots is an acceptable option in matters when good decision making is not possible.

We find another example of this when Prophet Jonah and his companions faced an impossible situation. They were on a ship that was taking on water and about to sink. It was necessary to lighten the ship's load, not only of cargo but also of people: a few passengers had to go overboard to save the rest. The only way such a tough decision could be acceptable was by drawing lots. Otherwise, there would have been a brawl, and the weak and the old would have been thrown overboard. Lots protected people from the injustice of each other. It was destined for Jonah, peace be upon him, to jump into the sea and be swallowed by a whale. He accepted Allah's choice. In fact, his praise of Allah was his salvation. Allah says:

Jonah, too, was one of the messengers. He fled to the overloaded ship. Then he drew lots with them, and he was one of those who lost, and a whale swallowed him for he had committed blameworthy acts. Had it not been that he was one who always glorified Allah, he would have stayed in its belly until the Day when all are raised up. (37:139-144)

Thus, we understand that Zachariah's guardianship was Allah's choice. He says, "Her Lord graciously accepted her and made her grow in goodness, and entrusted her to the care of Zachariah."

The verb "entrusted" is translated from the Arabic origin كَفَّلَهَا (kaffalaha). The word كفيل (kafeel) in general terms means "the guarantor," that is, the person who promises to pay the debt in case the borrower defaults on the loan obligation. Similarly, Prophet Zachariah was ultimately responsible for Mary's care and the fulfillment of her needs.

The verse continues, "Whenever Zachariah went in to see her in her sanctuary, he found her supplied with provisions." Prophet Zachariah used to bring Mary her daily food and drink as she secluded herself for worship. On multiple occasions, he was surprised to find food he did not bring or seen before in the market. Naturally, he questioned Mary, the sainted worshiper, who had never departed her chamber, "Mary, how is it you have these provisions?" Zachariah teaches us two important lessons. First, as you will see later from Virgin Mary's answer, Allah can overrule the laws of cause and effect and provide from nothing. Second, we learn to be watchful over our loved ones, and be proactive when we see signs of possible corruption. You should always be curious when you see suspicious matters of unexplained wealth. Simply stop and kindly ask, "Where did you get this from?"

For example, a wife can usually tell when her husband spends more than his salary or when her daughter wears something that exceeds her income. If she questions her family about how they obtained these goods, there will be little room for corruption. The question "Where did you get this from?" is a shield that protects the family's morals. Corruption spreads when we turn a blind eye to illegal acts and unlawful wealth. While having no doubt about Mary's piety, Prophet Zachariah still exercised vigilance and asked, "Mary, how is it you have these provisions?" She replied, "They are from Allah: Allah provides limitlessly for whoever He will."

As a last note, the word "sanctuary" is translated from the Arabic origin الْمِحْرَابَ (al-mihrab), which refers to places of worship or the area where the imam stands in the mosque. It also describes a room that is accessed through a staircase. You can see an example of its use in the following verse:

They made for him whatever he wished; sanctuaries, and figures of inanimate objects, and carvings, as well as basins like ponds and boilers built into the ground. "Work, O family of David, in thankfulness to Me." Few are genuinely thankful among My servants. (34:13)

Verses 38 & 39

Hunaaalika da'aa Zakariyyaa Rabbahoo qaala Rabbi hab lee mil ladunka zurriyyatan taiyibatan innaka samee'ud du'aaa'

There and then, Zachariah prayed to his Lord, saying, "Lord, from Your grace, grant me virtuous offspring: You hear every prayer." (Verse 38)

Fanaadat hul malaaa'ikatu wa huwa qaaa'imuny yusallee fil Mihraabi annal laaha yubashshiruka bi Yahyaa musaddiqam bi Kalimatim minal laahi wa saiyidanw wa hasooranw wa Nabiyyam minas saaliheen

While he was standing in prayer in the chamber, the angels called unto him: "Allah doth give thee glad tidings of Yahya, witnessing the truth of a Word from Allah, and (be besides) noble, chaste, and a prophet,- of the (goodly) company of the righteous."(Verse 39)

When Mary pointed out that Allah provided for her, she awoke the spiritual intuition of Prophet Zachariah and reminded him that "Allah provides limitlessly for whoever He will." In fact, it is enough for Allah to say about something "Be," and it becomes. Here Zachariah thought to himself, "If Allah's power can provide directly without means and causes, then I crave a son to carry on prophethood after me." At that moment, He supplicated his Lord about this issue that required absolute freedom from all physical laws. He wanted a child, but reproduction requires a young and fertile couple. Zachariah's wife was infertile even when she was young, and now they both were old. A matter like this is against the laws that govern humans, even by today's modern medical standards. Allah alone is capable of going beyond any set laws.

Zachariah knew that Allah could provide without account, but that thought was not at the center of his consciousness. This belief crystallized in his mind only after he witnessed Allah's provisions for Mary in her prayer chamber: the food she had was not available in the market and was of the sorts the prophet had never seen before. Mary's words, "They are from Allah: Allah provides limitlessly for whoever He will" struck the right cord and awakened certainty within Zachariah. He must have asked himself, "How did I miss this?" Then, right at that moment, right in Mary's sanctuary, our beloved Zachariah stood in prayer and supplicated the Almighty, "Lord, from Your grace grant me virtuous offspring: You hear every prayer."

Let's take a moment to appreciate what Zachariah asked for. Most of us want children to be the joy of our life, our pride in society, and our helpers in old age. We like them to carry our memory and be a legacy for the family. But was that what Prophet Zachariah asked for? No, because he was aware that a child could be evil and a burden on society. Zachariah asked explicitly for "virtuous offspring."

Let us look at the following verse:

"Lord, my bones have weakened, and my hair is ashen grey, but never, Lord, have I prayed to You in vain: I fear what my kin will do when I am gone, and my wife is barren, so grant me a successor —a gift from You— to be my heir and the heir of the family of Jacob. Lord, make him well-pleasing to You." (19:4-6)

Zachariah wanted a son who would continue the legacy of prophethood, carry the divine scriptures, and uphold heavenly values. His prayer "grant me" is evidence that he was well aware that he did not possess the requirements to conceive a child or make him or her righteous. Allah warns us against falling into the trap of believing that we have the ability to create or even raise children. He says:

Allah controls the heavens and the earth; He creates whatever He will —He grants female offspring to whomever He will, and grants to whom He wills sons. On some, He bestows both sons and daughters, and some He leaves barren. He is all-knowing and all-powerful.

(42:49-50)

So if you are young and healthy, do not be fooled by your superficial abilities: every child is a blessing from Allah. Zachariah's words "Lord, from Your grace, grant me" mean "Lord, give me a child despite my shortfalls," because Allah is the Creator of causes and laws, and He alone can overrule them.

Here it is worth taking a moment to study the difference between Allah's gifts through causes and Allah's grants. Take, for example, a man who learns engineering by spending four years studying in a University, and another who is talented from youth and can design world-renowned buildings on a napkin. Allah grants talent to some with no effort on their part, while He facilitates the circumstances for others to study hard and learn. Thus, Zachariah knew what to ask for when he prayed, "Lord, from Your grace, grant me virtuous offspring."

The supplication ends with, "You hear every prayer." Here we may ask, was Allah's hearing of the prayer intended or His acceptance of the prayer? We answer that Prophet Zachariah had pure faith in Allah. And because of the sincerity of his supplication, and because he wanted a child for Allah's pleasure alone, he trusted that Allah would respond to his prayers. The next verse in Al-Imran confirmed Zachariah's intuition. Allah says:

The angels called out to him while he stood praying in the sanctuary, "Allah gives you the glad tidings of John, confirming a Word from Allah. He will be noble and chaste, a prophet, one of the righteous." (Chapter 3: Verse 39)

Did all the angels gather and call out to Zachariah? Or was it the Archangel Gabriel? The prevailing scholarly opinion is that it was the Angel Gabriel who spoke to the prophet. The phrase "The angels called out to him" helps us understand that the angelic voice of revelation is different from the human voice. When your friend calls your name, you can tell where the voice is coming from. Your ears can distinguish between a voice coming from in front of you, from your left, or from another room. However, when an angel speaks to a human, the voice is all-encompassing and fills the entire world. It sounds as if all the angles in the universe are speaking in one voice. Nowadays, modern audio equipment can create room-filling sound to the extent that it is difficult to tell where the speakers are located. Thus, the phrase "The angels called out to him" means that the voice came to Zachariah from all sides.

Gabriel called him during his finest encounter with the Lord. It is a lesson we learn from all the prophets and messengers. Our beloved Muhammad would rush to prayer when a matter troubled him, so each one of us should try this when facing difficulty. But what qualifies as a troubling matter? We answer that issues are problematic when they are beyond your control or when you have tried to solve them with all the tools Allah gave you, yet you failed. In such cases, you should not worry yourself sick because you have a wise and capable Lord. Turn to Him using the best way possible: prayer. We said before that the child who has a father protecting him or her does not stress about problems; shouldn't the one who has a Lord be more at ease?

So turn to Allah in prayer and say, "My Lord, this matter has become too difficult for me. I have exhausted the means you put at my disposal, and You are the Creator of means and causes. Please help me." If you pray to the Lord with devotion, I guarantee that, even before you complete your supplication, you will be overcome with relief. Remember that the angels did not wait for the end of Zachariah's prayer to bring the good news. Allah says, "The angels called out to him while he stood praying in the sanctuary, "Allah gives you the glad tidings of John."

"Glad tidings" are good news that is yet to happen and predictions of a bright future. But, if someone predicts good fortunes for you, you should always take it with a grain of salt. Why? Because there are many unknowns and circumstances often change. If, for example, you are expecting a raise at work next month, there is always a chance you could lose your job: your boss may die, or the company may suffer a loss. There are too many variables outside of your control. But, if the glad tidings come from Allah, then you have nothing to worry about. Allah is all-competent, and the good news will happen without a doubt. He says, "Allah gives you the glad tidings of John, confirming a Word from Allah. He will be noble and chaste, a prophet, one of the righteous."

Allah gave Zachariah the blessing of a son and increased him with the gift of naming him "John." Above all, the phrase "confirming a Word from Allah" was proof that he would live abiding by Allah's teachings, walk the path of his forefathers, and carry on Allah's message. Prophet John was the first to believe in the message of Jesus, peace be upon them. Allah further described him as "noble and chaste" because he would abstain from all sins even when faced with sexual lust, the strongest of human instincts.

Verses 40

Qaala Rabbi annaa yakoonu lee ghulaamunw wa qad balaghaniyal kibaru wamraatee 'aaqirun qaala kazaalikal laahu yaf'alu maa yashaaa'

He said, "My Lord, how shall I have a son when old age has overtaken me, and my wife is barren?" "Just so," he said, "Allah does whatever He wills." (Verse 40)

Verse 41

Qaala Rabbij 'al leee Aayatan qaala Aaayatuka allaa tukalliman naasa salaasata ayyaamin illa ramzaa; wazkur Rabbaka kaseeranw wa sabbih bil'ashiyyi wal ibkaar

He said: "O my Lord! Give me a Sign!" "Thy Sign," was the answer, "Shall be that thou shalt speak to no man for three days but with signals. Then celebrate the praises of thy Lord again and again, and glorify Him in the evening and in the morning."

Let's begin by admiring the nobility and etiquette of prophethood. Zachariah, peace be upon him, was old, but old age is not a reason for the inability to have children. Many men in their eighties and nineties have impregnated women. However, if the woman is infertile, then there is no hope of conceiving. Yet, we find that our beloved Zachariah started his supplication politely. He said, "My Lord, how shall I have a son when old age has overtaken me?" He attributed the weakness to himself first and did not lay blame on his wife's condition alone.

We also note that Zachariah said, "old age has overtaken me," rather than the common "I have reached old age." This is because reaching something gives a sense of desire and achievement, but it is usually against your will when something overtakes you.

Zachariah was surprised when his prayers for a son were immediately accepted. He wondered, how could this be? Allah narrates this incident to teach us that the human soul is always in a state of flux, not absolute certainty. Allah also teaches us to turn to Him when matters are beyond our abilities. When Zachariah asked his Lord in wonder, the decisive statement, "Just so, Allah does whatever He wills," clarified that the Creator's absolute ability is above all obstacles.

The angels informed Zachariah that "Allah gives you the glad tidings of John," but they did not specify how. Was it through a new marriage to another woman? Was he to return to youth and be able to have better sexual relations? Thus, it was natural for the prophet to inquire further. He asked, "My Lord, how shall I have a son when old age has overtaken me, and my wife is barren?" because such a matter was supernatural to what was familiar to him. Allah confirmed with "Just so," meaning that the pregnancy would occur while both Zachariah and his wife were in their current state, old and barren. Allah does not need to return them to young age or bring Zachariah a new healthy woman: "Allah does whatever He wills." The moment the Lord said, "Be," the pregnancy began.

In the next verse of Al Imran, our beloved Zachariah asked for more.

"Lord," he entreated, "appoint a sign for me." "Your sign," He said, "is that you will not be able to speak to people for three days except by gesture. Meanwhile, mention your Lord much and glorify Him in the afternoon and the early hours of the morning."

(Chapter 3: Verse 41)

Why would Zachariah ask for a sign that a baby was created in his wife's barren womb? Did he doubt Allah's word? We answer that the prophet did not want to miss a moment of Allah's blessing. He wanted to feel Allah's power not only in his wife's womb but also within himself.

He feared that he might not show proper gratitude while waiting for his wife's belly to get bigger. Thus, he asked for a physical sign to start thanking Allah from the moment the pregnancy began.

Allah's gift fit what Zachariah had asked. " 'Your sign,' He said, 'is that you will not be able to speak to people for three days except by gesture. Meanwhile, mention your Lord much and glorify Him in the afternoon and the early hours of the morning.' "

There is a difference between choosing not to speak and not being able to speak. Allah told the prophet, "I will prevent you from speaking, and when you find yourself unable to speak, then know that it is your sign." Now, Zachariah could only communicate with people through hand gestures. But Allah knew that His servant wanted to spend every moment in gratitude; thus, the only words Zachariah could speak were the words of the Lord's praise. Allah told him, "And mention your Lord much and glorify Him in the afternoon and the early hours of the morning." It was as though the Almighty said, "Since you want to experience the blessing while being thankful, I will make you incapable of speaking anything but My praise."

The word "mention" is translated from the Arabic origin "Thikr," which is the remembrance of Allah, His favours, grandeur, and qualities of perfection. On the other hand, the word "glorify" is translated from the Arabic "Tasbeeh," which exalts Allah above everything else. Hence, when we say "Subhan Allah," we declare our Lord's transcendence above all things.

Mary pointed out to Zachariah that Allah provided her with food and provision directly, without means and causes. Now, Mary experienced firsthand how Allah overruled physical laws and provided Zachariah and his wife with a child. There is great wisdom behind these events because soon, Mary would bear a burden related to her chastity and honour as a woman. Thus, she needed to have the unshakable faith that "Allah provides limitlessly for whomever He will." Now, when Mary bore a child without a father, she was firm in her faith, and Prophet Zachariah stood by her side in support. They both knew that Allah provided Mary with food through His command "Be," and it was, just as He provided an old Zachariah and his infertile wife with a baby through His command "Be," and it was.

Allah further blessed Zachariah and his wife by naming their son. He says, "Allah gives you the glad tidings of John." Choosing a name is usually done by the parents. In many cultures, parents select a name full of optimism for their newborn in the hopes of giving their son or daughter a good start. For example, they may choose the name Kareem, which means "generous," in hopes of having a wealthy and kind child. But life does not unfold according to our wishes because humans have no knowledge or control over the future. A girl named Grace may not turn out to be graceful at all.

But what happens when the Almighty names a child? The situation is quite different. Allah chose the name "John" translated from the Arabic origin يَحْيَى؟ (Yahya), which means "the alive." A poet once said in eulogy of his son:

I have named him Yahya so he lives

But I cannot control what fate takes and gives

The poet had named his son "Yahya," hoping that he would live a long life, but matters of life and death were not in his hands. His son died as a young boy. But when Allah, the All-Capable and the Grantor of life, gives the name "Yahya," the intention must be a distinguished and eternal life. You and I may think that a long life means living for over a hundred years, but that is our limited human thinking. Our beloved Prophet Yahya was killed by his enemies, thus becoming a martyr. Allah says:

Do not think at all of those killed in Allah's cause as dead. Rather, they are alive; with their Lord they have their sustenance. (3:169)

Yahya lived on earth, and then when he was martyred, he was instantly transferred to the heavens to live eternally without interruption. That was the blessing of Allah Almighty naming a child "John."

Verses 42

Wa iz qaalatil malaaa'ikatu yaa Maryamu innal laahas tafaaki wa tahharaki wastafaaki 'alaa nisaaa'il 'aalameen

The angels said to Mary, "Mary, Allah has chosen you and made you pure, and then truly chose you above all women." (Verse 42)

All the events in the previous verses were centered around Mary, peace be upon her. More specifically, these events were meant to cement the creed that "Allah provides limitlessly for whomever He will."

While she was secluded for worship, Allah provided Mary with provisions directly and without account. This blessing alerted our beloved Zachariah to Allah's infinite ability, so he supplicated for a son to carry on the legacy of prophethood. Mary witnessed how Allah provided an old and barren couple with a child. Soon, she would be granted honour and responsibility that no other woman will have until the end of time.

The verse starts with "The angels said to Mary."

Did all the angels gather and call out to her? Or was it the archangel Gabriel? The prevailing opinion is that it was the angel Gabriel who spoke to Mary. The phrase "The angels said" helps us understand that the angelic voice of revelation is different from the human voice. When Gabriel's voice came to Mary from all sides, it was as if all the angels were speaking in one voice. What did Gabriel say? He conveyed the Lord's message: "Mary, Allah has chosen you and made you pure, and then truly chose you above all women." The verb "chosen" is repeated twice. It is translated from the Arabic origin اصْطَفَى (Istafa), which means "to purify from all contaminants."

Allah says describing Paradise: Rivers of honey strained and pure. (from 15:47) When Allah says, "Mary, Allah has chosen you and made you pure, and then truly chose you above all women," we see two levels of selection. The first selection is not followed by the preposition "above" while the second one is. Let's look into the difference. The first selection, "Mary, Allah has chosen you," means that Allah distinguished Mary by her untainted faith, good manners, and kind heart. But why was the selection mentioned without the preposition "above"? We answer that the omission of "above" means that other men and women can share these traits. Untainted faith, good manners, and a kind heart are not exclusive to Mary. The second selection, "then truly chose you above all women," was mentioned preceded by the preposition "above." The phrase "above all women" excludes men from the circle of selection and places Mary, peace be upon her, above all women. No other woman in history would ever share Mary's status because she was the only one who would get pregnant and give birth without a man.

Here we should ask, what are the benefits of Allah's selection? We answer that when Allah chooses a time, person, or place, it is not meant to favour such person, time, or location. Rather, it is a mission to serve humanity. For example, Allah chose messengers from among the people to serve as examples for all of us to follow. Those chosen by Allah did not have easy, comfortable lives: it was quite the opposite. They often suffered hardships and difficulties to help others. Likewise, Allah selected the days of Ramadan for fasting not to honour these days over the rest of time; instead, He wants the worship during Ramadan to serve as an example for the rest of the year. You often hear a person who just came back from the Hajj pilgrimage say, "When I was in Mecca, I felt the sweetness of faith and experienced great peace and comfort in my heart. It was like I had forgotten the entire world around me." If you were blessed with a Hajj or Umrah trip, you might have experienced these feelings yourself. Are these feelings exclusive to the holy places and cannot be experienced anywhere else? Or are these places supposed to serve as an example of what you can feel anywhere you choose? We answer that when you go to Mecca, you leave your life behind and focus on connecting with Allah. The moment you hear the Athan call for prayers, you rush to perform prayer with devotion. You take your time during prayer and listen carefully to every word of the Imam. This sincerity in worship is what brings you closer to Allah and His Messenger. Shouldn't you, then, adopt the same sincerity and rush to prayer in every place and at all times? If you do so, you will experience the same psychological tranquillity whether you are in Mecca, Paris, or Beijing.

Allah says: Behold, the first House of prayer established for humankind is the one at Makkah, a blessed place and a guidance for all peoples. (3:96) Allah's selection of a person, place, or time is for the benefit of humanity in all places and times. Hence, Allah chose Mary and assigned her a difficult task to serve as an example for all the women in the world. He prepared her for her mission and purified her faith. In fact, her life events were designed so she could reach the following conclusion:

"Allah provides limitlessly for whomever He will." From that point onwards, she was ready to carry the burden of bearing a child without a father and to face a hostile society that would accuse her of her honour and purity.

Allah says, "Mary, Allah has chosen you and made you pure, and then truly chose you above all women." Mary's purification was through the blessings of providing for her directly, assigning Prophet Zachariah to care for her, and granting Zachariah a son. These blessings filled Mary with gratitude to Allah.

VERSE 43

Yaa Maryamu uqnutee li Rabbiki wasjudee warka'ee ma'ar raaki'een

He says, O Mary, be devoutly obedient to your Lord and prostrate and bow with those who bow. (Verse 43)

A person chosen by Allah must be free of all questionable behaviours. Take the example of Allah's selection of our beloved Muhammad. He, peace be upon him, lived an exemplary life well before becoming a messenger. His fellow Meccans knew him as the most honest and truthful man decades before Islam. He continued to serve as a role model for morals and faith during his twenty-three years of prophethood. Similarly, Allah said to Mary, "O Mary, be devoutly obedient to your Lord" so she could be the perfect example for other women well before she became Prophet Jesus' mother. Allah continues with "prostrate and bow with those who bow." Prostration is an act of reverence in submission expressed by placing the forehead -which is the most honourable part of the body- on the ground. To bow, on the other hand, is a lesser form of submission. Yet, prostration did not exempt Mary from bowing to Allah. Why? Because doing something great is not an excuse to abandon a matter of lesser good. Allah's commands should be obeyed in all matters, big or small.

Verse 44

Zaalika min ambaaa'il ghaibi nooheehi ilaik; wa maa kunta ladaihim iz yulqoona aqlaamahum ayyuhum yakfulu Maryama wa maa kunta ladaihim iz yakhtasimoon

This is an account of the unseen that We reveal to you: you were not present among them when they cast lots to see which of them should take charge of Mary, and you were not present with them when they argued. Verse 44

The word "account" is translated from the Arabic origin أَنْبَاءِ (Anba'), which is only used for important news. The "unseen" is what is absent from the senses, and it generally falls under one of two types. First are matters absent from your senses but available to others like you, and second are matters absent from your senses and all those like you. An event may be concealed from you by time or space. For example, a war may have happened years in the past before your time, or it may break out years after you die. There may be wars happening right now in faraway places that you are not aware of.

If an event has happened in the past before your time, you can pierce the veil of the "unseen" by listening to those who witnessed it, like your grandfather, or read about it in a history book. If a military officer informs you of an attack planned for next month, then the officer has also pierced the veil of the future which is "unseen" for you. Lastly, devices such as satellites and televisions can show you live events happening in another country, thus piercing the "unseen" hidden from you by distance.

The events narrated in the verse under study happened centuries before the birth of Prophet Muhammad. As all Meccans knew, our beloved Prophet was illiterate, so he could not have read about these events in history books. There were no televisions to replay such events for him to see. Moreover, Prophet Muhammad did not sit with a teacher or have any formal or informal education during his childhood. This leaves one channel of acquiring knowledge, which is a revelation from Allah. Allah says:

This is an account of the unseen that We reveal to you: you were not present among them when they cast lots to see which of them should take charge of Mary, and you were not present with them when they argued. (Chapter 3: Verse 44)

To "reveal" is to inform someone secretly or quietly. For example, when a salesperson comes to your door, and you don't have the time to meet with them, you might motion to a family member to let that person go. In essence, you have revealed your wishes to your family member that you did not want to see the salesman.

There are many forms of revelation mentioned in the Quran. Allah has revealed to the angels, to people other than the prophets, such as the mother of Moses, and to many of His creation as stated in the following verse:

Your Lord revealed to the bees: "Build dwellings in the mountains and the trees, and also in the structures which men erect." (16:68)

Furthermore, the devils have revealed to each other and to human beings. Allah says:

In this way, We have appointed as enemies to every Prophet devils from both mankind and from the jinn, who reveal to each other alluring words of delusion. If your Lord had willed, they would not have done it, so abandon them and all they fabricate. (6:112)

However, when the word "revelation" is used, it usually takes the specific meaning of Allah revealing His message to His prophets. There are three forms that revelation may take, as mentioned in the following verse:

It is not fitting for a man that Allah should speak to him except by inspiration, or from behind a veil, or by the sending of a messenger to reveal, with Allah's permission, what Allah wills: for He is Most High, Most Wise. (42:51)

Let's take them one by one.

The first form of revelation is inspiration. When Allah inspires someone, He throws the idea into the person's heart, and the person would then act on it. However, as you know, many ideas pop into one's head. How do we know which one of them is true revelation? We answer that when true inspiration comes from Allah, the person finds him or herself completely content and at peace with that thought, even if such inspiration calls for an action that goes against the thoughtful mind.

Look at an example of this type of revelation from the Quran:

We revealed to Moses' mother, "Suckle him and then, when you fear for him, cast him into the river. Do not fear or grieve: We will return him to you and make him one of the Messengers." (28:7)

What woman -in her right mind- would throw her baby into a river when she fears most for its life? She would basically be throwing her son from grave danger into certain death. Yet Moses' mother felt entirely at peace with this action when Allah inspired her.

The second form is revelation from behind a veil. Whether it was Judaism, Christianity, or Islam, every major religion had its message delivered partly by this method. For example, when the prophet was commanded to start the five daily prayers, Allah spoke to him from behind a veil, the same way He spoke to Moses before.

Finally, the third form is revelation through a messenger sent from Allah. The Quran was exclusively revealed by sending a direct messenger, the angel Gabriel. The Quran was not revealed by inspiration to the prophet, nor through direct speech by Allah behind a veil. The Quran was delivered solely by the angel messenger, so there would be absolutely no doubt of its origin. The prophet heard a loud noise like the tolling of a bell before the angel came and became visible to him. The presence of

Gabriel would take a heavy toll on the prophet. His face would change colour and, if he were sitting next to one of his companions or resting his leg on them, they would feel the prophet's leg getting so heavy that they would describe it as a boulder.

The verse continues with, "you were not present among them when they cast lots to see which of them should take charge of Mary, and you were not present with them when they argued." The village elders had gathered to discuss who would be in charge of caring for Mary. Each member was eager to take on the responsibility. The discussion went on without an agreement, and tempers flared. The leaders feared chaos, so they resorted to drawing lots. People resort to chance when they fear that making a decision would end in conflict. Drawing lots completely removes personal desires and undue influence and leaves the final decision to Allah. It is said that the lots were pens used to write down the Torah. The elders cast them in the sea, then watched whose pen floated to the top and whose pen sunk. Mary would be entrusted to the person whose pen drowned. Turning to something completely out of everyone's control leaves no room for anger and resentment. Had someone taken on Mary's responsibility by force or coercion, he would have left the others with feelings of bitterness and rage. Instead, the matter is left to Allah's destiny because lots have no desires.

Verse 45

Iz qaalatil malaaa'ikatu yaa Maryamu innal laaha yubashshiruki bi Kalimatim minhus muhul Maseehu 'Eesab nu Maryama wajeehan fid dunyaa wal Aakhirati wa minal muqarrabeen

And when the angels said, "Mary, Allah gives you the glad tidings of a Word from Him, whose name will be the Messiah, Jesus, son of Mary; honourable in the world and the Hereafter, and one of those near-stationed to Allah." (Chapter 3: Verse 45)

The Virgin Mary had a great task ahead of her. She would be the only woman ever to bear a child without a father, thus becoming the target of accusations about her purity and honour. But our Lord is the most-merciful, so he prepared Mary well for her future task. The first stage of preparation was completed when Mary uttered the following words: "Indeed Allah provides whom He wills without account." While she was secluded in her prayer chamber, Allah provided her with food and drink, the likes of which no one had seen before. The second stage of preparation was completed when Mary witnessed the pregnancy of Prophet Zachariah's wife, who was old and barren. Now, she had firsthand knowledge of the limitlessness of Allah's power in all matters, especially provision and pregnancy. Then, Mary received Allah's revelation of her stature, as the following verse illustrates:

The angels said to Mary, "Mary, Allah has chosen you and made you pure, and then truly chose you above all women." (3:42)

Now, she was ready to enter a new stage. Allah says:

And when the angels said, "Mary, Allah gives you the glad tidings of a Word from Him, whose name will be the Messiah, Jesus, son of Mary; honorable in the world and the Hereafter, and one of those near-stationed to Allah." (Chapter 3: Verse 45)

People often ask, what did Allah mean by "a Word from Him?" We answer that Allah exercises His authority in His dominion with a word, not physically or through means and causes. For example, if you wanted to make a chair, you would have to gather the raw materials of wood and iron and then work these materials into the shape of a chair. Allah, on the other hand, does not work through elements or materials.

He says in the 47th verse of Al Imran:

This is how Allah creates what He will: when He has ordained something, He only says to it, "Be," and it is.

"Be" is a mere clarification and an approximation for us because we do not know of any word shorter than "be." Allah's power is so absolute that His will manifests even before the pronouncement of the letter "b." Take note that Allah did not say, "when He has ordained something, He only says, "Be," and it is." Instead, He said, "when He has ordained something, He only says to it 'Be' and it is." By adding the pronoun "it," Allah showed us that His will brings the matter into existence even before the word "Be" is pronounced. That is how Allah created Jesus, peace be upon him, in the womb of Mary with "a Word from Him."

The verse continues with "whose name will be the Messiah, Jesus, son of Mary." Note that the name consists of three parts: "Messiah," "Jesus," and "son of Mary." Let's take them one by one.

The word "Messiah" is derived from the Arabic root مَسَحَ (Ma Sa Ha) which means to wipe clean. The words "Messiah" may mean "the one whose sins are cleaned and wiped off." It may also be referring to one of his signs that, when he wiped his hand over the ill, the patient was cured. It is also used to refer to the blessed Christ, the leader of his people.

As for "Jesus," it is the prophet's actual name, while "the Messiah" is the nickname, and "the son of Mary" is his surname. It was customary in the Arabic language that a name comes in three forms: first name, last name —often referring to family heritage— and then a title. The title could be used as an indication of honour or as a sign of low status in the community. The three names of Jesus have great wisdom behind them that will appear to us later.

Our beloved Jesus will be "honourable in the world and the Hereafter." The word "honourable "is translated from the Arabic origin وَجِيهًا (Wajeeh). It refers to a person who is respected and never turned away when he asks for a favor. People would hesitate to deny his request. Would you turn away a prophet if he asked you for a favour? Of course not. Would you turn away a person who asks you for the sake of a prophet? You may hesitate. We see this in our daily lives. For example, a beggar may say, "Please give me some money for the sake of Allah." He asks you not to look at him but at the face of Allah, because Allah is the One Who created him. And when you help provide for the poor whom Allah has brought into existence, you become part of Allah's people, even when the poor person you are helping is a disbeliever.

This brings us back to the phrase, "honourable in the world and the Hereafter." We understand how a person may be distinguished on earth, but how about the hereafter? Why did Allah specify that day? Aren't all believers honoured then? We answer: yes, every believer will be honoured, but Prophet Jesus will have a special status because he will be asked the following question in front of all to see:

When Allah says, "Jesus, son of Mary, did you say to people, 'Take my mother and me as two Allahs alongside Allah?' " he will say, "May You be exalted! I would never say what I had no right to say. If I had said such a thing, You would have known it: You know all that is within myself, though I do not know what is within Yours, You alone have full knowledge of unseen things." (5:116)

The question in this verse is not a rebuke from Allah to Jesus. To the contrary, it is a vindication before all to see. Prophet Jesus' stature is above any doubts, as the following verse illustrates:

"Peace was on me the day I was born and will be on me the day I die, and the day I am raised to life again." (19:33)

Jesus' birth was controversial as some Israelites accused the Virgin Mary of her honour. Jesus' death was also controversial as the story of the crucifixion caused an uproar. Prophet Jesus was not crucified.

Allah says:

And for their saying, "We killed the Messiah, Jesus son of Mary, the apostle of Allah" —though they did not kill him nor did they crucify him, but so it was made to appear to them— indeed those who differ concerning him are surely in doubt about him: they do not have any knowledge of that beyond following conjectures, and certainly they did not kill him. (4:157)

It is Jesus, the son of Mary, whom Allah honours in life, death, and eternal life. Allah says, "honourable in the world and the Hereafter, and one of those near-stationed to Allah." Being close to Allah is indeed the highest degree of honour. More importantly, Prophet Jesus' stature will not be affected by those who came later and claimed him to be a Allah or the son of Allah. Such outrageous claims will earn the people who make them great punishment, but not our beloved Jesus. Allah says:

Some say, "The All-Merciful has taken to Himself a son." You have indeed uttered something monstrous. How terrible is this thing you assert: it almost causes the heavens to be torn apart, the earth to split asunder, the mountains to crumble to pieces, that they ascribe to the All-Merciful a child! It does not befit the Lord of Mercy to have offspring. (19:88-92)

Verse 46

Wa yukallimun naasa filmahdi wa kahlanw wa minassaaliheen

He will speak to the people in the cradle and in maturity and will be of the righteous. (Verse 46)

What a wonderful verse that refutes many of the falsehoods attributed to our beloved Prophet Jesus! Let's take a few moments to examine it.

Allah mentioned that Jesus will speak to people "in the cradle and in maturity" to direct our attention, but towards what? We answer that Allah wants you to know that Prophet Jesus, the son of Mary, was subject to change like each one of us. He started as a weak infant in the cradle and then went through boyhood and puberty to reach maturity. Since Jesus was subject to the effects of time, people must know that he is not fit to be a deity or the son of one. Allah says, explaining Jesus' mortality and needs for sustenance:

The Messiah, son of Mary, was only a messenger; other messengers had come and gone before him. His mother was a virtuous woman, and both ate food. See how clear We make these signs for them, see how deluded they are. (5:75)

We ask those who claim that Jesus is God, when was his divinity? In the cradle, during the teenage years, or at maturity? If his divinity were in the cradle, it would be incomplete because he did not remain in that state. Prophet Jesus, peace be upon him, was created subject to the effects of time and vulnerable to life's circumstances just like the rest of us. Thus, he cannot be God.

The phrase "He will speak to the people in the cradle" also refers to the miracle Allah granted our beloved Jesus while he was an infant. From the moment of his birth, Mary's honour and dignity were subject to accusations, and that was understandable. Thus, it was necessary to present an irrefutable sign to stop such allegations once and for all. How do you explain to rational people the wonder of an unmarried chaste, and righteous woman giving birth? The explanations came directly from the mouth of the infant. Allah says:

> She went back to her people carrying the child, and they said, "Mary! You have done something terrible! O sister of Aaron, your father was never a bad man, nor was your mother unchaste." Mary pointed to him. They said, "How can we talk to one in the cradle, an infant boy?" He said, "I am a servant of Allah. He has granted me the Scripture, and made me a prophet. He made me blessed wherever I may be, commanded me to pray, give alms as long as I live, and dutiful to my mother. And He has not made me arrogant or wretched. Peace was on me the day I was born and will be on me the day I die, and the day I am raised to life again." Such was Jesus, the son of Mary: in the words of the truth about which they have been doubting. (19:27-34)

An infant who speaks and argues eloquently is a wondrous miracle. But what is genuinely puzzling is that this miracle has been completely erased from Christian history. Why would people who glorify their prophet to a God status omit such a miracle from their books? The news of a talking infant must have spread like wildfire in the community at the time. It was probably the subject of conversation for months. But the first question anyone would ask about a talking infant is, "Well, what did he say?" And there lies the problem!

The first words that came out of Jesus, the infant, confirmed his humanity: "I am a servant of Allah." These words do not support those who came later and claimed that Jesus is God or the son of God. Thus, it was necessary not only to erase these words but also to deny the miracle altogether.

Now, let's look into the second part of the phrase, "He will speak to the people in the cradle and maturity." Maturity refers to the age from the late thirties and into the forties. As narrated in Christian history, the events of the crucifixion occurred before Jesus reached that age. In other words, Prophet Jesus' speech in maturity remains unfulfilled. Thus, a time must come for Prophet Jesus to return to earth and speak to people before the Day of Judgment. Allah says:

And when the son of Mary is presented as an example, your people turn from it in disdain; they say, "Are our Gods better or he?" They only cite him to you for the sake of arguing. Rather they are a contentious lot. Indeed, Jesus was not other than a servant, whom We favoured, and We made him a miraculous example for the Children of Israel. If We had so willed, We could have made some from among you angels, succeeding each other on the earth. He is certainly a sign of the approach of the Last Hour. So have no doubt about it, and listen to me. This is the straight path. (43:57-61)

The birth of our beloved Jesus and his speech as an infant were a miracle and a controversy. His death is also controversial. Jesus' return to earth will be another miracle and a sign for the approach of the Day of Judgment. Lastly, on the Day of Judgment, Jesus will have time to speak and clear his name and that of his mother from all the falsehoods people attributed to them. Allah says:

When Allah says, "Jesus, son of Mary, did you say to people, 'Take me and my mother as two Gods alongside Allah'?" he will say, "May You be exalted! I would never say what I had no right to say. If I had said such a thing, You would have known it: You know all that is within myself, though I do not know what is within Yours, You alone have full knowledge of the unseen matters.I told them only what You commanded me to: 'Worship Allah, my Lord, and your Lord.' I was a witness over them during my time among them. Ever since You took my soul, You alone have been the watcher over them: You are witness to all things." (5:16-17)

On the Day of Judgment, Allah will question our beloved Jesus before all humanity. This question is not a question of reprimand. To the contrary, it is an exoneration for Jesus and his mother, and a scolding to all those who deified them.

Let's look into Jesus' response to the question "Jesus, son of Mary, did you say to people, 'Take me and my mother as two Gods alongside

Allah'?" His comprehensive answer came in five parts that refuted all false claims.

In the first part of the answer, Jesus said, "May You be exalted! I would never say what I had no right to say." In other words, he, peace be upon him, denied having uttered such words and glorified Allah above the absurd claims of polytheism.

In the second part, Jesus not only denied to have said what he was not supposed to, but he also affirmed that he delivered Allah's message verbatim as instructed: "I told them only what You commanded me to: 'Worship Allah, my Lord, and your Lord.'"

Then, to complete this argument, the Prophet simply pointed out that "if I had said such a thing, You would have known it."

The fourth part of the answer is the most interesting. Jesus says, "You know all that is within myself, though I do not know what is within Yours, You alone have full knowledge of the unseen matters." What is the purpose behind this statement? The purpose is to give us insight into Jesus' thoughts. By pointing out that Allah has full knowledge of our thoughts and feelings, Prophet Jesus denies that even the idea of claiming divinity had never occurred to him.

Lastly, some people say that even if Jesus did not claim divinity, he might have smiled or nodded approvingly when he heard others attribute it to him. To refute such claims, Jesus says, "I was a witness over them during my time among them," meaning that he was watchful for any signs of corruption of faith around him.

Indeed, our beloved Prophet Jesus was one of the righteous.

Verses 47

Qaalat Rabbi annaa yakoonu lee waladunw wa lam yamsasnee basharun qaala kazaalikil laahu yakhluqu maa yashaaa'; izaa qadaaa amran fa innamaa yaqoolu lahoo kun fayakoon

She said, "My Lord, how can I have a son when no man has ever touched me?" The angel said, "So it is. This is how Allah creates what He will: when He ordains something, He only says to it, 'Be,' and it is."
(Verse 47)

Let's take a few moments to ponder over the words, "She said, 'My Lord, how can I have a son when no man has ever touched me?'" We ask, how did the Virgin Mary, who just received the news that she would bear a child, know that the child would have no father? Had she said, "My Lord, how can I have a son?" and then stopped, it would have made sense. Maybe she would get married soon and have a family, or perhaps the pregnancy would be a few years down the line. But by adding, "how can I have a son when no man has ever touched me?" Mary raised a very different issue. Did someone tell her that she would give birth to a child while a virgin? The angels did not tell her that.

We answer that Mary's intelligence and wisdom in receiving Allah's revelation gave her the answer. She heard the words "whose name will be the Messiah, Jesus, son of Mary," and then said to herself, "Allah has attributed this child to me, so he must not have a father." In the olden days, and even in many countries today, the child is assigned his or her father's name. We say, "Hussain, son of Ali" and "Fatimah, daughter of Muhammad." It is entirely out of custom to attribute a child to the mother. Thus, we see the insight of the Virgin Mary in receiving Allah's words. She immediately recognized the fact that her pregnancy with Jesus would not be through a father.

Naturally, she asked, "How can that be?" The Almighty answered, "So it is," which means, "Yes Mary, you understood correctly: the pregnancy will happen just as you are, a virgin that no man has ever touched."

Our Lord has the absolute ability in all matters, including creation, reproduction, and childbearing. This power is not dependant on the presence of a male and a female because, if that were the case, then how was Adam created from none? And how was Eve created only from a male? Allah says:

Verily, the case of Jesus in the sight of Allah is as the case of Adam. He fashioned him out of dust, then He said to him, "Be," and he came to be. (3:59)

And in another chapter:

Allah controls the heavens and the earth; He creates whatever He will —He grants female offspring to whomever He will, and grants to whom He wills sons. On some He bestows both sons and daughters, and some He leaves barren. He is all-knowing and all-powerful. (42:49-50)

So do not fall under the illusion that the elements of masculinity and femininity create a child. Creation only occurs by the will of Allah. He says," So it is. This is how Allah creates what He will: when He ordains something, He only says to it, 'Be,' and it is."

In your daily life, you deal with means and causes to get results, but the One Who created you and created the means and causes has the power to overrule them and create from nothing. Allah created the entire universe from nothing.

Now, let's move to the next verse in Al Imran. Allah says:

Verse 48

Wa yu'allimuhul Kitaaba wal Hikmata wat Tawraata wal Injeel

And He will teach him the scripture and wisdom, and the Torah and the Gospel.

The word "the scripture" is translated from the Arabic origin الْكِتَاب (Al-Kitab). This can be interpreted in one of two ways. First, the word الْكِتَاب (Al-Kitab) usually refers to the books revealed by Allah. But, as you continue reading the verse, you find that "the Torah and the Gospel" are already mentioned. Hence, Al-Kitab must be referring to something different. It could be previous holy books such as the Zabur of David and the Scriptures of Abraham.

The second possible interpretation of "And He will teach him Al-Kitab" is as follows. Some scholars have said that Jesus, peace be upon him, had the most beautiful handwriting of any human being. His calligraphy was a heavenly gift. This means that he, peace be upon him, received from Allah the ability to write beautifully along with the full understanding of the Torah and the Gospel.

Lastly, the word "wisdom" is usually mentioned in the Quran after the holy book. For example, Allah says addressing Prophet Muhammad's wives:

Remember what is recited in your houses of Allah's revelations and wisdom, for Allah is all-subtle, all-aware. (33:34)

We understand that the Noble Quran is the book, and the narrations of our beloved Prophet -also known as Hadith- are the wisdom. Allah reveals the scriptures to His messengers and, in addition, He blesses them with the ability to speak with wisdom.

Verse 49

Wa Rasoolan ilaa Baneee Israaa'eela annee qad ji'tukum bi Aayatim mir Rabbikum annee akhluqu lakum minatteeni kahai 'atittairi fa anfukhu feehi fayakoonu tairam bi iznil laahi wa ubri'ul akmaha wal abrasa wa uhyil mawtaa bi iznil laahi wa unabbi'ukum bimaa taakuloona wa maa taddakhiroona fee buyootikum; inna fee zaalika la Aayatal lakum in kuntum mu'mineen

He will send him as a messenger to the Children of Israel: "I have come to you with a sign from your Lord: I will create the shape of a bird for you out of clay, then breathe into it and, with Allah's permission, it will become a real bird; I will cure the blind and the albino, and bring the dead back to life with Allah's permission; I will tell you what you eat and what you store up in your houses. There truly is a sign for you in this if you are believers." (Verse 49)

A messenger necessarily requires a miracle because anyone can claim, "I am a messenger from Allah," but such a bold claim cannot go unsupported. For a messenger to stand a chance, he must bring a miracle from Allah that proves the authenticity of his message.

A miracle is a wondrous thing that disturbs the laws of the universe. When people contradict the messenger, they must face the question, "How do you explain the messenger's miracle that goes against everything we know?" The miracle puts deniers in a tough spot. They cannot explain it using human laws and cannot find anyone else who can do anything like it.

But for a miracle to be effective, it is necessary to be of the type in which the messenger's nation excels. Otherwise, people would simply say, "This is something we have not learned, and once we learn it, we can do the same." Say, for example, that you want to challenge someone to prove your superiority; to do so, you must challenge them in something they excel at. You cannot challenge a weak, disabled person in weightlifting because that would prove nothing: you must challenge a weightlifter. It is for this reason that the Almighty sent messengers armed with miracles suitable for their nation. Allah sent Moses, peace be upon him, to a people that excelled in magic and engineering. Who would appreciate the splitting of the sea more than the engineers who built the pyramids? Likewise, when the top magicians, who knew all the trade secrets of magic, saw a wooden stick turn into a live python, they immediately believed in Allah. They understood, more than anyone else, that Moses did not perform magic but a miracle. Allah says:

Throw down what is in your right hand, and it will swallow what they have conjured. What they have conjured is only a magician's trick, and the magician does not fare well wherever he may show up. And so it happened, and the magicians threw themselves down in prostration. They proclaimed, "We have come to believe in the Lord of Aaron and Moses!" (20:69-70)

And in another chapter:

"Moses, what is that in your right hand?" "It is my staff," he said, "I lean on it, restrain my sheep with it, I also have other uses for it." Allah said, "Throw it down, Moses." He threw it down and, lo and behold, it became a slithering snake! "Pick it up," He said, "and have no fear; We shall revert it to its former state." (20:17-20)

When Moses, peace be upon him, saw his wooden staff turn into a snake, he feared it. This fear separates his miracle from magic. How? We answer that when a magician makes a stick appear to the people as a snake, he –the magician– still sees it as a stick. Had the magician seen it turn into a real snake, he would have feared it just like the audience. Moses, peace be upon him, feared because his staff truly changed into a living snake.

This brings us back to the verse. The Israelites at the time of Prophet Jesus were famous for advanced medical treatments; hence he was granted miracles in the same field. Let's look at these miracles in ascending order.

First is the healing of the sick. The Quran says on the tongue of Jesus, "I will cure the blind and the albino." Why did Jesus mention these two diseases? Because they were incurable illnesses at the time and are still so up to this day. By "blind" the verse is specifically referring to people blind since birth. Albinism is a genetic disorder that causes the skin, hair, and eyes to have little or no color.

Some people have tried to downplay this miracle by claiming that Jesus, peace be upon him, was simply ahead of his time. In other words, modern medicine can cure some types of blindness by corneal implants or laser treatment, so what is the big deal? We answer that Allah's miracles will remain miracles until the Last Hour.

For example, today's ophthalmologists treat blindness with elaborate transplants. Jesus, son of Mary, used to cure the same disease with a prayer. No matter how much science advances, it will never cure diseases with a word. We can only treat patients through the chemistry of medicine and the physics of surgery.

The second miracle challenged the Israelites at a much higher level. Our beloved Jesus would "bring the dead back to life with Allah's permission." Doctors can treat the body, cure some ailments, and may even prolong life, but no one can bring back the dead.

Take note that, in the verse under study, the phrase "with Allah's permission" was mentioned after some miracles and omitted after others. More specifically, the miracles of curing the sick, raising the dead, and creating birds were all followed by the phrase "with Allah's permission," while the miracle of knowing what people stored in their homes did not, and that is significant.

We understand that Allah granted Jesus two types of miracles. The first were miracles inherent to the prophet, so he could perform them at will, such as knowing what people ate and what they hid in their homes.

The second were miracles, such as resurrecting the dead and breathing life into objects, that were not inherent to Jesus; rather, they required Allah's direct permission every single time. For example, Jesus could not raise every dead person at will; instead he, peace be upon him, raised the dead in a very limited scope. The purpose of such a miracle was to prove the authenticity of his message. It is said that the person would come back to life just to say a few words and then die again.

Before we study the highest miracle, that of creation, in detail, let's look into the miracle which was inherent to Prophet Jesus (that is, which he could repeatedly perform at will). He said, "I will tell you what you eat and what you store up in your houses." This miracle is different from the others because it is personal. How, you may ask? We answer that curing the sick or raising the dead was done publically because it affected the entire community. When people see a blind man regain vision, they appreciate the power of Allah.

On the other hand, what people eat and store in their homes is only known to them. This private knowledge is usually shared with one or two members of the family. Allah granted our beloved Jesus the ability to inform each person of what they ate and the treasures they stored in their homes. Thus, he would touch them at a personal level that others could not appreciate.

Verse 49

He will send him as a messenger to the Children of Israel: "I have come to you with a sign from your Lord: I will create the shape of a bird for you out of clay, then breathe into it and, with Allah's permission, it will become a real bird; I will cure the blind and the albino, and bring the dead back to life with Allah's permission; I will tell you what you eat and what you store up in your houses. There truly is a sign for you in this, if you are believers."

In the previous verses, we discussed Prophet Jesus' miracles, specifically the miracles of healing the sick and raising the dead. In today's session, let's examine the miracle of creation. The Quran narrates

Jesus' words: "I have come to you with a sign from your Lord: I will create the shape of a bird for you out of clay, then breathe into it and, with Allah's permission, it will become a real bird."

The verb "create" means to bring something into being with prior planning. To create something, you would imagine it first, plan its function, and then make it according to your plan. However, if the object deviates from your plan, then it is not creation. Similarly, if you take a piece of clay and mess with it for a while making different shapes, you would not be creating; you would be just playing. Creation requires purposeful planning.

For example, a glassmaker who takes sand and makes it into a glass cup is a creator. This person has the skill, a plan, and a goal. From collecting the sand, to melting it, adding chemicals, removing impurities, and shaping the glass, each step was according to the original plan. The glass cup did not exist and later came into being according to the glassmaker's vision. This is creation.

What about Allah's creation? Does He create with planning, or is it just play? He says:

We did not create the heavens and the earth and what lies between them for play. (21:16)

And in another chapter:

Does man think that he will be left alone without purpose? Was he not a drop of ejaculated sperm, then a blood-clot which Allah created and shaped, fashioning from it the two sexes, male and female? Does He Who can do this not have the power to bring the dead back to life? (75:36-40)

So Allah creates with planning and purpose. But there are big differences between the creations of man and those of Allah. We build from raw materials, while Allah creates from nothing. In fact, we need to use Allah's creations to make something new. In the example above, the glassmaker could not have made a glass cup from thin air; he or she had to use sand and fire —both creations of Allah. Allah, on the other hand, created the entire universe from nothing.

Another difference between man's creation and Allah's creation is that the Almighty instills in some of His creations a secret that humans can never give to theirs: life. Life fosters growth and multiplication. In our example, when a glassmaker creates a cup, it remains a cup. Have you ever seen two glasses get together and give birth to small shot glasses? Have you seen a chair grow up to be a bigger wiser couch? Man creates his craft, but it remains as is, while Allah's work contains life, growth, and learning. When the power of man touches dirt, it produces glass, but when the power of Allah touches dirt, it produces a human that changes the face of an entire planet. Allah says:

We created the human from an essence of clay, then We placed him as a drop of ?uid in a secure depository, then formed the drop into a clot and formed the clot into a lump and formed the lump into bones and clothed the bones in flesh. Then We have caused it to grow into another creation. Blessed be Allah, the Best of Creators! (23:12-14)

Allah did not deny humans the power to create, but He is the best of creators.

This brings us back to the verse. Our beloved Jesus said, "I have come to you with a sign from your Lord: I will create the shape of a bird for you out of clay, then breathe into it and, with Allah's permission, it will become a real bird." Anyone can make a bird-like figure from clay, but Allah gave Jesus the miracle of blowing life into it. The key phrase in this verse is "with Allah's permission." Jesus, peace be upon him, could not have created except with Allah's permission. Take note that the words "with Allah's permission" came from Jesus' mouth as a confession that he did not possess this ability.

Sadly, over the ages, people forgot these words and started attributing divinity to Jesus. They claimed him a Allah or the son of Allah. We say to anyone with such belief, if you were captivated by Jesus blowing life into a bird of clay, you should have equally been fascinated by Abraham when he butchered four birds into pieces, mangled them, and left parts of them on different mountains. Abraham then called them back to life, and they came rushing to him. He, peace be upon him, did not need to breathe life into them; he merely called them to life. Allah says:

And when Abraham said, "My Lord, show me how You will restore life to the dead!" Allah said, "Why? Do you not believe?" Abraham said, "Yes, but that my heart may be at peace." He said, "Then take four birds of different kinds, and tame them to yourself to know them fully. Then chop them into pieces, mix them, and put on every one of the hills a piece from each. Then summon them, and they will come to you walking in haste. And know that Allah is Almighty and All-Wise." (2:260)

Abraham's miracle is also a grant from Allah. He could not do so by himself, nor could Jesus, peace be upon them all.

Similarly, if you were captivated by the fact that Jesus came into the world without a father, then the creation of Adam and the birth of Eve should have been more fascinating. Adam came to be without a mother and a father, while Eve was created from a male without a female.

As we mentioned previously, the miracle of creation was not inherent to Jesus. In other words, it required Allah's direct permission every single time. Prophet Jesus could not blow life into any object at will; instead, he, peace be upon him, created in a very limited scope. The purpose of such miracle was to prove his message's authenticity so the children of Israel would believe.

The miracles of prophets and messengers prove the existence of a superior and overwhelming power. This power can overrule all laws and tear the fabric of the universe at will. Thus, when people see the effects of such power through miracles, they should develop faith in the message brought to them by the prophets and messengers. Jesus, peace be upon him, was sent to a people who were immersed in materialism. Their hearts were far from spirituality, and they did not believe in the unseen. Thus, it was necessary to present miracles that centred around the unseen —such as life and creation— to turn their hearts and minds back to the Lord.

Verses 50

Wa musaddiqal limaa baina yadaiya minat Tawraati wa liuhilla lakum ba'dal lazee hurrima 'alaikum; wa ji'tukum bi Aayatim mir Rabbikum fattaqul laaha wa atee'oon

"And to confirm that which is before me of the Torah, and to make lawful for you some of the things that were forbidden. I have brought you a sign from your Lord, so be mindful of Allah and obey me." (Verse 50)

Prophet Jesus' new message of Christianity reemphasized the teachings of the Torah. It was identical to the Torah in many aspects, which begs the question of whether there was even a need for his message. More broadly, if the heavenly books confirm one another, what is the benefit of having more than one?

We answer that it is true that Jesus' message confirmed Allah's teachings to Moses and David, but it also introduced some changes, as evident in the second part of the verse: "and to make lawful for you some of the things that were forbidden." Thus, confirmation was not the only purpose.

Second, heavenly books serve as reminders for those who strayed away from the previous messages. And, third, new heavenly books bring provisions that are more suitable for the times. Creed never changes, neither does historical narrations, but some of the rules governing people's movements in life do.

There is always wisdom behind what Allah allows and what He forbids, but His wisdom is not according to what you think. Thus, we caution against assuming that everything Allah forbids is harmful. He may prohibit things for other reasons, such as to discipline people. A believer may live his or her life while never understanding the harm behind what Allah has forbidden. If someone questions, "Why did Allah forbid that?" say, "It is the Lord's wisdom, not mine." Allah says:

So, because of the wrongs committed by the Jews, We made unlawful for them many pure, wholesome things which had been lawful for them, and because of their barring many from Allah's way. (4:160)

And the details are explained in the followed verse:

We forbade for the Jews every animal with claws, and the fat of cattle and sheep, except what is on their backs and in their intestines, or that which sticks to their bones. This is how We penalized them for their disobedience: We are true to Our word. (6:146)

Jesus, son of Mary, was sent to the Children of Israel to bring them ease and mercy, unburden them from previous sins, and "to make lawful for you some of the things that were forbidden."

The verse ends with Jesus' words, "I have brought you a sign from your Lord, so be mindful of Allah and obey me." As a messenger and a human being, Jesus brought Allah's teachings to the Israelites who were mired in materialism and corruption. Thus, Allah armed him with miracles to support His message. Glory be to Him Who caused these marvels to occur on the hands of His servant! Jesus, in turn, ordered his people to fear Allah and to follow his example in implementing Allah's commands, which brings us to the next verse in Al-Imran:

Verse 51

Innal laaha Rabbee wa Rabbukum fa'budooh; haazaa Siraatum Mustaqee

"Indeed, Allah is my Lord and your Lord, so worship Him. That is the straight path." (Verse 51)

Jesus said to the Israelites, "I did not bring the Gospel and perform miracles so I can rule over you. You and I are equal in servitude to the Almighty Allah." Jesus' words, "Indeed, Allah is my Lord and your Lord, so worship Him. That is the straight path," reemphasized to his people that he shared their humanity. He, peace be upon him, had been delivering this message since he was an infant. Allah says:

Mary pointed to him. They said, "How can we talk to one in the cradle, an infant boy?" He said, "I am a servant of Allah. He has granted me the scripture, made me a prophet, and made me blessed wherever I may be. He commanded me to pray and to give alms as long as I live." (19:29-34)

A straight path is the shortest distance between you and your goal. There are no detours, distractions, or crookedness. To stay on track, you have to be mindful of Allah at all times. In other words, you must keep your eye on the prize.

Our beloved Jesus wanted his people always to be mindful of Allah's teachings because they are the best guard against conflicts and desires. Allah's teachings are the short and straight path that leads directly to Him. The further people go from the Lord, the more conflicts arise. That is why Jesus advised, "Indeed, Allah is my Lord and your Lord, so worship Him." This is the summit of all heavenly religions.

Allah's teachings revolve around the commands of "do" and "do not do," but most people find that difficult. Why? Because, on the surface, such orders limit your freedom. The command "do" takes away from your free time and forces you to do something that you may otherwise choose not to do, and the command "do not do" prevents you from doing something you enjoy. There is apparent hardship in both commands.

Thus, religion is a hardship and an assault on personal freedom, right? Not exactly. Sadly, most people look at religion as rituals, and they lose sight of the actual goal. When you take your eye off the prize, you fail to appreciate Allah's teachings. In such cases, it becomes easy for anyone to tempt you away from the path.

Let's look at a student who gets up early every morning to go to school, then comes home and spends hours studying before going to bed again. That is a hard life with very few hours of freedom, right? Before giving this hasty judgment, we should ask, what is the goal of this student? It is to graduate with a respectable degree, enter a good profession, and live comfortably, enjoying decades of financial freedom. Now let's analyze the student's behavior based on this defined goal. Does waking up early in the morning bring him closer to his destination or away from it? How about studying for hours every day? Every action that brings him closer to becoming a highly paid professional is good, while activities like watching TV for hours or sleeping till noon are not.

This brings us back to religion. Your goal is to live in Allah's company, enjoying the eternal pleasures of paradise, right? Now, every action you take can be evaluated through the prism of this goal. If the action brings you closer, then it is good; likewise, every step that takes you away from your goal is a waste. By allowing you to reach your destination, religion is not a burden; it is eternal freedom.

Unfortunately, people often have different goals. They want money, fame, and instant gratification. Many chase after partners of the opposite sex and maximize pleasure through eating and drinking. For people with such goals, religion is a burden as it distracts them from their desires, so they often abandon it altogether. As long as people chase after goals different from the one Allah set for them, there will be turmoil and conflict in life. Allah says:

The life of this world is merely an amusement and a diversion; the true life is in the Hereafter, if only they knew. (29:64)

If your true goal is to be in Allah's company in paradise, then you should use that lens to evaluate all of life's events, even death. Should we grieve when a loved one dies? Yes, we are sad because we feel lonely and miss their company, but we are also happy because they moved closer to the ultimate goal. Genuine grief should only be over the person who wasted their life and missed the target altogether.

"Indeed, Allah is my Lord and your Lord, so worship Him. That is the straight path."

Verse 51)

The message of Jesus, peace be upon him, is the same eternal heavenly message of all the prophets and messengers:

"Indeed, Allah is my Lord and your Lord, so worship Him. That is the straight path." (3:51)

When you hear the phrase "the straight path," you immediately imagine one long road leading to your destination. No road exists for its own sake; it always leads to a destination. Allah's path is no different; it leads to eternal paradise in the Hereafter. He says:

This is My straight path, so follow it. And do not follow other paths, lest they scatter you from His path. This He has enjoined upon you, that you keep from disobedience to Him in reverence for Him and piety to deserve His protection. (6:153)

Thus, Jesus, peace be upon him, made it clear to his people which path to follow: "Indeed, Allah is my Lord and your Lord, so worship Him. That is the straight path."

By definition, "to worship" means to obey Allah's commands and avoid His prohibitions. Hence, when Allah says, "do," then I must do, and when He says, "do not do," then I must refrain. But worship is not limited to Islam's established pillars such as prayer, Zakat almsgiving, and fasting the month of Ramadan. These are the foundation on which

Islam is built, but a foundation without a building is meaningless. For example, it is not appropriate for you to dissociate yourself from Allah between the Maghrib sunset prayer and the Isha night prayer. The pillars of Islam are meant to recharge your faith and give you the energy to act righteously at all times. Worship encompasses every aspect of life because Allah wants a universe built by faith, not a few minutes of prayers. He says:

> O you who believe, when the call to prayer is made on the day of congregation, hasten to remember Allah, putting aside your trade—that is better for you, if only you knew. Then, when the prayer is finished, disperse in the land and seek out Allah's bounty. Remember Allah often so that you may prosper. (62:9-10)

Allah did not only order you to pray your Friday congregation prayers, but He also ordered you to go out and earn a living after the prayer is done. Both are acts of worship. He does not want you to be so involved in your trade and worldly affairs that you are late or forget your prayers. Likewise, Allah does not want you to spend all your time in the mosque and ignore your family's needs. Islam brings balance to your life. The ritual of Friday prayers is meant to connect you with Allah and charge your faith with the necessary energy to run your trade ethically for the rest of the week.

Take note that Allah chose "trade," not agriculture or manufacturing, because it is the moment a merchant, farmer, or industrialist collects profit. Selling is the ultimate goal of all businesses. The farmer can easily leave the land to pray because crops take months to mature. So, when Allah orders you to leave trade, then leaving other professions is implied. A buyer may buy out of necessity, but the seller is always happy to sell.

In fact, you can turn every action of your day into worship by obeying Allah's command "when the prayer is finished, disperse in the land and seek out Allah's bounty." If all Muslims obeyed their Lord's commands both in prayers and at work, the entire society would be prosperous. And this is how we understand the verse narrating the words of our beloved Jesus: "Indeed, Allah is my Lord and your Lord, so worship Him. That is the straight path." He, peace be upon him, called on his people to be mindful of Allah in all aspects of their lives. Sadly, the call to Allah did not go well with the Israelites. Allah says in the next verse of Al-Imran:

Verse 52

Falammaaa ahassa 'Eesaa minhumul kufra qaala man ansaaree ilal laahi qaalal Hawaariyyoona nahnu ansaarul laahi aamannaa billaahi washhad bi annaa muslimoon

And when Jesus sensed their faithlessness, he said, "Who will be my supporters toward Allah?" The Disciples said, "We will be supporters of Allah. We believe in Allah, so be our witness that we submit to Him."(Verse 52)

The phrase "when Jesus sensed their faithlessness" gives us a valuable lesson in leadership. Every person with a mission must be vigilant to the actions of those around him or her. This is especially true in matters of faith because faith is the salvation that brings people out of darkness and into the light.

Here you may wonder: why do people, even when in the presence of a messenger from Allah, choose darkness over light? We answer that many people gather power and riches by way of corruption and oppressing others. Thus, the call to faith and justice threatens their way of life. Such people detest the words of logic and often hate both the message and the bearer of that message.

Our beloved Jesus knew that the society of the Israelites was rife with corruption. While the oppressed were guided and comforted by his words, there were many others whom he angered. Jesus had to be vigilant, so he could spot those who plotted against Allah's message. Thus when he sensed that the supporters of injustice and transgression did not appreciate him, he wanted to assemble a sincere and faithful group to help him on Allah's path. He asked, "Who will be my supporters toward Allah?"

Prophet Jesus' mission was to deliver Allah's message to the Israelites. The heavens usually intervene with a new message only when the society is mired in corruption. The Israelites at the time of Jesus were no exception. Many of them had abandoned the Torah and enriched themselves by transgressing over the weak and the poor. Naturally, those were the same people who viciously opposed Jesus' message.

Thus, the call to faith necessitates a battle and requires sacrificing the precious, whether in wealth or life. From the moment Jesus began preaching, he was alert to those who were displeased with the call to justice. Often the signs of displeasure are subtle and have to be spotted by an acute observer.

He, peace be upon him, wanted to bring together a group of the faithful who could carry the torch of Allah's message. Jesus did not call specific individuals by name; instead, he called for supporters who were ready to sacrifice for Allah's cause. Allah says, "And when Jesus sensed their faithlessness, he said, 'Who will be my supporters toward Allah?'"

Take note of the accuracy of Jesus' call when he specified, "Who will be my supporters toward Allah?" making the goal very clear. In other words, he asked for help in reaching Allah while leaving the whims of this world behind. The goal was not victory, money, or status: it was Allah and Allah alone.

We find a similar example in what happened between our beloved Prophet Muhammad and the men of Medina during their pledge of allegiance in Aqaba. The Messenger, peace be upon him, asked, "Would you pledge to defend me from whatever you defend your own families from?" The companion Ibin Ma'rur held the Prophet's hand and said, "Yes, we swear by Allah Who sent you as a Prophet of the truth that we will defend you as we defend our own families." Then Abu Haitham interrupted, "O Messenger of Allah! Between the Jews of Medina and us, there are agreements which we would have to sever. If Allah grants you power and victory, should we expect that you leave us and return to your people of Quraish?" The Prophet smiled, "No, Abu Haitham, that will never be. Your blood is my blood. In life and death, I will be with you, and you with me. I will fight whom you fight, and I will make peace with those whom you make peace with."

Prophet Muhammad did not promise the companions victory, riches, or vast lands; rather, he said, "I am one of you, and you are of me." Why? Because Allah wants faith in the Hereafter, not greed in this world. Had Prophet Muhammad promised them the spoils of their enemies, then what about a companion who dies before that happens? All the believers needed to know was that the Messenger of Allah was one of them and that they were of him. As such, they will enter paradise with him, which is the ultimate goal. Likewise, when Jesus, peace be upon him, asked, "Who will be my supporters toward Allah?" he made the goal very clear: meeting Allah in paradise.

The word "supporter" is translated from the Arabic origin نصير (Naseer), which is the person who lends aids, effort, and power. Let's learn more about aid and victory from the Quran. Allah says:

You who believe! If you help Allah, He will help you and make you stand firm. (47:7)

We are Allah's supporters when we follow His teachings, and Allah is our supporter against our enemies. Prophet Jesus' call "Who will be my supporters toward Allah?" covers both meanings. It is as if Jesus said, "Support me in implementing Allah's teachings in this corrupt society, and Allah will support you against your enemies. Allah has placed the key to paradise in your hands: if you fulfill your promise to Him, He will fulfill His promise to you. But you have to take the first step."

The Disciples said, "We will be supporters of Allah. We believe in Allah, so be our witness that we submit to Him." The word "disciples" is translated from the Arabic origin الحواريون (Al-Hawariyoun), derived from الحور (Al-Hour), which means "the bright" or "the intensely white." That was the description of those whose faces shined of faith as if they were illuminated by light. It did not refer to fair complexion or the color of their skin. To this day, we use the common expression, "When he walks in, he lights up the room." The believer's pure soul reflects light on his or her face. Allah says:

Prophet Muhammad is the Messenger of Allah. Those who follow him are harsh towards the disbelievers and compassionate towards each other. You see them kneeling and prostrating, seeking Allah's bounty and His good pleasure: on their faces, they bear the marks of their prostrations. This is how they are pictured in the Torah and the Gospel: like a seed that puts forth its shoot, becomes strong, grows thick, and rises on its stem to the delight of its sowers. So Allah infuriates the disbelievers through them; Allah promises forgiveness and a great reward to those who believe and do righteous deeds. (48:29)

When all the human organs, senses, and emotions are at peace with Allah, the face reflects tranquillity and serenity. The Disciples of our beloved Jesus were pure in faith and in harmony with Allah's creation, and their faces showed it. They also had clean white deeds not tainted with corruption.

Many actions in life require faith in the outcome because, without faith, people lose their way. But what is faith? Simply put, it is the heart's contentment with an issue. For example, if a traveller from Damascus to Baghdad did not believe that he was on the right road, he would stop and ask for directions. Likewise, if a student did not have faith that studying would give her a better life, she would quit school. Countless matters in this world are built on faith.

The summit of faith is faith in Allah. It is the unshakable belief of the heart that Allah takes care of those who follow His teachings. And when the heart believes, the rest of the body follows. That is why the Disciples said, "We will be supporters of Allah. We believe in Allah, so be our witness that we submit to Him."

Here you may ask, why did the Disciples ask Jesus to testify to their faith? We answer that the messenger must convey Allah's message to the people on the one hand and make sure that the believers implement them correctly on the other. Allah says:

Strive in Allah's cause and purely for His sake in a manner worthy of that striving. He has chosen you and has not laid any hardship on you in the religion. This is the way of your father, Abraham. He named you Muslims previously and in this Book, so that the Messenger may be a witness for you and that you may be witnesses for people. So establish the prayer in conformity with its conditions, pay the prescribed purifying alms, and hold fast to Allah. He is your Owner and Guardian. How excellent a Guardian and an Owner He is, how excellent a Helper. (22:78)

Verse 53

Rabbanaaa aamannaa bimaaa anzalta wattaba'nar
Rasoola faktubnaa ma'ash shaahideen

"Our Lord! We believe in what You have sent down, and we follow the Messenger, so write us down among the witnesses." (Verse 53)

The disciples declared their faith to Prophet Jesus. But was that faith in the legislations of the previous heavenly messages? Did they mean faith in the Torah? No: the disciples were referring to the teachings of Christianity. Every messenger brings something new from Allah to renew people's faith and introduce new legislation appropriate for the times. The Quran relays to us the words of our beloved Jesus:

"And to confirm that which is before me of the Torah, and to make lawful for you some of the things that were forbidden. I have brought you a sign from your Lord, so be mindful of Allah and obey me." (3:50)

Creed never changes from one heavenly message to another. The narrated incidents of history do not change either. Allah says:

In matters of faith, He has laid down for you the same commandment that He gave Noah, which We have revealed to you and which We enjoined on Abraham and Moses and Jesus: "Uphold the faith and do not divide into factions within it." What you call upon the idolaters to do is hard for them; Allah chooses whomever He pleases for Himself and guides towards Himself those who turn to Him. (42:13)

Thus, the Disciples' words are a declaration of faith both in the creed -which was ever-present before Jesus- and in the new teachings of Christianity.

The Disciples' words, "We believe in what You have sent down," accurately describe that their faith was in a system of governance handed from above, rather than a man-made one. We do not submit to our equal but to our Lord, who created and provided for us. Their words were an affirmation of Prophet Jesus' message:

"Indeed, Allah is my Lord and your Lord, so worship Him. That is the straight path." (3:51)

We only submit to the Lord –the Most High– who created and provided for us. This theme is consistent throughout the Quran. Listen to the following invitation from Allah:

And when it was said to them, "Come to what Allah descended and to the Messenger," they said, "Enough for us what we found our fathers on." Even if their fathers were not knowing a thing nor being guided! (5:104)

The word "come" is translated from the Arabic origin تَعَالَوْا (Ta'alou), derived from the root على (Ala), which means above. The name "Ali," which we are familiar with, shares that same root and means "the high" or "elevated one." Thus, a more proper translation for تَعَالَوْا (Ta'alou) is not "come" but "rise." Allah is inviting you to rise, but towards what? We answer that you are invited to rise above all worldly legislations because they are often short-sighted and rife with corruption. Allah is asking you to rise towards the legislation set by Him, Your Creator. The divine teachings give humanity freedom, equality, and a path to paradise. Thus, the Disciples' words, "Our Lord! We believe in what You have sent down," were accurate.

They continued, "and we follow the Messenger." A faithful follower is someone who has aligned values, not someone who is coerced. To "follow" means to have a free will of the heart. A tyrant can hold a whip and subdue the weak to walk with him. He or she can subjugate the body but can never control the heart. Allah says:

Perhaps you will consume yourself away with anxiety because they do not become believers. If We had wished, We could have sent them down a sign from heaven, at which their necks would stay bowed in utter humility. (26:3-4)

Allah, the All-Merciful, consoles His messenger that none can escape His power. Had He willed, He could have made every human a believer by force. But Allah does not want bowed heads but loving hearts that come to Him voluntarily choosing devotion while capable of rejecting it. This is the true power of faith.

Prophet Jesus asked, "Who will be my supporters toward Allah?" and the Disciples said out of conviction, "We will be supporters of Allah. We believe in Allah, so be our witness that we submit to Him." They continued, "Our Lord! We believe in what You have sent down, and we follow the Messenger, so write us down among the witnesses," testifying that Jesus delivered Allah's message. They also chose to bear the duty of conveying that message to the people and asked the messenger to bear witness to their faith and actions.

We, the followers of our beloved Prophet Muhammad, have been entrusted to uphold and deliver Allah's teachings to the people till the last hour. He, peace be upon him, will be a witness to our actions before Allah. Allah says:

Strive in Allah's cause and purely for His sake in a manner worthy of that striving. He has chosen you and has not laid any hardship on you in the religion. This is the way of your father, Abraham. He named you Muslims previously and in this Book, so that the Messenger may be a witness for you and that you may be witnesses for people. So establish the prayer in conformity with its conditions, pay the prescribed purifying alms, and hold fast to Allah. He is your Owner and Guardian. How excellent a Guardian and an Owner He is, how excellent a Helper. (22:78)

Allah entrusted the nation of Muhammad to carry on the message after him. Thus, no prophets or messengers will come after our beloved Prophet, peace be upon him.

ADDITIONAL INFORMATION

ISLAM AND CHRISTIANITY

There are many similarities between Islam and Christianity. In fact, it is easy to think that there are more similarities than differences.

Both Islam and Christianity encourage their followers to dress and behave modestly, and both believe that being charitable and showing compassion are desirable qualities in a human being. They both place emphasis on prayer and communication with God, both call on people to be kind and generous, and both counsel treating others the way you would expect to be treated. The two religions expect their followers to be truthful, stay away from major sins and ask for forgiveness. And both religions respect and love Jesus and expect him to return to earth as part of their end of days narratives.

Members of both religions would have us believe that they are poles of apart but their histories begin in exactly the same place, in the Garden with Adam and Eve. It is in the life of Prophet Abraham that their paths begin to diverge and as if to add emphasis to their mutual beginning Islam and Christianity along with Judaism are known collectively as the Abrahamic faiths.

The Prophets

According to the Quran, Abraham was known as the beloved servant of God; because of his deep devotion, God made many of his descendants Prophets to their own people. The story of Prophet Abraham being commanded to sacrifice his son is known in both Christianity and Islam. In Islam, that son is Ishmael and it was through his lineage that Islam was established through Prophet Muhammad, may the mercy and blessings of God be upon him. In Christianity, the son in the sacrifice narrative is Isaac. Through the line of Isaac come many Prophets including Jacob, Joseph, Moses, David, Solomon and Jesus.

One of Islam's six pillars of faith requires that a Muslim believes in *all* of the Prophets. To reject one is to reject them all. Muslims believe that God sent many Prophets, one to every nation. Some we know by name and others we do not. Prophet Muhammad is known to have said that all the Prophets are brothers to one another. Thus you will find that all the Prophets mentioned in the Bible are respected and acknowledged by Islam. Many of them are mentioned by name in the Quran with detailed life stories. Islam treats all Prophet with respect and rejects the stories in the Bible that ridicule and tarnish some of the Prophets.

Christianity acknowledges that Prophet Muhammad existed but does not endow him with Prophethood. Throughout Christian history he has been called a liar and a lunatic; some people even associated him with the devil. On the other hand, Islam considers Prophet Muhammad to be a mercy from God to humankind. As far as Jesus is concerned Christians and Muslims have many similar beliefs. Both believe that his mother Mary was a virgin when she gave birth to him. Both religions believe that Jesus was the Messiah sent to the people of Israel and both believe that he performed miracles. Islam however says that such miracles were performed by the will and permission of God. Islam calls Prophet Jesus the slave and messenger of God and he is held in great esteem as one man in a long line of Prophets and Messengers all calling the people to worship One God. Islam rejects completely the notion that Jesus is God or is part of the Trinity.

The Trinity

The Trinity is the core belief of Christianity that says that there is One God who has three manifestations, the Father, the Son and the Holy Spirit. God has a son called Jesus who is also God and it is through Jesus that a person can reach the Father. The Holy Spirit, also God, is the divine force, that mysterious force responsible for faith. The Trinity is sometimes depicted as the wings of a dove or tongues of fire. It is a controversial doctrine that came about as an attempt to reconcile the teaching of the Bible and the early Christian church. Disputes over the nature of Jesus lead to the Roman emperor Constantine convening the Council of Nicaea in CE 325. And it was the doctrine of the Trinity that caused the split between the eastern and western churches. Even today many people are unable to understand or explain the doctrine that they profess.

Believing themselves to be monotheistic is something common to both Islam and Christianity. Monotheism is a word derived from the Greek words 'monos' meaning only and 'theos' meaning god. It is used to define a Supreme Being who is all-powerful, the Creator and Sustainer of the universe, the One responsible for life and death. Muslims however believe that they practice pure monotheism unadulterated by concepts such as the Trinity. The core belief of Islam is that there is no god worthy of worship but God; it is a simple concept in which worship is directed to God Alone.

The Scriptures

Muslims derive their understanding of the nature of God from the Quran and the authentic traditions of Prophet Muhammad. The Quran explains that all the divine books of Christianity, the Old Testament, including the book of Psalms, and the New Testament containing the Gospels of Jesus were revealed by God. Therefore, Muslims believe in the Bible when it does not differ from the Quran. Muslims believe only what has been confirmed in the Quran and the traditions of Prophet Muhammad because Islam says that much of the original text of both the Old and New testaments has been lost, altered, distorted or forgotten.

Muslims believe the Quran to be the last revealed text and the exact words of God brought down to Prophet Muhammad through the agency of Angel Gabriel. Christianity however believes that the Bible was inspired by God and written by a number of different authors.

"They schemed, and Allah also schemed. Allah is the best of schemers."

This verse is talking about the Jews who were plotting against Prophet Isa. They were the schemers and they schemed against him in the most terrible way. They were wicked and relentless.

What did they do?

They made all sorts of accusations against him and against his mother, the pure. They also accused Prophet Isa, may the blessings of Allah be upon him, of lying and taking advantage of people. They reported him to Pontius Pilate, the Roman Governor, describing him as an agitator who stirred up the masses and encouraged rioting and rebellion. They further accused him of being an impostor who tried to corrupt the faith of the masses.

They continued with this line of false accusations until Pilate granted them their request of punishing him themselves as they saw fit. Pilate, a pagan ruler, dared not take upon himself the responsibility of punishing a man whom he could not condemn on the basis of any real evidence. These are only a few examples of the endless scheming by the Jews.

"They schemed, and Allah also schemed. Allah is the best of schemers."

Here the verse is telling us that Allah swt is the "best of schemers".

What does this mean?

It means that no matter what the Jews were plotting Allah swt will protect Prophet Isa, may the blessings of Allah be upon him.

Their scheming will have to be set against what Allah schemes. How can their scheming be compared to what Allah plans? Indeed, how can their power be compared to Allah's might?

They wanted to crucify and kill Prophet Isa, may the blessings of Allah be upon him. Allah, on the other hand, willed to gather him and cause him to ascend to Himself. He further willed to purify and cleanse him from mixing with the unbelievers and remaining with them. Such a purification is necessary since all unbelievers are impure. It was also the will of Allah to elevate the followers of Prophet Isa, may the blessings of Allah be upon him, above the unbelievers until the Day of Resurrection. What Allah willed came true, and the scheming of the Jews was of no consequence whatsoever:

Allah tells us in the following Verse, Verse 55:

Verse 55

Iz qaalal laahu yaa 'Eesaaa innee mutawaffeeka wa raafi'uka ilaiya wa mutah hiruka minal lazeena kafaroo wa jaa'ilul lazeenattaba ooka fawqal lazeena kafarooo ilaa Yawmil Qiyaamati summa ilaiya marji'ukum fa ahkumu bainakum feemaa kuntum feehi takhtaliifoon

"Allah said: 'Prophet Isa, may the blessings of Allah be upon him, I shall gather you and cause you to ascend to Me, and I shall cleanse you of those who disbelieve, and I shall place those who follow you above those who disbelieve until the Day of Resurrection.'" (Verse 55)

How Prophet Isa, may the blessings of Allah be upon him was gathered and how he ascended to Allah are matters which lie beyond our human perception. They are unknown except to Allah. To try to pursue these matters is of no use whatsoever in respect of faith or its implementation. Those who pursue them will inevitably end up more confused, struggling with complicated and endless arguments, gaining no certainty or satisfaction whatsoever. For the whole matter is part of Allah's own knowledge.

It is not difficult, on the other hand, to explain Allah's statement that He has placed those who follow Prophet Isa above the unbelievers, and that this elevation continues until the Day of Resurrection. Those who follow Prophet Isa, may the blessings of Allah be upon him, are the ones who believe in Allah's true religion, Islam, or surrender to Allah. Every Prophet is fully aware of the true nature of this religion. Every messenger preached the same religion and everyone who truly believes in the Divine faith believes in it. These believers are indeed far superior to the unbelievers, according to Allah's measure, and they will continue to be so until the Day of Judgement. Moreover, they prove their superiority in our practical life every time they confront the forces of un-faith with the true nature of faith and the reality of following Allah's messengers. The Divine faith is one, preached by Prophet Isa, son of Mary, as preached by every messenger sent before him and by the messenger sent after him. Those who follow Prophet Muhammad (pbuh) at the same time follow all the messengers sent by Allah, starting with Adam until the last messenger.

This comprehensive outlook conforms to the theme of the surah and its presentation. It is also in conformity with the essence of faith.

Verses 56

Fa ammal lazeena kafaroo fa u'az zibuhum 'azaaban shadeedan fiddunyaa wal Aakhirati wa maa lahum min naasireen

As for those who disbelieved, I will punish them with a severe punishment in this world and the Hereafter, and they will have no helpers. As for those who believe and do good, righteous deeds, He will pay their rewards in full. Allah does not love the unjust. (Verses 56)

Verse 57

Wa ammal lazeena aamanoo wa 'amilus saalihaati fa yuwaffeehim ujoorahum; wallaahu laa yuhibbuz zaalimeen

As to those who believe and work righteousness, Allah will pay them (in full) their reward; but Allah loveth not those who do wrong

In verse 55 of Al Imran, Allah liberated His Messenger Prophet Isa from those plotting to kill him, then He promised all parties, "You will all return to Me, and I will judge between you regarding your differences." The verb "judge" indicates that there are disagreements, truth, and falsehoods. The wrongdoers may have power on earth because Allah granted them freedom of choice, but there will come a time when all their authority will be abolished. Allah says:

The Day when they will come forth, with nothing of them being hidden from Allah. To Whom belongs absolute sovereignty today? It is to Allah, the One, the Overwhelming. (40:16)

And in another chapter:

When those who have been followed disown their followers, when they all see the suffering, when all bonds between them disintegrate, the followers will say, "If only we had one last chance, we would disown them as they now disown us." In this way, Allah will make them see their deeds as a source of bitter regret: they shall not leave the Fire. (2:166-167)

A leader who misled others will come on the Day of Resurrection to find him or herself alone and disowned. Their followers will ask Allah for one more chance to return to earthly life to exact revenge on those who deceived them. This is how relations will break down between humans on the Day of Judgement.

A similar case happens within each human! Your body parts –in essence, your followers in earthly life– will disown you for the evil deeds you did. Your tongue, legs, and hands will testify against you if you abused your authority over them. Allah granted you freedom of choice and control over your body, but He will take away this sovereignty on the Day of Judgement. He says:

On that Day We shall seal up their mouths, but their hands will speak to Us, and their feet bear witness to everything they have done. (36:65)

On the Day of Resurrection there is no oppression, compulsion, or subjugation because the entire dominion belongs to Allah alone. People will testify freely, and so will their tongues and skins. Allah says, "You will all return to Me, and I will judge between you regarding your differences."

The fruit of Allah's judgment is compensation for one's actions in life. He says:

As for those who disbelieved, I will punish them with a severe punishment in this world and the Hereafter, and they will have no helpers. As for those who believe and do good, righteous deeds, He will pay their rewards in full. Allah does not love the unjust.

(Verses 56 & 57)

These two verses are interesting because Allah started with the disbelievers first and then mentioned the believers in the second verse. Why? Because the believers already know these facts and trust the Lord's judgment. It is part of their faith.

Another interesting fact is that when Allah addresses the disbelievers, He mentions punishment both in this world and the Hereafter. This is because some people think that the Hereafter is far off, while others do not believe in it at all. If Allah's punishment was limited to the Hereafter, then such people would spread evil on the earth as they see no consequence for their actions. An individual who has no faith in the Hereafter behaves accordingly and often causes suffering to those around them. Thus, Allah hastens some punishment so people would think twice before acting unjustly. But do not think that Allah's punishment in this world absolves them from the penalty in the Hereafter. It is a mere taste for what is to come. Allah says:

But whoever disregards My remembrance, he shall have life of hardship and, on the Day of Resurrection, We shall raise him blind. (20:124)

Some of the righteous people used to supplicate, "Dear Allah, the unjust people see Your Hereafter as being far-off, and Your patience has deluded them, so take them to task as only the Almighty Who controls all things can!"

Here, I would like to remind you that when you hear a phrase such as "I will punish them with a severe punishment," you should realize that the action is proportional to the doer. For example, if I tell you that my two-year-old son is angry and is coming to hit you would make you feel one way. But if I tell you that the world heavyweight champion boxer is mad and coming to punch you, you would feel quite differently. Similarly, if the one threatening severe punishment is Allah Almighty, you should expect a punishment befitting His limitless power. It will be unimaginable suffering. And, since Allah is the only One with the power on that Day, the residents of Hellfire will have no helpers.

Likewise, the pleasures and rewards of Paradise are proportional to Allah's limitless power and mercy. He says, in contrast to the previous verse:

As for those who believe and do good, righteous deeds, He will pay their rewards in full. Allah does not love the unjust. (Verse 57)

Verse 58

Zaalika natloohu 'alaika minal Aayaati wa Zikril Hakeem

That is what We recite to you, these verses, a reminder full of wisdom. (Verse 58)

The phrase "That is" refers to the preceding verses narrating the stories of the wife of Imran, the Virgin Mary, and Prophets Zechariah, John, and Prophet Isa. Each of them experienced wondrous signs from Allah that shattered the physical laws of the universe. The stories in the Quran are narrated by Allah, so they are free from falsehood and are precisely as experienced by the people who lived at the time.

Perhaps the most important story is that of our beloved Prophet Isa, peace be upon him, and we must lend a great deal of attention to it. We should take the time to weigh the evidence and consider the opinion of those who gave Prophet Isa his due right and those who assigned him a status opposite to what Allah commanded. This study aims not to claim victory over a group or religion, nor to say that Muslims are better and other groups are wrong. The matter is far more serious because it has severe consequences in the Hereafter that would land a person eternally, either in Paradise or Hellfire. Hence, we must filter each argument with reason, not biases and fanaticism, until the truth becomes clear.

Prophet Isa, peace be upon him, was sent to the Children of Israel. Judaism, at the time, had been distorted and heavily tilted towards materialism, with almost complete disregard for spiritual matters and the unseen. This obsessive materialism culminated in what they asked Moses, peace be upon him, as the following verse illustrates:

Remember when you said, "Moses, we will not believe you until we see Allah face to face." At that, thunderbolts struck you as you looked on. (2:55)

The Jews who accompanied Moses failed to recognize that a great deal of Allah's perfection and majesty is to be unseen. Had Allah been seen by humans, He would have been limited and enclosed. It would mean that the Almighty exists in one place, so He is absent from others. Allah is free from such descriptions because He is omnipresent in all places at all times. We do not see Him with the eye, but we see the effects of His presence and the majesty of His work throughout the universe. Thus, Allah is unseen because this is an essential part of His grandeur and perfection.

But the Jews of the time perceived all things as strictly tangible. This was made especially clear when it came to their food and provisions. While they wandered in the desert, Allah sent them their daily provisions in the form of manna and quail. Manna is a sweet exudate that appears on tree leaves at daybreak. It can still be found today in some regions of Iraq. The wandering Israelites used to collect this delicious dessert in the early morning by spreading white sheets under desert plants. The quail is a type of fatty bird that approached them and landed in flocks making it an easy catch. Allah sent both foods daily, providing the Israelites with great nourishment that did not require any work. It was a provision from the unseen, and that is exactly what made the Israelites uncomfortable and caused them to reject Allah's rations as narrated in the following verse:

Remember when you said, "Moses, we cannot bear to eat only one kind of food, so pray to your Lord to bring out for us some of the earth's produce, its herbs and cucumbers, its garlic, lentils, and onions." He said, "Would you exchange better for worse? Go to Egypt, and there you will find what you have asked for." They were struck with humiliation and wretchedness, and they incurred the wrath of Allah because they persistently rejected His messages and killed prophets, contrary to all that is right. All this was because they disobeyed and were lawbreakers. (2:61)

The Israelites wanted foods to sow with their hands and watch grow every day, even if it meant exchanging quails for onions. They doubted the provision of the unseen and said, "Who knows, maybe the manna would not appear tomorrow, and the quail flocks would stop coming." They had little faith in Allah, and wanted to handle all their affairs with pure materialism.

Such people, who were immersed in materialism and tangible gains and whose hearts were far from spirituality, needed a violent jolt to shake their belief system and bring them back to Allah.

Prophet Prophet Isa was the answer: a messenger whose entire life revolved around the unseen. His birth, death, and miracles were all matters of the unseen. He was born of a virgin woman without a father. His miracles were centered on healing the sick without physical treatment and raising the dead back to life. But, over time, the followers of Christ started to claim him as Allah or the son of Allah, and point to his birth and miracles as proof.

So, today we look into each argument of the Christians and weigh the evidence.

The first argument is that Prophet Isa is the son of Allah because he was born of a virgin mother. More specifically, since the masculine human element was absent and since Allah breathed the spirit into Mary, this implies that Allah is the father and Prophet Isa the son.

We answer that, if this were the case, then the creation of Adam would be more worthy of consideration than that of Prophet Isa, peace be upon them. Motherhood existed in the creation of Prophet Isa, but neither motherhood nor fatherhood existed for Adam. Thus, for those making a case for divinity, the creation of Adam is more substantial. Allah says:

Verily, the case of Prophet Isa in the sight of Allah is as the case of Adam. He fashioned him out of dust, then He said to him, "Be," and he came to be. (3:59)

But there is more to the Christian argument, specifically the claim that Allah is the father because He breathed His spirit into the Virgin Mary. To that, we answer that you must acquaint yourself with the following about Adam. Allah says,

Your Lord said to the angels, "I will create a mortal out of dried clay, formed from dark mud. When I have fashioned him in due proportions and breathed into him out of My Spirit, then fall down prostrating before him." (15:28-29)

Since the same conditions were present for Prophet Isa and Adam, why would you keep silent about Adam and only assign fatherhood to the advent of Prophet Isa?

The second Christian argument is as follows: Prophet Isa healed the sick, raised the dead, and breathed life into objects, and that is the realm of Allah. Here, we also bring forth the stories of other messengers of Allah, namely Abraham and Moses. First, let's consider the story of our beloved Abraham. Allah says:

And when Abraham said, "My Lord, show me how You give life to the dead," He said, "Do you not believe, then?" "Yes," said Abraham, "but just to put my heart at rest." So Allah said, "Take four birds and train them to come back to you. Then place them on separate hilltops, call them back, and they will come to you in haste: know that Allah is all-powerful and wise." (2:260)

Abraham, peace be upon him, did not need to breathe life into the birds; he merely called them back to life. On the other hand, Moses' miracle gave life to a wooden staff. Not only was this inanimate object given life, but it was also transformed from a dead plant to a live reptile, crossing species lines.

Thus, the miracles of Prophet Isa, peace be upon him, are not grounds to attribute divinity to him. Otherwise, we would have to include Abraham and Moses. Rather, Allah grants His messengers miracles that shatter the physical fabric of the universe to show people proof that these men are carrying a divine message from the Almighty. All such wonders only happen with a grant and permission from Allah. The miracles of Prophet Isa, Moses and Abraham should lead us to the path of Allah, not away from Him.

Now, let's move to the third argument. Our fellow Christians agree with us that Allah Almighty is unseen. However, they differ and say that Allah wanted humanity to be familiar with an image of Him, and Prophet Isa is the comforting image of Allah on earth.

To address this argument, we ask: which stage of Prophet Isa' life represents Allah's image? In other words, is the image of Prophet Isa as a baby supposed to represent Allah? Or was it his image during his teen or adult years? Also, if all these images represent Allah, then this means that Allah is subject to change and the effects of time.

Allah is the ever-present, ever-constant that does not change. Neither place nor time affect the Almighty. He has one image that we do not see or know. He says in the 11th verse of chapter 42:

There is nothing whatever like Him.

The second half of this argument states that Allah's descent to earth in Prophet Isa' form was to familiarize people with Him and ease any feelings of estrangement between people and their Creator. But Prophet Isa lived for just over thirty years. Was that the entire period of familiarizing people with the divine image? What about the generations who lived thousands of years before Prophet Isa or thousands of years after? Were they not worthy of knowing their Lord? This is a perception of an unjust God, and the Almighty is free from injustice. God is generous, and He would not make His image available for only thirty years.

Since the beginnings of humanity, Allah sent to each nation a prophet to show them the path to their Creator. He supported His prophet, from Adam to Noah, Lot, Isa, Muhammad, and countless others, with miracles to prove the authenticity of their message. Allah is the all-giving Lord Who treats humanity with love and justice.

The last argument is that of the crucifixion. It is an understandable argument. In fact, Allah has excused those who think that Prophet Isa was crucified in the Quran. He says:

And for their saying, "We killed the Messiah, Prophet Isa son of Mary, the Messenger of Allah," – whereas they did not kill him, nor did they crucify him, but so it was made to appear to them. Indeed those who differ concerning him are surely in doubt about him: they do not have any knowledge of that beyond following conjectures, and certainly they did not kill him. (4:157)

Christian scholars still argue about the actual events of that day. Allah excused those who said Prophet Isa was crucified because it appeared to be the case during the chaos of that time. A man who resembled Prophet Isa was captured and crucified. It would have been reasonable for them to seek clarification from future heavenly revelations, namely, Islam and the Quran.

Moreover, murder and crucifixion contradict the idea of Prophet Isa being a God or the son of God. Undoubtedly, the divine has the power to overcome His enemies and protect Himself or His son from harm. How could mere mortals overcome their Creator?

The second half of this argument states that Prophet Isa sacrificed himself to absolve humanity of its sins. But what about the generations who lived thousands of years before Prophet Isa? Were they not worthy of having their sins forgiven? Allah is fair, and such a claim is far from justice.

Islam has truly honoured Prophet Isa, peace be upon him, by explaining that he was not crucified; instead, he was saved by Allah and raised to the heavens. Just as the message of Christianity came to purify the corruption and materialism that crept into Judaism, the message of Islam came to purify the distortions of polytheism that crept into Christianity. Allah says in the 143rd verse of Chapter 2:

And thus, We have made you a middle nation that you will be witnesses over the people, and the Messenger will be a witness over you.

People are often much attached to their beliefs, and sometimes that makes arguments of reason unfruitful. In the next session, we learn how our beloved Muhammad dealt with situations when disputes between him and Christian scholars hit an impasse.

Verses 59, 60 & 61

Inna masala 'Eesaa 'indal laahi kamasali Aadama khalaqahoo min turaabin summa qaala lahoo kun fayakoon

Alhaqqu mir Rabbika falaa takum minal mumtareen

Faman haaajjaka feehi mim ba'di maa jaaa'aka minal 'ilmi faqul ta'aalaw nad'u abnaaa'anaa wa abnaaa'akum wa nisaaa'anaa wa nisaaa'akum wa anfusanaa wa anfusakum summa nabtahil fanaj'al la'natal laahi 'alal kaazibeen

The similitude of Jesus before Allah is as that of Adam; He created him from dust, then said to him: "Be". And he was.

The Truth (comes) from Allah alone; so be not of those who doubt.

If any one disputes in this matter with thee, now after (full) knowledge Hath come to thee, say: "Come! let us gather together,- our sons and your sons, our women and your women, ourselves and yourselves: Then let us earnestly pray, and invoke the curse of Allah on those who lie!"

A Christian delegation from Najran –an area south of Medina in Arabia– came to visit Prophet Muhammad. They wanted to discuss some differences they had with the Muslims and the Jews. The disputes between the Jews and the Christians had a long history going back hundreds of years. Allah says:

The Jews say, "The Christians have no ground whatsoever to stand on," and the Christians say, "The Jews have no ground whatsoever to stand on," though they both read the scripture, and those who have no knowledge say the same. Allah will judge between them on the Day of Resurrection concerning their differences. (2:113)

One of the issues of contention was their relation to our beloved Abraham. The Jews claimed that Abraham was Jewish, while the Christians refused and claimed that he was one of them. Allah answered:

People of the Book! Why do you argue concerning Abraham when the Torah and the Gospel were only sent down after him? Why do you not use your intellect? (3:65)

The disagreement between the Christians and Prophet Muhammad was regarding the status of Jesus, peace be upon him. Allah wanted to clarify this crucial matter once and for all, so it would not remain suspended and a source of corruption.

Two men led the Christian delegation: Al-Sayyid and Al-'Aqib, accompanied by priests and theologians. Prophet Muhammad(pbuh) asked, "What do you say about Jesus?" They said, "He is the son of God," to which the Messenger replied, "But Jesus said 'I am a servant of God.' He is God's servant, His messenger, and a word from Allah to the Virgin Mary." That upset the delegation, so they turned and said to the Prophet, "Have you ever seen a child born without a father? If you have seen something like that, then let us know!" At that point, Allah revealed the following verse:

Verily, the case of Jesus in the sight of Allah is as the case of Adam. He fashioned him out of dust, then He said to him, "Be," and he came to be. (Verse 59)

Allah distilled the issue down to the undisputed fact that Jesus was born without a father, and so was Adam. Actually, Adam was even born without a father and a mother.

Prophet Muhammad said to the delegation, "From your books, you know that I am the Messenger of Allah and the Prophet of this nation. Why don't you turn to Allah's book and enter Islam?" They said, "We need to discuss some matters, and we will be back tomorrow."

When disagreements represent two opposing views, Allah taught His Messenger to say:

One party of us must be rightly guided and the other clearly astray. (from 34:24)

In other words, there is no grey area: one side is right, while the other is deep in the wrong. When issues are contradictory, there is no middle ground. Allah says:

The truth is from your Lord, so do not be among the doubters. (Verse 60)

Most people view their religion through the lens of prejudice, not reason. That is why religious arguments are often fruitless. The truth comes from Allah in heavenly revelations leaving no room for doubt. Whoever wants to appeal or argue should resort to Allah, Who never rules unjustly.

The next day, the Christian delegation of Najran came back to Prophet Muhammad and informed him that they stand firm on their opinion of Jesus and reject Islam. At such a point, there was no need for further evidence or argument. Allah taught our beloved Muhammad what to do when matters hit an impasse. He says in the next verse of Al Imran:

If anyone disputes this with you now that you have been given this knowledge, say, "Come, let us gather our sons and your sons, our women and your women, ourselves and yourselves, and let us pray earnestly and invoke Allah's curse on those of us who are lying."

(Verse 61)

Both parties were invited to bring forth their closest family members, women, and children for prayers and supplication. Here you may ask, why involve the women and the children? We answer that families are the closest kinships that concern each person regardless of their beliefs. In other words, when you turn to Allah for critical matters, bring along the people dearest to your heart. Many warriors in the olden times used to bring their families along to the battlefield. It meant to show the enemy that they believed in what they were fighting for and would never retreat.

To "pray earnestly" is translated from the Arabic origin المباهلة (Al-Mubahala). It is a specific form of supplication for Allah to descend His curse on the liar or the wrongdoer. Both parties would get together and then invoke their Lord, "O Lord, descend your curse on the liar amongst us." This supplication carries absolute justice because only the true Allah can send down a curse, and those praying to the false God would lose. It is a plea to the irresistible power of the Almighty to act in the matter under dispute.

When Prophet Muhammad, peace be upon him, suggested to the Christian delegation that they all resort to المباهلة (Al-Mubahala) prayers, they said, "Give us until tomorrow, and we will come ready." The next morning, they sent one of them to see what Prophet Muhammad was doing. Was he really prepared for this, or was it a bluff? They found him with his grandchildren, Al-Hassan and Al-Hussein, along with his daughter Fatima and his cousin Ali bin Abi Talib, peace be upon them all. Only a man with absolute conviction would come along with his family in preparation to pray for Allah's curse.

The man returned to the delegation and told them. The leaders discussed the matter and decided against going forward with the prayers. They reasoned, "We will not be able to pray for a curse. By Allah, no nation has engaged in Mubahala with a messenger of Allah except that they were laid to waste."

They later met with the Prophet and tried to settle the matter differently. They said, "Muhammad, we will remain on our religion, and your followers will remain on your religion. We shall make peace with you that you will not fight against us, nor will you turn us away from our religion. We will also pay the Jizya taxes twice a year." Perhaps they decided against it because they doubted their position. As for the Prophet, he was sure of what Allah had revealed to him.

The three verses under study present the perfect solution from the heavens to the Muslim-Christian dispute about the divinity of Jesus. Allah gave the example of Adam, who was created without a father or a mother, to refute the argument that Jesus is the son of God simply because he was born of no father. This argument did not come from Prophet Muhammad. It came from the Almighty, Who is fair and has knowledge of everything. It came from Allah, the Lord of Abraham, and the Lord of the Jews, Christians, and Muslims. Thus, if you have a counter-argument, then bring it against the Almighty and pray for guidance and a curse against the wrongdoers. Is there a fairer process than this? Allah says:

Verily, the case of Jesus in the sight of Allah is as the case of Adam. He fashioned him out of dust, then He said to him, "Be," and he came to be. The truth is from your Lord, so do not be among the doubters. If anyone disputes this with you now that you have been given this knowledge, say, "Come, let us gather our sons and your sons, our women and your women, ourselves and yourselves, and let us pray earnestly and invoke Allah's curse on those of us who are lying." (Chapter 3: Verses 59, 60 & 61)

Verses 62

Innaa haazaa lahuwal qasasul haqq; wa maa min ilaahin illal laah; wa innal laahaa la Huwal 'Azeezul Hakeem

This is indeed the true narrative; and there is no deity but Allah, and truly Allah is the Almighty, the All-Wise. (Verse 62)

The words "indeed" and "true narrative" indicate that there are many false accounts of history. Allah wants to differentiate between His narrations and those of storytellers and historians that are often filled with additions, omissions, and fallacies. The word "narrative" is translated from the Arabic origin قصة (Qissa), which is often used for a story. In modern literature, a story frequently involves fictional events. But if you study the linguistic roots of the word قصة (Qissa), you will find its origin in قص الأثر (Qass Al-Athar), which means "to track the footsteps of others." When you track someone's foot trail in the sand or snow, you will follow the exact path they took and reach the same destination without deviation. Allah, the all-knowing, is the narrator of the stories in the Quran, and He guides us along the exact path of how the events unfolded. He says:

This is indeed the true narrative; and there is no deity but Allah, and truly Allah is the Almighty, the All-Wise. (Verse 62)

Since Allah is one, rest assured that there will be no other God who will come up with other stories or change history. And even though Allah has all the power, you can be comforted that He only uses His might wisely.

Given all the information from the previous verses, shouldn't the Christian delegation who debated our beloved Muhammad have followed the path of Allah and the Quran? Sadly, they did not. Allah says in the next verse of Al Imran:

Verse 63

Fa in tawallaw fa innal laaha'aleemun bil mufsideen

If they still turn away, be assured that Allah has full knowledge of those engaged in causing disorder and corruption. (Verse 63)

The phrase "if they still turn away" indicates that Allah knew from perpetuity that they would not accept the Prophet's invitation. By rejecting the truth and refusing to defend their opinion before Allah, they became corrupters. Yet, Allah commanded His Messenger to sit with them to find common ground as stated in the following next verse of Al Imran:

Verse 64

Qul yaa Ahlal Kitaabi ta'aalaw ilaa Kalimatin sawaaa'im bainanaa wa bainakum allaa na'buda illal laaha wa laa nushrika bihee shai'anw wa laa yattakhiza ba'dunaa ba'dan arbaabam min doonil laah; fa in tawallaw faqoolush hadoo bi annaa muslimoon

Say, "People of the Book, let us arrive at a statement that is common to us all: we worship Allah alone, we ascribe no partner to Him, and none of us takes others beside Allah as lords." If they turn away, say, "Bear witness that we submit to Him as Muslims." (Verse 64)

Our fellow Jews and Christians believe in Allah, and believe that the heavens sent messengers armed with holy books to guide humankind. For this reason, Allah extended an invitation to build on these shared beliefs.

It is a call to an equitable and clear statement indisputable by all parties: "we worship Allah alone." From this common ground we move to, "we ascribe no partner to Him." A business partner shares equal status as other partners and participates in the responsibilities of running the business.

Can anyone rise to the majesty and perfection of the One God? Does anyone share Allah's status as the Creator of the universe? Of course not; every creature that was ever ascribed as a partner to Allah came only after Allah created the universe. He says:

Had Allah willed to take Himself a child, He could certainly have chosen whatever He willed out of all that He has created. He is exalted above all that. He is Allah, the One, the Overwhelming. (39:4)

Now we question the second function of a partner: are partners needed in the management of the universe? Does Allah need help? This is the most trivial of reasons to justify polytheism because Allah is more than capable of managing this universe. He says in Ayat Al-Kursi:

Allah: there is no Allah but Him, the Ever-Living, the Ever Watchful. Neither slumber nor sleep overtakes Him. All that is in the heavens and in the earth belongs to Him.

And in another chapter:

Allah is the Creator of everything, and He is the guardian over everything. (39:62)

Allah revealed to us a scripture that, if followed, can make human life as harmonious and enjoyable as the rest of heavenly creations. Thus, ascribing partners to Allah is entirely unnecessary.

If we suppose that Allah had a partner, are they His equal? Or does one have better abilities than the other? Is there a flaw in one, and is that where the second Allah comes in? Allah is exalted above all such absurdities. He says:

Allah has never had a child. Nor is there any God besides Him—if there were, each God would have taken his creation aside and tried to overcome the others. May Allah be exalted above what they describe! (23:91)

This brings us back to the joint statement between all heavenly religions. We continue with, "and none of us takes others beside Allah as lords." In other words, we should not appoint from among us priests, imams, and lamas who rule what is permissible and what is forbidden. Permissions and prohibitions are only from Allah. He is the sole legislator. All our movements are guarded by Allah's commands to "do" or "do not do." If there were a Allah who said "do" while another commanded the opposite, this would ruin the universe. Likewise, if religious leaders ruled based on their desires, the universe would also go to ruin. Allah says:

But if the truth were in accordance with their desires, the heavens, the earth, and everyone in them would disintegrate. We have brought them their reminder and they turn away from it. (23:71)

Allah's instruction to His messenger ends with "If they turn away, say, 'Bear witness that we submit to Him as Muslims.'" A person who does not accept the worship of the One Allah without associating any partners or assigning other people as religious legislators indicates that his or her heart is not ready to accept faith.

Such was the call to Allah on the tongue of His beloved Muhammad: "People of the Book, let us arrive at a statement that is common to us all: we worship Allah alone, we ascribe no partner to Him, and none of us takes others beside Allah as lords." It is a simple yet beautiful and equitable call to all the followers of heavenly religions, and that is the essence of being a Muslim.

Verses 65

Yaaa Ahlal Kitaabi limaa tuhaaajjoona feee Ibraaheema wa maaa unzilatit Tawraatu wal Injeelu illaa mim ba'dih; afala ta'qiloon

People of the Book, why do you argue about Abraham when the Torah and the Gospels were not revealed until after his time? Do you not use your intellect? (Verse 65)

The Jews attribute themselves to Prophet Moses and the Christians to Prophet Jesus. So Allah asks, "Why do you argue in the matter of Abraham? He, peace be upon him, could not have been a Jew as the Jews claim, for Judaism came after Abraham, nor a Christian, because Christianity came even later." Then why the disagreement? Allah says:

Verses 66

Haaa antum haaa'ulaaa'i haajajtum feemaa lakum bihee 'ilmun falima tuhaaajjoonaa feemaa laisa lakum bihee 'ilm; wallaahu ya'lamu wa antum laa ta'lamoon

You argue about some things of which you have some knowledge, but why do you argue about things of which you know nothing? Allah knows, and you do not. (Verse 66)

Verses 67

Maa kaana Ibraaheemu Yahoodiyyanw wa laa Nasraa niyyanw wa laakin kaana Haneefam Muslimanw wa maa kaana minal mushrikeen

There were many disputes among the Jews and Christians over the authenticity and content of their scriptures, but that does not mean making a controversy out of every issue. Allah is your Creator and the Creator of Abraham, and He knows best. He says:

Abraham was neither a Jew nor a Christian, but he was one inclining toward the truth, a Muslim. He was never of those who associate partners with Allah. (Verse 67)

Abraham, peace be upon him, is Khalilu Allah ("the dearest to Allah"). He was neither a Jew nor a Christian because both faiths came well after him; instead "he was one inclining toward the truth," translated from the Arabic origin حَنِيفًا (Haneefan). The word حَنِيفًا (Haneef) is interesting because it is used to describe something curved, bent, or not aligned correctly. Medically, it represents a deformity in the feet called clubfoot.

So we ask, why was the word حَنِيفًا (Haneefan) used to describe Abraham's faith? Wasn't he, peace be upon him, on the straight path? We answer that yes, Abraham had the purest of beliefs, but he came at a time when idolatry and corruption were widespread. He was sent to correct this crookedness and deviate from it towards Allah. Thus, his misalignment to the corrupt society around him landed him on Allah's straight path.

Allah created every human with a healthy seed of faith within. This seed grows stronger when nourished with good deeds and weaker if you head in the wrong direction. When you sin, your healthy conscious steps in to deter you or make you feel regret after the fact. This self-blame is a sign of a healthy state because it brings you back to the Lord, seeking forgiveness.

Be careful, however, because if you persistently sin, then that part of yourself becomes weaker. At some point, the self-blame ceases and turns into an insatiable lust that chases after life's pleasures and leads you astray.

But all is not lost! Allah put another safeguard to bring you back to His path, which is the good people around you. If you go down the wrong way, your parents, relatives, and good friends usually step in and advise you. That is why it is critical to surround yourself with the right friends and community.

Sadly, at times, both the reproaching self is diminished, and the society is corrupt. Evil becomes widespread and even celebrated. Allah says:

They did not forbid each other to do wrong. How vile their deeds were! (5:79)

Who can correct this situation? This is when the heavens intervene with a new prophet or messenger to bring people back to the straight path. Allah made the nation of Prophet Muhammad the best of nations until the Day of Resurrection because He preserved within it groups that speak the truth and stir the society towards good. He says:

You are the best community singled out for people: you order what is right, forbid what is wrong, and believe in Allah. If the People of the Book had also believed, it would have been better for them. For although some of them do believe, most of them are lawbreakers. (3:110)

Since no prophet will come after Prophet Muhammad, we, as Muslims, are tasked with preserving the light of faith till the Day of Judgement. Our duty is to command good and forbid evil. Allah guaranteed that the nation of Prophet Muhammad would never lack people of integrity in any era. As for previous nations, it was necessary to send new messengers when all the candles of righteousness were extinguished within the community.

Prophet Abraham, peace be upon him, was sent to such a community, mired in corruption and idol worship. His task was to incline people back towards moderation and pull them out of ignorance. Allah sent His messenger to restore the flame of faith within each soul and within the community.

However, being on the straight path is difficult, especially when people all around you are corrupt. Allah warns us against abusing religion to fulfill worldly desires. He says:

The Jews and the Christians will never be pleased with you unless you follow their ways. Say, "Allah's guidance is the only true guidance." If you were to follow their desires after the knowledge that has come to you, you would find no one to protect you from Allah or help you. (2:120)

In the 135th verse of Surah Al-Baqarah, Allah instructed Prophet Muhammad to reply to those inviting him to leave his religion, "Say, 'Rather, the religion of Abraham, inclining toward the truth, and he was not of the polytheists.'"

Abraham is the father of the prophets, and heavenly religions do not differ in their core principles, so why can't we call the Jews and the Christians "followers of Abraham"? We answer that Judaism and Christianity have been distorted over time. Abraham, peace be upon him, could not have been a Jew considering the distortion that occurred in their creed. For the same reason, he could not have been a Christian; rather, "he was one inclining toward the truth, a Muslim. He was never of those who associate partners with Allah."

The word "Muslim" means "the one who surrendered his or her will to the Almighty willingly." Thus, when Abraham submitted his reins to Allah and faithfully adhered to all His commandments, he became, by definition, a Muslim. Likewise, if we apply this definition to all prophets and messengers, we find that Adam was devoted to Allah as a Muslim, and so were Noah, Jesus, Moses, and countless others, peace be upon them all. Allah says:

In matters of faith, He has laid down for you the same commandment that He gave Noah, which We have revealed to you and which We enjoined on Abraham and Moses and Jesus: "Uphold the faith and do not divide into factions within it." What you call upon the idolaters to do is hard for them; Allah chooses whomever He pleases for Himself and guides towards Himself those who turn to Him. (42:13)

Each prophet and messenger submitted his will to Allah and faithfully applied the scriptures. So the word "Muslim" is a befitting description. The heavenly religions were concluded with the message revealed to our beloved Muhammad. Islam became its official name, and its followers earned the permanent name: Muslims.

Verse 68

Innaa awlan naasi bi Ibraaheema lallazeenat taba 'oohu wa haazan nabiyyu wallazeena aamanoo; wallaahu waliyyul mu'mineen

Surely the people most worthy of associating with Abraham are those who followed him, and this Prophet, and those who believe. Allah is the guardian of the believers. (Verse 68)

Since the beginning of time, each messenger of Allah was sent to a specific nation. For example, Moses was sent to the Children of Israel, and so was Jesus, peace be upon them. In verse 49 of Al-Imran, Allah said about Jesus:

He will send him as a messenger to the Children of Israel.

And in verse 73 of Chapter 7:

To the people of Thamud We sent their brother, Saleh. He said, "My people, serve Allah: you have no Allah other than Him."

This fact held true until the message of Islam. Our beloved Prophet Muhammad was sent as a messenger to the entire humankind till the end of time. Many people of the previous nations, whether Jews or Christians, embraced Islam, and this procession of faith continued until it reached you and me today. Thus, the nation of Prophet Muhammad, peace be upon him, is a worldwide nation with no boundaries. Allah says about Prophet Muhammad:

We did not send you but as a mercy to all the nations. (21:107)

Islam is the culmination of all heavenly religions. Prophet Muhammad, peace be upon him, said, "My place in comparison with the other prophets before me is that of a man who built a house nicely and beautifully, except for one missing corner brick. People would tour the house and marvel at its beauty but say, 'When will this brick be put in its place?' I am that brick, and I am the last of the prophets."

Prophet Abraham, peace be upon him, is considered the father of all prophets. That is the reason behind the dispute between the Jews and the Christians about Abraham's religion. The Israelites wanted to claim him as Jewish, and the Christians said that he followed their faith. Both love to claim that they are his descendants and grandchildren. Faith, however, is not inherited by blood or kin. It is earned through hard work. Allah says:

Surely the people most worthy of associating with Abraham are those who followed him, and this Prophet, and those who believe.

Prophet Muhammad preserved the creed of Abraham, the creed of monotheism, while others had distorted the scripture and deviated. Allah addressed this issue in the following verse:

And when Abraham's Lord tested him with specific commandments, which he fulfilled, He said, "I will make you a leader of people." Abraham asked, "And will You make leaders from my descendants too?" Allah answered, "My pledge does not hold for those who do evil." (2:124)

Allah tested Abraham with orders and prohibitions, and he, peace be upon him, fulfilled them with the utmost care. Most of us fulfill our religious duties out of formality. For example, you rush to pray and go through the physical motions of the prayers without involving your heart. Only a few people look at each prayer as a precious opportunity to meet and connect with Allah.

Let's look at Prophet Abraham's example when he fulfilled Allah's command to raise the foundations of the Ka'aba. It would have been sufficient for him to implement the order by raising the building to the maximum height his hands could reach. But, out of love and dedication, Abraham looked for rocks to stand on so he could build Allah's house even higher. It was his best attempt at what we call scaffolding today. His footprints appear on one of the rocks he stood on. Allah honours those who perform religious obligations wholeheartedly; this is why the standing place of Abraham was made significant. Today it is a place of prayer for all Muslims.

Allah further honoured Abraham by entrusting him to be a leader. He says, "I will make you a leader of people." Abraham is a worthy man to follow because he performed his duties to perfection and led by example. The proof of his deep love for Allah's religion was immediately apparent when Abraham asked, "and will You make leaders from my descendants too?" He feared that the faith would be limited to his life and wanted to assure that his descendants inherited this treasure. The Almighty answered, "My pledge does not hold for those who do evil," teaching all of us that faith is not inherited by blood or kin. It is not who you are but what you do that counts.

There were grandchildren of Abraham who were unjust and unworthy of Allah's trust. And there were some who implemented Allah's teachings fully without distortion. Those are the true leaders of the people regardless of their nationality or skin colour. We had recently mentioned that Prophet Muhammad, peace be upon him, said to Salman, a companion from Persia, "Salman, you are one of us, the household of Muhammad." In other words, Salman belonged to Ahl Al-Bayt –the close family of Muhammad– by virtue of his faith.

We learn a similar lesson from the story of our beloved Noah when his son was about to drown.

Noah called on his Lord and said, "O Lord, my son is surely a member of my family, and verily Your promise is true, as You are the most just of all judges." (11:45)

To which Allah replied:

"O Noah! He is not of your family. He is one of unrighteous conduct. So do not ask of Me what you have no knowledge of. I caution you so that you do not behave as one among the ignorant." (11:46)

Allah informed Noah that his son was not worthy of being saved because he was not a part of Noah's family. Take note that Allah did not say that Noah's son was evil; instead, He specified that his actions were. Allah explained, "He is one of unrighteous conduct." Again, faith is not lineage or race, nor affiliation; it is all about your actions. If you sincerely work according to Allah's law, you can be a close member of Prophet Muhammad's family. This remarkable honour is exclusive to true believers.

How about material inheritance? Is that also exclusive to the believers? The answer comes from another lesson Allah taught Prophet Abraham. The following verse says:

And Abraham said, "My Lord, make this land secure and provide with produce those of its people who believe in Allah and the Last Day." Allah said, "As for those who disbelieve, I will grant them enjoyment for a short while and then subject them to the torment of the Fire —an evil destination." (2:126)

In olden times, people were afraid to travel to Mecca because the roads leading to it were unsafe, and the lands were barren, providing little to no food. When food is scarce, people often turn violent. Thus, Abraham supplicated, "My Lord, make this land secure and provide with produce those of its people." However, Abraham added a stipulation and prayed for provision only for the believers. He said, "Provide with produce those of its people who believe in Allah and the Last Day." Why? Because Abraham remembered that, when he supplicated Allah to bless his descendants with prophethood and leadership, Allah answered, "My pledge does not hold for those who do evil."

Did Allah respond by granting abundant provision only to those who believed from the people of Mecca? No: when it comes to material blessings, Allah provides for all, the believer and the disbeliever alike. He said to Abraham, "As for those who disbelieve, I will grant them enjoyment for a short while."

Allah brought us to life, and He guarantees material sustenance regardless of our faith. The sun rises on all humankind, the earth yields crops for everyone, and livestock serves the believers and disbelievers alike. As for the blessings of guidance and the scriptures, they are exclusive for the few who follow the footsteps of Allah's prophets and messengers. While these blessings come attached to duty and obligation in this world, their true and immense reward will be given free in the hereafter exclusively to the believers, as mentioned in the following verse:

Say, "Who has forbidden the adornment of Allah which He has brought forth for His servants, and the good things of provision?" Say, "These are for the faithful in the life of this world, and exclusively for them on the Day of Resurrection." This is how We make Our revelation clear for those who understand. (7:32)

Moses, peace be upon him, brought Allah's message to the Israelites, but they shunned it and chased materialism instead. Jesus, peace be upon him, came to restore spirituality to the Children of Israel, but they fought him, distorted Allah's scriptures, and injected polytheism into Christianity. The true inheritors of Abraham are the ones who followed him and the nation of Muhammad, who upheld the creed of monotheism.

Verse 69

Waddat taaa'ifatum min Ahlil Kitaabi law yudil loonakum wa maa yudilloona illaaa anfusahum wa maa yash'uroon

Some of the People of the Book would dearly love to lead you astray, but they only lead themselves astray, though they do not realize it. (Verse 69)

Why would anyone go out of their way to mislead others? Because misery loves company! When a sinner sees people acting righteously, it highlights his or her failings. Righteous people are able to control their desires and commit to Allah's teachings, while a sinner has little self-control. Thus, he or she says out of envy, "How are these people able to control themselves?" The righteous expose the sinners' weakness, so they feel the need to remove this nuisance from their way. Thus, you often see those who properly practice faith ridiculed in their community.

Take the example of a lazy student who sees her friend studying and preparing for exams. She starts wondering, "Why is my friend disciplined to study and succeed, and I cannot bring myself to sit down and focus?" No one likes to feel inferior to others. Sadly, for many people, the solution is not to sit down and study but to distract the good student from studying or make fun of her. This is exactly what happens when someone is upright in a corrupt society. Allah says:

Some of the People of the Book would dearly love to lead you astray.

And in another chapter:

The wicked used to laugh at the believers, wink at one another as they passed by them, and joke about them when they got back to their folks. When they saw them, they said, "They have indeed gone astray," though they were not sent to be their keepers. (83:29-33)

Sinners often try to lead good people towards sin and, when they fail, they resort to mock and ridicule. In essence, they work hard to adorn sin and undermine faith in society. Don't we see this scenario play out in our communities today? Corrupt people often make fun of scholars and ridicule those who adhere to Allah's teachings as squares or out of touch with modernity. And, when they get together with their family and friends, they share these fun stories. Allah assures the believers that they will have a day when they too will laugh:

So, today, the believers are laughing at the disbelievers as they sit on couches, gazing in wonder. Have the disbelievers been repaid for what they used to do? (83:34-36)

This brings us back to the verse. The phrase "would dearly love" indicates the disbelievers' deep wish to attract the believers to their camp. But not everything that a person desires happens. To wish is to demand something challenging or impossible to achieve. At times, you may even end up with the opposite result. Allah says, "But they only lead themselves astray, though they do not realize it."

Let's take a few moments to study the word "astray" translated from the Arabic origin ضَلَال (Dalal). When mentioned in the Quran, it holds a few distinct meanings. For example, Allah says:

They say, "What! When we have been astray into the earth, shall we really be created anew?" In fact, they deny the meeting with their Lord. (32:10)

In the verse above, "astray" refers to the death and obliteration of the body. In other words, the disbelievers are mocking the fact Allah will ever be able to resurrect bodies that decayed and vanished into the earth.

The second meaning of "astray" is "to be aimless without a clear goal." Allah says describing our beloved Muhammad before the advent of Islam:

Did He not find you astray and guided you? (93:07)

From his youth, Prophet Muhammad refused to worship the idols and rejected the practices of the pagans. Prophet Muhammad would seclude himself from the corruption of Quraish and meditate in the cave of Heraa outside Mecca. For years, he kept searching for the right path until Allah guided him with the revelation of the Quran.

The last meaning of "astray" describes a person who knows the proper path but intentionally deviates from it. Allah says:

Some of the People of the Book would dearly love to lead you astray, but they only lead themselves astray, though they do not realize it. (Verse 69)

It is a double tragedy when the person who knows the truth decides to reject it and works hard to mislead others. Rejecting Allah's teachings is a sin; leading others astray is a compound sin. This concept helps us appreciate the following two verses. Allah says:

No soul will bear the burden of another: even if a heavily laden soul should cry for help, none of its sins will be carried, not even by a close relative. You can only warn those who fear their Lord, though they cannot see Him, and keep up the prayer –whoever purifies himself does so for his own benefit. Everything returns to Allah. (35:18)

We understand that each person is fully responsible for his or her actions, so if you sin, no one will carry that load for you. Then we run across the following verse. Allah says:

Hence, they will bear their own burdens of sin in full on the Day of Resurrection and some of the burdens of those whom they, being ignorant, caused to go astray. Look now! How terrible is the burden they load upon themselves! (16:25)

So which is it? Are you just responsible for your own sins? Or can you also be responsible for the sins of others? We answer that the burden of sin Allah referred to in the first verse is that of your own sins. In contrast, the burden in the second verse is that of misleading others. Prophet Muhammad explained it best. He, peace be upon him, said, "Whoever calls for guidance will have a reward equal to the reward of those who follow him or her until the Day of Resurrection, without diminishing anything from their rewards. And whoever calls for misguidance will carry sins equal to the sins of all those who follow him or her until the Day of Resurrection, without diminishing anything from their sins." Allah says:

Some of the People of the Book would dearly love to lead you astray, but they only lead themselves astray, though they do not realize it. (Verse 69)

What the disbelievers do not realize is how catastrophic the burdens of their actions are. They will be held accountable for all those they mislead. Had they taken just a few moments to think, they would have left people alone and would not have tried to corrupt all those around them.

Verses 70

Yaaa Ahlal Kitaabi lima takfuroona bi Aayaatil laahi wa antum tash hadoon

People of the Book, why do you deny Allah's revelations when you can see they are true? (Verse 70)

In this verse, Allah questions the Jews and the Christians through the words of Prophet Muhammad, "Why do you disbelieve in the magnificent signs and revelations of Allah while you were witnesses to their authenticity?" Here you may ask, did the People of the Book see Allah's signs firsthand at the time of Prophet Muhammad? Yes! Years before the advent of the prophet, the Jews of Medina used to boast about the coming of an unlearned prophet in Arabia. They awaited him so they could fight with him and be granted victory. They prayed, "Our Lord, we ask you by the right of the illiterate prophet whom you have promised us. Send him so we may be victorious over our enemies." But when Prophet Muhammad (pbuh) was sent, just as they had asked, they were the first to reject him. Allah says:

When a scripture came to them from Allah confirming what they already had —even though before that, they were praying for victory over the disbelievers— even when there came to them something they knew to be true, they disbelieved in it: Allah rejects those who disbelieve. (2:89)

Why would they reject something they dearly prayed for? Because the new prophet threatened their governing authority and the clergy's power.

There was no shortage of evidence. Prophet Muhammad's attributes and detailed description were in the Torah. Abdullah bin Salam, a leader of Medina's Jewish community, said after he accepted Islam, "I recognized Muhammad the minute I saw him. I knew him as I know my own son. In fact, my knowledge of Muhammad was greater."

Sadly, most denied him out of greed for power and went as far as distorting the scriptures to deceive their followers into rejecting Islam. Allah says:

So woe to those who write something down with their own hands and then claim, "This is from Allah," in order to make some small gain. Woe to them for what their hands have written! Woe to them for all that they have earned! (2:79)

Allah says in the next verse of Al-Imran:

Verse 71

Yaaa Ahalal Kitaabi lima talbisoonal haqqa bilbaatili wa taktumoonal haqqa wa antum ta'lamoon

People of the Book, why do you dress the truth with falsehood? Why do you knowingly conceal the truth?

Let's start with the verb "dress." It means "to insert something into something else." For example, when you wear a jumper, you enter your body into it, and then your arms and head come out of it. In essence, your appearance changes because your body and the jumper become intermingled. That is the description Allah chose for those who muddy the truth with falsehood to obscure the reality of things.

Corrupt clergy distorted the Torah and the Gospel by adding their own words to them while omitting Allah's. In essence, they mingled the truth Prophets Moses and Jesus brought with falsehoods. One of their most brazen distortions was removing the good tidings of the advent of Prophet Muhammad from their heavenly books.

But when it comes to faith, you cannot pick and choose what is to your liking. Moses and Jesus gave glad tidings of Muhammad –the seal of the prophets who would bring the final heavenly message to humanity. Isn't that the worst example of dressing the truth with falsehood and knowingly distorting the truth? Allah says in the 85th verse of Chapter 2:

Do you believe in some parts of the Scripture and not in others? The punishment for those of you who do this will be nothing but disgrace in this life, and on the Day of Resurrection, they will be condemned to the harshest torment: Allah is not oblivious of what you do.

And in another chapter:

And they denied them out of malice and pride, though in their hearts they believed that they were true. See how those who spread corruption met their end! (27:14)

As if changing Allah's scriptures was not enough, some of the People of the Book devised new tricks to stop the new heavenly message. Allah says:

Verse 72

Wa qaalat taaa'ifatum min Ahlil Kitaabi aaminoo billazeee unzila 'alal lazeena aamanoo wajhan nahaari wakfurooo aakhirahoo la'alla hum yarji'oon

A group of the People of the Book says, "At the beginning of the day, you should claim to believe in what was sent down to those who believed, and then at the end of the day you should reject it, so that hopefully they will revert."

This trick was aimed at sowing doubt in the new Muslim community. The believers –many of them Arabs from Mecca and Medina– were largely illiterate. They trusted that the People of the Book had more knowledge about heavenly scriptures. Moreover, at that time, the Quran had not been revealed in its entirety.

Some of the Jews and Christians at the time wanted to exploit the Muslims' trust and illiteracy. They decided to declare their faith in the message of Muhammad and then reject it shortly after. The aim was to spread suspicion and confusion in the budding Muslim community. Some illiterate people may say, "The People of the Book have tested the new religion and, through their knowledge of heavenly scriptures, found it lacking." This was yet another form of confounding the truth with falsehood.

The phrase "At the beginning of the day" is translated from the Arabic origin وَجْه (Wajh), which means "the face." Generally, the morning and noon hours are intended, but the word وَجْه (Wajh) has other connotations. It is used to describe a storefront where the best goods are displayed to the walking public. Some sellers put the best and freshest fruits on top while hiding older or even rotten ones underneath.

The customers are tricked into thinking that the seller is offering top-quality fruit. Likewise, some of the People of the Book tried to deceive the believers by declaring faith early in the day while hiding their rotten intentions beneath. They could then say, "We are not biased or intolerant because we have accepted Islam but found it incompatible with what was revealed to our messengers."

It is also the opinion of some scholars that the verse under study was revealed regarding changing the direction of prayer (Qibla) for Muslims. The Prophet, peace be upon him, was commanded to change the Muslim Qibla from the Aqsa mosque in Jerusalem to the Ka'aba in Mecca. The disbelievers from the People of the Book and the hypocrites said, "Let's pretend to listen to Muhammad and face the Ka'aba for the early prayers, then revert back to Jerusalem for the end-of-the-day prayers." The aim was, again, to sow discord among the believers.

All these tactics were a form of psychological warfare against the Muslims. Allah revealed their tricks to us and highlighted how such people inadvertently admitted to joining the camp of the disbelievers. Their own words exposed them: they said, "At the beginning of the day, you should claim to believe in what was sent down to those who believed." They chose disbelief for themselves and labelled the Muslims as believers.

Verses 73

Wa laa tu'minooo illaa liman tabi'a deenakum qul innal hudaa hudal laahi ai yu'taaa ahadum misla maaa ooteetum aw yuhaaajjookum 'inda Rabbikum, qul innal fadla biyadil laah; yu'teehi mai yashaaa'; wallaahu Waasi'un 'Aleem

"But do not trust in any but those who follow your religion." Say, "Surely, the only guidance is Allah's guidance," that anyone should be given the like of what you were given, or that they should argue against you before your Lord. Say, "All grace and bounty is in Allah's hand; He gives it to whomever He wills." Allah is Infinite, All-Knowing. (Verse 73)

When Islam spread in Arabia, some of the Jews and Christians of Medina conspired to sow doubt within the Muslim community, as the following verse illustrates:

A group of the People of the Book says, "At the beginning of the day, you should claim to believe in what was sent down to those who believed, and then, at the end of the day, you should reject it, so that hopefully they will revert." (3:72)

They thought, "Let's declare that we have accepted Islam, and then renounce it shortly after. We are the trustees of the heavenly scriptures, and people trust our judgment. Hopefully, others would leave Islam with us." They aimed to demoralize the Muslim community. Of course, for such a plan to work, they had to keep it a secret. They said, "But do not trust in any but those who follow your religion."

Allah exposed their deception to the believers by revealing the verses under study. Thus, He spoiled their plan and turned the psychological war against those who ignited it. Allah further highlighted their fears:

Say, "Surely, the only guidance is Allah's guidance," that anyone should be given the like of what you were given, or that they should argue against you before your Lord.

The perpetrators of this scheme claimed that they were the only source of guidance and that they were entrusted to lead people to the heavens. It would have been understandable if their goal were to convert people from Islam to Christianity or Judaism. Sadly, they could not care less if people followed their religions. All they aimed for was chaos and delusion and to leave Muhammad with no followers. They conspired to keep their plans secret rather than bring forth an intelligent argument against Islam.

Here we should ask, what were they afraid of? For decades, they felt superior to others because of their connection to the heavens, and they used this knowledge to rule over the pagans. Now, with the new message revealed to Prophet Muhammad (pbuh), people around them established a more robust and untainted connection to the heavens. The People of the Book also knew that Islam is the final message and the Quran the final heavenly scripture, so the advantage they once enjoyed was lost forever. Rather than embracing the truth, they desperately wanted to deprive people of it. They feared that the Muslims would soon be able to hold their own while arguing against them in matters of faith.

All of that pointed to their foolishness and lack of faith. Why? Because they operated under the illusion that Allah was unaware of their secrets. They forgot that Allah knows what the hearts conceal, so their plans could never work. Allah says:

And the disbelievers schemed; Allah also schemed; Allah is the Best of Schemers. (3:54)

Sadly, the Children of Israel have littered their history with false narratives about Allah's knowledge. For example, when the Israelites left Egypt and went wandering in the desert, they claimed that Allah instructed Moses as follows: "Mark the homes of the faithful, for My punishment will descend soon and seize the whole country." That is to say, if they did not put signs on their doors, Allah would not know, and He would punish the wrong people.

Allah answers with, "Surely, the only guidance is Allah's guidance" and "All grace and bounty is in Allah's hand; He gives it to whomever He wills." As long as the grace is within the hands of Allah, people of deception will never be able to misguide others as they wish. Allah grants His guidance and grace to those who deserve such gifts, and no one can take that away except Him.

The verse ends with "Allah is Infinite, All-Knowing," meaning that Allah is not limited by supply, so He can grant grace to all His creations. Yet, Allah is also All-Knowing of who deserves the grace and whose heart is corrupt. He says in the next verse of Al-Imran:

Verse 74

Yakhtassu birahmatihee mai yashaaa'; wallaahu zulfadlil 'azeem

And He singles out for His mercy whoever He will. His grace is infinite. (Verse 74)

Every moment of life is a blessing –not a right– from Allah. He showers His mercy by granting the blessings of faith to whomever He wills. The disbelievers and some of the People of the Book wanted to subject Allah's scriptures and teachings to their whims. They did not hate Islam or the Quran; they simply could not stand the fact that it was not revealed to one of them. Allah says:

They say, "Why was this Quran not sent down to one of the great men of the two cities?" Are they the ones who hand out your Lord's grace? We are the Ones Who give them their share of livelihood in this world, and We have raised some of them above others in rank, so that some may take others into service: your Lord's grace is better than anything they accumulate. (43:31-32)

Allah replied that the disbelievers are not in charge of Allah's mercy: He, the All-Knowledgeable, the All-Wise, puts His message and mercy where He sees fit. In fact, the phrase "singles out" means that there is a selection. One party is chosen while all others are excluded, and no one except Allah has any say or influence on this decision. The jealousy and resentment of those who opposed Prophet Muhammad only distanced them further from Allah.

Allah says:

They seek to extinguish Allah's light with their mouths, whereas Allah refuses but to complete His light, even though the unbelievers detest it. It is He Who has sent His Messenger with the guidance and the religion of truth that He may make it prevail over all religions, however hateful this may be to those who associate partners with Allah. (9:32-33)

Verse 75

Wa min Ahlil Kitaabi man in ta'manhu biqintaariny yu'addihee ilaika wa minhum man in ta'manhu bi deenaarin laa yu'addiheee ilaika illaa maa dumta 'alaihi qaaa' imaa; zaalika biannahum qaaloo laisa 'alainaa fil ummiyyeena sabeelunw wa yaqooloona 'alal laahil kaziba wa hum ya'lamoon

Among the People of the Book are some who, if you entrust them with a weight of treasure, they will return it to you intact; and among them are some who, if you entrust them with one gold coin, will not return it unless you keep insisting on its return. That is because they claim, "We have no responsibility toward the unlettered people." Thus they speak lies in attribution to Allah, and do so knowingly. (Verse 75)

This verse is a display of absolute divine fairness. In the preceding verses, Allah exposed the plans some of the People of the Book devised to discredit Islam and weaken the followers of Prophet Muhammad. But this did not mean that Allah was waging a campaign against the Jews and Christians. Allah highlighted certain behaviours and simply singled out those who did them.

In the verse under study, Allah sheds light on the Jews and Christians who are distinguished with honesty, again pointing out behaviours rather than individuals. He says, "Among the People of the Book are some who, if you entrust them with a weight of treasure, they will return it to you intact."

The call of Prophet Muhammad, peace be upon him, was sent as a mercy to all humankind. The Jews and Christians are the closest to the believers because they recognize that the heavens send messengers armed with miracles and scriptures. More importantly, their books highlight the signs of the advent of Muhammad, peace be upon him. And among them are those who took the time to study these signs and consider the prophet's message. Many reverted to Islam because they saw it as an essential step of their Christian or Jewish faith.

Had Allah initiated a campaign against all the People of the Book, those who were considering Islam would have said, "We were thinking of believing and implementing Allah's teachings; How could Muhammad launch a war against us?" But, when Allah declared that some Jews and Christians were distinguished by honesty, He gave them comfort that Muhammad only spoke of what His just Lord informed him. Allah says:

Yet they are not all alike: among the People of the Book there is an upright community, reciting Allah's revelations in the watches of the night and prostrating. (3:113)

Allah reassured those who occupied themselves with studying the new religion, and there lies the divine justice in the phrase "Among the People of the Book are some who, if you entrust them with a weight of treasure, they will return it to you intact."

Some scholars tried to limit the phrase "People of the Book" to the Christians, excluding the Jews. We answer that such interpretation takes away from Allah's fairness. Among the People of the Book, whether Jews or Christians, are those with a healthy conscious and pure heart. In other verses of the Quran, Allah specified the Jews or the Christians by name; thus, the phrase "People of the Book" should be understood to include both. Allah recognizes the good and the vile in the Quran, which will be recited until the Day of Judgment. And, when people read verses that highlight the virtues of some Jews and Christians, they should also take seriously the verses that describe the evil characteristics of others among them. Allah only speaks the truth, and thus the Quran is a book of absolute fairness.

The word "entrust" is derived from the Arabic الأمانة (Amanah). The Amanah trust begins when something is given to you for safekeeping. It could be money, a car, or even a piece of information. Trust means that there are no guarantees, collaterals, or contracts. In other words, if I entrust you with some of my money for safekeeping, and then we sit down to write a contract or bring witnesses, then it is no longer known as the Amanah trust. By definition, trust relies exclusively on the entrusted person's consciousness.

Here, I would like to remind you of a critical point: there is a big difference between accepting the trust and performing the duties of the trust. I will explain with an example. A friend may come and ask, "I will be going overseas for four years. I have ten thousand pounds. Can I trust you to keep it safe until I come back from my studies?" You reply with, "Yes, of course." This is what we call accepting the الأمانة (Amanah) trust. It is the easy part because you may accept the responsibility and have full intention to safeguard your friend's money, but life is not predictable. What if you fall on hard times during the next four years and need money for a critical medical operation for your child? What if the only money available to you is the money your friend entrusted you with? Would you take some? Would you tell your friend? Would you procrastinate in giving the money back? That is the difference between accepting the trust and fulfilling the duties of the trust. Fulfilling the duties is the difficult part.

The issue of accepting the trust and bearing its responsibilities is not specific to this verse or financial dealings. It is a common pitfall of all human beings. In fact, this very issue has to do with the origin of our humanity as trustees in the universe. Allah says:

We offered the trust to the heavens, the earth, and the mountains, yet they refused to undertake it and were afraid of it; humankind undertook it —they have always been unjust and ignorant. (33:72)

The entire universe feared to bear the trust of free will. It understood the difference between accepting the trust of faith and fulfilling that responsibility. No one can guarantee to properly fulfil the trust when the time comes. Hence, the universe declined Allah's offer and chose to keep its will in the hands of Allah, the Creator. What was the result? A universe that performs its duties as Allah intended, working like clockwork. There is, however, an exception: humankind. Man accepted the trust and thought, "I am intelligent, and I will always choose the best between alternatives. I will earn my way to Paradise." Look around you: where does corruption come from? It comes from the places where people abused their Allah's Amanah, interfered in nature, and chose to follow their whims over Allah's teachings.

Always remember: you may be strong when accepting the trust, but what about at the time of fulfillment? Allah says, "Humankind undertook it –they have always been unjust and ignorant." If you commit yourself to something and do not do it properly, then you are unjust to yourself. Similarly, if you commit yourself to something without fully appreciating the time and effort it will take to be fulfilled, then you are ignorant.

This brings us back to the verse. The phrase "Among the People of the Book are some who, if you entrust them with a weight of treasure, they will return it to you intact" indicates that the treasure is only held by a word with no contract or witnesses. Such people did not allow the brilliant shine of gold to distract them from their duty towards the trust.

The phrase "a weight of treasure" is translated from the Arabic origin قِنْطَار (Quintar), which is a unit for measuring weight. In ancient times, a sign of a person's wealth was when he or she would own enough gold to fill the skin of a bull. This volume was called "Quintar." Later on, rather than using the word "Quintar" to refer to the volume of gold needed to fill a bull's skin, people started using it to refer to the weight of that amount of gold, which equals about 144 kilograms or 317 pounds.

قِنْطَار (Quintar) was the heaviest unit of measurement known at the time of the Prophet, and gold is the most precious metal. Allah used the example of the heaviest weight and the most precious metal to highlight for us that honesty is more valuable than either.

In Islamic jurisprudence, the minimum value over which the thief's hand is amputated is a quarter of a dinar, which equals about a quarter of an ounce of gold. However, the compensation due to a victim who lost his or her hand by accident is 500 dinars. Naturally, some have questioned, "How can you value a hand at 500 dinars in one law and a quarter of a dinar in another?" One of the scholars replied, "An honest and trustworthy hand is most precious, while a hand that betrays the trust of others is almost worthless."

Among the People of the Book are some who, if you entrust them with a weight of treasure, they will return it to you intact; and among them are some who, if you entrust them with one gold coin, will not return it unless you keep insisting on its return. That is because they claim, "We have no responsibility toward the unlettered people." Thus they speak lies in attribution to Allah, and do so knowingly. (Verse 75)

At the beginning of the verse, Allah sheds light on the Jews and Christians distinguished with honesty and integrity. The phrase "and among them are some who, if you entrust them with one gold coin, will not return it unless you keep insisting on its return" highlights the opposite side of the spectrum. You cannot entrust some individuals even with a single coin because, if you do not repeatedly ask for it back, you may never get it.

The reason behind such dishonesty comes from the mouths of the corrupt: they claim, "We have no responsibility toward the unlettered people." In other words, they have a double standard when dealing with people. At the time of our beloved Prophet Muhammad, the Jews of Medina used to treat the Arabs —especially the unlettered— from among their customers differently, often denying their rights.

The word "unlettered" is translated from the Arabic origin الأميون (Umiyoon). The root الأم (Um) means "the mother." Here are the different meanings the word الأميون (Umiyoon) carries.

First, it is used to refer to the gentiles, that is, the people who were not Jewish or Christian. Second, it refers to a person who had no education, because he or she is like the day they were born out of their mothers. Allah says:

It is Allah Who brought you out of your mothers' wombs knowing nothing and gave you hearing and sight and minds so that you might be thankful. (16:78)

Lastly, الأميون (Umiyoon) means the people of Mecca, because Mecca was considered the mother of all cities, or Umm Al-Qura.

Here we ask: who established the system for the People of the Book to treat people differently? Is it OK to deceive illiterate people? Do you cheat others based on their education, religion, or place of birth? What ethics permit honouring the contract of a Jewish customer while violating that of the non-Jews? Is it acceptable to charge interest on loans to non-Jews, while lending interest-free to Jewish borrowers? All of the above transactions are unfair and are surely against the teachings of the Torah, the Gospel, and all heavenly religions.

Allah, on the other hand, is fair to people regardless of their faith. He says:

Allah commands you to deliver trusts to those entitled to them and, when you judge between people, to judge with justice. How excellent is what Allah exhorts you to do; assuredly, Allah is All-Hearing, All-Seeing. (4:58)

Thus, the People of the Book who cheat others and then claim, "We have no responsibility toward the unlettered people" are acting against what Allah preached in the Torah and Gospel. Their excuses result from the distortions, omissions, and modifications perpetrated against Allah's sacred books. He says:

So woe to those who write something down with their own hands and then claim, "This is from Allah," in order to make some small gain. Woe to them for what their hands have written! Woe to them for all that they have earned! (2:79)

In other words, the corrupt among the clergy added to the Bible that which was not a part of it and then believed their own lies. Allah does not classify humans into two classes, one of Jews or Christians that deserves to be treated fairly and a second class of gentiles who have no rights. They should have known better or looked up to the Quran for how to treat others.

In the Quran, Allah did not issue a single ruling that includes all Jews and Christians; instead, He treated the righteous among them fairly, regardless of their faith. The people who put faith above all were recognized in the phrase, "Among the People of the Book are some who, if you entrust them with a weight of treasure, they will return it to you intact." And those who put worldly material desires above all were also documented in the phrase, "And among them are some who, if you entrust them with one gold coin, will not return it unless you keep insisting on its return."

For this reason, the righteous among the Jews and Christians knew that Islam brought the truth. Had Islam painted all with a single brush, then fair-minded people would have said, "We are upright and honest; why would a heavenly religion attack us?" But Islam came to do justice and give each person his or her due right. Allah, the Lord of Muhammad, Jesus, and Moses, wants all people to deal with each other fairly. The value of trust far outweighs any material gain.

The People of the Book in Medina who betrayed the trust of their faith forgot the fact that our beloved Prophet Muhammad gained fame for his trustworthiness well before the advent of Islam. Even the disbelieving enemies of Prophet Muhammad trusted him to safe-keep their valuables while they travelled.

All the religious legislations that differentiate between people when fulfilling trusts are human fabrications. Allah says, "They speak lies in attribution to Allah, and do so knowingly." It might have been acceptable for them to say, "These laws are from us. We choose to treat our tribe fairly and cheat others." Instead, they intentionally attributed such injustices to Allah and debased their religion. More shocking is the fact that such corrupt clergy were also aware of the punishment they will receive for lying about Allah. He says:

There are some who twist the Scripture with their tongues to make you think that what they say is part of the Scripture when it is not; they say that it is from Allah when it is not; they attribute lies to Allah, and they know it. (3:78)

Verses 76

Balaa man awfaa bi'ahdihee wattaqaa fainnal laaha yuhibbul muttaqeen

No indeed! Whoever fulfills his pledge and is wary of Allah —Allah indeed loves the Allah-wary. (Verse 76)

Which pledge is this? It is the covenant of faith that we chose to accept freely. When you believe in Allah and declare your faith, you accept every judgment issued by Him and vow to abide by what He asks of you. If you do not abide by Allah's commands, your faith is worthless; it is just empty words.

That is why many verses in the Quran start with the phrase, "O you who believe," then mention religious rulings. For example, Allah says:

O you who have believed, eat from the good things which We have provided for you and be grateful to Allah if it is Him that you worship. (2:172)

Allah, the All-Merciful, does not issue orders or assign obligations to the disbelievers. He only invites them to join the faith. Allah only assigns duties to those who willingly believed in Him and sought His guidance. Faith is a personal commitment you make to the Lord. Only after you declare your faith does Allah address you with the commands "do" and "do not do." This is made very clear in the Quran because all religious rulings can be found in verses that start with the phrase "O you who believe."

Many people misunderstand the statement, "Whoever fulfills his pledge and is wary of Allah —Allah indeed loves the Allah-wary." They incorrectly assume that Allah's love is referring to the person. In other words, they think, "If I fulfill the requirements of faith and be mindful of Allah, then He will love me, and I can do whatever I like after that."

But remember that Allah does not value a person for his or her own sake. Allah values the good deeds that you perform with sincerity. Thus Allah did not say, "Whoever fulfills his pledge and is wary of Allah — Allah indeed loves him." Instead, He said, "Whoever fulfills his pledge and is wary of Allah —Allah indeed loves the Allah-wary," pointing to piety as the object of love. So make sure that you always hold that quality within you, so you remain loved by the Lord.

We remind you of an example we gave before about Allah's promise to Noah to save his family from drowning. Noah was later surprised to find his son in grave danger and about to drown. He raised his hands towards the heavens and supplicated:

"O Lord, my son is surely a member of my family, and verily Your promise is true, as You are the most just of all judges." (from 11:45) to which Allah replied:

"O Noah! He is not of your family. He is one of unrighteous conduct. So do not ask of Me what you have no knowledge of. I caution you so that you do not behave as one among the ignorant." (11:46)

Note that Allah did not hate Noah's son; rather, He detested His actions and explained, "He is one of unrighteous conduct." Allah attributed the matter to the deed, not the person. Likewise, in the verses under study, Allah's love is attributed to the act, not the person.

Now we move to the next verse in Al Imran.

Verse 77

Innal lazeena yashtaroona bi'ahdil laahi wa aymaanihim samanan qaleelan ulaaa'ika laa khalaaqa lahum fil Aakhirati wa laa yukallimuhumul laahu wa laa yanzuru ilaihim Yawmal Qiyaamati wa laa yuzakkeehim wa lahum 'azabun 'aleem

As for those who sell out Allah's covenant and their own oaths for a small price, they will have no share in the life to come. Allah will neither speak to them nor look at them on the Day of Resurrection; He will not cleanse them of their sins; agonizing torment awaits them.

When a verse mentions buying and selling, we should take time to understand the transaction properly. In the olden days, people traded by exchanging items of direct benefit to each other such as food, wood, and livestock. For example, a person may exchange wheat for fabric. There isn't a buyer and a seller in such a scenario because both have bought and sold at the same time.

A buy and sell transaction is different because it entails exchanging an item of direct benefit, such as food, wood, or livestock, for money, which has no direct benefit. For example, when you buy a loaf of bread from a bakery, the bread benefits you directly because you can eat it, while the money does not benefit the baker directly. Money does not fill your stomach, quench your thirst, or clothe you. In a buy and sell transaction, a person pays a price of money to buy something of benefit. In other words, you sell money to purchase an item.

When you read the phrase "As those who sell out Allah's covenant and their own oaths for a small price," you realize that the transaction is upside down: someone bought a price! They exchanged what is directly beneficial –which are Allah's teachings– for something of little benefit. It is similar to a usurious interest transaction where money itself is the good sold and bought. A lender sells a hundred coins in exchange for a hundred and ten coins from the borrower. Money, although not of direct benefit to either party, becomes the commodity being traded. That is a prohibited transaction because it devalues work and makes money the sole object. Allah says:

Those are the ones who have purchased error in exchange for guidance, so their transaction has brought no profit, nor were they guided. (2:16)

This brings us back to the verse, which has a story behind it. During a period of drought and famine, a group of Muslim travellers came to Ka'ab Ibn Al-Ashraf, a prominent Jewish merchant, and asked for food and clothes. He asked, "Do you believe that this man –Muhammad– is the Messenger of Allah?" They replied, "Yes, we do." He said, "That is too bad. I really wanted to help you, but Allah has deprived you of much good." They wondered, "Why?" He said, "Because you have declared faith in Muhammad." When they found themselves in this situation, they said to Ibn Al-Ashraf, "Give us some time. We have some suspicions about the message of Muhammad, and we want to think things over." They returned shortly and said, "We did some reading, and you were right. Muhammad is not a messenger." In essence, this group of people preferred food and clothing over Allah's guidance.

Keep in mind that the verse is general as it applies to anyone who exchanges Allah's teachings for a price. It does not have to be food or clothes; some people exchange their religion to fit in and keep up with the times. Others sell out for a job or political gain. Whoever puts up his or her values for sale in exchange for worldly gain is included in the verse. Allah says:

As for those who sell out Allah's covenant and their own oaths for a small price, they will have no share in the life to come. Allah will neither speak to them nor look at them on the Day of Resurrection; He will not cleanse them of their sins; agonizing torment awaits them.

The phrase "Allah's covenant" could be referring to one of two pledges. The first is the covenant of instinct and creation. Allah instilled within each of us a drive towards faith, and He took an oath from entire humankind to seek His path. We all experience this drive through our instinct to search for higher power and seek our Creator. It is a documented drive across cultures, generations, and continents. Allah says,

And when your Lord took out the offspring from the loins of the Children of Adam and made them bear witness about themselves, He said, "Am I not your Lord?" and they replied, "Yes, we bear witness." So you cannot say on the Day of Resurrection, "We were not aware of this." (7:172)

The second pledge is the one Allah took from His prophets and messengers to inform their nations of the coming of Prophet Muhammad, peace be upon him. They pledged to support him and ask their followers to believe in him when he arrives, as mentioned in the following verse:

Allah took a pledge from the prophets, saying, "If, after I have bestowed the Scripture and wisdom upon you, a messenger comes confirming what you have been given, you must believe in him and support him. Do you affirm this and accept My pledge as binding on you?" They said, "We do.' He said, "Then bear witness and I too will bear witness." (3:81)

So anyone who dismisses these pledges in exchange for worldly gain has sold Allah's covenant for a small price. What a great loss! Such people, whether they sold Allah's signs for food, money, power, or the opposite gender, all share the common outcome of having "no share in the life to come. Allah will neither speak to them nor look at them on the Day of Resurrection- He will not cleanse them of their sins- agonizing torment awaits them.

Let's take a few moments to study the phrase "Allah will neither speak to them nor look at them on the Day of Resurrection." Some people pointed out other verses in the Quran that seem to contradict the above statement. Allah says,

They will say: "Our Lord! Our wretchedness prevailed over us, and we were people lost in error. Our Lord! Take us out of this suffering. Then, if we ever revert to evil, we will indeed be wrongdoers." He will say, "Away with you! In you go! Do not speak to Me!" (23:106-108)

So, on the Day of Judgement, does Allah speak to the people who sold out His covenant or not? We answer that it could be that Allah will not address them with any words of mercy, or He may only speak to them indirectly through the angels.

The verse continues with "nor looks at them." Whenever you run across an attribute of Allah that is shared by humans, such as eyesight, you should refer the matter to the following verse: Allah says in the 11th verse of chapter 42,

There is nothing whatever like Him.

When you dislike a person and run into them walking down the street, you turn your head the other way. On the other hand, when you fall in love, you stare into your lover's eyes. Thus, the gazing of the eye shows interest, while turning away shows resentment.

We cannot apply the same example to Allah because He is exalted above all similarities and analogies. When the matter is related to the Almighty, we believe that "There is nothing whatever like Him," and this is how we understand the phrase "Allah will neither speak to them nor look at them on the Day of Resurrection." Allah will ignore those who sell His covenant for worldly gain; He will not care for them, and He will distance them from His mercy.

The verse continues with, "He will not cleanse them of their sins." The verb "cleanse" is translated from the Arabic origin يُزَكِّيهِمْ (Yuzakeehm). التزكية (Tzakia) means purification, praise, and growth. This is the root from which the word Zakat, almsgiving, is derived. Zakat is meant to purify and grow wealth. Prophet Muhammad, peace be upon him, said, "A man's wealth will never decrease from Charity."

The fact that Allah will not speak to those who forgo His teachings for worldly gains, nor look at them or purify them from their sins, is only an introduction to what they will suffer on that day. Allah says, "agonizing torment awaits them." Why did Allah specify the final destination? Because some people may think: Well, it is not a big deal if Allah does not look at or speak to me.

Verse 78

Wa inna minhum lafaree qany yalwoona alsinatahum bil Kitaabi litahsaboohu minal Kitaab, wa maa huwa minal Kitaabi wa yaqooloona huwa min 'indillaahi wa maa huwa min 'indillaahi wa yaqooloona 'alal laahil kaziba wa hum ya'lamoon

Among them is a group who twist their tongues with the Scripture to make you think that what they say is part of the Scripture when it is not; they say it is from Allah when it is not; they attribute lies to Allah and they know it. (Verse 78)

If you take two or more strings and twist them together, you end up with a rope. By twisting the strands, you strengthen the overall structure. A rope has higher strengths than the sum of its individual strands.

That is the same reason some of the People of the Book twist their tongues with words and then claim them from their scriptures. They do so because they are corrupt and have a weak argument. In other words, they want to strengthen their position against the believers by fabricating words and then claiming that they are quoting parts of the Gospel.

Allah says,

Some among the Jews distort the words out of context and say: "We have heard and do not obey," and "hear without listening," and "listen to us," twisting their tongues and reviling the faith. But if they had said: "We have heard and obey," and "hear and regard us," it would have been better for them and more appropriate. But Allah has disgraced them for their lack of belief; and so only a few of them believe. (4:46)

And in another chapter,

When they were told, "Settle in this town and eat freely there as you will, but say, "Unburden us!" and enter its gate humbly: then We shall forgive you your sins, and increase the reward of those who do good." The wrongdoers among them substituted another saying for that which had been given them, so We sent them a punishment from heaven for their transgression. (7:161-162)

In the example above, the Israelites accompanying Prophet Moses were ordered to say "Unburden us!" translated from the origin حِطَّة (Hitta), asking for Allah's forgiveness and the unloading of their sins. In exchange, they would be pardoned and granted access to the Holy land. But some, out of arrogance and ridicule, distorted Allah's command and said "hinta," which is a type of grain. The casual listener may not recognize the subtle difference because they deliberately twisted their tongue as they said it.

This type of trickery was not only employed with the pronunciation of the words but the meaning of Allah's words was also twisted. The corrupt among the people of the book distorted the meaning of the Gospel away from what Allah intended. They did so to misguide the believers and sow doubt in their faith. Allah says, "to make you think that what they say is part of the Scripture when it is not."

Their assertion "it is from Allah" is perhaps the strongest evidence of their lies. They wanted to distance themselves from the lie and blame Allah. Isn't this tactic common among criminals? A guilty person goes out of his way to repeatedly and loudly blame others for the crime. Parents know that the child who volunteers to tell on others for no reason is often the troublemaker! Allah exposes the unjust. He says, "they say it is from Allah when it is not."

And just in case you want to give them the benefit of the doubt and say, "maybe they forgot the exact wording of the scripture, or maybe they made a mistake," Allah informs you that "they attribute lies to Allah and they know it." They are liars who know exactly what they are doing.

But what exactly is lying? Most people would answer that lying is saying something that does not match reality. It is the opposite of being truthful. We answer that lying goes a bit deeper than that. Every time I speak, my speech passes through three different levels. The first level is mental where, before I speak, I run the issue in my mind. The second level is lingual, which happens after my brain gives the signal to my tongue to speak. The third level is a question of whether what I say matches reality or not. Only when there is agreement on all three levels, I am being truthful; otherwise, I am lying.

To better understand this concept, listen to the following verse:

When the hypocrites come to you, they say, 'We bear witness that you are the Messenger of Allah.' Allah knows that you truly are His Messenger, and He bears witness that the hypocrites are liars (63:1)

This verse, often pointed out by the critics of the Quran, relates to the incident of the hypocrites coming to the Prophet Muhammad to declare their faith. Allah affirms that their statement is correct, yet at the same time, He calls them liars. How could this be? The answer is found within the hypocrites' hearts.

Let's measure the statement of the hypocrites against the three levels of speech. Does the statement "you are the Messenger of Allah" match reality? It does. Allah affirmed it in the verse: "Allah knows that you truly are His Messenger." Did the hypocrites voluntarily say this statement to Prophet Muhammad? Yes, they did. So, where is the lie? It is in the statement "We bear witness." The hypocrites only testified with their tongues that Muhammad is the Messenger of Allah, while their hearts denied it. For a person to be truthful, what he or she says must match what is in the heart. Thus, although the statement "you are the Messenger of Allah" is true, the hypocrites were liars.

This brings us back to the verse. The phrase "they attribute lies to Allah, and they know it" means that they intentionally say words that do not match the reality of things, and that is, by definition, a lie.

We should also distinguish between the reliability of the information and the credibility of the informant. For example, if you see your neighbour up all night reading a book the day before the exam, you would assume that he is studying. You may tell your friends that your neighbour was up all night studying while, in reality, he was reading a novel. In this case, you were honest; however, the information you had was inaccurate. You were not truthful because the information you delivered did not match the reality, yet you were not a liar because you honestly believed in what you said. But in the case of the verse, we find that the corrupt people of the book were intentionally lying. They knew their scripture by heart but decided to say something different.

Verse 79

Maa kaana libasharin ai yu'tiyahul laahul Kitaaba walhukma wan Nubuwwata summa yaqoola linnaasi koonoo 'ibaadal lee min doonil laahi wa laakin koonoo rabbaaniy yeena bimaa kuntum tu'allimoonal Kitaaba wa bimaa kuntum tadrusoon

No person to whom Allah had given the Scripture, wise judgment, and prophethood would ever say to people, "Be my servants, not Allah's." Rather, "You should be devoted to the Lord because you have taught the Scripture and studied it closely." (Verse 79)

There are three elements of Allah's guidance mentioned in this verse: "Scripture, wise judgement, and prophethood." Let's take them one by one.

Allah reveals His teachings to humanity in the form of a scripture. That also necessitates that the Almighty selects a human being to deliver the message. A Messenger comes with a scripture, applies it, and delivers it to the people. Allah chooses the messenger specifically for this task. A prophet, on the other hand, has a different mission. Allah selects a prophet to implement the existing scripture. In other words, a messenger carries a new heavenly message, teaches it to his people, and practices it among them. A prophet, on the other hand, does not carry a new message. He only serves as a practical example and a reminder of previous messages. People do not only need to hear the words of Allah, but they also must see these teachings in practice. A prophet is a behavioural model for people to follow.

Let's clarify. Prophet Muhammad, Jesus, Moses, Abraham, David, peace be upon them, brought new heavenly messages and new scriptures; thus, they were all messengers. They were also prophets because they practiced the new message and led by example. Prophets Solomon, Lot, John, and many others, peace be upon them, were sent to bring people back to the right path and adhere to the scriptures they already had. They were not messengers because they did not bring new revelations. Allah says,

We had never sent any messenger or prophet before you into whose wishes Satan did not insinuate something, but Allah removes what Satan insinuates, and then Allah affirms His message. Allah is all-knowing and wise. (22:52)

There are many instances, just like in our modern times, when the heavenly scripture is present with us, but people simply ignore it or only implement a is convenient for them. We all know what is permissible and what is forbidden, but how many of us truly follow the heavenly guidance.

We have now understood the meaning of scriptures and prophethood but what is meant by "wise judgment" translated from the Arabic origin الْحُكْم (Al-Hukm)? We answer that Allah wants you to know that wisdom in faith is not limited to messengers and prophets. Rather, wise judgment can be present in any member of the faithful community. When matters of faith are clear in mind, a person may choose to spread Allah's word to others. Allah gave us the example of Luqman, who had beautiful advice to his son, perfectly aligned with the heavenly teachings. So, it is possible that a righteous person, who is not a prophet, acts as a model to others in his or her behaviour. Here, we must emphasize that whoever is calling towards Allah and applying His teachings should be true to the faith and never add anything to it. Allah says, "No person to whom Allah had given the Scripture, wise judgment, and prophethood would ever say to people, "Be my servants, not Allah's."

But why was the verse under study revealed? This verse came after the Christians delegation of Najran and a group of the Jews of Medina met with Prophet Muhammad, peace be upon him. During the debate, they asked the messenger: "What do you believe in? and what do you command people to do?" Muhammad informed them of Allah's religion, its creed, prohibitions, and the principles of worship. They replied, "So, you wants us to worship you and make you a God?!" They assumed that Prophet Muhammad's words and the commands he conveyed to them are his own. Why? Because they were used to fabricating matters in their own religion, attributing them to Allah, and then ask people to obey. Their corruption made them forget the differences between the teachings of a Messenger who is truthful in delivering Allah's message, and the fabricated commandments of the corrupt clergy.

Their question, "So, you want us to worship you and make you a Allah?!" is a telltale sign of their own doings. When a person falsifies Allah's commands and then asks people to obey, then he is asking them to worship him; it is a form of polytheism. That was the first thought that came to the minds of the Christians of Najran and the Jews of Medina because they considered such corruption the norm. They assumed that Muhammad, peace be upon him, was after power and wealth just as their superiors violated Allah's rulings and replaced them with their opinions.

Prophet Muhammad never asked them to obey him; instead, he asked them to obey the teachings he brought. At that juncture, Allah revealed:

No person to whom Allah had given the Scripture, wise judgment, and prophethood would ever say to people, "Be my servants, not Allah's." Rather, "You should be devoted to the Lord because you have taught the Scripture and studied it closely." (Chapter 3: Verse 79)

Negligence had them doubt Allah's ability to select an honest Messenger. They also distrusted that the Messenger would deliver Allah's teachings verbatim and assumed that he would distort them for his own benefit. Allah answers, "No person to whom Allah had given the Scripture, wise judgment, and prophethood would ever say to people, "Be my servants, not Allah's."

The verse under study is also a reference to some of the Companions who not only revered and honoured Prophet Muhammad, but also wanted to elevate him to a higher status. Out of extreme love, some asked if they should greet Muhammad with a prostration. Muhammad never asked to be treated differently than others. We should treat Muhammad, peace be upon him, with the utmost respect but never elevate him to any status above his humanity. Allah teaches us the right balance. He says,

A Messenger has come to you from among yourselves. Your suffering distresses him: he is deeply concerned for you and full of kindness and mercy towards the believers. (9:128)

And in another chapter,

Do not regard the Messenger's summons to you like one of you summoning another- Allah is well aware of those of you who steal away surreptitiously- and those who go against his order should beware lest a trial afflict them or they receive a painful punishment. (24:63) lastly,

No person to whom Allah had given the Scripture, wise judgment, and prophethood would ever say to people, "Be my servants, not Allah's." Rather, "You should be devoted to the Lord because you have taught the Scripture and studied it closely." (Verse 79)

The word "rather" is used to reject the case before it and approve the case that follows it. In the verse under study, Allah employs "rather" to alert you against thinking that a prophet or messenger would ever overstep Allah's boundaries; instead, Allah's messengers faithfully carry His teachings and invite people to the worship of the One Allah.

The phrase "devoted to the Lord." is translated from the Arabic origin رباني (Rabani). The root رب (Rub) means the caretaker who nourishes, educates, and protects. In the Arabic language, the father is called the Rub of the family. The same word 'Rub' is the root of 'tarbia', which means raising and educating a child. 'Ruban' is the captain of the ship.

So, what is the meaning of the word رباني (Rabani)? We answer that if you like to attribute yourself to the Lord, you would say (Rubee). And if we want to exaggerate the attribution, say 'رباني'. Adding the letters A and N is the highest form of emphasis. For example, the Arabic word for "to read" is (Qara'); by adding A and N at the end of the word, it becomes (Quran) which is the most recited book on earth.

Similarly, the word 'Rabbani' means a believer who is overly attached to the Lord. This devotion has two signs. First, the believers take every part of his or her faith from the Lord's teachings and no one else. Second, the believer speaks and acts as an educator and caretaker of the society towards success and righteousness.

The verse ends with, "You should be devoted to the Lord because you have taught the Scripture and studied it closely." To have knowledge is to receive it from someone, but to study is to spend time going over it for deeper understating.

The word "study" is translated from the Arabic درس (Darasa), which has its origins in milling wheat. In the olden times, harvested wheat was placed between two large millstones in the shape of wheels. The top stone was then turned round and round until the grains separate from the hay and turn into flour. The process of going over the wheat helps extract the beneficial food and discard the rest.

Similarly, studying the scriptures is the process of going over the material and exchanging ideas between students until a more profound understanding is reached and all possible meanings of the text have been extracted. Studying is an essential part of being a Rabani who is "devoted to the Lord."

Verses 79

Maa kaana libasharin ai yu'tiyahul laahul Kitaaba walhukma wan Nubuwwata summa yaqoola linnaasi koonoo 'ibaadal lee min doonil laahi wa laakin koonoo rabbaaniy yeena bimaa kuntum tu'allimoonal Kitaaba wa bimaa kuntum tadrusoon-(Verse 79)

Verses 80

Wa laa yaamurakum an tattakhizul malaaa 'ikata wan Nabiyyeena arbaabaa; a yaamurukum bilkufri ba'da iz antum muslimoon (Verse 80)

No person to whom Allah had given the Scripture, wise judgment, and prophethood would ever say to people, "Be my servants, not Allah's." Rather, "You should be devoted to the Lord because you have taught the Scripture and studied it closely." He would never command you to take angels and prophets as lords. How could he command you to be disbelievers after you had devoted yourselves to Allah? (Chapter 3: Verses 79 and 80)

A person whom Allah, the all-knowledgable all-wise, chose to be a messenger would never say to people: "Worship me, or the angels, or worship the prophets." Allah grants His book, wisdom, and prophethood to those pure in heart and faith. He says,

He would never command you to take angels and prophets as lords. How could he command you to be disbelievers after you had devoted yourselves to Allah? (Verse 80)

This verse is related to an incident where some of the companions wanted to show their love and respect to prophet Muhammad. They suggested that the best way to greet him was with prostration. The Prophet, peace be upon him, made it clear that prostration is to Allah, and Allah alone. Had the messenger agreed to their suggestion, this would have meant that he was taking them out of Islam, and that can never occur from our beloved Muhammad or any other Prophet.

Now, we move to the next verse in Al-Imran. Allah says,

Verse 81

Wa iz akhazal laahu meesaaqan Nabiyyeena lamaaa aataitukum min Kitaabinw wa Hikmatin summa jaaa'akum Rasoolum musaddiqul limaa ma'akum latu'minunna bihee wa latansurunnah; qaala a'aqrartum wa akhaztum alaa zaalikum isree qaalooo aqrarnaa; qaala fashhadoo wa ana ma'akum minash shaahideen

Allah took a pledge from the prophets, saying, "If, after I have bestowed Scripture and wisdom upon you, a messenger comes confirming what you have been given, you must believe in him and support him. Do you affirm this and accept My pledge as binding on you?" They said, "We do.' He said, "Then bear witness and I too will bear witness."

This verse explains why the Almighty sends a chain of messengers. We all know that the first teachings were revealed to Adam, peace be upon him. They contained everything necessary for a harmonious and just life on earth. Adam faithfully delivered Allah's teachings to his children just as any good father would. His children passed their knowledge onto their children and so on from one generation to the next. But unfortunately, with the passage of time we find that some of the religious obligations are ignored and forgotten. In short, humanity failed at preserving the teachings of their Lord.

Humanity has always succeeded in passing on material knowledge. People have used the wheel from the day of its invention without fail. Every generation after Edison enjoyed light and electricity. But humans are short-sighted and look for instant gratification. We value material progress because we can immediately enjoy its benefits. But we often fail to see the advantages of Allah's teachings, even though ignoring them usually ends in wars and poverty.

People often neglect religion and then discard it altogether. This usually happens gradually. When you sin, your healthy conscious steps in to deter you or make you feel regret. This self-blame is a sign of a healthy state because it brings you back to the Lord, seeking forgiveness. However, if you persistently sin, then that part of yourself becomes weaker. At some point, the self-blame ceases and turns into an insatiable lust that chases after life's pleasures and leads you astray. Now, you can no longer self-correct, and you need the help of the society around you to guide you towards the right path. That is why it is critical to surround yourself with the right friends and community.

Sadly, at times, both the reproaching self is diminished, and the society is corrupt. Sin becomes widespread and even celebrated. Allah says:

They did not forbid each other to do wrong. How vile their deeds were! (5:79)

Who can correct this situation? This is when the heavens must intervene with a new messenger to bring people back to the straight path.

Allah created us while He possessed all attributes of perfection. Our creation did not add anything to His attributes. We cannot benefit Allah in any way even if we all perfectly follow His teachings. This means that religion is a mercy from the Lord for our own benefit, not His, and His teachings are meant to elevate our status not His. Allah is our Creator, and He wants the best for His creation. We stand to lose if we leave Allah's teachings behind. In a scared narration –Hadith Qudsi- narrated by Abu Dharr, may Allah be pleased with him, the Messenger, peace be upon him, relays to us the words of Allah. He said:

"O my servants, I have forbidden injustice for myself, and I have forbidden it among you, so do not oppress one another. O my servants, all of you are astray except for those I have guided, so seek guidance from me, and I shall guide you. O my servants, all of you are hungry except for those I have fed, so seek food from Me, and I shall feed you.

O my servants, all of you are naked except for those I have clothed, so seek clothing from Me, and I shall clothe you. O my servants, you sin by night and day, and I forgive all sins, so seek forgiveness from Me and I shall forgive you.

O my servants, know that you will not be able to cause any harm to me, and you will not be able to bring me any benefit. O my servants, were the first of you and the last of you, the human of you and the jinn of you, to be as pious as the most pious heart among you, that would not increase my dominion at all. O my servants, were the first of you and the last of you, the human of you and the jinn of you to be as wicked as the most wicked heart among you, that would not decrease my dominion at all.

O my servants, were the first of you and the last of you, the human of you and the jinn of you to rise in one place and make a request of me, and were I to give each all he or she has requested, that would not diminish what I have any more than a needle would diminish the ocean if dipped into it.

O my servants, it is only your deeds that I record for you and then recompense for you. Let he who finds good praise Allah, and let he who finds otherwise blame no one but himself."

Verse 81

Allah took a pledge from the prophets, saying, "If, after I have bestowed scripture and wisdom upon you, a messenger comes confirming what you have been given, you must believe in him and support him. Do you affirm this and accept My pledge as binding on you?" They said, "We do." He said, "Then bear witness, and I too will bear witness." (Chapter 3: Verse 81)

In the previous verse, we explained how Allah created us with all His attributes of perfection. Our life did not add anything to Him, nor can we benefit Him in any way. He says:

I want no provision from them, nor do I want them to feed Me. Surely, it is Allah Who is the Great Sustainer, the Lord of immense power, the Almighty. (51:57-58)

Hence, when Allah sends us a heavenly message, He does it for our benefit, not His. Sadly, many people look at Allah's teachings as a constraint on their personal freedom. A young man may think, "I would like to drink alcohol in moderation and have a girlfriend. I am not hurting anyone." We answer that such thoughts are misguided. Allah's teachings protect your freedoms and all those around you. For example, Allah commands you not to steal from others. If you like something that does not belong to you, such as a nice piece of jewellery, you cannot just take it. Yet, at the same time, Allah commanded millions of people not to steal from you. Hence, Allah did not restrict your actions; rather, He protected your wealth. He instructed you as an individual not to steal and, at the same time, instructed millions of people not to steal from you. Who is the true winner in this case? No doubt, it is you!

Similarly, Allah prohibited you from maritial relations with the opposite gender outside of marriage; that surely limits your freedom, right? Not exactly, because Allah's law is not just for you. Allah commanded every believer on earth to lower their gaze and not to stare at your wife, sister, and mother. Doesn't that give you comfort and peace of mind? In exchange for guarding your two eyes, Allah protected your family from the sin of millions of eyes.

These are just two examples of how Allah's teachings bring balance and comfort to your life. Allah, the All-Merciful, sent messengers armed with scriptures to benefit all human beings from the time of Adam till the message of Islam. Since the source of all heavenly messages is Allah Almighty, and since their common purpose is the protection and betterment of humankind, why do we have so many disagreements and wars? Where did all the conflicts between religions and even within every religion come from? We answer that Allah's messengers are absolved from contradiction. It is not possible for one messenger of Allah to contradict and fight another. Conflicts are manufactured by some of their followers who chase after worldly power and wealth.

When Prophet Jesus, peace be upon him, brought us Christianity, some rabbis objected. Why? Because their worldly authority was at stake. Had such rabbis been true to their faith, they would have welcomed the messenger of Allah with appreciation and said to him, "Help us deepen our understanding of Allah's teachings."

Conflicts only happen when people put their whims above Allah's teachings. The procession of heavenly messages since the creation of man is a collaborative one, not a contradictive one. Prophet Muhammad, peace be upon him, said, "My place in comparison with the other prophets before me is that of a man who built a house nicely and beautifully, except for one missing corner brick. People would tour the house and marvel at its beauty but say, 'When will this brick be put in its place?' I am that brick, and I am the final messenger."

At times, the fiercest enemies of Allah's messengers are those who claim to follow previous religions. When a messenger is sent to ignorant people, matters are easy because all the messenger needs to do is educate them about the One God. However, when a messenger faces corrupt clergy of previous religions, they act as zealots against the new faith because it threatens their authority. Allah says:

Have you considered those who were given a share of the scripture? When they are asked to accept judgment from Allah's Scripture, some of them turn their backs and walk away, all because they declare, "The Fire shall not touch us, except for a few days," and so the lies they forged in their religion have deluded them. (3:23-24)

Since the beginning of time, the procession of heavenly prophets and messengers continued to protect it from deviation. Allah chose the nation of Muhammad to carry the trust of the divine message till the end of time. No messenger will come after Muhammad because Allah guaranteed the subsistence of good within his nation. Thus, if you see people transgressing in disbelief, then rest assured that there are believers whom Allah has supported to restore balance. Allah says:

Let there be a community among you who call to the good, and urge the right, and forbid the wrong. They are the ones who have success. (3:104)

And in another verse:

You are the best community ever brought forth for humankind, promoting what is right and good and forbidding evil, and you believe in Allah. If only the People of the Book believed, this would have been good for them. Among them there are believers, but most of them are transgressors. (3:110)

And in another chapter:

By Time! Man is certainly in deep loss, except for those who believe, do good deeds, urge one another to the truth, and urge one another to steadfastness. (Chapter 103)

Take note that Allah used the phrase "urge one another," not "urge others," so we understand that giving good advice is a mutual matter. You may sometimes find yourself spiritually weak while your friends feel firm; hence, they push you in the right direction. On other occasions, you may advise your friend to stay away from sin.

Thus, no specific people, group, or agency has the job of enjoining good or preventing vice. Instead, the matter is the duty of every Muslim. This is solidarity in faith; it protects against the ever-changing state of the human heart. When we see a believer weakening in faith, we must urge him or her towards the truth, and we expect nothing less from our brothers and sisters.

As for the previous nations, corruption had crept in until no one minded sin. Thus, the heavens needed to intervene and send a new messenger with a new miracle to restore faith on earth. Allah says:

Those among the Children of Israel who defied Allah were cursed through the words of David, and Jesus, son of Mary, because they disobeyed, they persistently overstepped the limits. They would not restrain one another from any of the wrong things that they did. How vile were the things they used to do! (5:78-79)

All the messengers, peace be upon them, were instructed to include the following covenant in their message: when the heavens intervene with a new messenger, people of faith must follow him and abandon intolerance, because Allah always guides people towards good. He says, "If, after I have bestowed scripture and wisdom upon you, a messenger comes confirming what you have been given, you must believe in him and support him."

Here, you may ask, is this covenant only valid when two messengers are contemporaries of the same era? For example, prophets Abraham and Lot were present at the same time; so were our beloved Shuaib and Moses, peace be upon them all. We answer that Allah's covenant applies to all messengers, whether contemporaries or centuries apart.

As long as people believe in their messenger and follow Allah's teachings, they should accept any new messenger who comes to confirm and expand on the Lord's teachings. People must be aware that the heavens may intervene at any time, and they should discard fanaticism and welcome the messengers of their Lord. Allah asked, "'Do you affirm this and accept My pledge as binding on you?' They said, 'We do.' He said, 'Then bear witness, and I too will bear witness.'"

Let's take a moment to study the phrase "A messenger comes confirming what you have been given." All heavenly messages share the same creed of monotheism and accountability for one's actions. Allah is One; to Him belongs absolute perfection; He is glorified in His essence and actions. Heavenly messages differ, however, in the matters regulating daily life. As life progressed, new circumstances arose that were not an issue in the previous era; thus, Allah sent new messengers confirming the creed and introducing new legislation better suited for the times. He says:

In matters of faith, He has laid down for you the same commandment that He gave Noah, which We have revealed to you and which We enjoined on Abraham and Moses and Jesus: "Uphold the faith and do not divide into factions within it." What you call upon the idolaters to do is hard for them; Allah chooses whomever He pleases for Himself and guides towards Himself those who turn to Him. (42:13)

When it comes to the day-to-day teachings, we see that Prophet Jesus brought rulings different from the previous prophets, as did Moses and many before them, peace be upon them all. Thus, it was imperative for people to support any messenger that came with miracles and a scripture that confirmed the creed of "There is no Allah but Allah."

Prophet Muhammad(pbuh) was sent to restore faith and guide the People of the Book back to Allah's path. He, peace be upon him, brought a clear scripture confirming the heavenly messages before him and containing the undistorted stories of previous prophets. This, however, presented a real threat to those who held religious and political power at the time.

The Jewish rabbis of Medina recognized that Muhammad was Allah's messenger beyond any shadow of a doubt because they had his description in their books. Some upheld their pledge to Allah and became Muslim, while others did not. Allah says:

Those to whom We gave the scripture know him as they know their own sons. But indeed, a party of them conceal the truth while they know. (2:146)

Prophet Muhammad extended an invitation to every person who followed previous scriptures.

Those who felt that Islam threatened their authority chose intolerance and fanaticism over faith. They followed the distortions in their faith even though Islam came to clarify much of the matters they disagreed about.

Allah wants to protect humankind from the evils of fanaticism that arise from blindly following a messenger while rejecting all else. You should not use one of Allah's messengers as a barrier against another or set one heavenly message as the enemy of another. Such actions are precisely why atheism is becoming widespread in our times.

Nowadays, atheists use the rifts between heavenly religions and within each religion to sow doubt in people. How come that so many groups who claim to follow divine guidance do not agree with one another? How come that people who claim to be of the same faith are fighting each other? If these religions were the truth, they would have agreed and not differed! These types of arguments are only made possible by the people who ignored their pledge to Allah. He says:

Allah took a pledge from the prophets, saying, "If, after I have bestowed scripture and wisdom upon you, a messenger comes confirming what you have been given, you must believe in him and support him. Do you affirm this and accept My pledge as binding on you?" They said, "We do." He said, "Then bear witness, and I too will bear witness." (Chapter 3: Verse 81)

If the followers of each prophet adhered to this covenant, then atheists would be stripped of their strongest argument. People of faith should not be enemies to each other. Instead, they should form one solid wall to confront the deniers of Allah. Sadly, in our times, we often see that the enmity between people of faith is stronger than the enmity between the atheists and the faithful.

Verses 81

Wa iz akhazal laahu meesaaqan Nabiyyeena lamaaa aataitukum min Kitaabinw wa Hikmatin summa jaaa'akum Rasoolum musaddiqul limaa ma'akum latu'minunna bihee wa latansurunnah; qaala a'aqrartum wa akhaztum alaa zaalikum isree qaalooo aqrarnaa; qaala fashhadoo wa ana ma'akum minash shaahideen

Allah took a pledge from the prophets, saying, "If, after I have bestowed scripture and wisdom upon you, a messenger comes confirming what you have been given, you must believe in him and support him. Do you affirm this and accept My pledge as binding on you?" They said, "We do." He said, "Then bear witness, and I too will bear witness." (Verse 81)

We start with the question, who is the witness and what is being witnessed in the phrase "Then bear witness, and I too will bear witness"? We answer that, since Allah said to the prophets, "bear witness," then they are in the position of the witness. So, what is being witnessed? Do the prophets bear witness against themselves? Does every prophet bear witness against others? Or does each prophet testify that he delivered the covenant to his nation? Allah's covenant is inclusive of all the meanings above. Each prophet vows to support future heavenly messages and promises to teach his people the necessity of believing subsequent messengers and Holy Scriptures.

The word "binding" is translated from the Arabic root الإصر (Al-Isr), which is the strongest bond. It is followed by "We do," which is the strongest affirmation. This pledge is then documented by multiple witnesses: the prophets, who bear witness to one another and their nations, and Allah, Who bears witness above all the others. This leaves no room for doubt or claims of misunderstanding.

Hence, when the followers of previous heavenly religions display fanaticism against a later one, rest assured that they have intentionally betrayed Allah's covenant. Allah wants the call to faith to be in complete harmony. Hence, a messenger cannot be a fanatic to himself or his nation. Likewise, the people should not be zealots in their community or religion. The only one we should follow is Allah. In this manner, all heavenly religions are consistent in source and united in goal. They all share the creed of "There is no Allah but Allah."

Allah says in the next verse:

Verse 82

Faman tawallaa ba'da zaalika fa ulaaa'ika humul faasiqoon

Then whoever after this turns away, those are the transgressors. (Verse 82)

The phrase "turn away" is translated from the Arabic origin تولى (Tawalla). It is similar to the common expression "He gave me his back." When you support Allah's messengers, you turn towards the All-Merciful Lord. As for people who fight them, they are the ones turning their back to the Lord. Allah says, "Those are the transgressors," translated from the Arabic origin الْفَاسِقُون (Al Fasiqoun).

The word فُسُوقٌ (Fusuq) originated from the desert environment where the Arabs lived at the time of the Prophet. When a date ripens on a palm tree, its skin stays attached to the fruit and protects it from the elements. As the date ages, the skin separates from the fruit, making it easy to peel. The word فسق (Fasaqa) describes the detachment of the protective skin from its natural place, exposing the fruit to harm and causing it to spoil. Similarly, Allah used the same word فسق (Fasaqa) to describe a person who distances him or herself from Allah's teachings, thus exposing him or herself to harm and ruin. Since Allah's teachings are the shield protecting you in life, you expose your soul to rot whenever you abandon them.

What kind of transgression are we facing in this verse? Is it a major fisq, or a minor one? A minor transgression is when you have faith in Allah but weaken and commit a sin. As for the fisq referred to in the verse "Whoever after this turns away, those are the transgressors," it is the ultimate transgression because it represents defiance against Allah and rejection of faith at its core. It is a rejection of the covenant that was affirmed by the people, the prophets, and then confirmed by the Almighty. Does that leave any excuse for you to turn your back?

If you reject Allah's teachings, then you have to follow a system set by other people. Keep in mind: such people are your equal, and they have the same abilities as you. None of us is perfect, and none of us has superpowers.

However, when the legislation comes from Allah, things are different. As a Muslim, you declare faith in Allah and have conviction in His ultimate wisdom and perfect knowledge; you entrust that He is free of need and that has your best interest at heart. It is from Allah's grace that He sent us messengers armed with miracles and scriptures, so no man has to follow another human being. Allah saved you from slavery and exploitation and gave you the ultimate freedom in this world and the next.

So now we ask, why would any person turn their back on a system that was approved by Allah, the prophets, and the messengers? The answer is simple: people abandon Allah's teaching to follow their desires. They want money, fame, and the opposite gender regardless of the cost to themselves or the society around them. A thief does not care about those he steals from. A drunk driver wants to have fun with complete disregard for endangering the lives of others. Similarly, a person who abandons Allah does not care about the corruption they will cause.

Allah says:

Had the truth been subject to their whims, the heavens and the earth and all those within them would have been ruined. In fact, We had sent them their reminder, but they turned away from good advice. (23:71)

Verse 83

Afaghaira deenil laahi yabghoona wa lahooo aslama man fis samaawaati wal ardi taw'anw wa karhanw wa ilaihi yurja'oon

Do they seek a religion other than Allah's, while to Him submits whoever is in the heavens and on the earth, willingly or unwillingly, and to Him they will be returned?! (Chapter 3: Verse 83)

The verse begins with a rhetorical question,

"Do they seek a religion other than Allah's?".

Let us look at some of the reasons why someone might do so.

Human Free Will and Choice:

Humans are endowed with free will, allowing them to make choices, including choosing to follow or deviate from Allah's guidance.

Influence of Satan and Ego:

The verse suggests that some people may be influenced by Satan, who tempts them with worldly desires and veils them from the truth. This can lead to ego-centric thinking and rejection of Allah's path.

Disbelief and Ignorance:

Some individuals may choose not to believe in Allah or His guidance due to ignorance, lack of knowledge, or stubbornness.

Following Personal Desires:

People may prioritize their own desires and worldly pleasures over the guidance of Allah, leading them to stray from the path of Islam.

Influence of Wrongful Beliefs:

Individuals may be influenced by false beliefs or traditions, leading them away from the true religion of Islam.

Attachment to Material Wealth:

Some people may become overly attached to material wealth and worldly possessions, neglecting their spiritual obligations and distancing themselves from Allah's path.

Ego and Pride:

Some may become prideful and arrogant, believing they are superior to others or that they don't need Allah's guidance.

In essence, the verse highlights the human propensity to choose paths other than Allah's due to a combination of free will, external influences, internal biases, and a desire for worldly gratification.

Why you should follow the religion of Islam

Allah has made you trustees in the universe, and He made everything subservient to you. Let us reflect about the different types of creation at your service. Livestock bend to your will, so does the earth and all the plants it produces. The sun rises and provides you with light and warmth, and the stars help you navigate all corners of the planet. We dig mines to extract metals and energy while the oceans provide us with rain and food. The oxygen we breathe and the medicines we take are the products of forests. Even your body parts do whatever you want. Thus, every type of creation, as far as the eye can see, was created to serve you whether you are a believer in Allah or not.

Have you ever heard the sun saying, "I will not shine on earth today?" or "I will only give my warmth to the believers in Allah?" Has the air ever revolted and said, "This person is corrupt and no longer deserves to breathe, so I will not allow him the benefit?"

Some people object and say, "Many animals are not tame, and some may even attack humans. We had droughts where the earth did not produce anything, and our livestock died of thirst!" We answer that wild animals, droughts, and disasters should serve as a wake-up call that it is not your strength or intelligence that controls nature; rather, it must be something more powerful than you that makes animals, rain, and the soil subservient to you.

Allah says:

Have they not seen how We created for them, by Our own handiwork, livestock which are under their control? And made them tame for them, so that some can be used for riding, some for food, some for other benefits, and some for drink? Will they not give thanks? (36:71-73)

Here is another point to ponder. Everything in life has a task. For example, with a leather cushion and a silver bridle, you can use a horse to fulfill its task as a ride. Yet on another day, you can use the horse to carry your belongings to the market; and if you pay close attention, you will find that the same horse you are riding is fertilizing the earth with its droppings. Hence, this horse has fulfilled its task as a ride, a hauler, and a fertilizer, all with silent obedience to make your life easier.

Inanimate objects serve the plants and provide them with food and energy. Likewise, plants serve the animals as food and shelter, while you stand at the apex as the master of creation with everything at your service. Which begs the question, who do you serve? What is your task? Some people are quick to answer, "I serve no one. I am the master of my own destiny." But that is not true. You did not create the sun, earth, plants, and animals. You don't control your time and place of birth or death. You did not make livestock subservient to you because, if that were the case, then why can you tame a dog but not a wolf? Even your body parts may stop serving you with age or after an accident.

So isn't it logical to wonder about the force that brought you to life and made you king? Once you answer this question, you will figure out who to serve and where to turn for guidance about your task in life.

Let's start by asking: if everything in the universe serves you, is it appropriate for you to follow another human or a man-made system? Of course not, because that does not befit your status. It would be best if you searched for a boss who suits your authority and position.

Allah asks,

Do they seek a religion other than Allah's, while to Him submits whoever is in the heavens and on the earth, willingly or unwillingly, and to Him they will be returned?! (Verse 83)

Allah is your Creator, and He takes care of His creation regardless of their faith. If you work hard and use the means at your disposal, you will benefit. For example, a hard-working farmer will reap great crops from the earth even if he is a disbeliever. A lazy believing farmer, on the other hand, will harvest nothing. All these material blessings are Allah's gifts of lordship, and they are available to everyone. As for Allah's gifts of divinity, they are more precious and only available to the believers who follow His path and respond to the call of the messengers.

Let's take a moment to examine what happens when people function outside of Allah's teachings. For thousand of years, the environment was a self-sustaining, peaceful, and thriving place. Take a look around you today; wherever you see pollution and the destruction of nature, you see human greed. Why do we suffer from food shortages but not air shortages? Because food production and distribution are controlled by our lust for profit and power, while air and wind are not. We have intervened in freshwater management and, as a result, polluted and exhausted much of the supply. In fact, corruption is often proportional to the extent of human intervention. When modern governments want to preserve the beauty and resources of an area, they declare it a natural protected zone. In other words, they set laws to keep human and commercial activities out because such activities equal corruption.

Here you may ask, does that mean that we should just sit around and do nothing? Should we bring progress and innovation to a halt? Of course not. We should work with Allah's creation according to Allah's teachings. If you keep the creator's instructions in mind as you work, then everything will thrive. Just as the sun fulfills its duty, you too are required to perform your duty and obey Allah in all your actions. He says:

He erected heaven and established the balance; that you should not violate the harmony and balance. And observe the balance with full equity, and do not fall short in it. (55:7-9)

Everything managed by Allah functions like clockwork; and if you want your life to run in similar harmony and precision, then you need to align your actions with Allah's teachings just as the heavens and earth do. Let your Creator be the standard for your deeds. Haven't we learned enough from our own mistakes that caused corruption and conflict?

Let us read the verse again:

Do they seek a religion other than Allah's, while to Him submits whoever is in the heavens and on the earth, willingly or unwillingly, and to Him they will be returned?! Verse 83)

Let's start by exploring the meaning of the phrase "willingly or unwillingly." "Willingly" refers to obedience and humility. Allah says:

Then He turned to the sky, which was smoke, He said to it and the earth, "Come into being, willingly or not," and they said, "We come willingly." (41:11)

"willingly" applies to all creations that have no freedom of choice; each follows Allah, the Creator, with obedience and humility. Some scholars specified that "willingly" includes the angels, inanimate objects, plants, and animals because they all perform their duties and do not possess the ability to disobey.

But when it came to "unwillingly," translated from the Arabic كرها (Kurhan), the same scholars explained that it refers to people who were slaves or forced into Islam. We answer that this understanding is neither correct nor appropriate because it allows the opponents of Islam to label it as a violent religion imposed by force or claim that it allowed the subjugation of humans. Allah answers:

There is no compulsion in religion: true guidance has become distinct from error, so whoever rejects false Allahs and believes in Allah has grasped the firmest hand-hold, one that will never break. Allah is all-hearing and all-knowing. (2:256)

Since Allah never forces anyone to believe in Him, why would He allow humans to do it to others? Thus, we must understand the word "unwillingly" in its true sense.

Allah informed us that the entire universe is subjugated to Him because He is the One Who created it; there are no other God but Him. He says:

Allah has never had a child. Nor is there any Allah besides Him - if there were, each Allah would have taken his creation aside and tried to overcome the others. May Allah be exalted above what they describe! (23:91)

And, since He is the only Creator, no one will ever be able to rebel against His will. Allah granted you the immense blessing and responsibility of freedom of will. All other creations, from the sun to the grain of sand, have no choice. Thus, Allah did not command them with 'do' or 'do not do.' Religious instructions are part of the blessings of your freedom of choice. Allah granted you autonomy and guidance on how to best exercise your freedom. When He commands you to 'do,' He knows that you have the option not to.

Take your hand, for example. Allah created it and put it at your service so you can move it any way you like. But always remember that your hand is a gift not inherent to you because, at any time, it may be paralyzed through an accident or disease. Allah also sent you guidance on how to best use your hand for good. He instructed you not to steal or strike an innocent person with it.

By following Allah's teachings, you can be in perfect harmony with all other creations because they, too, act according to Allah's will. He says:

Do you ever consider that all who are in the heavens and all who are on the earth prostrate themselves to Allah, and so do the sun, the moon, the stars, the mountains, the trees, and the beasts, and so do many among human beings? Whereas many others are deservedly condemned to punishment. Whoever Allah humiliates can have none to give him honour. Assuredly, Allah does whatever He wills. (22:18)

All creations are humble before the Almighty, from the sun and moon to the mountains, trees, and animals. Many people also recognize Allah as their Creator and Lord, and they prostrate to Him in gratitude. Sadly, there are just as many who do not and believe they are self-sufficient. In fact, we, as humans, often glorify our intelligence and overestimate our abilities. Take, for example, how we marvel at scientific advancements such as the internal combustion engine. It is a great invention that allowed us to travel from one place to another, have great cars, and even fly. The scientists who developed the engine had the best intentions, but they did not have full knowledge. The internal combustion engine is perhaps the biggest polluter of air and water, and it has caused great harm to the environment. Now the same scientists are searching for ways to clean the mess. Similar was the case for pesticides. We solved one problem but created many more down the road, including a rise in cancer. Many pesticides that were hailed as great inventions are now banned. Allah says:

We offered the Trust to the heavens, the earth, and the mountains, but they refrained from bearing it and were fearful of it. But man undertook it. He is indeed prone to misjudging and acting out of ignorance. (33:72)

The point is that we often fail to see the big picture. Whether in science or in government, people have tried over and over only to end in corruption and ruin. Allah says:

Say: "Shall We inform you who are the greatest losers in respect of their deeds? They are those whose efforts in this world are misguided, even when they think they are doing good work. It is those who disbelieve in their Lord's messages and deny that they will meet Him.

Their deeds come to nothing: on the Day of Resurrection, We shall give them no weight." (18:103-105)

So how do we understand Allah's words that there are those who submit to him unwillingly? We answer that Allah did not grant us freedom in all matters. He kept many in His hand. For example, you have no control over the time of your birth, nor over accidents or diseases that may befall you, whether you like it or not.

Our life in this world is like a sentence between two parentheses. The first parenthesis is Allah bringing us into existence, and the second parenthesis is our death. The journey of life is what we have between these two boundaries. The beginning and end belong to Allah.

Allah could have subjugated you in matters of faith, just like He subjugated you in matters of life and death. The intelligent person recognizes these facts and lives his or her life according to the guidance of the Creator. That is the secret behind the phrase "to Him submits whoever is in the heavens and on the earth, willingly or unwillingly." If you disbelieve in Allah, then do not challenge Him only in matters of faith! Rebel and prove that you are in control of every little detail in your life and destiny: Stop yourself from dying, falling ill, or try controlling the function of your kidneys or spleen. No one can escape Allah. The believer takes this point and says, "I want to be in harmony with the universe and follow Allah's teachings even in matters where I have free will. I know that I will stand before Him on the Day of Judgment." Allah says, "and to Him they will be returned."

In the preceding verses of Al-Imran, Allah presented you with a perfectly logical argument. He began by informing you that His messengers —who were sent to serve you- are honest and trustworthy. Then He told you that all the heavenly messages are complementary building blocks for the betterment of the human race. There is no disagreement or competition. These facts were sealed by a covenant between Allah, the messengers and humanity. Isn't that a Lord and a system of living worth following? Allah says:

No person to whom Allah has given the scripture, wise judgment, and prophethood would ever say to people, "Be my servants, not Allah's." Rather, "You should be devoted to the Lord because you have taught the Scripture and studied it closely." He would never command you to take angels and prophets as lords. How could he command you to be disbelievers after you have devoted yourselves to Allah? Allah took a pledge from the prophets, saying, "If, after I have bestowed scripture and wisdom upon you, a messenger comes confirming what you have been given, you must believe in him and support him. Do you affirm this and accept My pledge as binding on you?" They said, "We do." He said, "Then bear witness, and I too will bear witness." Then, whoever after this turns away, those are the transgressors. Do they seek a religion other than Allah's, while to Him submits whoever is in the heavens and on the earth, willingly or unwillingly, and to Him they will be returned?! (Chapter 3: Verses 79-83)

Verse 84

Qul aamannaa billaahi wa maaa unzila 'alainaa wa maaa unzila 'alaaa Ibraaheema wa Ismaa'eela wa Ishaaqa wa Ya'qooba wal Asbaati wa maaa ootiya Moosaa wa 'Eesaa wan Nabiyyoona mir Rabbihim laa nufarriqu baina ahadim minhum wa nahnu lahoo muslimoon

Say, "We believe in Allah and in what has been sent down to us and to Abraham, Ishmael, Isaac, Jacob, and the Tribes. We believe in what has been given to Moses, Jesus, and the prophets from their Lord. We do not make a distinction between any of the prophets. It is to Allah that we devote ourselves." (Verse 84)

The verse begins by stating belief in Allah and the Quran, which is the final revelation to Prophet Muhammad.

It then extends this belief to include the messages given to all previous prophets, such as Abraham, Ishmael, Isaac, Jacob, Moses, Jesus, and others.

The verse emphasizes that Muslims make no distinction between any of these prophets, recognizing them all as messengers of Allah.

The verse concludes with a statement of submission to Allah, signifying that Muslims are those who willingly and fully submit to His will.

Now let us take a deeper look into this verse.

We find that Allah combines the Messenger, the believers, and the heavenly message and speaks to them as a single unit of faith. The verse starts with the command "say," which addresses one person: our beloved Muhammad. It then continues with the phrase "we believe," which includes both the Prophet and all Muslims. This highlights the harmony between the messenger and the nation that believes in him. Allah used this mixed address to clarify that Prophet Muhammad (pbuh) was not appointed king above his nation, but he came to deliver the message and serve his people. He, peace be upon him, will also intercede for the forgiveness of his nation on the Day of Judgment. Allah says:

A Messenger has come to you from among yourselves. Your suffering distresses him: he is deeply concerned for you and full of kindness and mercy towards the believers. (9:128)

Thus, the phrase "Say, 'We believe'" perfectly embodies the unity and love between Prophet Muhammad and all Muslims. Grammatically, the verse would be more appropriate to state, "Say, I believe,'" but Allah chose the perfect words to reflect that Prophet Muhammad is one with his nation. When the command "say" comes to Muhammad, we all implement it as one people. This unity also signalled the Prophet's enemies that they would be up against fierce loyalty and resistance if they tried to harm him. Allah says:

When Allah's help comes and victory, when you see people embracing Allah's faith in crowds, then glorify your Lord with His praise, and ask Him for forgiveness, for He surely is One Who returns repentance with vast forgiveness and reward. (110:1-3)

Now we look into the phrase, "We believe in Allah and in what has been sent down to us." More specifically, we should consider its variations in the Quran.

Coming back to the verse, Allah says,

"Say, 'We believe in Allah and in what has been sent down to us and to Abraham, Ishmael, Isaac, Jacob, and the Tribes. We believe in what has been given to Moses, Jesus, and the prophets from their Lord. We do not make a distinction between any of the prophets. It is to Allah that we devote ourselves.'"

This verse clarifies that Prophet Muhammad, peace be upon him, came to restore the previous heavenly messages and build on their foundation. Islam has within its folds the creed of all divine messages and the unadulterated stories of previous nations.

In verse 81 of Al-Imran, Allah took a covenant from the previous nations and prophets to support future messengers and believe in them. More specifically, Allah provided Muhammad's description and glad tidings. Likewise, in the verse under study, Allah instructed the Muslims to believe in the earlier messengers and recognize the shared creed among faiths. Now the circle is complete!

Allah says in the third verse of chapter 5(Surah Maidah):

This day I have perfected your religion for you, completed My favour upon you, and am pleased to assign Islam as the religion for you.

The reins of all heavenly messages ended with our beloved Prophet Muhammad. Allah took a covenant from others to believe in him and took a covenant from Prophet Muhammad to believe in those before of him. Islam is the final message and the summit of heavenly revelations to humanity.

Allah ended the verse with, "It is to Allah that we devote ourselves." In other words, there is nothing that gives the followers of previous heavenly religions enduring power or an excuse to be zealots against new revelations; instead, the whole matter begins with Allah and ends with Allah. By submitting your will to Allah in Islam, you choose to be in harmony with yourself and all the creations around you, from the animals to the plants and inanimate objects. In this way, we all share in our humbleness before the Creator. And as long as we move in the same direction, there will be no conflict or room for opposing whims.

Do they seek a religion other than Allah's, while to Him submits whoever is in the heavens and on the earth, willingly or unwillingly, and to Him they will be returned?! (3:83)

Nowadays, we see the world making remarkable advances in science and technology. Each one of us holds the world in his or her pocket via a smartphone. We have been to the moon and reached the outer limits of the solar system. But has the world become peaceful? Are we freer and less stressed? Quite the opposite. The scientists have exhausted themselves inventing new products to bring everyone comfort, but it seems we have less time to enjoy life. Why? Because we manage our worldly affairs based on greed for money and power. Every nation, corporation, and group follows its own desire to dominate others. This creates endless conflicts. Many people escape their reality through drugs and other addictions.

We have put our reins in the hands of our whims and are not the faithful hand of Allah. He says:

Have you seen him who has taken his desire to be his Allah and whom Allah has led astray knowingly, and set a seal upon his hearing and his heart, and put a blindfold on his sight? So who will guide him after Allah? Will you not then take heed? (45:23)

Allah sent us heavenly guidance with our sole interest as a goal. Once we all share the path of "It is to Allah that we devote ourselves," the world will find peace.

Verse 85

Wa mai yabtaghi ghairal Islaami deenan falany yuqbala minhu wa huwa fil Aakhirati minal khaasireen

If anyone seeks a religion other than Islam, it will not be accepted from him: he will be one of the losers in the Hereafter. (Verse 85)

This verse is telling us that whoever seeks a religion other than Islam will have it rejected by Allah, and will be among the losers in the afterlife.

Islam is the final and complete revelation of God's will, making it the only acceptable path after the Prophet Muhammad's time.

Islam involves not just a belief system, but also a commitment to following God's laws and guidelines, which are believed to be revealed in the Quran.

A fundamental aspect of Islam is the belief in one God (Allah), and the rejection of any other gods or deities, which is also a core principle of the faith.

Peace and harmony can only be achieved through the heavenly religion of Islam.

If a person does not like the laws of his or her Creator, then they have lost this world and the next. Many people claim that divine laws are cruel. They point to rulings such as the amputation of the thief's hand or the death penalty as examples. We answer that a car crash or a building collapse results in loss of life and limb far more than the people who lost their hands or died under Islam.

Let's talk about those who stand against the death penalty because they claim it is inhumane or excessive. We ask, what is it that makes you defend a person whose life is to be taken justly over the person who was murdered wrongfully? More importantly, the true purpose of the penalty prescribed by Allah is to prevent the heinous act of murder from occurring in the first place. We implement fair retribution not only to bring justice to the victim but also to deter whoever is thinking about committing murder. Allah says, "And there is life for you in fair retribution, o people of understanding."

In matters of justice, Allah addresses the people of intellect, not those who focus on the superficial and sensational. Laws and punishments are legislated not with enforcement in mind; instead, they aim for prevention. In other words, the true goal is for both the crime and the punishment to disappear. This is similar to building a formidable army equipped with the best weapons to instill fear in the enemy and prevent war from occurring in the first place. Allah says:

Fair retribution saves lives for you, people of understanding, so that you may guard yourselves against what is wrong. (2:179)

Whoever sets laws that contradict what Allah has prescribed is claiming that Allah has erred. We ask, do you really think you are more affectionate to the creation than the Creator? To claim that you are better is defiance at its worst. In order to enjoy peace and justice, we must defer all matters to our Creator. Now, you can understand the sound logic behind the statement, "If anyone seeks a religion other than Islam, it will not be accepted from him: he will be one of the losers in the Hereafter."

The verse continues with, "it will not be accepted from him." Some people point to such statements and say, "Why should I do anything good, if there is no guarantee that Allah will accept it from me? Why should I perform acts of worship when Allah may choose to accept or reject them?" We answer that you will return to your Creator and stand before Him whether you like it or not, so there is no point behind your question. If you were able to escape Allah, then it would make sense for you to say and do as you wish, but you cannot! So be logical and do not rebel against the command of the Almighty.

The verse ends with "he will be one of the losers in the Hereafter." Loss is the departure of capital and the disappearance of investment. And since the afterlife is the true everlasting life, you are a true loser if you do not attain paradise. Allah says:

Say, "It is Allah I serve, dedicating my worship entirely to Him." You worship whatever you wish besides Him. Say, "Indeed the losers are those who ruin themselves and their families on the Day of Resurrection. Look! That is the manifest loss!" (39: 14-15)

Lastly, we should take a moment to understand the name "Islam." The word "Islam" comes from the Arabic root "Sa La Ma," the meaning of which revolves around peace and protection from corruption. It refers to integrity, righteousness, and harmony between a person and his soul, his Lord, and the universe. Since the word "Islam" holds all these meanings within, isn't it worth following?

The literal translation of the word "Islam" is "complete devotion to Allah." It means to be a servant of Allah, a slave of Allah. I understand that these words hold very negative connotations in human terms, but they mean the exact opposite when it comes to Allah. How, you may ask? Let's compare the most negative of these terms," slavery," as it relates to humans and to Allah. A human slave is held against his or her will. He or she is exploited for labour to benefit the master who reaps all the rewards, while the slave gets the absolute minimum for sustenance. The children of slaves are born into slavery, and they are often denied education to keep them ignorant about their condition. A slave is severely punished for every mistake. In short, the human master-slave relationship is most unjust.

On the other hand, submission to Allah is a source of pride and elevation. I am a proud slave of Allah because my Lord is just. Allah sent me prophets and messengers to educate me so I could choose Him freely. He prepared for me an entire universe and put it at my service. Allah did not ask anything of me until I chose to come to Him. Allah does not need my labour, and He rewards me tenfold or more for every deed I do. I have made countless mistakes, and I found my Lord to be the most forgiving. My children are free to choose their way in life. Allah does not ask anything of them until they reach the age of maturity so they can make a thoughtful decision. They have the Quran to show them the exact consequences of their choices. Yes, I am a very proud servant of Allah, and I willingly submit to Him and only to Him. It brings me peace and harmony. This is the essence of the word "Islam."

Verse 86

Kaifa yahdil laahu qawman kafaroo ba'da eemaanihim wa shahidooo annar Rasoola haqqunw wa jaaa'ahumul baiyinaat; wallaahu laa yahdil qawmaz zaalimeen

Why would Allah guide people who deny the truth after they have believed and acknowledged that the messenger is true and after they have been shown clear proof? Allah does not guide the unjust. (Verse 86)

The verse begins by posing a rhetorical question:

"How shall Allah guide a people who disbelieve after their belief and had witnessed that the Messenger is true and clear signs had come to them?".

Who is this verse addressing:

The verse specifically addresses those who, having initially embraced faith and witnessed its truth, subsequently choose to reject it; emphasizing that these individuals had already acknowledged the messenger as true and received clear proofs of the truth, and yet they chose to disbelieve.

The conclusion statement is highlighting that Allah will not guide those who persistently reject the truth and engage in wrongdoings.

However, whilst the verse speaks of the difficult situation of those who apostatize, it also implies that repentance and a genuine return to faith can lead to forgiveness and guidance. We also learn that those who stubbornly remain in disbelief will face harsh consequences, including condemnation from Allah, angels, and humanity.

Let us reflect:

How can anyone after tasting the sweetness of devotion accept disbelief for him or herself?

Let us look at some of their excuses:

They point to phrases like "Allah guides whomever He wills" and claim that "I cannot help myself from doing sin. If Allah wanted me to be good, He would have guided me!" We answer that this is a poor justification for sin because, interestingly, such statements are never uttered regarding obedience. In other words, when a person sins, he or she says, "Allah wanted me to sin; it is not my fault, I couldn't help it." But, after they help a poor person, they never say, "Allah wanted me to be good; I couldn't help it, so I do not deserve a reward." Why do you only attribute your sin to Allah, and not your virtue? You cannot demand a reward for your obedience and escape the punishment for your sins.

Let us now look at Guidance.

Guidance has two levels. To guide means to highlight the path which takes you to the desired destination. The first level of guidance is general. An example of this are road signs which clarify the direction and distance you need to travel to reach your destination city. Such signs are placed for general guidance.

Similarly, Allah guided all people, the believers, and the disbelievers, and showed them the correct path to paradise. He sent prophets, messengers, and scriptures to guide everyone. After that, people became divided into two groups based on their choice: a group that accepted the path shown by Allah, and a group that rejected it.

Allah supports those who follow His general guidance with the second level: His divine guidance. He endears faith and piety to their hearts and facilitates the actions that lead to paradise. It is as if the Almighty says to them, "You have believed in Me and followed My teachings, so you have earned another prize: I will come to your aid and ease matters for you." This is the divine guidance that Allah gives only to those who follow His general one.

Let's clarify the difference between general and divine guidance with an example. Say that you were lost and asked a policeman for directions towards your destination. The policeman hands you a map; it is the same general map he gives to everyone. Here, you show your appreciation and say, "Thank you, officer, for your help; you have made things so much easier for me." Now, the policeman decides to offer help beyond the general map. He highlights the best way for you to take and warns you about the roads under construction and the areas that are not safe at night. Then, he volunteers to ride with you and shows you through the best exits and roads.

Hence, guidance sometimes means "indication" and, at other times, it means "aid." I repeat this statement to make it clear that Allah comes to the aid of those who believe in Him. He says:

As for those who follow true guidance, He leads them far ahead in their right ways and grants them piety and restraints from evil suited to their condition. (47:17)

Just as Allah comes to aid those who chose Him, He abandons those who reject His teachings or associate partners with Him. He asks:

Why would Allah guide people who deny the truth after they have believed and acknowledged that the Messenger is true and after they have been shown clear proof?

Always remember that Allah only abandons a person after he or she rejects His general guidance, as illustrated in the phrase "after they have believed and acknowledged that the Messenger is true and after they have been shown clear proof."

Here you may ask, who are the people implicated in this verse? We answer that it refers to a few people who embraced Islam then reneged but, mainly, this verse refers to the People of the Book who were given Prophet Muhammad's description in their books. Take the example of Abdullah bin Salam, a Jewish Rabbi in Medina, who said, "I knew Muhammad the moment I saw him as I know my own son; in fact, my knowledge of Muhammad was stronger." Allah says:

Those who follow the Messenger, the Prophet who can neither read nor write, whose description they will find written in the Torah and the Gospel with them. He will enjoin on them that which is right and forbid them that which is wrong. He will make lawful for them all good things and prohibit for them only the foul, and he will relieve them of their burden and the fetters that they used to wear. Then those who believe in him, and honour him, and help him, and follow the light which is sent down with him, they are the successful. (7:157)

The Quranic expression "they will find his description written in the Torah and the Gospel with them" indicates that it was not hearsay or an oral tradition; rather, both holy books described Prophet Muhammad in black and white. It was common knowledge among the People of the Book. Allah says:

When a book does come to them from Allah, confirming what is with them —even though before they were praying for victory over the disbelievers— when there came to them something they knew to be true, they disbelieved in it: Allah's curse is on those who disbelieve. (2:89)

Before the advent of Prophet Muhammad, the Jews and Christians of Arabia sought Allah's support over the disbelievers. They used to threaten the pagan Arabs and say, "A prophet will come whom we will follow. We will fight along his side and kill you like the killing of Iram and 'Aad." Thus, they believed in the Messenger, peace be upon him, before his arrival. But when he came, they rejected him. Allah answers:

Those who disbelieve say, "You are not a Messenger sent by Allah." Say: "Allah suffices for a witness between me and you, and anyone else who has knowledge of the Book." (13:43)

It is as if those who took the time to study the Torah and the Gospel would be able to see Muhammad right before their eyes. Thus, with such strong evidence at hand, isn't fair for Allah to say, "Why would Allah guide people who deny the truth?" What more do they need to believe? Haven't they already said that a prophet would come, and they would be by his side? Such people are not worthy of Allah's help because they put their desires before Allah's love. He says:

As for those who disbelieve, it makes no difference whether you warn them or not: they will not believe. Allah has sealed their hearts and their ears, and their eyes are covered. They will have great torment. (2:6-7)

And, in verse 88 of Chapter 4:

If Allah leaves anyone to stray, you will never find the way for him.

Allah laid the foundations of faith before you, and He will respect whatever choice you make. If you willfully ignore His general guidance, He will abandon you to whatever you choose for yourself. Allah will not hold anyone's hand and drag them to His path. On the other hand, if you want Allah's help, all you need to do is take the first step and follow the guidance of the messengers; Allah will then rush to your aid.

Let us read this beautiful Hadeeth:

"I treat My servant as he hopes that I would treat him. I am with him whenever he remembers Me: if he remembers Me in his heart, I remember him in Mine; if he remembers Me in a gathering, I remember him in a gathering far better; if he draws near towards Me a hand's span, I draw near towards him an arm's length; if he draws near to Me an arm's length, I draw near to him a mile; and if he comes to Me walking, I go to him running."

Allah wants to grant you more but, first, you have to be deserving of such gifts. So make sure you do not fall into the categories of people Allah does not guide. The Quran clarified to us three types of people who are deprived of Allah's divine guidance. They are listed in the following three verses:

That is because they preferred the worldly life over the Hereafter and that Allah does not guide the disbelieving people. (16:107)

That will make it more likely they will give true and proper testimony, or fear that their oaths might be refuted by others afterwards. Be mindful of Allah and listen; Allah does not guide those who are corrupt. (5:108)

Why would Allah guide people who deny the truth after they have believed and acknowledged that the Messenger is true and after they have been shown clear proof? Allah does not guide the unjust. (Verse 86)

We understand that the disbelievers, the corrupt, and the unjust are the ones who are expelled from Allah's divine guidance.

Verses 87

Ulaaa'ika jazaaa'uhum anna 'alaihim la'natal laahi walmalaaa'ikati wannaasi ajma'een

The reward of such people is that Allah's curse is on them and that of the angels and of all humankind.
(Verse 87)

In the previous session, we discussed people who received Allah's guidance and recognized the truth beyond any doubt, yet decided to reject it.

This verse is highlighting the consequences of disbelief. And what may that consequence be?

Let us look first of all at "Allah's curse", as the verse states. What does this really mean?

It means the expulsion from Allah's mercy. And, because Allah rejects them, the angels, the believers, and the entire humankind will do the same. Here you may ask, will the disbelievers curse such people too? We answer: yes because human nature recognizes what is right and wrong. A thief does not respect other thieves; in fact, he or she will look for an honest person to deposit money with. A sinful woman will leave her newborn by the door of a mosque or a church because she knows where righteous people usually are. Likewise, a disbeliever recognizes the sin of others even if he or she is committing the same. Thus, disbelievers will curse one another because the human instinct does not approve of such behaviour.

On the Day of Judgement, the disbelievers will exchange curses, and all people will curse them as well. They will remain in this wretched state eternally for their intentional deviation from Allah's path.

Verse 88

Khaalideena feehaa laa yukhaffafu 'anhumul 'azaabu wa laa hum yunzaroon

And so they will remain, with no relief or respite for their suffering.

This verse discusses the eternal punishment of those who disbelieve in the afterlife. It states that they will remain in Hell forever, their torment will not be lessened, and they will not be given any further reprieve.

"They will be in Hell forever." (Khaliduna fiha):

This emphasizes the permanent nature of their punishment, indicating that they will remain in Hell throughout eternity.

"Their punishment will not be lightened." (La yukhaffaf 'anhumu al-'adhab):

This highlights the severity and unrelenting nature of their suffering, meaning there will be no respite or reduction in their torment.

"Nor will they be delayed." (Wa la hum yuntharun):

This signifies that they will not be given any postponement or delay in facing their punishment, and they will not be allowed to return to the world or be given another chance.

Some people mistakenly assume that entering Hellfire means that they will burn like a wood log, and then all will be over, as narrated by the following verse:

They say, "The Fire will only touch us for a few days." Say to them: "Have you received a promise from Allah - for Allah never breaks His promise - or are you saying things about Him of which you have no real knowledge?" (2:80)

Allah answers these claims with the following verse. He says:

We shall send those who reject Our revelations to the Fire. When their skins have been burned away, We shall replace them with new ones so that they may continue to feel the pain: Allah is mighty and wise. (4:56)

Modern science proved that the skin is the center of pain receptors. A person becomes less sensitive to pain after their skin calluses or breaks. Thus, Allah will create a new skin for the people of Hell, so their suffering will continue forever.

However, it is crucial to keep in mind that Allah is not out to punish people. Quite the opposite, He sent you messengers, scriptures, and countless warnings to guide you towards Paradise and save you from sin. Allah leaves the door of repentance open even for the worst sinners and deniers.

Verse 89

Illal lazeena taaboo mim ba'di zaalika wa aslahoo fa innal laaha Ghafoorur Raheem

Not so for those who afterward repent and mend their ways - Allah is most forgiving and merciful. (Verse 89)

Allah is your Creator, and He wants you to do well. He likes you to be pure even after sin, so He opened the door of repentance wide before you. Our beloved Prophet Muhammad said, "Allah is happier with the repentance of His servant than one of you finding his horse after it had strayed away in the middle of the desert." This narration illustrates a man traveling with all his wealth, food, and water, packed on the back of his animal. Amid a barren desert, the horse gets away. He searches for days to no avail. He has lost all the necessities for survival, and he knows that an agonizing death is one or two days away. Suddenly, he turns around and finds the horse standing before him. Imagine the amount of happiness, joy, and relief this man feels. This pales when compared to Allah's delight when you repent to Him and seek forgiveness for your sins; "Allah is most forgiving and merciful."

Sincere repentance means to cease from sin, feel remorseful for what you did, and determine to never return to that sin again and, lastly, to make amends and return what you have wrongfully taken from others.

Our beloved Muhammad said, "Verily, Allah stretches out His hand by night to accept the repentance of those who sinned by day, and He stretches out His hand by day to accept the repentance of those who sinned by night; until the sun rises from the West."

Allah legislated repentance to save you and the society around you because if repentance were not allowed, then a person may despair after the first sin. Once a sinner loses hope of forgiveness, they would continue on that path and cause suffering to society. It is for this very reason that Allah legislated repentance so that you do not despair from His mercy. At every turn in your life, you can ask for forgiveness and be close to your Creator again.

A common saying goes, "Perhaps a sin that causes humility and regret is better than obedience that provokes pride and arrogance." This is because the most generous members of society are often those who wronged themselves and sinned before. When they remember their past sins, they hasten towards good acts hoping that Allah will overlook their mistakes. Allah turns the former disobedience of the individual into a permanent flame that provokes his or her conscience to do good continually.

So, whenever you see a person who has excessively wronged him or herself, take a moment to pray for their guidance because they may turn out to be a great source of good for the society. Quite often, people who go after sin with intensity will do the same when they reform themselves and try to erase their evil past with good deeds.

Verses 90

Innal lazeena kafaroo ba'da eemaanihim summaz daadoo kufral lan tuqbala tawbatuhum wa ulaaa'ika humud daaalloon

Indeed those who turn faithless after their faith and then advance in faithlessness, their repentance will never be accepted, and it is they who are the astray. (Verse 90)

In the previous verse, Allah highlighted the way to salvation through repentance and good deeds to erase the mistakes of the past. In this verse, He speaks about those who disbelieved after faith and then went even further. Such people have lost all access to Allah's mercy.

Here you may wonder, how could a disbelieving person increase in disbelief? We answer that some people are not satisfied by rejecting faith; they want others to join them, so they try to corrupt their family and friends. This is an increase in disbelief.

This verse addresses some of the Jews who believed in the glad tidings which foretold the arrival of our beloved Jesus, yet, when he came, they disbelieved and fought him. They did the same regarding Prophet Muhammad. They disbelieved in Jesus first and then increased in disbelief by denying Prophet Muhammad; at the same time, they claimed to be Allah's chosen children and beloved.

A common adage says, "The person who breaks the promise of repentance is a person who ridicules his Lord." In other words, some people declare repentance with their tongue but never correct their mistakes or embrace faith sincerely. May Allah protect us all.

Verse 91

Innal lazeena kafaroo wa maatoo wa hum kuffaarun falany yuqbala min ahadihim mil'ul ardi zahabanw wa lawiftadaa bih; ulaaa 'ika lahum 'azaabun aleemunw wa maa lahum min naasireen

Indeed, those who disbelieve and die as disbelievers, no ransom even if it were as much gold as to fill the earth will be accepted from any of them. For them, there will be an agonizing punishment, and they will have no helpers. (Chapter 3: Verse 91)

Allah points out the disbelievers who never repent and then die as such. Here, we should take a moment to explain the phrase "no ransom even if it were as much gold as to fill the earth will be accepted from any of them." Does it refer to this life or the hereafter? We answer that the phrase applies to both.

Suppose a disbeliever died but spent enough gold to fill the entire earth on good causes during his life. We say that such spending will not benefit you in the hereafter because you have committed the greatest disloyalty. Since you were not a believer in Allah, then you did not spend this money for His sake but had some other goals in mind. So do not expect a reward or even recognition from the One you denied. Thus, Allah will not accept this person's charity even if it equals the weight of the earth in gold.

Some people wonder, is it conceivable that a person who comes up with an invention that saves millions of lives will not benefit from it on the Day of Judgment? Could great inventors and philanthropists end up in Hellfire if they are disbelievers? We answer that you earn your reward from the one you worked for. We gave the example of an engineer who works for BMW and designs an outstanding safety feature. Would he or she expect to get a salary from Mercedes Benz or Pepsi? Of course not; that is not who he or she worked for. Similarly, disbelieving inventors and philanthropists do not work with Allah in mind, so they should not expect any reward from the Lord. They worked for humanity, money, and fame, and they have received their compensation in full. University halls were named after them; they have statues and books commemorating their work, and some have earned great wealth. Allah says:

But the actions of the disbelievers are like a mirage in the desert. A thirsty man mistakes it for water but, when he reaches it, he finds it to be nothing at all, and he finds Allah there. He will pay him his account in full. Allah is swift at reckoning. (24:39)

A mirage is an optical phenomenon where the reflection of sunlight off of the desert sand appears as a pool of sparkling water. The thirsty traveller rushes towards it filled with hope to only find more sand and heat. Similarly, the disbeliever is deceived by the illusion that life will end at death, only to be surprised by the hereafter and the existence of Allah. Even then, there is hope that the charity and good deeds he or she did in life will be enough for salvation, but that too is an illusion. Such a person will not be saved by good deeds, nor by anyone who steps up to intercede, even with enough gold to fill the earth. Allah says:

The Day when they will come forth, with nothing of them being hidden from Allah. Whose is the absolute Sovereignty on that Day? It is Allah's, the One, the All-Overwhelming. (40:16)

And in another chapter:

If the evildoers possessed the earth's assets twice over, they would offer them to ransom from the terrible suffering on the Day of Resurrection: Allah will show them something they had not reckoned with. (39:47)

Lastly:

And beware of a Day when no soul can stand in for another. No compensation will be accepted from it, nor intercession is of use to it, nor will anyone be helped. (2:123)

The verse ends with, "For them, there will be an agonizing punishment, and they will have no helpers." We have explained before that the severity of an action is directly proportional to the power of the doer. In this case, the punisher is the Almighty, so the severity of the punishment is proportionate to His power. Can anyone withstand such a penalty?

Verse 92

Lan tanaalul birra hattaa tunfiqoo mimmaa tuhibboon; wa maa tunfiqoo min shai'in fa innal laaha bihee 'Aleem

None of you will attain true piety unless you spend out of what you cherish: whatever you give, Allah knows about it very well. (Verse 92)

Verse 92 underscores that genuine righteousness is not merely about performing good deeds, but also about sacrificing that which is most cherished in the way of Allah. This includes spending from what is dear, beloved, and valuable to oneself. This verse is meant to convey that true piety and devotion are demonstrated through self-sacrifice and a willingness to give from one's most valued possessions for the sake of Allah's pleasure. Hence, verse 92 encourages Muslims to reflect on their priorities and be mindful of their spending habits. It urges them to ensure that their expenditures are directed towards righteous causes and that they are not overly attached to worldly possessions.

Now let us look at the phrase "True piety".

"True piety" is translated from the Arabic origin بِرَّ؟ل؟ (Al-Birr). The root "Ba Ra Ra" refers to something large and open. We use the word Barr to describe vast lands.

In the verse under study, بِرَّ؟ل؟ (Al-Birr) refers to righteousness and obedience. It also means Paradise. All these meanings converge because righteousness leads to vast comfort in the heart, while Paradise is the ultimate comfortable home.

Here, we should take a moment to appreciate the Quranic style. Verse 91 of Al-Imran ended by describing the severe punishment awaiting those who ignore Allah's guidance and die as disbelievers. Here, you may wonder, why did Allah discuss charity right after talking about the punishment of the disbelievers? We answer that Allah often brings contrasting issues to motivate you. He mentioned charity right after punishment to encourage you to rush towards pleasure and Paradise. Allah, who abandons the disbelievers, will rush to the aid of the believers. What a beautiful contrast.

The Quran is the miraculous word of Allah, and such contrasting statements are parts of its beauty and impact. Our Creator knows the best way to speak to us. Every person is made up of many faculties that are closely intertwined. For example, when you listen to slow music, you often have romantic or relaxing emotions, and your eyes may even tear up. Likewise, when you see a picture of an old friend, you recall the good times together and remember images of family and friends. One action stirs up many thoughts and emotions. Allah's speech nourishes all of our mental and emotional faculties at once.

Let's look at a few examples. The polytheists used to enter the Sacred House in Mecca freely. Many travelled long distances to visit Mecca during the pilgrimage season and brought their wealth and goods to trade. This Hajj season was the main driver of all economic activity in Mecca. Allah wanted to prevent the polytheists from entering His Sacred House. He started the address to the Muslims as follows:

O you who believe, those who associate partners with Allah are impure. So, after the expiry of this year, let them not approach the Sacred Mosque.

But Allah is our Creator, and He knows how our faculties and emotions interact. You could imagine the anxiety of Mecca's merchants when they heard of the prohibition on non-Muslims entering the Sacred Mosque. How would they earn their living? Who would buy their goods? Thus, in the very same verse, Allah immediately addressed the issue on everyone's mind. He continued:

And should you fear poverty, Allah will enrich you out of His bounty if He so wills. Surely, Allah is All-Knowing, All-Wise. (9:28)

This is the magnificence of the divine speech: Allah addresses concerns and emotions even before the listener is aware of them. The phrase "should you fear poverty" is a perfect example of that. When you and I speak, we may miss the emotional impact of our words on the listener. In fact, many family and social problems are the result of misunderstandings. But Allah does not miss anything. Let's look at two other examples. Allah says:

They say, "Should we follow the guidance with you, we will be driven out of our land by force." Did We not establish a secure sanctuary for them where fruits of all kinds are brought as a provision from Us? But most of them do not know. (28:57)

Here again, Allah gives the people of Arabia peace of mind, specifically addressing their economic concerns. He reminds everyone that He is the One Who provides and grants economic security.

In another verse, Allah says:

Have you not seen how those who have been forbidden to hold secret conversations go back afterward and hold them and conspire with one another in what is sinful, hostile, and disobedient to the Messenger? When they come to you, they greet you with words Allah has never used to greet you and say to themselves, "Why does Allah not punish us for what we say?" Hell will be punishment enough for them: they will burn there - an evil destination. (58:8)

Take note that Allah informed the disbelievers not only of their secret conversations but also of the thoughts and words they have within themselves. He said, "They say to themselves, 'Why does Allah not punish us for what we say?'" Allah has full knowledge of what we conceal and how our psychological faculties interact. So next time, when you read the Quran, pay close attention, and you will find that its verses are interconnected and arranged in a beautiful manner. Allah addresses your mind and emotions, so all of your faculties are satisfied and nourished.

This brings us back to the verse. Allah says, "None of you will attain true piety unless you spend out of what you cherish," bringing up the issue of the type of charity that is acceptable immediately after He highlighted those who spent tons of treasure and earned no reward at all. Allah knows that, when you hear the phrase in verse 91 of Al-Imran, "no ransom even if it was as much gold as to fill the earth will be accepted from any of them," you will wonder about your charity and if it would be acceptable to Allah. Thus, Allah immediately addresses your concern with:

None of you will attain true piety unless you spend out of what you cherish: whatever you give, Allah knows about it very well. (Verse 92)

Allah is guiding you towards generosity because He knows of our tendency to be greedy and stingy. He says:

Be mindful of Allah as much as you can; hear and obey; be charitable - it is for your own good. Those who are saved from their own stinginess will be the prosperous ones. (64:16)

Both greed and stinginess stem from our fear that life's circumstances will change for the worse. Hence, when people earn money or buy goods, they save some for a rainy day. This is especially true when resources become scarce. Let's clarify with the following example: Suppose you have three children and brought home twenty oranges. Every child can eat his or her fill with no need to worry about the others. But if you only get two oranges, then you would have a problem with the competing kids. You have to slice the oranges to ensure that one child does not deprive the others. Likewise, most of our problems today are fought over insatiable greed and dwindling resources.

Such was not the case at the beginning of history. In the olden days, the population was low, and resources were plenty. If you wanted a piece of land, you simply took it to build and farm. You could pick all the fruit you need from wild trees. But, as the population increased and people had more tools at their disposal, resources seemed scarcer. Circumstances were ripe for greed.

Allah wants you to keep Him in the equation of your wealth. Let's take a realistic look at the money you earn: you use the intellect Allah granted you and the body He gave you to make a living. You eat from the animals and plants Allah created for you and use the energy and metals He deposited in the earth. Since everything belongs to Allah, your role is minimal when it comes to earning provision and money. Don't you owe Allah His right from all He gave you? Allah does not ask for His sake; He is free of need. Allah's right is for your brothers and sisters in humanity who are down on their fortunes. More importantly, just as Allah asks you to give from what you like, He will ask everyone to give their best if you fall on hard times. Isn't that the best insurance policy of all?

None of you will attain true piety unless you spend out of what you cherish: whatever you give, Allah knows about it very well. (Verse 92)

I am sure that you have done this before, probably more than once! You opened your closet, looked through your clothes, and picked the old shoe and the out-of-style sweater to give to charity. People typically give away the things they do not like. But Allah commands you to do the opposite. Let's see how the Companions of our beloved Muhammad understood the verse, "None of you will attain true piety unless you spend out of what you cherish."

Abu Talha was one of the wealthiest residents of Medina. He owned an orchard called Bayruhaa across the mosque of Prophet Muhammad. He, peace be upon him, used to enter this garden to rest under its shade and drink from its water. When Abu Talha heard the verse "None of you will attain true piety unless you spend out of what you cherish," he came to Prophet Muhammad and said, "O Messenger of Allah, the most beloved property to me is Bayruhaa. I want to donate it for the sake of Allah. Please take the proceeds from its sale and give it where Allah guides you." Prophet Muhammad replied, "This is a winning trade, this is a winning trade! I suggest that you find poor relatives of yours and give it to them."

When Zaid bin Harithah heard the verse, he immediately thought of his majestic horse, Sabal. He grabbed the horse's rein, rushed to Prophet Muhammad, and said, "Messenger of Allah, you know how much I love my horse. I want to give it to charity." He, peace be upon him, took the horse from Zaid and gave it to his son, Osama ibn Zaid. Zaid felt unease in his heart and said, "O Messenger, I wanted to offer my horse in Allah's path, and you gave it to my son?!" The Prophet replied, "Allah accepted your charity, Zaid." He, peace be upon him, always gave the poor relatives of the donor priority.

Ibn Omar had a beautiful servant girl from Persia which he loved. When he heard the verse, he said, "I value nothing more than my servant, and I have now freed her for the sake of Allah." Ibn Omar could have married this servant after he freed her, but he said, "I want to keep my intention pure for Allah, and not taint it by marrying the woman I just freed."

The Companions rushed to give their most prized possessions to the poor. This may seem odd nowadays, but they understood that Allah's reward is none other than Paradise. Prophet Muhammad, peace be upon him, said, "Indeed Allah's product is very expensive. Indeed, Allah's product is Paradise." In a sacred narration (Hadith Qudsi), Allah says, "People paid each other with common goods in worldly life, and today I pay them with Paradise."

Lastly, we tell the story of Abu Dhar, who owned herds of camels and wanted to offer his most beloved camel for charity. He had a prized male stud that he used to fertilize all the female camels. When a poor guest came to his door, Abu Dhar said, "I'm sorry, brother, but I am too busy. Please go and select the best of all the camels from my herd so I can slaughter it for you." The guest returned shortly with a skinny camel. Abu Dhar looked up and said, "My friend, you have betrayed me! I asked you to bring the best camel, and you brought me this!" The guest replied, "I found the male stud to be the best of all, but I left it for the day that you might need it." To which Abu Dhar smiled and said, "The day I would need it the most is the day I am lowered into my grave. Please go back and take that camel."

The great Companion Abu Dhar understood that the day a person dies is the only day worth preparing for. He also understood not to trick or lie to himself. When the guest chose a camel that was not dear to Abu Dhar, he asked him to go back and bring his favorite because he remembered Allah's words, "Whatever you give, Allah knows about it very well."

In fact, Abu Dhar, may Allah be pleased with him, taught us the most beautiful lesson about managing wealth. He explained that there are always three partners who share your wealth. The first partner is life events that do not consult with you or ask for permission before grabbing your wealth. Life often forces you to spend when you do not want to or cause your investments to fail. If your child ends up in the hospital, you may spend all your money to help them recover. The second partner who shares your wealth is your heirs. They wait for your death, then dip in and take everything you own. They look at your money as a free gift to enjoy life. The third and last partner is you. You have control over your wealth as long as you live. Abu Dhar advised, "Try not to be the weakest of all partners. Spend in Allah's cause before life's events or death take your money away!"

The companion Abdullah Ibn Amrou came to our beloved Muhammad and asked him about reading the Quran. He, peace be upon him, said, "You should read the entire Quran in a month," to which Abdullah replied, "I think I can do better." Prophet Muhammad said, "Then read it in twenty days." Abdullah said, "I think I have the strength to do better." Prophet Muhammad said, "Then read it in ten days." Abdullah said, "Can you do more?" Prophet Muhammad then replied, "Read the entire Quran in a week but do not burden yourself with more than that."

The Quran is primarily divided by chapter (sura) and verse (aya). Chapters vary in length and are generally arranged from longest to shortest. The Quran is additionally divided into 30 equal sections, each called "a Juz." These divisions make it easier for you to pace the reading of the entire Quran over one month: reading a relatively equal amount of one Juz each day. It is particularly helpful during the month of Ramadan when it is recommended to complete one full reading of the Quran from cover to cover.

Verse 92 of Sura Al-Imran marks the end of the third Juz of the Noble Quran.

Verse 93

Kullut ta'aami kaana hillal li Baneee Israaa'eela illaa maa harrama Israaa'eelu 'alaa nafsihee min qabli an tunazzalat Tawraah; qul faatoo bit Tawraati fatloohaaa in kuntum saadiqeen

All food was lawful for the tribe of Israel except what Israel made unlawful for himself before the Torah was sent down. Say: "Bring the Torah and recite it if you are telling the truth." (Verse 93)

This verse is part of a larger section in Surah Al-Imran that addresses the claims and beliefs of the Jewish people, challenging them to support their positions with evidence from the Torah. The verse refutes a specific Jewish claim about initial prohibitions on certain foods, emphasizing that before the revelation of the Torah, all food was lawful, except for the personal prohibition made by Jacob(Israel) himself.

And what food did Jacob made lawful for himself?

Jacob, in a personal vow, forbade the consumption of camel meat due to an affliction he suffered when he consumed it.

Let us now remind ourselves about the misdemeanours of the People of the Book.

Some of them rejected Prophet Muhammad, peace be upon him, at the beginning of his call to Islam. They denied the glad tidings of his coming mentioned in the Gospel and Torah and went as far as erasing his description from their books, although they used to announce it loudly just a few years prior. Allah says:

When a Book does come to them from Allah, confirming what is with them - even though before that they were praying for victory over the disbelievers - when there came to them something they knew to be true, they disbelieved in it: Allah's curse is on those who disbelieve. (2:89)

They worked hard to ensure the distortions they made to the Torah remained hidden, but Allah wanted to expose them. We had mentioned before the story of the Jewish Rabbis of Medina who faced the problem of an intimate affair between a man and a woman from very prominent families. The Rabbis wanted to conceal the ruling in the Torah, which is stoning. So, they suggested that the families should go to Prophet Muhammad, hoping that he would circumvent the Torah and find a socially acceptable solution to them.

When the Jewish group sat with Prophet Muhammad, they said, "O Messenger of Allah, judge between these people." He, peace be upon him, replied, "Don't you have a clear ruling for this matter in the Torah? I will judge according to your scripture." They reluctantly replied, "That would be fair." Prophet Muhammad first explained that the ruling for adultery in Islam is stoning, and then he asked for a part of the Torah to be brought in. Prophet Muhammad, an illiterate man, pointed to a section in the Torah and a man from the Jewish tribe began to read; when he reached the verse about stoning, he covered it with his hand and skipped ahead. A companion named Abdullah bin Salam said, "O Messenger of Allah, did you see him covering the verse with his hand!?" It became clear to everyone that the Jewish leaders wanted to override Allah's ruling. In fact, whenever they faced a matter they did not approve, such as the coming of a new prophet from the Arab tribes, they rushed to alter the scriptures to match their whims.

Likewise, in the verse under study, Allah exposes another example of the corrupt Jewish clergy for all to see. When Prophet Muhammad, peace be upon him, said that camels and their milk are permissible to consume, some Rabbis objected and said, "These were forbidden since the days of Abraham, and even before him from the days of Noah. We cannot accept that eating and drinking from a camel is permissible." Prophet Muhammad replied that whatever Allah made lawful is permissible, and there was no need for discussion.

It should have been enough for any clergy to accept that a new messenger from Allah should be welcomed and supported. Any new legislation from the heavens overrules all previous rulings. Allah says:

Allah took a pledge from the prophets, saying, "If, after I have bestowed scripture and wisdom upon you, a messenger comes confirming what you have been given, you must believe in him and support him. Do you affirm this and accept My pledge as binding on you?" They said, "We do." He said, "Then bear witness, and I too will bear witness." (3:81)

Interestingly, camel's meat and milk were never prohibited before. In other words, the legislation brought by Prophet Muhammad perfectly aligned with the ruling in the Torah. Thus he, peace be upon him, asked the Rabbis to refer to their book. He could not say, "Go back and look in the Torah" unless he was confident it supported his case. This was the light of our beloved Muhammad. He was an illiterate man that never read the Torah, but his Lord guided him to the truth. They brought the Torah and found its words identical to what the Messenger said. Allah says:

All food was lawful for the tribe of Israel except what Israel made unlawful for himself before the Torah was sent down. Say, "Bring the Torah and recite it if you are telling the truth." (Verse 93)

Some of us choose not to eat certain foods because we do not like them. Some people stay away from specific foods when they diet or for medical reasons, such as lactose intolerance. Similarly our beloved Prophet Jacob, who was also known as Israel, chose not to eat certain foods; that did not mean that such foods were religiously unlawful, it was simply his personal choice. So why did the Rabbis insist that these particular foods were unlawful? We answer that they did so to cover an ugly episode in their history. Allah says:

We forbade for the Jews every animal with undivided hoof and the fat of cattle and sheep, except what is on their backs and in their intestines, or that which sticks to their bones. This is how We penalized them for their disobedience: We are true to Our word. (6:146)

Allah informed us that some things - which had always been lawful - were forbidden for the Jews because of their sins. The phrase "with undivided hoof" means that the toes of the animal are not separate; we find such examples in camels, geese, and ducks. The prohibitions here were not because these things are harmful; rather, they were a punishment for the injustice the Children of Israel committed against their prophets. In other words, the camel's meat was made unlawful only for the Israelites, as a punishment. Abraham, Noah, and all their followers had always enjoyed such meats.

When something is forbidden (Haram), people often rush to rationalize that it must be harmful to their health. We answer that, if you insist on finding a reason why something is forbidden, then you have sinned! There is always wisdom behind what Allah allows and what He forbids, but His wisdom is not according to what you think. Thus, I caution you against assuming that everything Allah forbids is harmful. He may prohibit things for other reasons, such as to discipline people. For example, you may tell your children that they cannot eat chocolate this week because they broke the neighbour's window while playing ball. Allah says:

For the wrongdoings done by the Jews, We forbade them certain good things that had been permitted to them before: for having frequently obstructed others from Allah's path, taking usury when they had been forbidden to do so, and for wrongfully devouring other people's property. For those of them that reject the truth, We have prepared an agonizing torment. (4:160-161)

Thus, you should not rush and judge why Allah made certain things permissible (Halal) or forbidden (Haram). It is not your business. A believer may live his or her life while never understanding the harm behind what Allah has forbidden. If someone questions, "Why did Allah forbid that?" say: "It is the Lord's wisdom, not mine."

Why do people transgress over Allah's teachings? Why do they take usury? Why do they unlawfully take the property of others? They do so to please themselves and indulge in money and power. For this reason, heavenly legislations sometimes come to deprive them of other pleasures, just as they deprived people of their rights. For example, in Islamic legislation the murderer is deprived of the victim's inheritance because they want to enjoy the inheritance sooner. This legislation intends to protect you from your heirs who may value greed more than your life.

This brings us back to the verse. The Jews of Medina, at the time of Prophet Muhammad, wanted to hide their past. More specifically, they wanted to deny that Allah had punished them for obstructing others from His path, dealing in usury, and wrongfully taking other people's property. So, they claimed that certain foods, like the meat and milk of camels, were always forbidden since the time of ancient prophets such as Noah. Allah wanted to expose their lies, both in the Torah and the Quran. He says:

All food was lawful for the tribe of Israel except what Israel made unlawful for himself before the Torah was sent down. Say, "Bring the Torah and recite it if you are telling the truth." (Verse 93)

Here we ask, why did this verse come after the verse that said, "None of you will attain true piety unless you spend out of what you cherish"? What is the connection between acceptable charity and foods that are permissible? This verse seems out of place. We have mentioned earlier that Allah is fully aware of our thoughts and emotions, and He takes everything into consideration. When you hear a verse talking about food, you may react in one of two ways. If you had just had a big meal, you would not pay much attention. But, if you are poor or hungry, you would start thinking about the foods you like to eat.

Thus, right before Allah awakened the desires of the hungry and the deprived with words about meat and milk, He encouraged the rich to give from the best they have. Thus, Allah brought balance to the world. He is our Creator Who does not forget the needs of His creation. Our beloved Moses said:

"My Lord alone has knowledge of them, all in a record; my Lord does not err or forget." (20:52)

Everything that ever happened or is destined to happen is in Allah's knowledge as He decreed it; He deprived some of wealth, and He knows the wisdom behind it, while He gave prosperity to others, and He knows the wisdom behind it. But Allah did not leave the poor to suffer; He encouraged the rich to provide for them from the best of their possessions because they know that Allah is the One who gives and withholds.

Always remember that your ability to earn a living is a fleeting state. You could fall ill or be disabled tomorrow. If you keep this real possibility in mind, you will rush to help the needy so you can guarantee that someone capable will help you if you become weak. That is the divine insurance plan. Allah orders the capable to give, so if one of them becomes weak, others will help out.

This brings us back to the verse. Allah says, "All food was lawful for the tribe of Israel." The word "lawful" is translated from the Arabic origin حلّ (Hill). When Allah said, "except what Israel made unlawful for himself," it meant that Prophet Jacob deprived himself of some foods not out of religious obligation, but for other reasons which he was free to follow. The key phrase in this verse is "before the Torah was sent down," because it reminds us that these dietary restrictions were not forbidden by Allah, as the Jews claimed afterward. Noah, Abraham, and all the followers of previous heavenly religions were free to eat and drink from camels. Thus, when they challenged Prophet Muhammad, he, peace be upon him, said, "Bring the Torah and recite it if you are telling the truth." Allah exposed their lies.

Verse 94

Famanif taraa 'alal laahilkaziba mim ba'di zaalika fa ulaaa'ika humuz zaalimoon

Now, those who fabricate lies against Allah, they are indeed the most unjust. (Verse 94)

This is a clear warning against attributing any lies or fabrications to Allah, the messengers, or the sacred books. Anyone who does so has committed great injustice against him or herself. Allah says:

So woe to those who write the scripture with their own hands, then say, "This is from Allah" in order to exchange it for a small price. Woe to them for what their hands have written and woe to them for what they earn. (2:79)

Verse 95

Qul sadaqal laah; fattabi'oo Millata Ibraaheema Haneefanw wa maa kaana minal mush rikeen

Say, "Allah speaks the truth, so follow the way of Abraham as people of pure faith. He was never of those who associate partners with Allah." (Verse 95)

At the time of our beloved Prophet Muhammad, there were two superpowers: Rome and Persia. While the Muslims were being persecuted in Mecca, the Persians - who worshiped fire - won a major victory over the Roman Christian army. The infidels of Mecca were overjoyed, and they mocked the Muslims that the same would happen to them soon. At that time, Allah revealed the following verse:

The Byzantine Romans have been defeated in the lands close by, but they, after their defeat, will be victorious in a few-years time. Allah is in command, first and last. On that day, the believers will rejoice. (30: 2-4)

Linguistically, the word "few" means any number between three and nine. When Abu Bakr Al-Sideeq heard the verse, he said, "Allah will not let the idolaters rejoice for long. By Allah, the Romans will be victorious over Persia after three years." Abu Bakr chose the lowest number of years in the range because he knew that Allah would not burden the believers with the hardship of patience for nine years.

Ubayy bin Khalaf, a disbeliever, overheard Abu Bakr. He rushed to him and said, "Would you bet me over what you have just said?" Abu Bakr replied, "Absolutely! Name your price." He said, "I bet you ten young camels if the Romans are victorious in three years, and you will give me the same if they are not." Abu Bakr agreed.

When he went to Prophet Muhammad, he, peace be upon him, said, "O Abu Bakr, why don't you increase your bet in price, but make it over a longer period of time?" Abu Bakr went back and did just that. He increased the bet to one hundred young camels and the years to nine.

During the following months, the maltreatment of Muslims in Mecca intensified, so Abu Bakr decided to migrate. Ubayy bin Khalaf saw him and said, "Where are you going? Are you abandoning your bet?" Abu Bakr replied, "Don't worry, my son Abd-ul-Rahman will pay you when the time comes."

The following year, while Ubayy bin Khalaf was saddling up to go to Badr and fight the Muslims, Abd-ul-Rahman caught up with him and said, "Where are you going? You may be killed in battle. Are you abandoning your bet?" Ubayy laughed and replied, "Don't worry, my son will pay you when the time comes."

In Badr, Ubayy sustained a wound from our beloved Muhammad and died. On the same day, the Romans won a major battle against Persia, and Ubayy's grieving son had to deliver one hundred young camels to Abd-ul-Rahman, son of Abu Bakr. Prophet Muhammad, peace be upon him, told Abu Bakr, "Why don't you give these camels to charity in Allah's cause?" And so it was done.

Here I would like to ask you, can you show me a supercomputer in our modern world that can predict the outcome of a battle that will take place after three years? Is there a think-tank or a government agency that could do that? Not even close. Muhammad, an illiterate man, residing in Arabia in the seventh century, had no information about the strength of the Romans or the Persians, nor access to data, satellite images, or spy information. Yet, he told us the result of a battle to be won by a defeated army three years in the future as if it were a foregone conclusion.

This prediction was documented in the Quran, so there was no way to deny it if the events did not unfold favourably. How could this be? Allah answers, "Allah speaks the truth." Prophet Muhammad received from his Lord, the Creator, and the Manager of the universe. Allah says:

Will they not study this Quran? If it had been from anyone other than Allah, they would have found much inconsistency in it. (4:82)

Speaking the truth occurs when the spoken words match reality. When Allah, Who knows everything from pre-eternity, speaks, the reality must come to match exactly what the Almighty said. Would a true God speak words conveyed by messengers and recorded in the scriptures only for life's events to contradict these words? That could never be. Thus, when Allah decrees a matter of faith or life, He knows from perpetuity that it will occur precisely as He said, even if the circumstances at the time do not instill confidence or support understanding.

When Islam began in Mecca, Muslims were few in number and heavily persecuted. Many of them had to leave their homes and possessions and migrate to protect their lives. At that time, Allah revealed the following verse:

Their forces will be routed, and they will turn tail and flee. (54:45)

How can we believe a message promising the defeat of the strongest army in Arabia by a group incapable of protecting itself? We answer, "Allah speaks the truth" because, for such a message to hold any weight, it can only come from the One Who possesses absolute power and complete knowledge and has control over time, space, and creation. When Muhammad, peace be upon him, conveyed Allah's message, Omar ibn Al-Khattab wondered loudly, "What army?" He knew that the Muslims could not safely assemble in a small group to worship, let alone put together a force to face Quraysh. But Prophet Muhammad was not talking about the means available to the believers; rather, he was talking about the Lord of the means. In a few short years, the events of the battle of Badr came to prove the authenticity of Allah's words: "Their forces will be routed, and they will turn tail and flee." He says:

Say, "Allah speaks the truth, so follow the way of Abraham as people of pure faith. He was never of those who associate partners with Allah." (Chapter 3: Verse 95)

Allah and Muhammad asked people to believe in the religion of Abraham. This emphasizes that all heavenly religions share the same creed and that all the messengers and prophets belong to a single convoy of divine delegation to humanity. There are no differences in faith, nor room for disagreement. In fact, our beloved Abraham called all the believers in Allah "Muslims."

We have explained earlier that "the way of Abraham" is the straight path of faith and Allah gave it the name حنيفا (Haneef). Linguistically, "Haneef" means "crooked or off the main path." How could this be? We have said before that the heavens do not interfere by sending messengers except when corruption is widespread. At such times, the one who deviates away from corruption is the one who is guided to the straight path. Thus, the description "Haneef" accurately describes a person who avoids the corrupt crowds and deviates away towards righteousness.

It is strange that the People of the Book, whether Jews or Christians, quarrel about Abraham, peace be upon him. Each side claimed Abraham as its own, although both Judaism and Christianity came after his time. Allah says:

People of the Book, why do you argue about Abraham when the Torah and the Gospels were not revealed until after his time? Do you not understand? (3:65)

Such arguments only come from extreme ignorance. Our beloved Abraham is the grandfather of the prophets, and he belongs to every monotheistic believer. Thus, Allah added, "He was never of those who associate partners with Allah," pointing out that both the Jews and Christians have gravely erred in their faith. How, you may ask? We answer the Jews claimed that Uzair was the son of Allah and the Christian made a similar claim about Jesus; they both ascribed partners to the Almighty.

Similarly, the Meccans and the Arabs before Islam worshiped idols and, at the same time, claimed to follow in the footsteps of Abraham. They pointed to the fact that they were preserving the Ka'aba and the rituals of Hajj taught by Abraham. Allah absolves Abraham from such ridiculous claims. He says:

Say, "Allah speaks the truth, so follow the way of Abraham as people of pure faith. He was never of those who associate partners with Allah." (Verse 95)

And in another verse:

The people with the strongest ties to Abraham are those who followed him and this Prophet and those who believe. Allah is the Protector of the believers. (3:68)

Verse 96

Inna awwala Baitinw wudi'a linnaasi lallazee bi Bakkata mubaarakanw wa hudal lil 'aalameen

The first House of worship to be established for humankind was the one at Bacca. It is a blessed place and a source of guidance for the whole world. (Verse 96)

Abraham, peace be upon him, was the first prophet associated with the Sacred House. He raised the foundations of the Ka'aba after it was ruined by the flood of Noah, peace be upon them.

In the previous verse, Allah invited all the believers to look at their shared heritage in faith. More specifically, Allah addressed the Jews and Christians who had distorted the Torah and the Gospel and asked them to return to the religion of Abraham, the religion of monotheism. It is the same message of our beloved Prophet Muhammad and the Noble Quran: there is no God but Allah.

Faith and values are centered in the heart, and that's where Abraham's convictions resided. But that is not enough; faith has to be reflected in physical actions to implement Allah's teachings. Just as Allah directed your heart to share the faith of Abraham and Muhammad in verse 95, He also directs your body towards a shared destination, Qibla. He says:

The first House of worship to be established for humankind was the one at Bacca. It is a blessed place and a source of guidance for the whole world. (Verse 96)

Now, when you pray, your heart is tuned to the presence of the Lord, and your body is turned towards His Sacred House. In other words, your entire being is one with its Creator.

Moreover, you are now united with every believer on earth. Your heart shares the faith of all the believers since the time of Adam, and your body turns to the same destination as Adam. In this manner, you are in the perfect state to receive Allah's grants, mercy, and blessings.

All heavenly religions before Islam required a designated place for prayers, such as a church. In other words, meeting with Allah in prayer could not be achieved outside places of worship, such as churches and synagogues. Allah blessed the Muslims by making the entire earth a place of worship. Prophet Muhammad, peace be upon him, said, "I have been given five things which were not given to anyone else before me. Allah made me victorious by fear after a march of one month. The entire earth was made a place for prayer and its soil pure, so any of you can pray wherever you are. The spoils of war are lawful for me, and they were not for anyone else before me. I have been given the right of intercession on the Day of Resurrection. Every prophet before me was sent to his nation, but I was sent to all humankind."

Now, every place where Allah is worshiped in Islam is considered a mosque. Even the soil of the earth is pure, so if you cannot find clean water for the wudu ablution, you can use the soil and dust as means for -purification in tayammum. Adam was created from clay, a mix of water and soil; thus, Allah made water and soil as means to purify yourself and return to your original untainted state. Why all this ease, you may ask? We answer that Allah wants every Muslim to meet Him effortlessly, at any place and time, regardless of the circumstances. What a great blessing and honour!

But there is a difference between a random place where you worship Allah and a mosque dedicated to worship. For example, you may pray at your place of work, whether in an office or a factory, and then get back to your work. You may pray in your classroom and then resume studying. But when a place is dedicated as a mosque, you are prohibited from engaging in any other activity besides worship. A mosque is not a place for business or gossip: it is a place of prayer. A business transaction that takes place inside the mosque will not be blessed.

A man who lost his camel entered the mosque of our beloved Prophet and loudly said, "Has anyone seen my red camel?" Prophet Muhammad replied, "May you never find it! This is not what mosques are built for."

Isn't it enough that you spend twenty-three hours of your day busy with worldly affairs? Shouldn't you devote just an hour to Allah alone? I advise you to leave all worldly worries at the door of the mosque just as you leave your shoes there. It is not good manners that you occupy your heart with something other than Allah at the time of prayers. In fact, it is of the etiquette of worship to avoid speaking to others in the mosque - even greeting them with "Salam."

Allah gave us the freedom to construct mosques wherever we like. But all the mosques on the planet, chosen by people, have to face the one mosque chosen by Allah, the Sacred Haram; It is the Qibla that all mosques face.

Some people question why a Qibla is needed if Allah is everywhere. They point to verses such as the following:

The East and the West belong to Allah: wherever you turn, there is His Face. Allah is all-encompassing and all-knowing. (2:115)

We answer that, when you look at the Ka'aba, you find that people are lined around it in a circle, facing one another. Some people face the Ka'aba while the east is behind them and the west in front. Others are facing north while the south is behind, and so on. In this way, all directions are covered, supporting the verse "The East and the West belong to Allah: wherever you turn, there is His Face." In other words, there is no direction specific to Allah and preferred over others; He is "all-encompassing and all-knowing."

The first House of worship to be established for humankind was the one at Bacca. It is a blessed place and a source of guidance for the whole worlds. (Verse 96)

Imam Ali, may Allah be pleased with him, said that a man came to our beloved Muhammad and asked: "Is this, the Ka'aba, the first House of Allah?" He, peace be upon him, explained that there were many Houses of Allah before that, but it is the first House established for humankind.

Prophet Muhammad clarified that Allah made the Ka'aba the first House of worship for humans, but for the creations before humans, there were surely many Houses of Allah which we are not aware of. This is also consistent with geological discoveries. When we hear of fossil discoveries dating back millions of years, some people question: how can it be possible when Adam is much more recent? We answer that you are right. The family tree of all our beloved prophets and messengers tells us that, approximately, there were five generations to reach Idris from Adam, then three generations to Noah, eleven to Abraham, and about thirty to Muhammad, peace be upon them all. This means that our human experience is measured in the tens of thousands of years, not millions.

But who said that Adam was the first creature to inhabit the earth? Religion did not say that! Quite the opposite. Allah says that Adam was the first of the human race, but there were many creations before.

The following verses say:

Do you not see that Allah has created the heavens and the earth with ultimate reason? If He so wills He could take you away from the earth and raise a new creation. (14:19)

And in another chapter,

And the Jinn We created before, from the fire of scorching wind. (15:27)

Lastly,

When your Lord said to the angels, "I am putting a successor on the earth," they said, "Why put on it one who will cause corruption and shed blood when we glorify You with praise and exault You?" He said, "I know what you do not know." (2:30)

It is clear that the angles had observed other creations, before Adam, that caused corruption and bloodshed. We know that, at a minimum, the Jinn were created before us. Thus, there is no room for debate that there were many Houses of Allah before the Ka'aba, and that the Ka'aba was the first House of worship built for human beings.

Had Allah wanted to teach us that the Ka'aba is the very first House on earth, he would have said, "The first House of worship to be established on earth was the one at Bacca," but He did not. Instead, Allah informed us that "The first House of worship to be established for humankind was the one at Bacca."

But what does 'first' mean? Is it the beginning? And so there must be a second, a third and a last? No, some things have a beginning but do not have an end. For example, the number one is first, but you can count from there to infinity and beyond. Paradise has an entrance but has no ending in space or time.

How about the phrase "established for humankind"? This is our clue for how old the Ka'aba is! Allah specified that His House was established for humans, and since our beloved Adam is a human, he had the same heavenly rights as all other humans. Allah would not deprive him or his family of the House of Allah. Thus, we understand that the Ka'aba must have existed before Adam.

Some people are quick to point out that prophet Abraham, peace be upon him, was the one who built the Ka'aba. They recite verses such as the following as proof,

As Abraham raised the foundations of the House with Ishmael: "Our Lord, accept it from us! Indeed You are the All-hearing, the All-knowing." (2:127)

We answer that such understanding is incorrect. What does it mean to raise a foundation? To 'raise' is to elevate or to move something to a higher position. All architectural structures have specific lengths, widths, and heights. Abraham was commanded to raise the foundation, suggesting that the length and width were already established, and all he had to do was increase the third dimension: height. In other words, the

House existed before Abraham, but its structure was lost -probably after the flood in Noah's time-. Thus, Allah wanted it rebuilt so its location could be seen by people again.

Another proof are the many extensions and levels that have been added to the Sacred House since. If you were blessed with a visit to Mecca and you prayed on the top level of the Haram, you know that you did not prostrate towards the Ka'aba directly because it was below you. However, your prayer was complete because all you have to do is face the direction of the foundation of the Ka'aba; the height does not matter. The Ka'ba is not the House; rather, it is the landmark that guides us to the location of the House of Allah.

Perhaps the strongest evidence that the Sacred House existed before Abraham and Ishmael raised can be found in the following verse narrating the supplication of Prophet Abraham when He left his wife and, then infant, son Ishmael behind,

Our Lord, I left some of my offspring in an uncultivated valley, close to Your Sacred House, Lord, so that they may keep up the prayer. Make people's hearts turn to them, and provide them with produce, so that they may be thankful. (14:37)

Clearly, this supplication was made when Ishmael was an infant, many years before helping his Dad raise the foundation of the Ka'ba. Yet, in his prayer, Abraham mentioned that he left his wife and son near the Sacred House of Allah. Allah says,

The first House of worship to be established for humankind was the one at Bacca. It is a blessed place and a source of guidance for the whole worlds. (Verse 96)

Here is a fascinating question: since the Ka'aba was built before Adam, who built it? We note that the passive phrase "established for humankind" was used in the verse. In other words, the subject was not named. So, who established the House? Was it the angels? This could be true; the angels may have received a command from Allah to establish the site. But we also note that Allah describes the Ka'aba as "a source of guidance for the whole worlds," a phrase that includes the angels. Thus, we conclude that the most likely answer to the question "Who established Allah's House on earth?" is Allah Himself!

Now we ponder over the location of the Sacred House, which Allah refers to as "at Bacca." We know that the city of the Sacred House today is known as "Mecca."

Let us look at the explanation that considers the linguistic origins of both words, "Mecca" and "Bacca." "Bacca" is derived from Bak, which refers to a very crowded place. This is a perfect description of the location of the Holy Ka'aba because it is always packed with people. If you were blessed with a visit to Mecca for Hajj or Umrah, you know well that the circumambulation (Tawaf) close to the Ka'aba can be a very challenging proposition.

"Mecca," on the other hand, is derived from Mak, which refers to a hungry calf that dries up the mother's milk. Mecca is a city in the middle of the barren desert that does not offer much water or food. Visitors often arrive hungry and thirsty and draw on its resources. Thus, we understand that Mecca refers to the city that houses Bacca, while Bacca is the ground where the Sacred Haram is built.

As for the word "blessed," derived from the Arabic root ك ر ب (Ba Ra Ka), it means something that is steady and stable. We often say, "This money is blessed" (or "has barakah"), meaning that there always seems to be more, no matter how much you spend. We use similar words to describe a pond that collects rainwater and continually replenishes itself. Likewise, "blessed is Allah" means that Allah is the truth; He is the ever-constant and perpetual, the One and Only. Allah described the location of His Sacred House as blessed. How, you may ask? We answer that the Ka'aba is the most generous place to its visitors because it multiplies the rewards of good deeds by a thousandfold or more. Is there a blessing better than this? It is also "guidance for the whole worlds," because it guides people to Paradise.

Prophet Muhammad, peace be upon him, said, "He who performs Hajj and refrains from obscene or immoral acts, will return to his family free from sin as the day his mother gave birth to him." And, in another

Hadith, "Allah will expiate the sins committed between performing two Umrahs. A Hajj, performed properly, has no reward but Paradise." Lastly, Aisha, may Allah be pleased with her, said that she heard the Prophet say, "There is no day in which more people are pardoned from Hellfire than the Day of Arafa. Allah is close to the pilgrims on that day. He boasts before the angels and says, 'Look at my servants: they made it here from all places, ragged and tired, seeking My mercy. I want you to bear witness that I have forgiven them.' The angels would say, 'Our Lord, among them is so and so who has overburdened himself with sin.' Allah answers, 'I have forgiven them.'"

We ask, is there a more blessed place, or a place that guides people to their salvation more than this? Allah says:

The first House of worship to be established for humankind was the one at Bacca. It is a blessed place and a source of guidance for the whole worlds. (Verse 96)

Verse 97

Feehi Aayaatum baiyinaatum Maqaamu Ibraaheema wa man dakhalahoo kaana aaminaa; wa lillaahi 'alan naasi Hijjul Baiti manis tataa'a ilaihi sabeelaa; wa man kafara fa innal laaha ghaniyyun 'anil 'aalameen

In it are clear signs – the standing place of Abraham. Whoever enters it is safe. Pilgrimage to the House is a duty owed to Allah by all who can afford a way to it. And whoever rejects, Allah is independent of all creation. (Verse 97)

Allah talks about the clear signs of His Sacred House, yet, only one sign is mentioned: "the standing place of Abraham." Shouldn't the verse start with "In it is a clear sign"? We answer, no. Allah wants to turn your attention to the fact that "the standing place of Abraham" includes many signs. Let's explore.

Abraham, peace be upon him, searched for a large rock to stand on so he could raise the foundation of the Sacred House. But was that necessary? No, it was not! Allah asked Abraham to raise the pillars of the House, so it would have been sufficient for him to raise it as high as his hands could reach. Had he done that, he would have fulfilled his duty. But Abraham approached all of Allah's commands with love and devotion. Allah says:

When Abraham's Lord tested him with specific commandments, which he completely fulfilled, He said, "I will make you a leader of people." Abraham asked, "And will You make leaders from my descendants too?" Allah answered, "My pledge does not hold for those who do evil." (2:124)

Abraham thought to himself, "Why don't I raise the house as high as possible?" At the time, the concept of scaffolding did not exist. So he, peace be upon him, searched for the largest rock he and his son Ishmael could carry and then placed it next to Ka'aba's foundation. That is the first sign that teaches us how Allah's commands should be respected.

If you were blessed by visiting the standing place of Abraham, you know that the stone was only large enough for one person to stand. Thus, we understand that Ishmael passed the bricks to his father, who was building the Ka'aba. As for the imprints of Abraham's feet on this stone, we know that to carry such heavy bricks, Abraham needed stability and balance while on the rock. You can see the imprints of Abraham's feet in the stone. Is that possible? Of course. By going the extra mile to carry out Allah's command perfectly, Allah sent His divine support to Abraham. He softened the rock to support and protect Abraham from falling. That is another clear sign of how Allah helps those who help Him. As for people who find it hard to comprehend such a miracle, we say to them, "If it makes you more comfortable that Abraham carved a place for his feet in the stone so he could maintain his balance, so be it." You can take whatever aligns with your understanding and learn the lesson from it.

Allah helped Abraham because he, peace be upon him, did the best job he could. As you know, Allah's guidance is of two types: guidance of indication and the guidance of assistance. Allah comes to the aid of those who follow His teachings. He says:

As for those who have accepted Allah's guidance, He strengthens them in guidance and gives them piety and protection from sin. (47:17)

The verse continues with, "Whoever enters it is safe." Mecca is where the Arab tribes met during the Hajj season. Among these tribes were conflicts, bloodshed, and wars. Allah commands that whoever enters His Sacred Mosque is safe. Why? Because it is not appropriate for anyone to shed blood or conduct worldly affairs in the House of the Lord. Even if a person has committed a major crime, he or she should be safe in Allah's House. However, you can always make life very difficult for the criminal and pressure them to leave the Haram. Omar, may Allah be pleased with him, said, "If I were to find the murderer of my father around the Ka'aba, I would not confront him."

We can apply a more beautiful interpretation of the phrase "Whoever enters it is safe" in regards to the Hereafter. Those who visit Allah's House and properly perform the Hajj pilgrimage will find safety on the Day of Resurrection. It is a high degree of Allah's mercy and grace.

Another great sign of Allah's House is the black stone. You see people eager to touch or kiss it, even though stones do not hold much value in our world. We know that humans are Allah's successors in the universe, and He granted us the highest status of all creations. We are higher than animals, plants, and inanimate objects, including stones.

Here we should take a moment to erase any possible misconception that Muslims give rocks and stones a special status. We point that, during Hajj, Allah commands us to debase and stone another rock, the three Jamarat representing the devil. In other words, this is not about stone worship because we can highlight examples of honouring one stone while disdaining another. We only assign value to Allah's teachings. When He commands us to glorify, we do so out of obedience to Him, and when He commands us to disdain, we obey His will.

We say to the critics who claim that Islam has retained some pagan practices by idolizing the Black Stone, "Why do you remember the glorification of the Black Stone, and do not mention the stoning of the devil represented by the three Jamarat stones? Allah took us out of the depths of idolatry and the peak of polytheism to the honor of Islam which holds only one thing sacred: the teachings of our Creator. Are these not clear signs?"

In it are clear signs – the standing place of Abraham. Whoever enters it is safe. Pilgrimage to the House is a duty owed to Allah by all who can afford a way to it. And whoever rejects, Allah is independent of all creation. (Verse 97)

On a scorching hot summer day, our beloved Abraham arrived at the empty valley of Mecca with his wife Hajar carrying her infant

Ishmael. Abraham found a place to settle his family near the location of Allah's Sacred House, and planned to return to the area of modern-day Jerusalem the next day. With the sun beating down on their heads, Hajar looked around and saw nothing but sand. There was no water, plants, or people. As Abraham got ready to leave, she stopped him and asked him to stay. He, peace be upon him, said nothing. Hajar, may Allah be please with her, grabbed his clothes and pulled him back. She pointed out that there wasn't any food or water for them! Abraham, again, was silent. Finally, Hajar asked, "How can you leave us here? Is this your decision, or did Allah instruct you to leave us here?" Abraham answered, "My Lord directed me to this place," to which she replied, "Feel free to leave, Abraham. Allah will never abandon us."

Hajar let go of all her worries because she knew that Abraham obeyed Allah's command. This is faith at its summit and a conviction more powerful than a mother's instinct. Hajar, through her faith, felt at peace as the father of her child traveled, leaving her in the barren desert. She did not believe in Abraham, but she believed in the Lord of Abraham.

Now that she was alone with her Infant, Hajar left the location of the Ka'aba to look for food and water. She looked to the sky: maybe she could spot some birds to guide her to water. But there were none. Nearby, she saw two hills, Al-Safa and Al-Marwa. She put Ishmael down and rushed to Al-Safa, climbed to the top, then looked around, hoping to spot a caravan or water. When she saw nothing, she ran towards the Marwa hill and did the same. Hajar knew that there was not much as her son was crying louder out of thirst. She completed seven rounds between the two hills in the hopes of finding a bird, a person... anything! She was becoming desperate. When she climbed Al-Marwa for the fourth time, a sound grabbed her attention. Hajar fell silent and listened closer: Ishmael's cry had changed! His hunger and thirst were so severe that he began to squirm. Panicked, she ran down to Ishmael's side and was shocked to find water seeping from the sands where he was kicking his feet. She pooled some of the water with her hands and drank. Water kept seeping, then gushing out. Hajar drank her fill, then breastfed her son.

Here we ask, had she found water on the Al-Safa or Al-Marwa in the first round, would that have been a confirmation of her statement to Abraham, "Allah will not abandon us"? Probably not. Allah wants to teach you a fundamental lesson: you have to work hard to earn a living, but do not, for one minute, think that earning money and provision is the result of your effort. Provision comes from Allah. Hajar had to strive and run seven times between the two hills, but that did not produce any water. Allah granted her water from under Ishmael's feet. She believed with all her heart that "Allah will not abandon us," yet Allah made her complete seven rounds, a feat not easy for a woman of her age who recently gave birth. Allah wants you to utilize all the means at your disposal to earn a living, but your heart must remain connected to the Lord of the means. In this manner, Allah extinguishes greed and desperation from our hearts. Zamzam, the spring which is still found in the bosom of the Kaaba, is the spring of Hajar and Ishmael. Are these not clear signs for humankind?

Here we should take a moment to address a common problem. Placing your trust in Allah to provide you with money and provision is very different from laziness and stupid dependency. Reliance on Allah, also known as Tawakul, means to work hard with your hands while your heart is at peace that whatever provision Allah has decreed for you will reach you in time. But laziness and neglect, also known as Tawaakul, is to sit around doing nothing while declaring your trust that Allah will provide for you. We say to such a person, "If you truly believe that Allah will provide you with food while you do no work on your part, then do not even extend your hand to eat when people place food in front of you. Wait for Allah to make that food jump into your mouth. Do you even need to chew, or should Allah do that for you too?"

Prophet Muhammad, peace be upon him, said, "If you genuinely rely on Allah, He will provide for you as He provides for a bird. It leaves its nest hungry and comes back full." We know that the vast majority of bird species do not store any food. Every day, each bird wakes up hungry and has to find food, and Allah provides for each of them. There are many fascinating stories among the scholars regarding this beautiful Hadeeth. Let's consider two of them.

Imam Malik disagreed with Imam Al-Shafi'i, may Allah be pleased with them, on the issue of sustenance. The first saw that sustenance could come to you with no effort on your part because Allah can provide for you as he provides for birds. While Imam Al-Shafi'i argued, "Had the bird not left its nest, it would have stayed hungry." Al-Shafi'i wanted to prove this to his teacher, so he left the mosque and found an old man struggling with a heavy bag of dates. He said to him, "Let me help you carry this." When he reached the house, the old man thanked him and gave him a few dates as a token of appreciation. Al-Shafi'i went back to Malik, put the dates in his hands, and said, "See! If I did not go out and help the old man, I would not have earned these dates." Malik smiled, took a date and put it in his mouth, and said, "And you brought my provision to me, and I did not lift a finger!"

When you enter the Sacred House of Allah in Mecca, you immediately shed all attachment to the world and become preoccupied with the worship of the Lord. The moment you see the Ka'aba, you forget about your children, money, and work. It is a magnificent feeling of tranquillity that can rarely be experienced anywhere else. Just ask anyone who was blessed with a Hajj or Umra trip. May Allah grant it to every Muslim. That is the meaning behind the phrase, "Whoever enters it is safe."

Here we must understand that there is a difference between the phrase "Whoever enters it is safe" being an informative one or a religious duty. In other words, is Allah informing us of a universal fact that whoever enters His Sacred House is safe, or is He requiring us to make it a safe sanctuary? History tells us that "Whoever enters it is safe" is not an informative statement but a religious duty.

The verse continues with, "Pilgrimage to the House is a duty owed to Allah by all people who can afford a way to it." When you hear the phrase, "John owes money to Miriam," you understand that Miriam has the benefit while John carries the liability. In other words, if you Based on this explanation, the phrase "Pilgrimage to the House is a duty owed to Allah by all people who can afford a way to it" means that people have the burden of Hajj, while Allah stands to benefit. However, matters are very different when it comes to the Almighty. Allah does not benefit from anything that you and I do. The Hajj pilgrimage does not help Allah; we alone will enjoy all its rewards. In short, Allah assigns you both the obligation and the reward.

Our Creator is well aware that some duties are difficult. For example, Hajj requires planning, money, time, and physical effort. When you find a religious commandment burdensome, here is my advice: try to remember the reward. When you recall the immense benefits of Hajj, the obligation becomes easy. Obedience is difficult for the person who does not see the end result; likewise, sin is easy for those who do not remember the punishment.

This brings us back to the verse. Allah says, "Pilgrimage to the House is a duty owed to Allah by all people who can afford a way to it." The phrase "a way to it" is translated from the Arabic origin سبيل (Sabeel), which is the road leading to the destination. When you set out for Hajj, you have some planning to do: you must arrange for travel, food, and accommodations. If you are traveling by land, you have to find a route free of danger. Still, that is not enough! How about your family and children? You have to ensure they are taken care of while you are away. Thus, Allah addressed all these concerns with the phrase, "all people who can afford a way to it."

The most alarming phrase in this verse is, "And whoever rejects, Allah is independent of all creation." The word "reject" is translated from the Arabic origin كَفَرَ (Kafara), which is usually reserved for the disbelievers. So we must ask: if you have the means to perform Hajj but choose not to, does that make you a disbeliever? Here the scholars took a pause. First, we explain that the Kufr (disbelief) falls under one of two categories. First is the rejection of Allah, and second is the rejection of His blessings. For example, Allah says:

Allah presents the example of a town that was secure and at ease, with provisions coming to it abundantly from all places. Then it became ungrateful for Allah's blessings, so Allah afflicted it with the garment of famine and fear for what its people had done. (16:112)

We must be careful in distinguishing between rejecting Allah on the one hand and denying His blessings on the other. In our example we ask, does the person oppose the mandate of Hajj? Or do they believe in it but do not implement it?

If you ask any Muslims, "Do you believe that Hajj is a duty?" he or she will respond with "Yes, of course." However, some believers are keen to fulfill Allah's command, while others procrastinate. Such lazy believers fall under the category of the disobedient, not the disbelievers.

Here I would like to take a moment to warn you against rejecting Allah's commands. For example, if you do not pray, do not say, "I do not pray because there is no benefit to prayers." Likewise, if you take a usurious loan, do not say that the prohibition of usury is unfair or incompatible with modern life. Because, when you say such statements -in essence turning your back to Allah's teachings- you will become a disbeliever and lose all access to Allah's mercy.

Instead, if you cannot bring yourself to implement Allah's teachings, then say, "My Lord, the obligation of prayers or the prohibition of usury is the truth, but I cannot bring myself to do these duties because my faith is weak. My Lord, please shower me with mercy and help me come back to Your path in this life and the next." If you sincerely mean these words, you will only be considered disobedient, not a disbeliever, and you will have access to Allah's mercy. So, be very mindful when distinguishing between sinning while accepting Allah's orders on the one hand and rejecting Allah's commands altogether on the other.

Verses 98

Qul yaaa Ahlal Kitaabi lima takfuroona bi Aayaatillaahi wallaahu shaheedun 'alaa maa ta'maloon

Say, "O People of the Book! Why do you deny the signs of Allah, while Allah is witness to all you do?"
(Verse 98)

Our beloved Prophet Muhammad is trustworthy and the truthful. These were the names Meccans gave him before Islam. When he became the Messenger of Allah, he delivered Allah's message in the most authentic and accurate form, precisely as he received. It would have been sufficient for the Prophet to go to the disbelievers and say to them, "O People of the Book! Why do you deny the signs of Allah, while Allah is witness to all you do?" But that would leave room for doubt as to the source of the message. Is the question from Muhammad or Allah? Thus, by delivering the message accurately, the Prophet informed everyone that he was conveying a verse from Allah. He passed the entire text verbatim as delivered to him by the Angel Gabriel.

Another interesting fact is that many verses in the Qur'an address the People of the Book. Still, not all of them start with the word "say." This is because, at times, Allah addresses His creation affectionately and makes them worthy of His direct speech by saying "O People of the Book." And, on other occasions, He says to His Messenger, "Say to them, O Muhammad," because they did not rise to the level of being addressed directly.

Here we ask, why are the Jews and Christians addressed as the "People of the Book," but Muslims are not addressed as the "People of the Quran"? We answer that Allah wants to remind the Jews and Christian that all the heavenly rules they violate are written down in their books. Matters are as clear as black and white, so their calls for polytheism and denial of Prophet Muhammad are a clear contradiction of what is written in the Bible. Thus, it is foolish for them to violate the scriptures because the Bible will be a witness against their actions on the Day of Judgement.

This brings us back to the verse. Allah asks, "O People of the Book! Why do you deny the signs of Allah?" Does denying Allah's signs mean disbelieving in them from the beginning, or does it mean denying them after belief? The word "deny" is translated from the Arabic origin تَكْفُرُونَ (Takfurun), which comes from the root ك ف ر (Ka-fa-ra). It means "to cover" or "to conceal." This is interesting because a person can only hide something that already exists. The Jews and Christians of Medina believed in Prophet Muhammad before his advent, but they denied him when he came. Allah says,

When a Scripture came to them from Allah confirming what they already had, and when they had been praying for victory against the disbelievers, even when there came to them something they knew to be true, they disbelieved in it: Allah rejects those who disbelieve. (2:89)

They chose disbelief because Prophet Muhammad was a threat to their worldly power. The new heavenly religion shifted authority away from priests and rabbis, and they could no longer issue rulings that served their interests and exploited their followers. Allah says in the next verse of Al-Imran,

Verse 99

Qul yaaa Ahlal Kitaabi lima tasuddoona 'an sabeelil laahi man aamana tabghoonahaa 'iwajanw wa antum shuhadaaa'; wa mallaahu bighaafilin 'ammaa ta'maloon

Say: "O People of the Book! Why do you bar from Allah's way those who believe, seeking to make it appear crooked, when you yourselves are witnesses to the truth? Allah is not heedless of what you do."
(Verse 99)

The only thing worse than losing your way is dragging others down with you. Isn't it enough that you defied your Creator? Why would you carry the burden of misleading others? Allah says,

On the Day of Resurrection, they will bear the full weight of their own burden and some of the burden of those they misled with no true knowledge. How terrible their burden will be! (16:25)

In Islam, every person is responsible only for his or her sins, except those who dragged others into sin. They will be bear the burden of their sins and the burden of every person they misguided. Prophet Muhammad, peace be upon him, said, "Whoever calls for guidance will have a reward equal to the reward of those who follow him or her until the Day of Resurrection, without diminishing anything from their rewards. And whoever calls for misguidance will carry sins equal to the sins of all those who follow him or her until the Day of Resurrection, without diminishing anything from their sins."

The word "crooked" is translated from the Arabic عِوَج (Iwaj), which is the corruption of morals and values, while عَوَج (Awaj) refers to crookedness in physical matters such as a wall or a stick. We know from geometry that a straight path is the shortest and easiest link between two points. On the other hand, bends and curves extend the distance to the destination. It is as if those who misguide people away from the Lord's straight path no longer seek Allah or Paradise.

Such people have committed a compound sin: they deliberately went astray after knowing the truth and then strived to mislead others. These terrible actions would have been excusable if they were done out of ignorance, but they were not. The Rabbis of Medina intentionally discarded their books, then worked hard to lead their followers away from the truth. Allah says, "You yourselves are witnesses to the truth."

Verses 100

Yaaa ayyuhal lazeena aamanoo in tutee'oo fareeqam minal lazeena ootul Kitaaba yaruddookum ba'da eemaanikum kaafireen

O you who believe! Were you to obey a party of those who were given the Book, they would turn you, after your faith, into disbelievers. (Verse 100)

The verse warns believers that if they listen to a group from among the People of the Book, those groups will attempt to turn them back from the faith.

This occurs because certain individuals from the People of the Book may harbour resentment or envy towards the Muslims and seek to undermine their faith.

The verse emphasizes the need for believers to remain steadfast in their faith and not be swayed by the temptations or false teachings of those who wish to lead them astray.

The verse also asks how believers could disbelieve while still being guided by the verses of Allah and having the Prophet (peace be upon him) among them. This highlights the importance of the Prophet's guidance and the verses of the Quran as a source of strength and wisdom.

In the previous verses, we learnt how Allah addressed the People of the Book who turned their back on their faith and disregarded the scriptures. They knew the truth yet deliberately went against it. And, as if that were not enough, they spent their time dragging others away from Allah's path. Thus, in this verse, Allah turns to the believers to warn them: some of the People of the Book will not rest as long as you are committed to Allah.

Here, we should take a moment to appreciate heavenly fairness. Note that Allah specified "a party of those who were given the Book." In other words, He identified a group of troublemakers and did not paint all the Jews and Christians with the same brush. Amongst them are people of integrity and honesty who are keen on following the truth. Islam is a religion without prejudice: it does not discriminate against people. It only discriminates against specific behaviours.

The phrase "they would turn you, after your faith, into disbelievers" does not necessarily mean that such people would prevent you from entering Islam or ask you to abandon your faith. Sometimes matters are more dangerous because the enemies of faith often try to corrupt your beliefs and keep you away from implementing Allah's teachings. In other words, they try to distract the believers from Allah's path.

Allah asks:

How can you disbelieve when Allah's revelations are being recited to you, and His Messenger is living among you? Whoever holds firmly to Allah will be guided to the straight path.

www.ingramcontent.com/pod-product-compliance
Lightning Source LLC
Chambersburg PA
CBHW030259080526
44584CB00012B/369